ERNST KÄSEMANN

NEW TESTAMENT QUESTIONS OF TODAY

new testament library

THE NEW TESTAMENT LIBRARY

ERNST KÄSEMANN

NEW TESTAMENT QUESTIONS OF TODAY

SCM PRESS LTD
BLOOMSBURY STREET LONDON

Translated by W. J. Montague
from selections from the German
Exegetische Versuche und Besinnungen, Zweiter Band
(2nd edition, Vandenhoeck und Ruprecht, Göttingen, 1965)

Chapter XII, 'Paul and Early Catholicism',
translated by Wilfred F. Bunge for
(and reprinted from)
Distinctive Protestant and Catholic Themes Reconsidered
(Journal for Theology and the Church, vol. 3)
Harper and Row, New York, 1967

334 01133 7
FIRST PUBLISHED IN ENGLISH 1969

PRINTED IN GREAT BRITAIN BY
W & J MACKAY & CO LTD, CHATHAM

To my old friends
Hans Kirchhoff
Ernst Haenchen

CONTENTS

PREFACE

As in the first volume, my labours in these essays are concerned with the multiplicity and range of New Testament proclamation. I have, however, made more strenuous efforts than before to trace the historical development involved and to see the crucial points of content in clearer outline against this background. This cannot be done without raising disputes in many quarters; I consider such disputation to be an indispensable element in theology and to be particularly necessary in the situation in which we find ourselves today. I have often been praised for sparing neither my teachers nor my friends. But this kind of praise has, for the most part, mistaken my motives. Controversy seems to me most meaningful when carried on with the strongest protagonist available and with one's closest intimates. In a time of confusion of voices, there is an obligation to give some answer to those whose work demands to be taken seriously, even if we cannot accept all they say. Disagreement is in this case the outward form of gratitude in the critical field, and is primarily designed to indicate those who must at all costs be heard and heeded. I do not really mind what effect it has on others, unless it is to drive them likewise to critical thought. There can, of course, be no true fellowship without the tensions and agonizings which are the inevitable price of freedom in human relationships.

Although more than half the essays that follow are about Paul, they are not intended to be in any sense programmatic. Yet the Apostle, more than most other New Testament writers, compels us to face the particular nexus of problems which he was the first to raise and reflect upon thematically. Thus he forces Protestantism, at least, to exercise perpetual self-criticism. If German theology appears to many foreigners to be nothing more or less than a permanent historical and theological revolution, this is only possible because Paul stood godfather at its cradle. We are in danger of giving up our own identity if we do not remain faithful to this tradition, which has so often been viewed with great suspicion. In our own generation, the managerial side, if not the creative leadership, of New Testament work has been taken over by the 'common sense' of English theology. But even this quality only displays its glamour for as long as it is subjected to disturbance by those who have accepted radical reappraisal and continual renewal as the divine promise to them and the divine necessity laid upon them.

I conclude with some essays which have a practical origin, namely, the confrontation which we now cannot avoid with Pietism; these essays are in no sense to be understood as an appendix. My questioning and my listening have never been directed exclusively to academic theology. In the last resort, what they are really about has to be expressed succinctly and in language that the ordinary man can understand. This has always been my view: when I wrote my dissertation *Leib und Leib Christi*, I tried to keep in mind that theology was not only or primarily a necessary tool for the clarification of my own faith, however little I succeeded in achieving this degree of detachment and however chaotic the final result turned out to be. Theology has both the commission and the capacity to summon the Church to take up the promise which is given to her and the service which is laid upon her, whatever else it may accomplish on the way. So I do not hesitate for a moment to say that for this reason my work is intended to have doctrinal implications. If it were to be content with less, it would be merely pretentious. Certainly, it is legitimate to ask whether doctrine can be taught at all, if critical study remains always in a state of flux and its findings have continually to be revised by the next generation.

But does not the answer run like this: 'How else can doctrine actually be taught, if Christ is to be the real Teacher?' The Protestant view is that it is only the man who is still learning who is fit to teach. Conversely, we miss the point of the mission which has been laid upon us if we deliberately confine the purpose of our learning to our own edification. True obedience may indeed presuppose radical thinking; but equally, thinking, however radical it may be, does not dispense us from obedience and communication. We are learning today on our own pulses of the dangers and the impoverishment which ensue in the Church of the Reformation when the will to think dies out and the essential leisure in which to think is denied. Yet it would, of course, be absurd if thinking were to be a substitute for action. It is for the very purpose of liberating the Church for decisive action that theology has to carry out its work of radical and critical questioning. It is my wish that my readers may work through my essays with an independent mind, but may also receive from them the impetus to involve themselves in our common mission.

In sending out this English edition of my work, I must again warmly thank Canon Montague for the care he has devoted to the translation.

This book is dedicated to the friends who, for forty years, have accompanied me along my way, often acted as my guides, kept me within reasonable bounds, and encouraged me to persevere.

ERNST KÄSEMANN

TRANSLATOR'S PREFACE

Most readers of this book will, I suspect, have read the earlier volume, *Essays on New Testament Themes*. For the benefit of any who have not, it may be helpful if I repeat here what I said in the translator's preface on that occasion about the word 'Enthusiasm' and its derivatives: namely, that it is used as in Bishop Butler's famous rebuke on the subject to John Wesley or in the title of the late Monsignor Ronald Knox's book on the sects.

New Testament citations are usually taken from the Revised Standard Version, but have occasionally been translated directly from the author's German. For the convenience of those who read German, the equivalent page numbers in the German edition appear at the top of each page.

Perhaps, in view of the fact that this is my second contribution to the privileged task of introducing Professor Käsemann's work to English readers, I may presume to make a short excursion outside the traditionally impersonal role of the translator. My own greatest gain from this involvement has been at the points at which confrontations occur between critical New Testament work and the life of the congregation. We do not seem to be very good at this in England: the 'scholars' seem reluctant to make the attempt, and the reactions of the 'pastors' (and the pews) when the attempt is made provide some justification for this reluctance! Yet it may well be that this is an indispensable next step in the process of renewal.

W.J.M.

ABBREVIATIONS

BFCT	Beiträge zur Förderung christlicher Theologie
BZ	*Biblische Zeitschrift*
BZAW	Beihefte zur *Zeitschrift für die alttestamentliche Wissenschaft*
EvTh	*Evangelische Theologie*
FRLANT	Forschungen zur Religion und Literatur des Alten und Neuen Testaments
HNT	Handbuch zum Neuen Testament
ICC	International Critical Commentary
JBL	*Journal of Biblical Literature*
NF	Neue Folge
NTD	Das Neue Testament Deutsch
NTS	*New Testament Studies*
RAC	*Reallexikon für Antike und Christentum*
SAW	Sitzungsberichte der Akademie der Wissenschaften
SBT	Studies in Biblical Theology
TLZ	*Theologische Literaturzeitung*
TWNT	*Theologisches Wörterbuch zum Neuen Testament*
ZST	*Zeitschrift für systematische Theologie*
ZTK	*Zeitschrift für Theologie und Kirche*

I

NEW TESTAMENT QUESTIONS OF TODAY*

(for Friedrich Gogarten on his seventieth birthday, 13 January 1957)

WHAT I PROPOSE to do in this essay is to some extent superfluous, in that it is not very long since I gave utterance on the theme 'Problems of New Testament Work in Germany'.[1] Neither the state of research nor the outlook of the person concerned normally changes so much in barely five years that a further meditation is likely to bring anything fundamentally new to light. On the other hand, it is nevertheless reasonable to take frequent account of the point at which we have arrived, of the possibilities and urgent tasks which are opening up before us, of the dangers which threaten us, of the supplementations and corrections which need to be made to what has been said earlier and, last but not least, of improper tendencies and developments by which we do not want to be simply taken in tow unresisting. Clarity over methods and aims seems generally not far from being an objective as universal as the preoccupation in the scientific field with the increase of productivity and the fulfilment of the daily and yearly quota. The gulf between fruitful knowledge and the fearsome process of conceiving useless hypotheses is growing inexorably deeper; but the faculty of detachment, which is the basic presupposition of all science, is not increasing correspondingly.

With this statement, I am already well into the task of delineating the situation of the professional New Testament scholar today. To a

* 'Neutestamentliche Fragen von Heute', first published in *ZTK* 54, 1957, pp. 1–21. Even though I should describe the German situation today in considerably different terms, nevertheless the essay delineates in programmatic form the nexus of problems, out of which the investigations that follow have grown during the last decade.

[1] 'Die Freiheit des Evangeliums und die Ordnung der Gesellschaft', *Beiträge zur evangelische Theologie* 15, 1952, pp. 133–52.

degree unthinkable even half a century ago we are determined in our work by the fact of a world which has grown smaller. The international character of scholarship, which ought to be ground for joy and thankfulness, is gradually growing into a pest and is causing nightmares. The time when German exegesis dominated the field is gone for ever. It has become an isolated voice in a chorus composed of many members. Not every country has yet its own series of full-scale commentaries, but the flood of monographs and the ever-increasing number of specialist periodicals overwhelm us from every side. The demands made simply by the task of reading can scarcely be met by the individual. For us also team work is becoming the solution. The advent of specialists, who simply record and card-index, was bound to come before long. The art of reviewing is bound to fall correspondingly into decay: a mere mention is bound to replace substantial discussion. One's own eye and independent judgment are in danger of losing the battle with the wilderness of paper. Even in our ranks the manager is appearing, to say nothing of the simplifiers who are opening up the market for popularizing literature.

Justice obliges us to admit that modern Catholic exegesis, at least in Germany and its immediate neighbourhood, has attained a standard which, generally speaking, is no longer inferior to Protestant work and indeed not infrequently outdoes it in careful scholarship. This state of affairs is proof that the historical critical method has in principle become common property. It no longer distinguishes one exegetical camp from another but now in fact simply divides scholarly work from speculation or primitive thinking. The assimilation of the different fronts is perhaps the characteristic mark of our epoch.

Concrete experiences undergone together have contributed not a little to this assimilative process. The scholarship of a generation which, with greater or lesser degrees of involvement, has lived through the Church Struggle, cannot but be determined thereby. The experience of war and of the concentration camps is equally a distinctive mark of this generation. They utterly destroyed in it the attitude of bourgeois individualism and of detached historicism. Naturally we cannot deny out of hand the tradition from which we came. It is the Liberal tradition, devalued and suppressed as it now is practically everywhere in the Church, which yet almost alone still prevails in the realm of academic theology. But even there all kinds of counter-movements have created new assumptions within our lifetime. To say the least, the very scholars who engage in this work from within our own theological tradition do not for the most part themselves breathe any longer the atmosphere of Liberalism. Confession, Church and Ecumenical Movement are for them not merely ineluctable realities but, in general, the positive foundations of their work and they find in their experience that this is not the case in Germany only. This proves, however, that alongside the ecclesiastical community of the Ecumenical Movement a theological community is appearing which, although differences of origin and confession and also actual individuality prevent it from becoming too much of a closed shop, nevertheless through its connection with the life and purposes of the churches is beginning to take shape as a valuable form of proclamation. It would be premature, to say the least, to speak of an ecumenical theology and it is questionable whether the differences in tradition, confessions and individuality will ever allow things to get that far. But we cannot help seeing that the attitude just described, carefully nourished both by the individual churches and by the Ecumenical Movement, is acquiring for a theology structured in a particular way international currency and a weight of influence such as formerly it would not have been able to secure in Germany itself. In plainer language, historico-critical radicalism is becoming increasingly isolated and confined. In some countries which were never particularly inclined to this outlook, this state of affairs may make no essential change in the perspective of the total picture. Not so in Germany.

We need only to think of our New Testament scholars in the period before and after the First World War to recognize that here was gathered together an extraordinary wealth of sharply defined figures, highly idiosyncratic in their historical or systematic work. It is evident that, in contrast to all this, a levelling-off has taken place; which is not merely to be explained in terms of the disappearance of great creative conceptions but must also be looked at in its connection with the present *rapprochement* among the churches; that is, if it is to be analysed without deference, except (I hope) to the facts. Understandably, confessional traits do not appear in such sharp relief here as in dogmatic theology. Equally, we cannot exactly speak of the upsurge of an ecclesiastical and theological conservatism, like, for instance, that embodied for the preceding generation by Zahn. The description 'theological pietism' fits the not easily comprehensible phenomena better to this extent, that personal commitment to faith and the intention of facilitating and deepening such commitment in others go hand in hand with a more or less developed biblicism and a great power of adaptability (not to say indifference) over against the various formulations of doctrine. Our contemporaries strive for unity in what is central which is seen to consist in personal commitment to faith – and allow freedom in what is alleged to be peripheral, i.e. dogmatic formulation; and this attitude is common to conservative and radical. This positive and even positivistic basic approach in no way excludes the use of an historical critical method applied with varying degrees of gentleness and gives plenty of scope to all styles of ecclesiastical involvement.

Now we have every reason not to adopt a belittling attitude to Pietism. A theology which did that, would have to abstract in a remarkably unrealistic fashion from the actual situation, which is that our church life still continues to draw its nourishment from its roots in pietism, that recruits to the ranks of theological workers even today are drawn from bourgeois pietistic circles, and that its weakening is undoubtedly leading to a very threatening crisis over the whole area of the Church's activity. We have every cause to approach the energies present in these circles with the deepest respect and to treat them with great delicacy if we do not wish foolishly to saw off the branch on which, whether willingly or unwillingly, we are now sitting. Certainly this does not mean that we can be happy over the penetration of Pietism into the field of academic theology at the precise moment when its impetus in congregational life is sensibly diminishing; nor that we can regard a pietistic theology propagated and furthered under ecumenical auspices otherwise than as a menace. If my estimate of the situation is a just and sober one, a thorough clarification is necessary here. Pietism's legitimate claim and limit must be mapped. The question of its limit comes under consideration when we ask ourselves why the work of Schlatter has made such a remarkably small impact on contemporary German theology. That is a quite astonishing and at the same time absolutely undeniable fact. Thousands sat at the feet of this great teacher, at least two generations of Würtemberg pastors were trained by him, the influence of his writing and lectures radiated far and wide into the whole realm of German Christendom, his theological work has, for the discriminating reader, lost nothing of its actuality and fascination. He, if anyone, seemed to be called to head the movement I have just described and to provide it with a definite shape. This simply did not happen. The fact that Schlatter is little esteemed abroad can be explained to a large extent by the idiosyncratic nature of his language. But why is it that our own students hardly read him any more and are obviously given very little encouragement to do so? Why, while there are not lacking those who value him and say that he has stimulated them on individual points, are there none who have resolutely taken up and carried on his work? Why, in the very place in which his memory is kept green, is he numbered among the ranks of the merely edifying writers or typically conservative theologians in which he, one of the most valiant and liberated spirits of his generation, emphatically does not belong? Even though he himself may not have sufficiently guarded against this kind of misunderstanding, it is an injustice to him and a loss to us that his portrait, which has come down to us in this present time only in a touched-up version, is increasingly taking on the lineaments of the mediocre. When his heirs admittedly do not themselves any longer possess his own originality, freedom, lust for battle and resolution, things could hardly turn out otherwise. Consequently, both the generous lines of his theological design and the explosive potential of his most daring ideas cannot help being buried under the pall of the ordinary and banal. This process seems to me symptomatic: the outlook which I have called the theological pietism of today lacks the courage and the drive for spiritual adventure, the readiness to think something through to the end come what may, in brief the most important presupposition of systematic thinking. Here, however, this movement differs not only from Schlatter but from the most distinguished representatives of the preceding epoch.

It is not an accident that we are experiencing in our own time in the camp of relatively conservative scholarship itself a late blooming of historicism at which we can only marvel. We must concede at once that the preceding generation over-reached itself with its systematic conceptions and constructions. It is comprehensible that the pendulum is now swinging towards the other extreme. We need also to understand that an epoch in which after two wars human existence has become profoundly uncertain is seeking a foothold in a very limited area and is not inclined to risk its neck in experiments or to contract vertigo by flying too high. But, even granting all this, one fact must not be forgotten nor glossed over in silence: everything spiritual, and to some extent all science likewise, including theology, is and remains an adventure demanding courage even more than discipline or perseverance. The *via media* is not the way of science, at least it is not to be adopted as the magic formula. Science draws its life from a passion (perhaps deeply hidden) and an unending process of radical questioning, concerned not with surface phenomena but with the ground of reality. Scientific theology also draws its life from the same sources if it is to be worthy of its name. At this point there can be no compromises or concessions or limitations. In true Greek fashion Pathos and Ethos are here identical. As I see it, the danger which threatens us is that we should consciously or unconsciously follow the solution of the *via media* which offers a way of escape where common sense is on the throne, churches are aspiring to establish ecumenical connections, the traditions of individual countries are intermingling, the wealth of material is crying out for administration and the impression is given that personal piety can be used as a labour-saving device in the work of systematic thinking. The churches may in general have no objection to such a development. They would be delivered by it from a seat of permanent disturbance and be confirmed in their existing continuity. Whether such a development would be a healthy one for them is another matter. For besides all this the churches – at any rate the churches of Europe – certainly stand in the twentieth century in danger of becoming a publicly recognized nature reserve set apart in the midst of the technical, social and political world. It must be the task of theology for the sake of the Church to move towards a confrontation with this danger rather than to increase it. Theology practised according to a prescription will surely not achieve this.

The foregoing remarks already touch upon that problem the existence of which I have previously established by pointing to the gulf between contemporary systematic theology and New Testament exegesis – a problem which can be simplified and brought within methodological compass by reducing it to the formula of the antithesis of Barth and Bultmann. It is true that such a formula circumscribes the most instructive example of the problem and not the whole problem. For it is not the case that Barth perhaps prefers some other New Testament scholar to Bultmann as crown witness. On the contrary, Bultmann still seems to be for him the dearest and most fruitful partner for dialogue. Conversely, neither would it be possible to maintain that any New Testament scholar was determined by Barth or any other contemporary systematic theologian in the same way in which this was true of liberal exegesis in regard to the systematic theology of the Idealists. In general, each side goes its own way without bothering too much about the other, although they find themselves bound to tread each other's territory without hesitation. The systematic theologian cannot forgo exegesis and historical analyses. Conversely, the exegete may imagine that he is not a systematic theologian and that there is no necessity for him to become one; indeed, it is one of the most remarkable effects of historicism that a number of exegetes with thoroughly misplaced modesty actually suppose that they merely do the historical donkey work for the systematic theologian. But systematic theology as the unconscious background of the historical scholar is a most dangerous exercise ground for narrow-mindedness and presumption, just as on the other side disrespect for historical critical method in systematic theology gives free course to speculations of the most diverse kinds. Wherever one thinks it can do without the other we find that in reality two forms of systematic theology and exegesis are failing to establish contact; and the result at times is that the representative of the one discipline formulates his judgments in the other field more or less by rules of thumb or else out of his own wishful thinking.

I do not need to go yet again into the causes of this state of affairs and its effects among students of the New Testament and in the Church. But we should be careful not to regard this temporary theological expression of schizophrenia as anything but a sickness which we are bound in the last resort to overcome with all the energy at our disposal. In any case, no one ought to go on making theological capital out of it. The rightness and necessity of historical criticism are no longer matter for debate. It may well be that a certain type of incarnational theology is being propagated which is enjoying great popularity today and which is declaring the brute facts of 'salvation history' and the church tradition deduced from it to be sacrosanct. But each trade has its own theory of method, determined by suitability for the purpose, and anyone who utters on this point from outside usually succeeds in proving only that he knows nothing of the trade. Scripture is essentially a document of the past before it is anything else and to this extent is subject to historical criticism as the universally tried and tested way into documents of the past. That it is God's Word is a pronouncement of church proclamation which may not as such be mistaken for a methodological principle. Faith therefore is not based on theological work which rather, when it is rightly understood and done, belongs to the sphere of good works. As faith liberates for service in the secular world, so the Church also releases into that thoroughly secular service what is called historical scholarship and does not set limits to this service by making conditions about methods and results. She risks her members and herself, just in virtue of her mission to the secular, in the worldly calling and profession of living in the world. If she did not do this, she would be concealing the fact that the world is her sphere of activity and that revelation is not glossolalia. The presence of revelation in Scripture is not a timeless presence, but one which is always being reconstituted by compounding with the past and by translation into the present which is there to be won or lost. The man who is not prepared to take the risk of failure cannot but make Scripture into the book fallen directly from heaven and its message into a timeless truth – and therefore a truth which does not call any man to any specific responsibility.

Conversely, it is precisely today that we have seriously to ask ourselves the reason why completely arbitrary historical reconstruction which does violence to the text is attaining such grotesque proportions. A deep uncertainty has set in as to the conditions under which historical judgements are possible and by which they are limited, in what sense historical work can lay claim to the nature of a science, i.e. accountability. His freedom from limitation by ecclesiastical tradition has undeniably furnished the individuality of the historian with a degree of free play in which any excess is possible and the rules of the business are not merely disregarded but become problematical. The passion for reality, that peculiar driving force of the historian, is only too often replaced by whimsy, the constant refuge of the dilettante. The indirect claim of truth from within reality increasingly loses the power by which it limits the individual and obligates to the whole. The tyranny of intuition succeeds the tutelage of tradition: and this is undoubtedly to fall out of the frying-pan into the fire. In view of this state of affairs which can no longer be overlooked, who can blame systematic theology if it adopts a generally suspicious or sceptical attitude towards historical work and at the very least requires that the rules of the business should be clearly promulgated in a newly thought-out hermeneutics. The dialogue on this subject, which has been begun by Bultmann, Gogarten, Diem and Fuchs must in no circumstances come to a stop. It will have equally to break with the romantic ideal of interpretation and to think itself back into the major concern of Reformation hermeneutics. Historical processes may well be demarcated by reference to individuals, yet they must not be reduced to the interplay of individualities. The history of primitive Christendom is not exclusively, indeed not even primarily, the history of the great theologians and of the self-understanding and understanding of existence attained by them, however attractively it is reflected and delimited therein. The element of obligation in the nature of the canon is not done away with simply by giving proof of its historically more or less accidental definition, its blurred frontiers and its diverse and partly contradictory individual testimonies. For in this same canon there is the steadfast affirmation and the manifold refraction of that history in which the comfort of tempted hearts by the Gospel became and sustains reality: a reality which is at the same time always being denied anew and, even within the ranks of the witnesses themselves, misunderstood and yet ever anew of itself creating acknowledgment for itself. The witness to this reality hides within itself in exemplary fashion the whole range of possibilities open in coming to terms with this reality. It is anything but uniform. Jacob and Esau go their separate ways within it. The Gospel does not appear on the scene without arousing the reaction both of legalism and of enthusiasm. But it is precisely in this way that the canon remains for us the witness of the history which is given and assigned to us: this is the only way in which in the last resort, it can be so. Otherwise it would not be concerned with our human reality but with an illusion.

If this is admitted to be the case, biblical interpretation can only be carried out critically; indeed, the criticism here must be a radical criticism, arising out of the demands of the Gospel itself, a content-orientated criticism casting its shadow over historical criticism. Historical criticism only indicates the complex of problems bound up with what we may designate the variability of the kerygma. Theological criticism alone is able to deal faithfully with the question as to what this problematic evokes and what it means for us. The obligatory character of the whole Scripture lies in this: namely, that exemplary witness to the reality of that history which is grounded in the Gospel is found only in the whole Scripture. But the total of all the individual biblical testimonies is not the Gospel. Otherwise, the Bible would be the book which fell from heaven and docetism would determine our conception of revelation. The tension between Gospel and Scripture is the indispensable presupposition of all theological interpretation and the inner meaning of those problems of Scripture of which historical criticism takes account. Whatever motive may have caused the taking over of historical criticism into the exegetical sphere, any retreat from this criticism in the present must necessarily make the problems of Scripture more obscure, reduce the diverse utterances of Scripture to a single level, remove the tension of Gospel and Scripture and endanger the proper historical character of revelation. Radical historical criticism is the logical consequence (not drawn before the modern era) in the methodological field of that theological criticism which is constitutive for Scriptural interpretation. In its attainment of independence this connection has been forgotten, the servant function has become the final objective of exegesis, and alien ideals have usurped the place of legitimate origins. The validity of this process must be questioned. For, so far as its proper task and scope is concerned, the theological clarification of historical criticism has so far been only inadequately undertaken, although this criticism is very widely treated as indispensable in practice and acknowledged as valid in principle. But this is just the point where lies the origin of the crucial tensions between exegesis and systematic theology. It cannot be left to the individual to experiment in this field in any way he likes; and it is inconceivable that in the realm of a *theologia crucis* at least some far reaching understanding should not be arrived at, impossible as this admittedly seems to be in the case of a theology of salvation history.

No contribution to the preparation and advance of this questioning process has been greater than that of the work of Rudolf Bultmann. I hope it will not merely be ascribed to the fact that I was his pupil if I characterize the necessity of coming to terms with this work of his as the most pressing task of the present generation of New Testament scholars in Germany. Only an immature judgment could assign to Bultmann, whose work is studied and debated about the world over, the role of a mere specialist, even if a leading one. Quite apart from the unusual width of his horizon in which the erudition of the outstanding New Testament scholar is combined with a passion for systematic theology and a life-long concern with questions of classical philology and philosophical problems, it has to be acknowledged that, in addition, he represents, as does no other contemporary exegete, continuity with that past in which we have our theological origins and which we cannot simply forget about. His work is given both binding and disruptive force by the fact that, he, like F. C. Baur in the nineteenth century, makes a determined effort to come to terms with the historical and theological problem of this past. I do not believe that we are uncritically to accept Bultmann's solutions as correct. Indeed, perhaps it is just precisely the pupil who cannot help being the predestined adversary of the teacher, inasmuch as their mutual dialogue about the truth always shows up the limitations of the earthly teacher and in any case liberates the pupil into independence. As it is not uncommon today to speak of the 'school of Bultmann', it may be allowable to emphasize that there is probably none of Bultmann's older and better-known pupils who do not adopt a thoroughly critical attitude towards the master. But this tells in favour of the master and not against him. For this state of affairs which is really very rare today only proves that the master has succeeded in supplying that Socratic midwifery which leads to truth and freedom. From this standpoint alone the anathematization of Bultmann as a heretic even to the extent of denunciations from the pulpit is manifestly ridiculous. Quite apart from the fact that this process of delation employed for the most part arguments that were not exactly judicious and indeed were sometimes embarrassingly trivial – the publication of a charge framed in biblical texts[2] was calculated to give the impression of embarrassment rather than of the Spirit and of power – today less than ever can the churches afford to dispense with a teacher who is able to educate his pupils into criticism of himself. There is quite enough marching and drilling in columns of route, although the church struggle showed us that there is seldom any future in *that*. The anathematization of Bultmann is, however, also foolish because it merely places obstacles in the way of a relevant and fruitful debate. The theological crisis of which Bultmann's work has enabled us to become freshly aware has been endemic in Protestantism for the last two hundred years. Bultmann the exegete has outlined the dimensions of it, Bultmann the systematic theologian has sought to open up ways by which it may be overcome. In any event, those who have graduated out of his school, will have to give up their life's work to going over again the historical presuppositions of Bultmann's conception of systematics, as a whole generation was similarly occupied with the work of F. C. Baur.

It seems to me necessary and profitable to discuss a little those lines of questioning on which the greatest weight falls in this matter. I am not specially anxious to embark on the problem (of which I have previously treated) of the historical Jesus and the relation of his proclamation to that of his first disciples. However, we have to postulate that, according to all the indications, violent controversies are to be expected on this point. Neither the Anglo-Saxon nor the French-speaking lands have ever really come to terms with the question

[2] Reference to a recent happening in the Church.

of the Jesus of history. On the contrary, they exercise towards radical German criticism, and in particular towards the work of the form-critics, what is no more than just a sceptical attitude towards such an endeavour in principle. In Germany itself the debate, which had been becalmed for decades, is once again in motion. It might be permissible to quote as characteristic facts in the situation that Stauffer does not shrink from the enterprise of laying before us a new outline of the 'life' of Jesus; that Joachim Jeremias has been trying for a long time not merely to illuminate from *ipsissima verba* the self-consciousness of Jesus but also to interpret primitive Christian history and New Testament theology as a reflection of the historical facts about Jesus; and finally that Ernst Fuchs, Günther Bornkamm and I myself see ourselves as being obliged to set limits to the proposition that the event of Easter was the foundation of the Christian kerygma and compelled to enquire as to what the significance of the historical Jesus for faith may be. The reconstruction of a 'life' of Jesus from the angle of salvation history will be found to be as incapable of providing a solution to the problem as a portrayal of Jesus in the role of a model for the believer, although both were attempted as early as the New Testament itself. We must cling obstinately to the knowledge that the first road – excluded in any event by the unsatisfactory nature of the sources – will end in a flat rationalism or a belief in (arbitrary) miracle, the second in moralism or mysticism. On that point, the story of the 'quest of the historical Jesus' should really have convinced anyone who is capable of drawing any conclusions at all from so long and laborious a history. A past happening, in so far as it does not vanish into thin air, takes on the form of a polychromatic piece of reality. It can only be rendered unequivocal and given power in the present by the Word which accompanies, determines and perhaps originates it. Only the proclamation of Jesus can enable us to encounter the historical Jesus and to comprehend his history. It is therefore meaningful to put this proclamation to the question concerning its relationship to the proclamation of the community. In this process the difference, which the emphasis on the events of Passiontide and Easter produces in the latter, may in no circumstances be obliterated. This means, however, that Christian preaching is not to be understood simply as the continuation and reflection of the *ipsissima verba*, certain though it is that the two are not placed in arbitrary juxtaposition. Thus everything will depend on defining in a new and better way the relationship of the message of Jesus to the proclamation about the Crucified and Risen One. We shall however be unable to do this without taking due account beforehand of the specific intention of the primitive Christian preaching of the Cross and Resurrection. Indeed, the message of Paul and John certainly proves that it is not just brute facts which are being proclaimed here. It was because Bultmann recognized the full impact of the task which now lies before us that he was able (as he had done for the Synoptists with his *History of the Synoptic Tradition*[3]) to introduce a new epoch in the study of Paul and John.

The distinctive feature of his interpretation of Paul is the manner in which he makes the doctrine of man the central point. This corresponds to the foundation text in that nowhere else in the New Testament is anthropology treated in this systematic fashion. At the same time Bultmann thus places himself within the continuity of the exegetical tradition begun by F. C. Baur, in which the problem of anthropology was for the first time clearly recognized. Admittedly, the classically-orientated interpretation of this tradition has been now replaced by the existentialist interpretation. In Paul anthropological terms exhibit throughout not idiosyncrasy but a definite orientation and an historical evaluation of human existence. From this angle alone, they constitute a systematic unity, which is not characterized by a conceptual foundation of dualism. From this angle, too, the dissection of Pauline theology into an Hellenistic and sacramental and a Jewish and forensic strand is surmounted, however impossible it may be to deny the assimilation of both Jewish and Hellenistic images by the apostle, whose home ground is the synagogue of the Diaspora. Paul's characteristic antithesis of flesh and spirit is to be seen then as directed neither towards the contrast of transitory and everlasting nor towards the experience of withdrawal from an earthly to a heavenly state. This antithesis connotes rather the attitude of the man who is delivered over by the sin of disobedience to the powers of the world without thereby being lost to his true Lord; or the state of the Christian who, being within the realm of Christ's lordship, yet at the same time remains constantly exposed to temptation. The historical dialectic of human existence BC and AD is therefore the ground and the burden of the Apostle's dualistic mode of expression and the sacrament is not an act of consecration which imparts a new nature, but the erection of the lordship of the Kyrios, and the turn of the ages in the life of

[3] *Die Geschichte der synoptischen Tradition* (FRLANT 29), 1921; 3rd ed., 1958; ET of 3rd ed., *The History of the Synoptic Tradition*, 1963.

the individual. In consequence, the doctrine of justification appears no longer as a secondary element of Pauline theology, as Wrede and Schweitzer maintained, but as its central point. For this doctrine is concerned with that very claim of lordship which God makes in regard to his creatures on earth and with the establishment of the *nova obedientia* in grace, and yet for this very reason in the shadow of persisting temptation. Those who today would make a heretic out of Bultmann have obviously not the least understanding of this part of his exegetical and systematic theology, while a witness so little open to the charge of partisanship as Schniewind frequently declared that, in his judgment, no one in the past generation of New Testament scholars with the exception of Schlatter had done so much for the rediscovery of the Reformation doctrine of justification as Bultmann.

The possible objections to this interpretation of Paul arise as the converse of its advantages. Bultmann has judged himself obliged to conclude from his premise that Pauline theology is essentially anthropology, not in the sense that every theology contains an anthropology within itself, but exclusively. I find it more than doubtful that such a conclusion is actually permissible, and in any event I cannot see that the apostle himself drew it. I should regard the anthropology which incontrovertibly characterizes Paul neither as the sum total nor as the central point, but as a specific and, of course, highly important function of this theology: through it the reality and radical nature of Christ's seizure of power as the Cosmocrator comes to expression. This seizure of power applies to the whole world, as both Paul's conception of the Church and his apocalyptic demonstrate. It seems to me that, although Bultmann has naturally seen this point, he only allows it weight in the realm of ethics – more accurately, of the I-Thou relationship. Otherwise he could not very well interpret the new understanding of the self as the specific gift of redemption. The fact is that in Paul the depth of redemption as it affects the individual corresponds to its cosmic breadth. If this were not so, the apostle would be presenting us with a myth. But the essential thing is this, that this individual be regarded as the concrete piece of worldly reality that I myself also am. Individualism, however well concealed, must in no circumstances be allowed any place here. The world and history are not the sum of potential and actual I-Thou relationships, as the Church is not the sum of its members. If they were, we should be able to reduce world, history and Church to an unending and manifold but, in the last resort, very superficial relationship of isolated individuals to each other. The profound involvement of all individuals in a common destiny, whether it is produced by nature or by matter or by some alleged event of revelation, would no longer be sufficiently evident. The moment of decision would then have to be emphasized so strongly that history would rest on a foundation clearly incapable of doing justice to the reality of any history which implies a doctrine of the Fall or of divine preservation. This is not the place to carry out a thorough exegetical and systematic exposition of this objection. We need do no more than raise the critical question whether the equation of theology with anthropology does not necessarily lead to a modified form of individualism. Even the anthropological limitation placed by Bultmann on Paul's doctrine of justification must be seen in this light. In fact, it is concerned only with the justification of the individual. But Paul can discuss Rom. 9–11 under the heading of the righteousness of God and expound this righteousness not merely as an antithesis to the works of the Law, which challenges the individual, but equally as the fulfilment of the promise given to the people of God. Further, his doctrine of justification, standing though it undoubtedly does under the sign of his eschatology, cannot be understood at all without his apocalyptic in which it is not a question of reward or completion but, according to I Cor. 15.28, a question of God's becoming all in all. Correspondingly, temptation may be the sign manual of the Christian condition in the present, but it is at the same time the expression of the fact – established only by groaning and travailing – that in this present God still meets with contradiction and his enemies do not yet lie definitively under his feet. Paul was unable to allow redemption to end in earthly contradiction. Apocalyptic is therefore not less meaningful in his theology than anthropology. It proclaims that the apostle was very deeply moved by the quest of the Johannine apocalypse for the revelation of the godhead of God, and his doctrine of justification revolves around the rightful claim which God will make good on his own created world. If that sounds mythological, the same is true in the last resort of all utterances about the work of redemption and in any event is no good reason for the elimination of this nexus of ideas. The interpretation of it will however play a real part in the determination of the total outlook of Pauline theology.

It is no less important to come to terms with Bultmann's interpretation of John. Once again the first thing to be said is that this interpretation will still be studied and have influence when even the names of Bultmann's contemporary opponents are scarcely remembered. It belongs to the line of classic interpretations even if the fourth-form mind of our own time does not recognize this. But the complex of problems contained in such a confession may not be concealed. It may even be that there is no contribution to the almost limitless flood of Johannine literature in the presence of which we are made so aware of the problematical nature of each and every Johannine interpretation. In the whole New Testament it is the Fourth Gospel which presents the greatest and most difficult riddles. Just as all that King Midas touched turned to gold, so almost everything which has any connection with this Gospel seems to become a problem. Thus nowhere in the New Testament have such opposed interpretations been possible as here. Apostle or heretic, the seamless robe of Christ or a conflation of sources, a dramatically constructed and skilfully articulated composition or a formless and monotonous chaos of repetitive utterances, Aramaic language and imagery or Hellenistic spirituality, mysticism or rudimentary Church dogmatics – these are only some of the alternatives which are still being canvassed. It is therefore characteristic of the situation that within one decade two contemporaries of such international standing as Bultmann and Dodd have presented us with two interpretations of which one takes its inspiration from Kierkegaard, the other from Platonism. Bultmann's interpretation, with which alone I am concerned here, stands and falls by the theory that the Evangelist has used, worked over and glossed a pagan source consisting of speeches purporting to be revelation and has employed at the same time a source consisting of signs, so that the gift and the claim of the revealer may be illustrated from the wonders contained in it. Only thus can Bultmann come to terms with the undoubtedly mythological matter to be found in the Gospel as well as the crude belief in miracles shown by the Evangelist. Only thus can he both cling to the thesis that the incarnation of the Word is the theme of the Gospel and allow, following Kierkegaard, the Incarnation to maintain the incognito of the Revealer and, by reason of this very incognito, to set up a stumbling-block for the world. But will the foundation really bear the burden of proof? I must confess that I cannot convince myself of the existence of the above mentioned 'revelation source' and find it not merely offensive but also incredible when, for very long stretches of the Gospel, the Evangelist is made into the Christian commentator of a pagan source. Above all I am unable to see the incognito of the Revealer as being maintained in a Gospel which begins with the wedding at Cana, sees the Passion narrative as arising directly out of the raising of Lazarus and reaches its culmination in the shout of victory from the Cross. This being the case, the stumbling-block seems to me to consist exclusively in the demand for obedience in the face of a world in revolt and the sole purpose of the Incarnation to be the opening up of the possibility of communication with the heavenly glory. It only provides the premise on the strength of which it can be said 'We saw his glory'. It is a very remarkable fact, and one worthy of further consideration, that Bultmann the exegete sees himself compelled, on the presuppositions of his own systematic theology, to interpret the Pauline eschatology on the basis of the Johannine and, conversely, to interpret the Johannine christology on the basis of a christology of incarnation and humiliation which is at least very near to the Pauline. The question of the reasons for this state of affairs and of whether such a procedure is justifiable should determine the continuing dialogue with him. If I am not to get lost in the problems of detailed research, I must in conclusion confine myself to indicating two constellations of questions which deserve more general interest. It is one of the special characteristics of our contemporary situation that the formulation of questions in the field of the comparative study of religions, once so energetically and frequently vilified, is enjoying the very highest popularity and indeed is triumphing all along the line since the Dead Sea texts have come over the horizon of our knowledge. But we should be well advised to suppress any ironical meditation on the subject of fidelity to principles and of prejudices about the application of any given method in the theological camp. We have to be grateful for the comprehensive, wearisome, laborious and fidgety work of editing and interpreting the new texts. If it is the details which have for the most part occupied the foreground, then we need only paint here with broad sweeps of the brush. An orthodox community with a highly-strung apocalyptic and messianic hope, which has liberated itself from the Temple and its sacrifices and is conscious of itself as standing out in polemical relief as the holy remnant and the fellowship of the New Covenant – such a community causes us to ask questions of a hitherto utterly undreamed-of sharpness about the presuppositions and possibilities governing the advent of the religion of John the Baptist and of Christianity. Historical and theological parallels to the motifs of almost the whole New Testament literature present themselves in profusion. I am thinking in this connection of eschatology, of the doctrine of predestination, of dualism, as well as ecclesiastical discipline, rites of initiation, catechetical and hymnological material conveyed from the sects; but also of details such as their cultic meals, their peculiar form of communism, the idea of a holy *militia*. The eschatological mode of exegesis approaches very closely indeed to that employed in the New Testament, while, conversely, the stark legalism of this literature distinguishes the sects from the New Testament and allows the specific characteristics of Christianity to emerge more clearly. It is incontestable that there is influence on the young Christian community, even if it is still unclear whether this derives directly from the sects themselves or stems from a source flowing widely on Jewish soil and becoming visible in the life of the sects.

In proportion as general participation in the study of the Qumran literature has increased, the thesis which maintained the existence of a pre-Christan mythological gnosis and its significance for the New Testament has been increasingly discredited. In general, scholars have been prepared to admit nothing except the existence of a widespread idealistic world-view. The genesis of gnosticism within the Church is widely explained as the result of a connection between such a dualism and Christian soteriology. This is to relapse into the way of thinking which sees the gnostic movement as a phenomenon of decadence in the life of the Church. However comfortable this attitude to the problem may be, it is an impermissible simplification of the facts and of New Testament problems. In any investigation in the sphere of the comparative study of religions we must definitely start from the knowledge that primitive Christian soteriology, christology and ecclesiology do not present themselves in the form of a self-contained unity, but rather fall apart into a multiplicity of divergent conceptions which can only reflect the changed historical situation of the community. Of course, the community of each age desires to describe the being and work of the one Jesus Christ. But it does this always with new means which are offered to it by its spiritual and religious environment. It is bound to do this if only because otherwise its proclamation would be utterly incomprehensible to its contemporaries. It is bound to do it even more because it is itself subject to historical change, in which continuity and discontinuity are interwoven in the strangest fashion. The one biblical theology, growing from a single root and maintaining itself in unbroken continuity, is wish-fulfilment and fantasy. The Hellenistic community did not hesitate to deliver its proclamation with the help of means drawn from its own time and milieu. Its principal difference from Jewish Christianity lies in the fact that it puts the main weight of its message on the present nature of salvation. But that alters the structure of all its dogmatic pronouncements. At this point there appears, instead of the Messiah and the Son of Man (in the role of Daniel's universal judge), the Kyrios, the Son of God, the Cosmocrator; the Church is seen as analogous to the fellowship of a mystery religion and, correspondingly, the Sacrament is made to effect a transformation of the Christian's existence or to bring him into close association with the multitude of the blessed, redemption is understood as liberation from the power of Ananke and eschatology becomes deliverance from this world. The process was certainly not completed smoothly: this would have been impossible in the face of the Jewish Christian tradition, which could not be sloughed off in its totality on the spot, and of the influence of the great theologians, whose chief service is to have taken up a critical posture towards the enthusiasm of the religious life of the community. But the slippery slope of this development requires to be perceived and acknowledged for what it is. Its first literary document is I Corinthians, in which we find the views and motifs of the religious life of the Hellenistic community springing up to meet us on every side. Nothing is more characteristic of this piety than the denial of the corporeal resurrection. The resurrection of Christ is not denied and the Corinthians are anything but rationalists: thus this denial cannot be derived simply from the Hellenistic 'Enlightenment'. The only remaining explanation, however, is that the Corinthians have appropriated to themselves at least in part the words of the gnostics of II Tim. 2.18: 'The resurrection has already taken place.' In baptism they have experienced rebirth, they have achieved the breakthrough from death to life, they have put on the new man, they have escaped from the power of the forces of fate and entered into association with the hosts of the blessed; as the undoubted quotation from a hymn in Eph. 2.6 formulates it, they are enthroned with Christ in the heavenly places.

If these facts are borne in mind, the logic of the foregoing theory of the origin of Christian gnosis seems to me to appear in a light at once hopeless and grotesque. How could anyone possibly start out from purely Jewish presuppositions, from the impression of the historical Jesus so gladly and frequently conjured up, above all from a nakedly dualistic world-view, and thence arrive at conceptions of this kind? For the Corinthians and their religious practice certainly show that there is more here than just pleasing imaginative theories. The dualism which is undoubtedly present is combined with the motifs and forms of expression of a redemption mythology paralleled only in the Hellenistic mysteries. And since the Corinthians boast of their 'illumination', and their fellows of II Tim. 2.18 are described unmistakably as gnostics, I do not see how we can escape the conclusion that the enthusiasm of the Corinthians is to be classified as a Christian variety of a mythological gnosis. Christian gnosis is therefore just as old as the Hellenistic community which grew up alongside, but independently of, Jewish Christianity; it is no product of an age of decadence but the possibility present on Hellenistic soil from the beginning of understanding Christianity as an analogue of the redemption religions of the mystery cults. We come up against the limits of its expansion only when we find ourselves back within the orbit of Palestinian Jewish Christianity or else already within that of nascent early catholic orthodoxy. This is why we practically never come upon traces of it either in the Synoptists on the one hand or in Acts on the other. Even these writings are in no way untouched by the dualistic world-view. If Christian gnosis had been the product of the combination of an ethical dualism with the Christian idea of redemption, as for instance K. G. Kuhn assumes, it is above all the Synoptists who would certainly bear witness to this, whether by way of affirmation or of denial. For ethical dualism can only flower, as the Qumran texts show, in the soil of a piety which stands in the shadow of the law conceived as the road to salvation. From this standpoint we might even ask whether the dualism of the Qumran texts is anything more than the typically Jewish expression of the metaphysical dualism represented by religious Hellenism. In any case we do not encounter anywhere in the New Testament a dualism which is limited to the ethical sphere. It is always projected into this sphere from eschatology, christology and soteriology. Because Christ stands over against Adam, the body of Christ over against the old aeon and justification is understood as the action of the God who raises the dead, there follows the parenetic call to put off the old man and put on the new, to renounce the lie, darkness and death in order to serve life, light and the truth. If the New Testament really represented only an ethical dualism clothed in the garments of a world-view, Christianity would become a Judaism which believed that the Messiah had already come. The Law would then necessarily triumph over the Gospel. The questions which concern us today in the field of the comparative study of religions have a depth which is not usually seen for what it is. The decision for Law or Gospel is already implicit in the attitude we take to these questions. Anyone who really maintained that they could be solved so far as the New Testament is concerned from the study of the Qumran texts would, in my opinion, incontrovertibly end up with a legalistic understanding of the Christian message. My incursions into the subject of gnosis were designed to demonstrate that it is precisely because of the present rush of new insights and problems in the field of the comparative study of religions that we need to guard ourselves from this kind of one-sidedness.

Only when we see gnosis as a possibility which was seized on by the Hellenistic community from its beginnings, do we also comprehend the genesis of early catholicism, which is nothing but the Church's defence mechanism in the face of the threat of a gnostic take-over. It seems to me one of the most significant steps forward in our work that we are already beginning to see this process more clearly in the New Testament. The recently published commentary on Acts by Ernst Haenchen opens a new chapter in the study of Acts inasmuch as it directs itself resolutely to this particular task. Here the analyses made by Martin Dibelius in his *Studies in Acts*,[4] by Philipp Vielhauer in his article on the *Paulinism of Acts*[5] and by Hans Conzelmann in his monograph *Die Mitte der Zeit*[6] are brought together into a closer relationship. Luke is not, as Dibelius still believed, a late pupil of Paul, but the first representative of nascent early catholicism. His attempt to present the history of the Christian religion including that of Jesus as secular history shows how far back the beginnings of this movement lie; on the other hand, it only becomes possible where primitive Christian eschatology, the dynamic force of New Testament preaching, is in eclipse and survives solely in the treatment of the 'Last Things'. Luke takes as his own peculiar theme the hour of the Church as the mid-point of time. Eschatology is replaced by a salvation history which is remarkably well organized and connected but which, in spite of the sheen imparted to it by miracles, remains confined within the limits of immanence. Its content is the world mission of the Church, foreshadowed as early as the speech of Jesus at Nazareth; it throws into even sharper relief the isolation of the parable of the Sower and articulates Acts thematically into the sub-sections

[4] *Aufsätze zur Apostelgeschichte*, 1951; ET, *Studies in the Acts of the Apostles*, 1956.
[5] 'Zum Paulinismus der Apostelgeschichte', *EvTh* 10, 1950/51, pp. 1–15.
[6] *Die Mitte der Zeit*, 1954; ET, *The Theology of St Luke*, 1960.

'Jerusalem', 'Samaria' and 'the ends of the earth'. The mission, however, is no longer regarded primarily as the testimony of the Christ who proclaims himself through his messengers but as the way and the work of the world-wide Christian organization for salvation. To put it in a nutshell: the Word is no longer the sole criterion of the Church, but the Church is the legitimation of the Word and the apostolic origin of the Church's ministerial office provides the guarantee of a valid proclamation. Of course, behind such conceptions there lies not the arbitrary judgment of an individual but the pressure of historical circumstances. Just as the Church, of which Luke is the representative, is having to arm itself for the imminent struggle with the Empire, so, on the other front and as a matter of priority, it is being compelled to throw up a dam against the flood of enthusiasm. Luke saw this necessity with great clarity and carried out his self-appointed task brilliantly. He is not only the first Christian historian and a cultural writer of the highest order; he represents a well defined theology, and one which has to be taken seriously. Admittedly, it is a theology which is essentially different from that of primitive Christianity and must be characterized root and branch as early catholic. Dibelius and even Haenchen have made the problems of this theology the matter of debate more indirectly than explicitly. We can only make a just estimate of it if we approach it from the aspect of the antithesis between *theologia crucis* and *theologia gloriae* and, in so doing, raise the central problem of all Christian proclamation.

Yet I should like to conclude my survey at this point. It has called attention to only a few of the questions out of the wealth of work which we have before us at this time. Others will probably plot the position differently from their particular coign of vantage, even if it seems to me that in what has been said the field of the real decisions in New Testament exegesis has been sufficiently mapped. Even this small contribution will already have shown that more or less all the basic problems of our subject are today once again at issue and open. We can no longer, as happened to a colleague before 1914 at the hands of an influential member of the faculty, advise our degree student to choose a thesis subject out of the Apostolic Fathers, with the observation that all the essential work on the New Testament has been done already but that what remains is so difficult that a beginner would be well advised to leave it alone. It is precisely in the open state of all the fundamental questions today that I should myself see the characteristic mark and the promise of our situation.

II

BLIND ALLEYS IN THE 'JESUS OF HISTORY' CONTROVERSY*

ANYONE WHO HAS followed the debate about the historical Jesus during the last decade must have been astonished or even horrified to observe how, as in a volcanic area, the earth was suddenly everywhere spewing forth fire, smoke and differently-sized masses of lava, where, for a generation past, pleasant gardens had been planted on the slopes of ancient craters. Exegetes and systematic theologians, Protestants and Catholics, one's own school and its opponents (not least what was once the New World), our students and even the so-called lay people have been drawn into the uproar and have made strenuous efforts to extend the firework display. The discussion on demythologizing receded into the background in the face of the new problem and the hermeneutic question raised by this discussion altered its sights considerably. It may well look as if the net result, here as elsewhere, will be in inverse proportion to the passion expended – very meagre, consisting in little else but general confusion. But at least we have an unusual opportunity of studying the various eruptive powers in our situation. Admittedly, not every jet of steam is interesting, and many such are dissipating of their own accord. But what should, more than anything else, provide grounds for serious concern is that while the technique of the historical critical method is being used on all sides, yet at the same time, the sense for historical dimensions is being lost. The 'new question' only merits being called 'new' because the theological relevance of the historical element has become, to a quite unprecedented extent, an acute and decisive problem which no one has really succeeded in mastering. This is a point which I should like to clarify by the use of two detailed analyses. I have chosen extreme examples; the advantage of this

* 'Sackgassen im Streit um den historischen Jesus', a hitherto unpublished lecture.

procedure is that a particular train of logic has been followed to its end and – at least as I see it – the conclusion is in direct contradiction to the premisses. Polemics, which are at a discount today, are an inevitable concomitant of this method. But they may well recall us from some blind alleys with which we are threatened. Any methodology which is not based on rigid principles can only learn from errors committed in the past and see in them ways which it might have taken for itself but which others have explored already.

I. THE CONTINUATION OF THE OLD TYPE OF 'LIFE OF JESUS' STUDY

The old type of 'Life of Jesus' study still blooms richly, if somewhat autumnally, wherever dialectical theology, thorough-going eschatology and the form-critical method – that strange, peculiarly German combination of questionings, rejected for the most part on the rest of the European continent – have not succeeded in penetrating. Its most significant representative and, at the same time, the mediator of a certain accommodation between the camps is, so far as we are concerned, undoubtedly Joachim Jeremias, whose whole life's work lies anchored in these waters. Since it is the question of methodology and its roots in, and implications for, systematic theology with which we are concerned, we can leave out of account his profusion of historical and exegetical studies and concentrate on the short programmatic work entitled 'The Present Position in the Controversy Concerning the Problem of the Historical Jesus'.[1] A short survey of the history of the question in Germany leads to the declaration, made with concealed yet unmistakable passion:

> We are in danger of surrendering the affirmation 'The Word became flesh' and of abandoning the salvation-history, God's activity in the Man Jesus of Nazareth and in His message. We are in danger of approaching Docetism, where Christ becomes an idea. [We are in danger of substituting the preaching of the apostle Paul for the message of Jesus.][2]

[1] This essay, which has appeared in slightly varying forms in a number of different contexts, is here quoted in the English version which appeared in the *Expository Times* 69, 1958, pp. 333–9. [Sentences in square brackets are from the version used by Professor Käsemann in the German original, 'Der gegenwärtige Stand der Debatte um das Problem des historischen Jesus', which appeared in *Der historische Jesus und der kerygmatische Christus*, ed. H. Ristow and K. Matthiae, 1960, pp. 12–25.]

[2] *Art. cit.*, p. 33.

Of course, these statements are not to be understood as overlapping completely in content, as the parallelism in the introductory formula might lead us to suppose. Nevertheless, this juxtaposition is peculiarly characteristic; to name the loss of the doctrine of the Incarnation and of salvation history in the same breath as docetism and a predominance of the Pauline preaching is so incongruous and puts Paul into such strange surroundings that such a combination of imminent dangers can only be explained and justified by a highly arbitrary plotting of New Testament theology. A second passage, of which I once again quote the core, leads us closer to the heart of the matter:

> Every verse of the Gospels tells us that the origin of Christianity is not the Kerygma, not the Resurrection experience of the disciples, not the Christ-idea, but an historical event, to wit, the appearance of the Man Jesus of Nazareth . . . and His message. I must specially emphasize these last words – and His message. The Gospel that Jesus proclaimed precedes the Kerygma of the primitive community. [Jesus refuses to be simply absorbed into an anonymous primitive community.] The Kerygma . . . refers us back from itself at every turn. . . . Whatever utterance of the Kerygma presents itself to us, its origins are always to be found in the preaching of Jesus.[3]

Jeremias exemplifies this by reference to the Pauline doctrine of justification by faith and goes on to distinguish kerygma as mission preaching from didache as the further instruction of the community, the precipitate of which we have in the Gospel narratives about Jesus and without which there would never have been any primitive kerygma.[4]

Some critical observations on detail are unavoidable at this point. For already the terminology used by Jeremias not only presupposes a very definitely slanted understanding of the particular issues, but also arouses objections to the whole approach. In the New Testament, didache is not so separated from kerygma as to be associated primarily with the transmission of the tradition about Jesus. It is primarily, as the later *Teaching of the Twelve Apostles* clearly shows, the presentation of liturgical, doctrinal or parenetical material indiscriminately, and sometimes also as, for example, in Hebrews and the Epistle of Barnabas, as a specific function of the διδάσκαλος, the interpretation of the Old Testament. Rom. 1.16ff. and I Cor. 15.3ff. show that in just the same way 'Gospel' may not be restricted to the

[3] *Ibid.*, p. 335. [4] *Loc. cit.*

message of the earthly Jesus or even only to the narratives concerning him. This kind of arbitrary restriction and distinction tends to make us think of different strands of tradition – a concept which would not seem to be at all tenable for the Synoptists. Further, no one is proposing to deny that Jesus was the origin of Christian existence and no one can seriously envisage his being absorbed into an anonymous original community, just because he is, and remains, the irreplaceable 'origin'. But the historicizing language used by Jeremias at this point puts the question-mark in the wrong place. It is not a matter of what role we do or do not ascribe to Jesus, but of what weight we give within the framework of New Testament proclamation to the 'historical' reports about Jesus. If exegetes who employ critical methods are to avoid the charge of making illegitimate encroachments on others' territory, these two issues may neither be simply identified nor confused with each other. Yet it cannot well be denied that the New Testament letters provide us with surprisingly little material about the historical Jesus. Still more important, Jeremias himself admits, and indeed demonstrates in *The Parables of Jesus*,[5] that narrative material about Jesus is found embedded in the community witness and nowhere else. Why is this? Why does this give the kerygma, which is in no sense merely mission preaching, precedence or, rather more carefully put, a significance which Jeremias' thesis is bound to diminish. To pick up his own phraseology: unless all critical analysis of the Synoptists, including that pursued by Jeremias himself, rests upon a fallacy and begets further fallacies, surely the primitive communities from the beginning absorbed the Jesus tradition into their own testimony? Can there, in the last resort, be any doubt that it was Easter which first called forth that Christian proclamation into which the Jesus tradition was then bedded?

All this indicates that Jeremias is swimming against the stream of New Testament tradition and its course and that therefore the onus is on him to demonstrate the theological validity of his procedure. He cannot push off this onus on to the critical scholars who pay due regard to this course and make it their starting-point. Nor is it permissible for him to transform the theological problem – that the New Testament offers us the Jesus tradition solely in the form of the testimony to the Christ yielded by this tradition after it has been worked over – into the historical problem as to whether Jesus was in

[5] *Die Gleichnisse Jesu*, 1947; ET, rev. ed., *The Parables of Jesus* (from 6th German ed. of 1962), 1963.

fact the origin of Christian existence and whether all Christian tradition is in fact to be referred back to him. It is not the 'that' but the 'how' which has to be considered here. For this very reason we are bound to want information as to why primitive Christianity did not make such a clear-cut distinction and separation between a 'didache' of the Jesus tradition and the kerygma, thus giving an unmistakable primacy to the former. This is not an unreasonable demand, because Jeremias has taken considerable pains, in his analysis of the parables for example, to find the way back to Jesus. Furthermore, Bultmann in particular has set out as clearly as anyone could wish the problem which arises here, so that an answer could not well be evaded. Must we not reproach Jeremias with embarking with extraordinary irresponsibility on our complex of questions, in that he simply passes over the original problem in a manner quite incompatible with his previous recognition and articulation of it in his book on the parables? Is it legitimate to substitute another problem, which in any case is logically dependent on the first, and to tack on to it theses for the categories of which no proper foundation or justification has been established?

Am I perhaps doing Jeremias an injustice? After all, he does provide us, if a little belatedly, with a further theological basis for his statements:

> The Incarnation implies that the story of Jesus is not only a possible subject for historical research, study and criticism, but that it demands all of these. . . . If it be objected that we fail to apprehend the essential nature of the act of faith if we make historical knowledge the object of faith, and that faith is in this way sacrificed to such a dubious, subjective, and hypothetical study, we can only reply that God has sacrificed Himself. The Incarnation is the self-sacrifice of God, and to that we can only bow in assent.[6]

But if this is really the case, it becomes still more puzzling that the New Testament does not draw the same conclusions as Jeremias. If it had done, it would have had to produce an exclusively, or at least primarily, historical narrative and, further, not to have worked over and altered this narrative so drastically at all points as Jeremias himself shows to be the case in his book on the parables. Actually, Jeremias does not attempt to answer our question by deriving and demonstrating the correctness of his own position from the New

[6] *Art. cit.*, p. 336.

Testament, but by appealing to a dogmatic judgment from which the New Testament deliberately does not draw the same historically illuminating implications. It is on this that Jeremias bases the necessity for critical study and here we ought to respect the expert. But he goes far beyond this. If critical research, dominated as it is by a complex of problems generally acknowledged to be fundamental to it, is reckoned to convey knowledge of the historical Jesus, this knowledge, then, means for Jeremias knowledge of the object of faith. Thus he does not shrink from really allowing faith to be dependent on insight mediated by scholarship. I cannot recall that the logic of this position has ever been pursued so radically by any other colleague of mine in this field. His endeavour, therefore, takes on a significance which it is impossible to overestimate and which has been long denied it. It is certainly not his intention to embark on a particularly hazardous enterprise. We are, he says, better equipped today than previous generations were. Literary criticism of sources and of tradition, form-criticism, the history of the age and its environment, new knowledge about Jesus' native tongue and, above all, about his eschatology have refined our methods and kept us from making mistakes which were once unavoidable We can no longer modernize Jesus and create him in our own image as easily as our fathers did.[7]

But can this – should this – be enough for Jeremias, even if his judgment should prove to be justified? Is it only the result that is decisive or does the method of working by which that result is reached count for anything? What of those generations who also engaged in critical study, but did not reach our present peak and fell into those errors which Jeremias censures? Are we to reproach them for having been unable to jump over their own shadow and that of their time and are they to be held responsible for what, in the nature of things, lay beyond their powers of attainment? Is Jeremias not aware of the dilemma which threatens him? On the one hand we say: 'We must follow along the way of the historical Jesus and his message, exactly where it leads us.'[8] This is to give sanction in principle to the whole history of error and confusion over the last two hundred and fifty years with all its catastrophes, although Jeremias expressly dissociates himself from this period. The logic of this, in turn, is that in each individual phase faith was dependent on the state of historical knowledge. But in actual fact such has only too often been the path to superstition. In view of this, are we justified in

[7] *Ibid.*, p. 337. [8] *Ibid.*, p. 336.

saying that the general direction was right and only its means and objectives were inadequate? Or – the other horn of the dilemma – is the postulate in question itself false? 'Regardless of where it may lead us.' Is it not a counsel of desperation to talk like this after the tragic history of the 'quest of the historical Jesus', as A. Schweitzer has portrayed it? Which generation in it did not boast of its refined methods and its spiritual achievements? It is here if anywhere that Jeremias reveals his spiritual forebears and his obligation to them. Here he enters on the inheritance of the past – that past which was motivated by liberal impulses and fascinated by the magic of evolutionary belief, but which ended in positivism and its polar counterpart, speculation. Note that I am not blaming Jeremias for this; on the contrary, I admire his resolution. For we must all in fact enter into this heritage and any of us who refuses to do so is not merely denying his fathers who, in the field of New Testament study, belong – and not accidentally – less among the ranks of the orthodox than among those of the liberals and perhaps even of the heretics. He is suspending himself in empty air, in a historical vacuum. I should certainly *not* say:

> We can venture on [this road] with confidence, nor need we fear that we are embarking on a perilous, fruitless adventure.[9]

Can we for a single moment forget that we are dealing every day with a flood of dubious and even abstruse attacks on the exegetical, historical and theological fields and that our study is gradually degenerating into world-wide guerilla warfare? (That is, if the past does not scare us enough by itself!) Can we, of our own power and without getting involved at all, disengage ourselves from the *massa perditionis*? Can we ply our trade otherwise than in the knowledge that the feet of those who will carry us out have already long been at the door and indeed are there all the time?

Quite unmoved by such questions, Jeremias declares that, protected by these various methods as by ramparts, we encounter along the road of critical study the same challenge to faith put to us by the kerygma; we are led into the realm of the One for whom there are no analogies in 'comparative religion'; we are set before God himself. But because the claim to sovereignty by which we are here confronted is the *fons et origo* of the Christian religion, we stand before him as before the central task of New Testament study.[10] We

[9] *Loc. cit.* [10] *Ibid.*, p. 338.

concede that the critical scholar, like every other reader of the New Testament, is able, over and above the boundaries of his work, to discover and to hear the Christian message. But it simplifies things too much to speak of the starting-point's being the same. For even the demand for faith does not wholly transcend the historical situation, and the kergyma has taken many forms which cannot easily be separated from the decisive content nor, on the other hand, identified with it. That apocalyptic claim to sovereignty, which, in the time immediately after Easter, was addressed to Israel alone is, however, no longer binding on us in the same way as is the other, made in the context of the Hellenistic community; not, at least, without some distortion of the problems involved. Does this not show that the historian never uncovers anything but relative claims? Further, true though it may be that the claim of Jesus to sovereignty cannot be derived from, nor compared with, anything in the comparative study of religions – once again, the historian will want to add 'so far' – this cannot be said of every verse of our Gospels, as Jeremias maintains.[11] On the contrary, the miracle stories and the parenesis, to name only two examples, offer a profusion of parallelisms and of adapted material from that field. Finally, even those words and actions which have no analogies there are seen in the context of a claim to sovereignty which as such is in thorough-going competition with other such claims, however different it may be in detail. In the last resort, the Gospels do not lead us anywhere except into the world of religion. This has to be stressed because Jeremias concludes that we are set before God. The believer may be convinced that even the critical study of the New Testament – indeed, this study above all – forces the reality and claim of God upon us. But this is not a possibility of critical study as such – to maintain this would be to place an intolerable strain upon it; it is a possibility to be encountered only along this, as every other road, *ubi et quando deo visum est*. Jeremias has no hesitation in expressing himself in an over-simplified, ambiguous and careless way or in omitting essential links in his chain of reasoning. This is on a par with the optimism we have already seen to be characteristic and, just because it occurs in a 'popular' lecture, is, to say the least, open to grave objection.

Before we embark on our summing-up, however, we have still to explore the third part of the essay, which deals with the relationship between preaching before and after Easter. It is rightly laid down that

[11] *Loc. cit.*

the two may not be separated, because otherwise the Gospel would become dead history and the kerygma – once again this antithesis we noted previously – would become an abstract idea. On the other hand, the two are not on the same footing and may not be reduced to the same level, but belong together in the relation of call and response.

> The call, not the response, is the decisive thing. . . . According to the testimony of the New Testament, there is no other revelation of God but the Incarnate Word. The preaching of the Early Church concerning this is the divinely inspired witness to the revelation, but the Church's preaching is not itself revelation. Revelation does not happen on Sundays from ten to eleven. The doctrine of continuous revelation is a gnostic error. . . . Jesus is the Lord. The Lord is above the messenger. For faith there is no authority but the Lord. The historical Jesus and His message are not one presupposition among many for the Kerygma, but the sole presupposition of the Kerygma. . . . Only the Son of Man and His Word can give authority to the message – no one else and nothing else.[12]

Here Jeremias formulates very clearly the dogmatic which, for him, generates New Testament work. Unfortunately, I see no alternative but to declare publicly that the New Testament enterprise is only discredited by a dogmatic theology of this kind. To begin with, the key term 'continuous revelation' is a questionable one in the context of the history of dogma. Have we here a new phrase, coined after the analogy of 'continuous creation'? This is really crucial. However strange a phenomenon a controversy about dogmatic theology between New Testament scholars may be, I cannot yield an inch in my contention that what Jeremias describes as a gnostic error is for me a fundamental doctrine of the Bible and the Reformation. When Luther, in his explanation of the Third Article, says that we are called by the Spirit through the Gospel, he certainly does not understand by 'Gospel', as Jeremias does, the message of Jesus but the Word which is preached on Sunday morning between ten and eleven; and when he begins 'not of my own reason or power', he is undoubtedly pointing towards revelation. Indeed, throughout the whole New Testament the Spirit is the power of revelation. The distinction – which is not a New Testament one – between Gospel and kerygma – in fact boomerangs because it ends by separating the testimony generated by the Spirit from the message of Jesus and

[12] *Ibid.*, p. 339.

ultimately, therefore, the Spirit from the Christ. Do not the Johannine farewell discourses teach that Christ, Spirit and preaching come together in the promised Paraclete and the revelatory function of the Spirit manifests itself in proclamation? It would thus not be easy to prove that the incarnate Logos of the Fourth Gospel is to be identified without reservation with the historical Jesus. In II Cor. 2–4 Paul speaks of his gospel as the medium of revelation and even for the Synoptists it is true that 'He who hears you, hears me'. In my view, to say that revelation is confined to the years 1–30 is to create a completely new doctrine. Neither must we overlook the fact that not infrequently, in the name of a genuine or a metamorphosed biblicism, private dogmatic theologies are minted out of the New Testament which bypass both the history of dogma and the doctrine of the writers' own reformation Church. I can only protest bitterly when this is done even by professional theologians. Of course, it is the heritage of liberalism which is reappearing here – liberalism, which together with pietism, has caused the disintegration of dogmatic theology within the Evangelical Church.

It will be useful to orient my concluding analysis and summary around the striking likeness which exists between the structure of these statements about revelation and those which, according to Schlier,[13] the Praesymbola, and the apostolic tradition assembled therein, present as the Gospel itself or, more exactly phrased, as at once the essence and the norm of the Gospel. In both cases, the preaching of the Church and the witness of Scripture are treated as the unfolding of the fundamental revelation and receive their unity from it. This fundamental revelation is prior to, and sovereign over, Scripture; equally, it enters into Scripture and becomes its centre in such a way that out of it specific points of Scripture may be both validated and criticized. Not the least important agreement between these two schemes is that both invest a historical phenomenon with such weighty significance and ground this procedure in an appeal to the Incarnation. The difference between them can be seen in the fact that Schlier does not touch at all on the problem of the historical Jesus, while Jeremias, on the other hand, does not explicitly tackle the question of the place occupied by the Resurrection and the exaltation of Christ in his own framework of reference. Where ecclesiology is the fulcrum of a theology, the earthly Jesus is so incapsulated in the

[13] H. Schlier, 'Kerygma und Sophia', *Die Zeit der Kirche* (Exegetische Aufsätze und Vorträge), 2nd ed., 1958, pp. 206–32.

self-revelation of Christ that there is no longer any need for him to make a direct personal appearance. As against this, we owe Jeremias a debt of gratitude for preserving the specifically Protestant heritage by the absolutely definitive way in which he has expounded Christology as the point and content of 'Scripture alone'. In his usual amazingly self-critical fashion he certainly acknowledges the danger that the christology he defends, in its isolation from the preaching of the primitive Church, may end in Ebionitism.[14] Resurrection and exaltation seem here to be nothing more than the vindication of the earthly Jesus and, as such, a part of the content of faith, not faith's very ground.

The Protestant heritage is preserved here, just at the deepest point of its modification by the Enlightenment. For it was the Enlightenment which, for the first time in the history of the Church, discovered the problem of the historical Jesus *as* a problem and, withdrawing it from the jurisdiction of the Chalcedonian dialectic, made it the measure of Christology. We can still see in Jeremias the same radicalism with which the Enlightenment set this question of the historical Jesus in opposition to the preaching and dogmatic theology of the Church. Never before had the earthly Jesus as such been made the object of faith. This only became possible with the deliberate and rigorous application of the tools of historical criticism, the same tools which still make it possible for Jeremias to say: 'Back behind the primitive Church to Jesus.' Now as then historical criticism serves the purpose of liberating the earthly Jesus from the ecclesiastical and dogmatic over-painting which has already begun in our New Testament. This is why so much hangs for Jeremias upon the *ipsissima verba*. *Ipsissima verba* – what is this phrase but the Enlightenment's version of '*Christ* alone' which is, likewise, meaningful only as an antithesis to ecclesiastical tradition. But if the '*Christ* alone' of the Reformers was intended to convey the uniqueness of the Gospel, then the term *ipsissima verba* alters the sense into that of the originality of the Christian message. There is further searching for, and exposition of, the Gospel. This orientation towards the Word reveals a genuine continuity. Yet the Gospel is being historicized. The *Verbum* is replaced by the words and works of the earthly Jesus, held together by the unity of his person. Paradoxically, this process of historicization is most obvious when Jeremias asserts with pride that the possibility of modernizing interpretations of Jesus is now excluded because of the

[14] Jeremias, *art. cit.*, p. 339.

knowledge we now have of his environment, the language he spoke, etc. As if archaizing exegesis were not a specifically modern phenomenon, and archaeology itself not the youngest branch on the tree of historical study!

I admit, of course, that Jesus is not for Jeremias, as he was for the Enlightenment, mere man, but the incarnate Son of God. For this reason he invariably speaks with very great emphasis, but from the New Testament point of view with very questionable propriety, of encountering the Son of Man. But this is to complicate things unbearably. For this Son of Man is to be recovered by the tools of historical criticism from the stratum of community tradition under which he has been concealed. The implication, as we saw previously, is that the historian has an access road to God himself, provided by the methodology of his specialism. The accessibility of God in the person of the incarnate Son follows immediately from this premise, as is shown in the theological conclusion to *The Parables of Jesus*. We certainly cannot complain of any lack of logical follow-through or courage here. On the other hand, we cannot escape the conclusion that, in the last resort, it is historical criticism which decides the content and the limits of the Gospel. Of course Jeremias can only take this position if he can at the same time be certain that the preaching of Jesus coincides in essentials with that of the Church. This is why he is so passionately concerned for the Messianic consciousness, especially for Jesus' knowledge of the necessity of his saving death and his resurrection. Otherwise a gap would open between the historical and the preached Lord such as would compel explicit criticism of the content of what was preached. Both the unity and the truth of revelation and faith depend on the absence of such a gap, and this absence can only be established by the methods of historical criticism. Thus historical criticism has a double function in the eyes of Jeremias: it is necessary in order to get back to the origin of the Christian religion in the historical Jesus and it must, at the same time, defend the continuity between this origin and the preaching of the Church. All this produces a gripping drama! In his own celebrated words, Bultmann can look calmly on while all that cannot be held to be historical in the Gospel narrative is burnt up in the critical bonfire. Jeremias must use the fire to burn a clearing for the historical Jesus, but dare not let a single spark jump out on to the portrait of Jesus. Yet this comparison will not do. For Jeremias strips away, with the help of the fire, the dogmatic overpainting from the original picture in order to be able to maintain ultimately that this original picture is fire-proof. The point is not whether such an endeavour can succeed, or not. What is important is its radical nature which cannot but fill the spectator with equal proportions of fascination and terror. It would be impossible to be more revolutionary in theory, yet more conservative in practice. Radical historicism is brought into the service of apologetic. This highly individualized method of working is the presupposition for a dogmatic theology which sees in the Spirit not the medium of revelation but of testimony divorced from revelation and in the Scripture a source-document – the oldest Church tradition about Jesus; finally, it understands faith as immediate access to the Son of Man in that historicity of his as Jesus of Nazareth which is open to discovery by critical methods.

2. BULTMANN'S CONTROVERSY WITH HIS PUPILS

The purpose of my essay on the historical Jesus[15] was to re-animate the discussion among the circle of Bultmann's pupils and to produce, so far as possible, a certain self-criticism on the part of the master, whose historical scepticism at this point seems to me to be exaggerated and the theological outcome of this scepticism dangerous. The discussion which has, in fact, ensued has had two main effects. It became apparent that Bultmann's pupils were, on the whole and in principle, moving in the same direction, although Ernst Fuchs immediately proceeded to give to the 'new quest' a central importance which Günther Bornkamm and I myself in particular were not prepared to grant it. It also became apparent that while Bultmann found himself obliged to clarify his views, he was however, in spite of various concessions in detail, totally unwilling to alter his basic attitude. Rather, in his essay *Das Verhältnis der urchristlichen Christusbotschaft zum historischen Jesus*,[16] he has gone over from defence to attack. So we had the very unfamiliar spectacle of master and pupils, as in the New Testament seminar in days of yore, now conducting a critical discussion with each other in the full glare of publicity. For Bultmann's essay by no means ended the discussion. On the contrary, it seems that something like a neuralgic nerve in Bultmann's

[15] 'Das Problem des historischen Jesus', *ZTK* 51, 1954, pp. 125–53, reprinted in *Exegetische Versuche und Besinnungen* I, 2nd ed., 1960; pp. 187–214; ET, 'The Problem of the Historical Jesus', in *Essays on New Testament Themes* (SBT 41), 1964, pp. 15–47.

[16] SAW Heidelberg, phil.-hist. Klasse, 1960. 3 (cited as *Christusbotschaft*).

theology was touched, and that the problem cannot possibly be allowed to rest there, because it is not a matter of keeping a system intact but of theological truth. The issue is more important than the personalities involved, and the strength of a fellowship can only be measured by what happens when internal stresses have to be tolerated.

I begin my analysis of the answer given to us by Bultmann by stating that I simply do not understand the extraordinarily radical antithesis of historical and material continuity between Jesus and the primitive Christian preaching which permeates his whole essay; indeed, our ways probably begin to diverge here at the very outset. It is certainly true that, frequently, what is still historically knowable about a happening or a particular series of events is not what is really essential; while, on the other hand, an interpretation may not seldom largely conceal the historical reality or even cast it away altogether. In the process of understanding historical connections, we are in fact always exposed to the possibility of a cleavage between the historical and the material. Yet Bultmann does not speak of the difficulties and dangers of historical interpretation but of the relationship of the historical phenomenon to the material question which is being put to us; he thus makes a fundamental separation between things which seem to me fundamentally to belong together. For the material question surely arises out of the encounter with the historical phenomenon, even if only in the form of 'I do not know what to make of this'. I completely fail to understand how it is possible, within the field of the historical, to maintain the existence of material continuity without immediately thinking at the same time of historical continuity; the latter may be buried over certain stretches and taking, as it were, an underground course, but nevertheless it will remain relevant.

Certainly there is disagreement among us in certain cases as to the meaning of 'continuity'. In his essay 'Der historische Jesus',[17] Ebeling has raised objections to the use of the correlatives continuity – discontinuity. He argues that real discontinuity means a total lack of connection which would put an end to the asking of all historical questions. Therefore, he says, in present-day discourse either the correlatives will be used dialectically, in which case discontinuity will be an integrating factor in, or a modification of, continuity; or it will remain formal, so that continuity will signify only the brute fact

[17] G. Ebeling, 'Der historische Jesus', *Theologie und Verkündigung* III. 3, 1962, pp. 51–82, esp. pp. 57f.

of proximity, but beyond the concrete relationship of neighbourhood in time will express nothing specific or important. In actual fact, one is inclined to assume that Bultmann takes up the second position. If so, this would make sense of the antithesis between continuity and discontinuity which he maintains with such consistency. The dialectical interpretation seems to me all the more important in that I am only able to picture a historical series at all as the resultant of the tension between continuity and discontinuity. For this very reason, I cannot myself dispense with these two categories. Otherwise I should no longer be able to talk of history at all, because changes of direction, setbacks, breakthroughs and new beginnings are essential components of the historical process. Accordingly, I must postulate 'material' continuity wherever historical continuity maintains an incipient trend. Any other distinction seems to me to come to the same thing as the idea-reality dualism. Presumably Bultmann will reproach me on the grounds that such an outlook leaves me stranded in the realm of objectifying thinking. This, however, I cannot admit, since I have no intention of underestimating the historical element nor is it my view that the existence of continuity can be either established or refuted apart from the decision of the historian; for these reasons, the expression 'objectification' seems to be inappropriate.

The immediate purpose of these observations is merely to focus attention on inconsistencies and contradictions in the linguistic margins of our discussion. But the implication of these is that different conceptions of the essence of the historical may well lie behind them. This has never been made clearer to me than at the point where Bultmann expressly adopts as his own H. Braun's statement: 'The constant is the self-understanding of the believer; christology is the variable.'[18] I hold this judgment to be, quite simply, false and, to pick up Bultmann's own distinction, false both historically and materially. Almost nowhere in the New Testament except in Paul and, to a very limited degree in the Fourth Gospel, is there any explicit anthropology. It and, *a fortiori*, its continuity within the New Testament is accessible only by inference, so that the conditions are no more favourable for method or for results than in the case of christology. But if anyone does go so far as to use terms like 'constant', it is simply incomprehensible how he can talk in the same breath of the self-understanding of an apocalyptically determined Christianity

[18] *Christusbotschaft*, p. 22; H. Braun, 'Der Sinn der neutestamentlichen Christologie', *ZTK* 54, 1957, pp. 341–77.

with that of the Fourth Gospel, the Epistle of James, the Lucan writings or the Hellenistic enthusiasts. The range of variations in christology itself could hardly be wider; in fact, it corresponds exactly to that in anthropology. Doubtless the variations in christology arose in direct relationship with the current variations in the Christian self-consciousness, and *vice versa*. The language in which H. Braun defines the criteria for this judgment of his, fraught as it is with important consequences, differs, if at all, only in degree from that of Jewish self-consciousness as it is found in the Thanksgiving Psalms of Qumran; and the 'most constant' element in the primitive Christian anthropology of the believers, the theme of belonging to Christ, is never mentioned at all. Braun derives the evidence for his assertion from Jesus, Paul and John only, and it is never explained whether this is a representative or an exclusive selection. Supposing it to be exclusive, nothing much would be gained materially because then the discrepancy over against the other New Testament writers would relativize Braun's thesis and would therefore demonstrate factually the variability of the self-understanding of the believer. Or is Braun's intention to radicalize his case to the extent of maintaining that it is neither possible nor legitimate to speak of an authentic believing self-understanding outside the circle he draws? If, however, the reference to Jesus, Paul and John is meant to be exemplary only, may we hope that this thesis will be extended within the framework of a New Testament theology, in which case a conflict with Bultmann's theology is surely inevitable? But even if we accept the more restricted interpretation of Braun's appeal to the New Testament evidence, we have problems enough. Can we and should we, when considering the self-understanding of faith in Paul, abstract from the fact that the Apostle, overstepping in apocalyptic vein the limits of anything that could be reasonably imagined and attained, reckons his task to be the conversion of the Gentile world; and that he further transcendentalizes this conception by proleptically crowning the success of his work with the conversion of Israel? Such abstraction would, however, reduce this self-understanding to an inner perspective which would then in practice degrade it further, making it a mere intellectual scheme. Paul himself, according to Gal. 1.15f., was never able to separate from each other the revelation of Christ, his own conversion and his call to his work. Is it not engaging in this very process of schematizing if we regard the Johannine self-understanding as expressing the same constant as the Pauline, even though within it futurist eschatology shrivels away into insignificance? There is little meaning in speaking of the historical Jesus while the interpretations of this term remain so diverse. After all, it is hardly satisfactory when the two themes of radicalized law and radicalized grace are merely juxtaposed to produce a paradox, because this paradox is very open to misunderstanding, as Braun's well-known formula 'I may and I should' clearly shows. The whole of Christian theology stands and falls by the resolution – and the correct resolution – of this paradox. While there is any doubt left on this score, nothing at all can be said about the 'constant' common to Paul and John which could not equally be applied to a relationship with a non-Christian theology.

But the series of logical inconsistencies does not end here. Bultmann especially is affected by it, since he takes over Braun's thesis without reservation. Any historian of the Church and its dogma who was charged with establishing the constant nature of the believing self-understanding throughout two thousand years, would certainly despair before he had well begun his work, which itself could only end by invalidating the premises on which it was based. In practice, nothing is so variable as the self-understanding of the believer when left to function within its given historical setting, and not forced into some schematized pattern of the interior life. Liturgical actions and formulae, dogmas and theological pronouncements, institutions and ecclesiastical ideologies all maintain a much steadier constancy than this very doctrine of man which is wont to be so tightly bound up with the individual. The questionable value of self-understanding as a means of communication between the generations is clearly revealed when we see how sons for the most part rebel against their fathers and how fathers are very seldom able to explain themselves to their sons. Surely, then, the saying that the foot of the man who stands in the river is never washed twice by the same wave is true?

What follows from what I have so far said? I must reply that there is no such thing as a constant in the historical field and that there is no continuity without a dialectical relationship with discontinuity. Continuity can only signify that process within change which, under the pressure of factors of discontinuity, maintains a particular trend and works itself out among different men in the degree of solidarity which is historically feasible. The historian cannot demonstrate continuity in the strict sense; he can only probabilify it with greater or less assurance, just as solidarity also has always to be grasped afresh. His activity, then, in so far as it is concerned with continuity and discontinuity, is anything but one of 'objectifying'; and even the material with which he works only exists 'objectively' in the minimal sense that it is isolable within the stream of history, despite all the currents of ambiguity. The existence of the constant can only be maintained in faith and with one's eyes fixed on the reality of miracle, as in the relation of the Bible to the Word of God. No assertion of continuity can ever be wholly exempt from contradiction. But if this is true, then the apodictic thesis of the constant within the believing self-understanding is either a judgment of faith needing doctrinal verification, or it is absurd. The problem of the continuity and discontinuity between the preaching of Jesus and the primitive Christian kerygma cannot, then, be solved by means of a simple antithesis, whether methodological ('historical' *v.* 'material') or based on content (the sharp separation of the historical Jesus from the kerygma). Indeed, this problem exemplifies the problem which is continually recurring in all history and so determines the whole of church history. Admittedly, we must add immediately that it has an exceptional title to this exemplary status. For as surely as the dialectic of continuity and discontinuity is always going to reappear in the preaching of the Church, we can say with equal certainty that, when it does, it will be, theologically speaking, under the shadow and, if things go well, under the promise of that fundamental process by which the historical Jesus becomes the preached Christ. The Easter event is the bridge between Jesus and the whole of the later kerygma; it both divides and unites them.

The New Testament expression of its unifying function can be seen in the inclusion of both the history of Jesus and that of the Christian kerygma under the comprehensive concept 'Gospel'. It is very remarkable how Bultmann, at least in his more recent writings, has come to ignore this. Of course, I am not saying that the question at issue is thereby settled once and for all. Yet surely so outstandingly an important deliverance of primitive Christianity, without which the very existence of the Johannine Gospel would be unthinkable, deserves to be discussed at depth and in detail; and all the more so, where the writer finds himself no longer able to accept it. Bultmann's whole argument is surely at risk here twice over: it is his own principal witness, John, who deliberately casts the kerygma in the form of a Gospel of the earthly Jesus, even though it contains, according to Bultmann, nothing authentic at all. The Gospels are thus, as Gospels, the outward expression not of an original form of preaching in early Christianity but of a relatively late one. Perhaps, we are entitled, even obliged, to go so far as to say that, not in regard to the traditional material they contain but as Gospel genre, they represent a reaction already in process against primitive Christian enthusiasm which thought itself, at least in part, able to do without the earthly Jesus. In any event, it is not permissible simply to shelve this problem by arguing that Paul and John had no interest worth mentioning in the historical Jesus. If this were really the case, it would be essential for the historian and of great interest to the theologian to ask why these two did not carry the day and whether what, on this hypothesis, was a retrograde development must not, in fact, be classed as significant and necessary. But if John felt himself under constraint to compose a Gospel rather than letters or a collection of sayings, Bultmann's argument is revealed as very one-sided. For it seems to me that if one has absolutely no interest in the historical Jesus, then one does not write a Gospel, but, on the contrary, finds the Gospel form inadequate. Yet this clear-cut decision is precisely what we do not find in Bultmann's presentation. I should not wish in any way to restrict his right of interpretation, so far as it is exercised within proper limits. But this right is abused when he embarks on generalization and the primitive Christian counter-current is deprived of *its* rights – historical and theological – particularly as it ultimately remained in possession of the field.

We have at this point to examine Bultmann's argument in detail. Among the things to which I took the greatest objection was the statement[19] in which he goes to some lengths to defend his categorization of the preaching of Jesus as a presupposition of New Testament theology and as belonging historically to Judaism.

> Was Jesus – the historical Jesus – a Christian? Well, if Christian faith is faith in him as the Christ, then certainly not; and even if he was conscious of himself as the Christ ('Messiah') and went so far as to require faith in himself as Christ, he would still not have been a Christian nor would it be correct to designate him a subject of Christian faith, of which he is in fact the object.

None of us doubts that Jesus was a Jew. But so were the first Christians as a body, not only as regards their physical descent but also as regards their outlook. This is no less true even if my objection that Jesus decisively broke through the limits of the Jewish religion brings

[19] *Christusbotschaft*, p. 8.

the reply that 'it was only as a Jew that he could radically overcome Judaism'. But Paul and John also operate, even if in very different ways, within the framework of Jewish eschatology and ethics and are not themselves thinkable without the questions these raise, as Bultmann maintains that Jesus is.[20] Are they also therefore to be assigned to the province of Judaism? Is it valid to pre-empt this possibility by defining Christian faith as faith in the Christ and so cutting off the first disciples from the historical Jesus? But Bultmann has just been at pains to establish that, even if Jesus had held and required this faith, he would still not have been a Christian. Such a separating process is thus not necessary in the case of this kind of faith, as we can see from the historical parallel of the Jewish faith in Bar Kochba as Messiah. But a further point demands attention: Bultmann defines faith here wholly in terms of dogmatics, which he does nowhere else and indeed in other contexts professes to regard as highly questionable. Are we not obliged in the last resort to conclude from this highly uncharacteristic distinction made by Bultmann between subject and object that his theology is therefore being moulded by christology rather than anthropology? One logical inconsistency thus cancels the other out. But this shows that Bultmann's fundamental opposition of Jew to Christian, which in his sense does not even apply to the first disciples, does not help us with Jesus. The question is not whether he was *a* Jew or *a* Christian, but whether this Jew is, as the common consciousness of Christendom asserts, the pioneer and the perfecter of faith, the archetype of obedience, the New Adam and, as such, not the presupposition but the centre of the New Testament. Without him, as Ebeling rightly states,[21] there would be no Christian kerygma. Can we make of the man of whom this has to be said a displaced person by setting him among the presuppositions of New Testament theology and thus assigning him out of hand to Judaism, without severely distorting the total problem, and indeed trivializing it? We get the same result if we look at the question from another angle. If Jesus had really been the wild apocalyptic figure that Albert Schweitzer saw in him, he would hardly have generated that self-understanding of the believers which, according to the views expressed elsewhere by Bultmann, is explicated by the predication 'Christian'. But if, on the contrary – as has already been conceded to me – Jesus did really break through out of Judaism, this breakthrough also involved those who had been following him in his earthly life,

[20] *Ibid.*, p. 9. [21] *Theologie und Verkündigung* III.3, p. 59.

even if the complete meaning of what had happened did not immediately come home to them and they therefore fell into confusion after the Crucifixion. To maintain that there was no such thing as the kerygma until after Easter because the eschatological self-understanding of the believer was a product of the Easter event is to deprive the following of the earthly Jesus of any solid content. In any event, I cannot see why this break in continuity which is dated at Easter could not be associated with the first appearance of Jesus; this is what happens both in the New Testament itself and in the chronology of the Christian era. Discipleship is not thinkable without eschatological self-understanding; but to say this is to leave open the precise nature of the change in the situation which Easter unquestionably brought about. This break in continuity following Easter is not in dispute. All that is being said is that it should not be treated in isolation. To adopt the simple opposition of Jew to Christian is to by-pass all these problems which first elicited our question. The argument is concentrated so exclusively on establishing discontinuity that Easter remains as the one solitary turning-point in the whole of Christian history. For this turning-point is not marked by the space the Easter event creates for itself within history but by the eschatological self-understanding made possible since Easter and now stretching away into the future to the end of time; so that Easter begets this self-understanding in a mode more or less miraculous and therefore opaque to the historian and not really meaningful for the theologian.

Bultmann undergirds this structure with his doctrine of the theological sufficiency of the '*that* of the coming of Jesus' as the necessary presupposition of the Christian self-understanding: he holds that there is no need, and no proper historical justification for going beyond this '*that*'.[22] We have to ask ourselves whether the brevity which prevails here is the kind of brevity with which a writer lays down a self-evident axiom or whether it is more a sign that Bultmann is taking refuge behind this axiom from a species of problem which he would prefer not to face and which does not fit into his framework of reference. Of course, to graft continuity on to a mathematical point is not a serious proposition. But does the New Testament permit us to make the earthly Jesus into a mathematical point? It seems to me that it is essential for us to forbid any over-simplification. I do not need to repeat Ebeling's observations on this point,[23] with which I agree. Bultmann has expounded in many different ways the end

[22] *Christusbotschaft*, p. 9. [23] *Art. cit.*, pp. 59ff.

which his thesis is designed to serve: it is to prevent faith from being rocked to sleep in a false security based on the assumption that bare facts can provide at once its justification and its inevitability. This objective of his is ours also. We have, up to a point, taken up residence with him in the realm of radical historical criticism; but the danger against which he is concerned to guard is hardly the greatest threat to us. From our standpoint, this threat lies rather in the possibility that we may be superimposing the predication 'Christian' on an understanding of existence and of the world, in which Jesus acts merely as the occasioner and Christ merely as the mythological cipher. It is certainly not by chance that Braun[24] has formulated the matter thus: 'We are not dealing, therefore, with a relationship between two persons . . . the relationship is not personal but dynamic.' There is no doubt that the use of the concept 'person' is dangerous and loaded, as the history of dogma shows. What concept in theological tradition is not, if it is of any significance at all? But to replace it with that of 'dynamic' is to fall out of the frying-pan into the fire. If you are going to look for support for this move to the Pauline 'in Christ', you would be well advised to find out, especially from Bousset's *Kyrios Christos*[25] and the comparative work of the days before the First World War, where this is likely to land you. I had assumed that this was just the kind of interpretation which could not possibly take on a new lease of life after dialectical theology and the more recent research on Luther. But here I see the Hercules myth and the Christ hymn in Phil. 2, the obedience of Christ and the virtue of the son of Zeus, assimilated so closely to each other, not only as parts of a pattern in the history of religion but in their actual content, that I find it very difficult logically to postulate Christology as a distinct entity;[26] and almost anything becomes possible, even the transformation of the Christian message into an abstract idea. Braun defends himself against imputations of this kind by pointing out that, in the Christian context, it is not a matter of conveying a universal truth but of preaching a specific truth which effects a judgment.[27] But is not this truth true of all truths and was there ever any idea worthy of the name which did not find itself a preacher? The sermons one is accustomed to hear do not normally display these excellences.

[24] *ZTK* 54, p. 343.

[25] W. Bousset, *Kyrios Christos. Geschichte des Christusglaubens von den Anfängen bis Irenaeus* (FRLANT 21), 1913.

[26] Braun, *art. cit.*, pp. 362f. [27] *Ibid.*, p. 372.

But I myself still do not think the preaching of *per aspera ad astra* to be Christian preaching, even though it is often heard in Christian circles, and I am therefore less open to the temptation of confusing Christology and the Hercules myth. Any interpretation of Phil. 2 which ended by doing this I should go so far as to call grotesque. Certainly, theology cannot and may not be forbidden to experiment, although I should have thought that our fathers had done all the experimenting there was to be done in this particular direction. Interpretation will always be subject to error. This we shall have to put up with, personally and collectively. But in any case we ought not to concentrate on the mote in our neighbour's eye to the exclusion of the beam in our own, which is steadily becoming more obvious. The self-assurance of faith is one thing and on this point we in our circle are all agreed. But in protest against it, we must not lose sight of, or render unanswerable, the further question as to who is the Lord of faith. I have to say that I simply cannot be satisfied by finding out who, as First Cause, set faith in motion. If my interest in this further question and my determination to pursue it brings me under suspicion of engaging in apologetics, I shall declare quite bluntly that, if this is apologetics, then I cannot give it up and still have the courage to call my understanding of existence Christian. If the '*that* of the coming of Jesus' is really the last theological word on my question, it is possible that the other question, that of eschatological self-understanding, need not necessarily be affected, although I should myself not like to maintain this with any degree of certainty. The predication 'Christian', however, would then become for me a mere trade name, prescribed by tradition but, in the last resort, of purely historical interest, where 'historical' is used to describe what happens in the history of an idea, even though that history may include some relentless preaching. I hear the note of challenge and the demand for decision in the histories of other ideas than the Christian, and today the preaching which exercises the strongest magnetic force on the greater part of mankind certainly radiates not from Christianity but from Marxism.

That is the nexus of the problems with which, under the general label of the 'historical Jesus', the school of Bultmann is currently concerned, just because we have followed in our teacher's footsteps and cannot throw overboard all we have learned from him. For that very reason his exaggeration of his doctrine arouses in us the inevitable reaction which distinguishes the true pupil from the learner by rote.

Every dialogue and every dispute eventually comes up against a finding which possesses absolute binding force for the one who is under fire, but represents for the questioners but one stage in their own development. We pupils owe it to our teacher to dissent from his statement that the '*that* of the coming of Jesus' is the sole identification mark of the Gospel and to refuse to accept his justification of it as a defence against a 'secure' faith, even if he insists on abiding by this justification. This is the only way to prevent the premature closure both of the discussion and of our own road into the future. Ebeling has formulated both our anxieties and our arguments. In what has gone before here I have brought to bear the witness of the New Testament and the general trend of primitive Christian history (the two of them speaking with one voice) and confine myself now to taking a closer look at one point in particular. Among the most astonishing things about the New Testament are these: that the earthly Jesus plays so insignificant a role, apart from the Gospels; that, secondly, except for a few sayings and a few allusions to the life history of Jesus, only the Cross is deemed theologically relevant; and, thirdly, both the narrative and the Cross are made less rather than more historically comprehensible by the mythology and parenetic applications through which they are filtered. All these phenomena undoubtedly acquire their coherence from the way in which the Easter event dominates the whole presentation, even in the Gospels themselves. Once again there is, I hope, complete agreement among us on this point, and this is presumably why Bultmann's interpretation of the situation seemed to us for so long to be convincing and his formula, the '*that* of the coming of Jesus', to be wholly apt. The fact that this is no longer generally true is, in itself, at once the indication that there has to be a new approach to the problem and the core of the problem as it must now be put. We have arrived at this necessity to change course partly from our further pursuit of the work of form-criticism, in which the material about Jesus which could with some degree of assurance be called authentic came to stand out in sharper relief and it became clearer that there were historicizing as well as kerygmatizing tendencies in the Synoptists, and possibly in other New Testament writers. Because we had learned not to separate historical insights from the question of their theological interpretation and because, with Ebeling,[28] we understand rigorous thinking to be a specific task of the theologian, we could not well do otherwise than reopen the

[28] *Art. cit.*, p. 61.

theological problem of the historical Jesus and of historicization in the Synoptic Gospels. By the very act of putting the question, we simultaneously rendered inoperative Bultmann's argument that it was unnecessary to go beyond the '*that*'. We had to go beyond the 'that' if our question were not to be shown to be meaningless and, as Bultmann has correctly analysed the situation, we had to attempt to make this advance first of all in the historical field, by first giving priority to a more accurate evaluation of the relevance of the earthly Jesus for the kerygma and then by asking whether the kerygma were not in fact already contained in essence in the words and works of Jesus. The methodological consistency of this procedure as a whole and of each individual step within it cannot be disputed. Bultmann therefore found himself obliged to make some contribution to our enterprise, although he obviously expected nothing material to result from it. What is decisive, of course, is the way in which he has done this. The more one studies his answer, the more difficult it becomes to escape the impression that he trivializes the historical problems involved and either mistakes the nature of their hermeneutical significance or denies that they have any. The problem of the historical Jesus thus becomes, between him and his pupils, a test case for historical understanding and for the relevance to human existence at any given time of what has happened in the past; in other words, a test case for the fundamental problem of hermeneutics.

It may readily be conceded that the kerygma has preserved some essential traits of the earthly Jesus. But Bultmann immediately proceeds to class this fact as material for the discussion about the possibility of a portrait of Jesus, whether of his person or his character, and goes on to condemn it as an attempt to validate the kerygma.[29] The very mode of expression he adopts reveals that Bultmann is not really addressing himself to his own pupils but to the representatives of the traditional 'Life of Jesus' school. Personally, I find these themes not merely theologically uninteresting but also totally beside the point in so far as any conceivable validation of the kerygma by scientific research, in particular by character studies, is concerned. My own questioning is aimed at finding out whether the earthly Jesus is to be taken as the criterion of the kergyma and, if so, to what extent. Whether the kerygma is historically verifiable is not important to me. On the contrary, in view of the content of the kerygma, I should call such a procedure absurd and, indeed, feel it to be blasphemous. Yet

[29] *Christusbotschaft*, pp. 10ff.

this kerygma, of which Bultmann never wearies of speaking, exists, not in some autonomous 'objective' form, but under the forms of very diverse 'kerygmata', as comes out most clearly in the case of eschatology. No philosophy, whether of ancient or of modern vintage, can exempt me from the 'discerning of spirits'. I therefore need criteria, as Christendom has always needed them, and to this extent the question of legitimacy is involved; not a historically guaranteed legitimacy, but one sustained by critical theological work. We can now put our problem in a nutshell: does the New Testament kerygma count the historical Jesus among the criteria of its own validity? We have to answer this question roundly in the affirmative. The fact that neither Paul nor, in his fashion, John seems to provide any support for our contention derives from their historical position in which, inevitably, the principal criterion of the Christian message is the Spirit. Yet this criterion was, of course, already proving to be inadequate, as we can see from the anti-enthusiastic conflict in which each of them, in his own way, has to engage. Even 'Spirit' has to be interpreted over again. Paul interprets it by reference to the service or the hope of those who are still undergoing the ordeal of temptation and, just as much, by his preaching of the Word of the Cross. But in so doing he calls men into the shadow of the earthly Jesus. Certainly the Cross is for him a saving event and, to this extent, mythologically decked out, transfigured and overpainted. Yet his eyes do not see the 'cross of light' of the gnostics, but that folly and shame in which the historical Jesus suffered. In precisely the same way, it cannot be doubted that the Christ of Phil. 2.5ff., in and despite all the luxuriant mythology of the hymn, was for Paul no mere symbol which, on better acquaintance with Greek mythology, could then be replaced by Hercules or, in all essentials, equated with Hercules; he was the Jesus whose place no man can take. As I see it, Paul does not resort to the '*that* of the coming of Jesus' to find a historical foothold for the eschatological kerygma; he connects this kerygma indissolubly with this irreplaceable Jesus.

The position with John is more complicated and I am not in a position to do justice to the totality of the problem; but I should like at least to indicate the general direction of my questioning. The Fourth Evangelist, too, has to provide some interpretation of 'Spirit', and does so by reference to the Word. But this Word is not just, in a kind of circular argument, the gift of the Spirit. It is the actualization of a clearly-defined tradition which, as such, is not validated by the

Church, as we might have supposed, but, as the word of Jesus, is evidently distinct from all other church tradition. To this end John puts it into the mouth of Jesus as he goes about on earth, and casts it in the form of a Gospel, the framework of which is composed of the conventional and traditional narrative of mighty works, Passion and Easter. It does not make any difference that nothing in this Gospel is historical in the sense of being authentic. The historicizing design of the whole cries out for explanation. Is any such explanation possible without presupposing a polemic intention in which 'Jesus' is pitted against the prevailing preaching of the Church? But if this is so, it emerges very clearly that the object of the exercise is not legitimation of the kerygma by a water-tight factual narrative; yet, at the same time, the Evangelist is maintaining the relevance of historical tradition in order to set out what is in the legitimate succession (sc. of apostolic faith) and to contrast it critically with other material that has been transmitted.

This process is therefore of the greatest significance because it enables us to acquire a right understanding of the Synoptists as being composers of Gospels and not merely the gatherers of certain material which happened to be circulating at the time. Doubtless they are dominated by the interests of kerygma. But they express this in the form of Gospels, which are essentially *not* preaching but reporting. Equally certainly, they are not historians in the modern sense and are totally devoid of any claim to scientific method; and this must be held to be true even of Luke. At the same time they supplement the kerygma with historical touches and employ a historicizing mode of presentation. Put another way: while in Paul and John the dimension of the past of the Gospel and of Christology is liable to be overshadowed, though admittedly not totally annihilated, by the present and the future, this same dimension of the past dominates the proclamation of the Synoptists, however true it may be that kerygmatic and parenetic interests are also pursued. I discern here a very important theological problem, especially as the Synoptists belong to the same Hellenistic community as Paul and John and, like them, worship Jesus as the exalted Lord. The role of earthly teacher appears, in the face of these presuppositions, to be a totally inadequate form of Christology, but is nevertheless indispensable if this very dimension of the past is to be opened up; so that our problem is also seen to be a problem from this angle as well. I have already hinted at the solution: the material transmitted by the first disciples and all that has grown up along with it is acquiring an unwonted theological importance for the whole of the Christendom of the time in the face of the preaching of the enthusiasts within the Hellenistic community. As this Christendom understands it, what has been thus transmitted and added makes it possible to distinguish between legitimate and illegitimate forms of the message and to discern the spirits. The teaching Christ is the criterion of the Spirit and it is thus (put summarily) not accidental that (sc. in the Synoptists) we see him displacing the Spirit who in Paul and the enthusiasts is the author of the kerygma. But the teaching Christ is the Jesus who speaks in the historical tradition. Once again it is true that this tradition possesses very little evidential value for us so far as authenticity is concerned and that therefore the kind of legitimation which Bultmann is looking for cannot be gained from it. What is even clearer, however, is that to approach the matter from this side is to conceal the real problem and its solution. The real problem is not how to give faith a historical foundation; it is how to use the critical method to separate the true message from falsifications of it, and to do this we need the help of the very One who was at that very time the historical Jesus, not by accident but by divine necessity. The measure of faith, then, was not ill-chosen. It has always been binding within Christendom and I think it must always be so in the future. For it does not, admittedly, make possible the kind of constant for which Braun is looking; but it does make possible that continuity of direction and that solidarity of faith which I feel bound to make the central object of my concern.

In order to explicate this last sentence, I now turn to Bultmann's second question: 'Does the history of Jesus – his words, works and suffering – already contain the kerygma in essence?' This must be so, unless the New Testament master concept 'Gospel' to denote the sum of the history of Jesus and of Christian preaching is theologically misleading. Here Bultmann himself has made very extensive, and what I myself feel to be very astonishing, concessions. They are not concerned with details and leave unaltered the total historical and critical perspective which has maintained itself in being since *The History of the Synoptic Tradition*. We might wish to provide correctives at some points. For instance, the open break between Jesus and the Baptist, from whose circle he originally came, seems to me to receive too little attention. I should, further, not myself wish to characterize the Cross simply as the result of a political misunderstanding on the part of the Romans, and I should raise the question as to whether it must not rather be understood as arising out of the internal logic of Jesus' own activity.[30] The misunderstanding of the Romans and the hate of the Jewish religious leaders, though individual details of the relationship may remain obscure, can hardly be separated, according to our sources. But the hate of the Jewish religious leaders goes back to Jesus' attitude to the Law and to his understanding of grace and the fellowship with sinners which derives from it, so that activity and fate can, historically speaking, hardly remain unconnected. However, Bultmann's reserve towards the drawing of any conclusions going beyond this seems to me to be thoroughly proper and even necessary. I, too, doubt whether there is a case for believing that Jesus went self-consciously to his death, and hold that talk of the 'faith of Jesus' has no sufficient basis in the Synoptic Gospels. Like Bultmann, I further see Easter as the decisive event of primitive Christian history and am not minded to smooth out the profound differences between the message of Jesus and that of the post-Easter community. Just as I am unable to understand Jesus as an apocalyptic figure, so I can ascribe to him neither an explicit christology nor an ecclesiology nor any mission beyond the frontiers of Palestine. I saw the reduction of the Gospel to the Jesus of history as by no means a remote possibility when I entered into controversy with my teacher. I should consider such a reduction to be a relapse into an Ebionite Jewish Christianity; and it seems to me urgently necessary that, in the face of many remarkable dialogues with Israel and of still stronger Judaizing tendencies in theology, we should today be very well aware of this danger.

What I find most astonishing is that Bultmann derives 'the historical continuity between the activity of Jesus and the kerygma' without any reservations, from the eschatological self-understanding and 'claim to sovereignty' of Jesus, as Bultmann has himself newly expounded them; and that he suddenly calls it comprehensible 'how the preacher became the object of preaching'.[31] We shall not forget that his essay began with the same assertion,[32] but neither shall we overlook the fact that shortly afterwards the continuity of the kerygma with the 'what and how of his (Jesus') history' was said to be doubtful and, in any event, confined to the '*that* of the coming of Jesus'.[33] A precisely similar reservation is immediately made here: namely, that what has been said does not establish material unity. In logical contradiction to what has gone before, Bultmann then denies that the

[30] *Christusbotschaft*, p. 12. [31] *Ibid.*, p. 17. [32] *Ibid.*, pp. 7f. [33] *Ibid.*, p. 9.

activity of Jesus can be put on the same footing as the kerygma 'in the sense that the kerygma is already present in essence in the words and works of Jesus'.[34] I could understand this odd mixture of concessions and restrictions better, if Bultmann did not combine it with an unremitting offensive. For is it really possible to get any historical understanding of the transition from preacher to object of preaching without needing to go beyond the unadorned '*fact* of the coming of Jesus'? Is it legitimate even to speak of this bare '*fact*', while at the same time establishing historically the eschatological self-understanding of Jesus and his claim to sovereignty? Does not historical continuity necessarily imply a certain material unity? Conversely, must we speak of 'equating', if Jesus does really anticipate in essence the kerygma? To conflate all these questions, can we not simply say that, while admittedly what the historical Jesus brings with him is by no means the kerygma in its later form nor indeed the whole gospel, on the other hand his words, his works and what happened to him do point us towards keystones of the later gospel; and to this extent they can be used as criteria of this gospel by a community engaged in conflict with enthusiasts? Legalism cannot be made compatible with his specific self-understanding, nor theosophy and refusal to love one's neighbour with his belief in a gracious God, nor any *theologia gloriae* with his Cross. His words and works are signs that salvation is present. Easter renews the bonds which bind to him those who had followed him before; he is still the way, the truth and the life which the disciples of the earthly Jesus had sought. Because I cannot read the facts in any other way, I hold strongly to the 'in essence' and can yet without contradiction bring out as clearly as I am able the differences between Jesus and the community after Easter; but equally I guard myself both against the dichotomy between historical and material continuity and against all talk of the bare '*fact* of the coming of Jesus' and feel obliged to combine continuity and discontinuity dialectically, because this is the mode which corresponds exactly to the reality.

Bultmann provides the greatest surprise for his readers when, in Section V, which deals with the existential encounter with the history of Jesus and the existentialist interpretation which arises from it, he not only raises these same questions but answers them with a resounding affirmative. Braun and J. M. Robinson, if nobody else, have convinced him that 'the material unity of the kerygma concerning Christ

[34] *Ibid.*, p. 17.

with the preaching of Jesus', 'the identity of the activity of Jesus with the kerygma', can be demonstrated[35] if we take this road of encounter and interpretation. One's inclination is to say, 'All's well that ends well.' For we seem finally to have reached the basis of agreement for which we were looking. There is an express acknowledgment that historical research is the presupposition of this existential encounter and this existentialist interpretation and thus the validity and necessity of our historical questioning and, in part, of our answers are implicitly conceded. But I confess to being somewhat unhappy about this agreement. So many obstacles have been raised along the road by which we have arrived at this point, that one has little breath left. So many harsh and problematical alternatives have opened up like chasms that it is impossible to get the proffered bridge working immediately. Surely Bultmann's principal argument was precisely this, that a material unity cannot be established and that the historical continuity has only a very limited significance. How can he suddenly maintain just the opposite when he is approaching the problem from a different angle? I believe, however, that it would be doing Bultmann an injustice to accuse him of lack of logic or even of self-contradiction. We have to assume that, on the contrary, he has remained completely true to himself all the way, in spite of many twists and turns; and that the danger of misunderstanding him has never been greater than it is now. What is the core of the solution he proposes? Shall we not have to answer in some such terms as these: contemporary man can, if and so far as he lives from the Christian message, receive instruction from the teaching of Jesus about the structures which constitute his existence and hear the summons to live in accordance with these structures? Thus far the preaching of Jesus actually coincides in content with the corresponding purpose of the kerygma. The kerygmatic statements about Christology and probably about other areas of Christian theology remain, however, untouched. In consequence, the historian cannot establish that material unity which only reveals itself to the hearer who takes hold of Jesus' words existentially out of his knowledge of the Christian proclamation and applies them to himself as the existentialists do, rather like an echo bouncing back off the kerygma. The historian establishes that there actually are walls there from which the echo can be bounced back and which are so constructed as to break up the sound. Without them there would be no echo. But if the historian

[35] *Ibid.*, pp. 22f.

treats these walls as an object of research in themselves, they remain more or less dumb, mute witnesses of a past to which we no longer have immediate access, which is not in the primary sense *our* past and which provides us with more riddles than solutions. The echo would not be possible without the walls. But for it to come into existence and be heard, a voice must previously have sounded forth – the voice we hear in the kerygma after Easter. Every metaphor limps, and I do not know whether Bultmann will find this one at all apt. But with its help – and only with its help – can I clarify for myself the logical structure of his essay, and, further, integrate satisfactorily the conclusion of the essay with the whole.

We come to yet another *volte-face*, although this time it is not wholly unforeseen. In his discussion of historical continuity, Bultmann had already asked whether the claim of Jesus to sovereignty extended beyond the time of his earthly activity.[36] He now asserts with crystalline clarity:

> Thus the Christ-kerygma demands faith in the Jesus present within it who does not merely, like the earthly Jesus, promise salvation, but who has already brought it.[37]

He goes further: the kerygma is the presence of Christ himself. It 'has taken the place of the historical Jesus. It represents him'. The natural reaction to this is to ask what theological significance the kerygmatic narrative of the Synoptists can now have as the 'recapitulation' of the history of Jesus. Is this narrative in fact not superfluous and anachronistic, since Bultmann speaks at this point[38] only of the possibility, not of the necessity of the 'recapitulation'? His answer is:

> Because the recapitulation is primarily the proclamation of the will of God and of his summons, it immediately raises the problem which has caused a permanent disturbance in the history of the Church – the relationship of Law and Gospel.[39]

The essay closes with the provocative acceptance of a criticism that has been made of Bultmann, namely, that in his writings Jesus is raised up into the kerygma.[40] That means, he says, that there is 'no faith in Christ, which is not bound to be faith in the Church as the bearer of the kerygma – in terms of dogmatic theology, faith in the Holy Ghost. But faith in the Church is at the same time faith in Jesus and Christ – a faith which the historical Jesus did not demand.'[41] The

[36] *Ibid.*, p. 17. [37] *Ibid.*, p. 25. [38] *Ibid.*, p. 26. [39] *Ibid.*, pp. 26f.
[40] *Ibid.*, p. 27. [41] *Ibid.*, pp. 26f.

next step is to say that 'the Church in its kerygma represents the historical Jesus' and that faith in the Church as the bearer of the kerygma *is* the Easter faith, which 'consists precisely in this belief that in the kerygma Jesus Christ is present'. We may legitimately call this conclusion, the abrasiveness of which certainly cannot be ignored, the centre and the key of the whole essay. This is the point of departure Bultmann takes in his attack on the problem we have raised and to which he here provides his own personal solution. It is precisely at this point, however, that the individual questions involved cluster together, and, with them, the possibilities and the necessities of criticism.

Bultmann's uninhibited and provocative mode of expression at this stage is indeed remarkable. If it ever looked as though he had got himself into difficulties,[42] there is nothing of this now. On the contrary, this counter-offensive applies an extraordinarily aggressive closure to all that has been said. But where is this attack of Bultmann's going to lead? I begin with two special problems. Even although the recapitulation of the history of Jesus by the Synoptic kerygma is only called 'a possibility', this recapitulation is still asserted to be meaningful on the grounds that what is primarily conveyed in it and by it is the summons of God. The expression 'primarily' leaves room both for limitation and for supplementation; but it does reveal what, in Bultmann's view, appeared to the Synoptists to be particularly important and worthy of transmission in the preaching of Jesus, and what Bultmann himself sees as the fulcrum in the history of Jesus for the existential encounter and the existentialist interpretation – namely, the demand of the divine will. He underlines this by asserting that it creates the problem of Law and Gospel. I am not certain whether we ought to press these words, and whether in fact the genesis of the problem of the Law really is being derived from the message of Jesus. The form of words suggests it, as does the fact that ever since his book on Jesus,[43] Bultmann has characterized this message in terms of its emphasis on the call to decision. Does he therefore see Jesus as 'primarily' a preacher of the Law and thus, materially, as 'Jew'? The question is of unusual significance and, so far as I am able to discover, has never been satisfactorily cleared up. It does not help to say that of course Jesus also brought the Promise;[44] for it is just this 'also'

[42] So Ebeling, *Theologie und Verkündigung* III.3, p. 61.

[43] *Jesus*, 1926; ET, *Jesus and the Word*, New York: 1934; London: 1935; reissued, 1958.

[44] *Christusbotschaft*, p. 25.

which is itself the problem. For the two are combined both in the Old Testament prophets and in the Baptist, and everything depends on the mode of their union in Jesus. Also I should not be prepared to class as Law either Jesus' radical demand for obedience or Paul's parenesis or John's commandment of love. For, while it is true that Jesus does not lead the disciples out of the realm of Judaism or to a decisive break with the inheritance they have grown up in, so that consequently the Jewish Christian community, in the course of its development, began by understanding the demand of Jesus as a pure sharpening of the Law and was therefore prone to relapse into legalism – while all these things are true, it is still my considered opinion that it is impossible for a historian not to acknowledge Jesus' fundamental critique of the Law and of the Jewish exegetical methods indissolubly connected with it. The Torah is indivisible, says Judaism. But Jesus refused to accept this indivisibility. For me, this is where his transcendence of Judaism is most clearly revealed and I should not hesitate to speak of a break with Judaism at its decisive point, a break which the Hellenists certainly seem to have been the first to discern. Here, too, in my judgment, is the point of the break with the Baptist; it is not fortuitous that John was primarily a preacher of imminent judgment which Jesus quite obviously was not – certainly not in the first instance. In other words, it is my view that the relationship of indicative and imperative in Jesus is the same as it is in Paul. Life and work under grace, radically understood, finds its embodiment and its verification in obedience, service and love, all of which must be understood in equally radical terms. But the situation changes completely if the two sides of this relationship are reversed, or, as sometimes happens, the meaning of 'Gospel' is held to be exhausted by the call to decision which has now become eschatologically possible. I have never been able to resolve all my doubts about where Bultmann actually stands on this. I therefore emphasize with all the force at my disposal that for me Jesus was primarily the 'Evangelist' (without qualification), so far as that can be said before Easter, and that any dialectical combination with the 'preacher of the Law',[45] much less any primacy of the latter is, as far as I am concerned, out of the question. There is here a fundamental choice which may well condition one's whole conception of the proportions of New Testament theology.

I now return to our starting-point. Even if Bultmann's hypothesis

[45] Like 'sharpening of the Law', intended in the Jewish sense.

is the right one, there would still be no sufficient motivation for the writing of the Gospels. Collections of sayings for parenetic purposes would have been enough. But neither the motif of narrative nor that of 'recapitulation' can be adequately accounted for on this basis. The theological problem of a Gospel which is more than a collection of traditional material remains to puzzle us. Once the existence of the question is acknowledged, the solution has to be sought elsewhere. It is for this very reason that I have called attention to the fact that the theological relevance of history in the controversy with the enthusiasts was not a discovery of early Catholicism but achieves its real breakthrough there, as we can see from Acts. For Bultmann, on the other hand, the writing of Gospels remains in the last resort an incomprehensible and superfluous sport in the natural history of the kerygma, which is, however, itself threatened with diminished status if no theological justification can be found for the wide range of mutations which occur within it.

Secondly, this talk of faith in the Church as the bearer of the kerygma seems to me equally dangerous, especially when it is used as a definition of the Easter faith. Bultmann has attempted to protect himself against misinterpretation by stating in a note:

> It is self-evident that 'Church' here is not an institution but an eschatological happening. It is not the guarantor but itself the object, of faith. It is a scandal, in exactly the same sense as the Cross is a scandal.[46]

I do not find this note at all reassuring. Once again I cannot accept this typical either/or – not an institution, but an eschatological happening! Can there be an eschatological happening without a substratum, without embodiment and even without institutional forms, if it is really to occur on earth and not to remain suspended between heaven and earth? Can we really talk of the Church like this? Is there not a dualism evident here, even more profound than that of the subject-object scheme, and does it not finally become evident at the same time that for Bultmann nothing historical really has any theological substance or meaning? Do we not see instantaneously, as though the whole thing were illuminated by a flash of lightning, why the historical Jesus cannot possibly, on the basic presuppositions of this thinking, have any independent significance whatever? Further, as good Protestants could we go on saying, as the wording of our confession demands, '*Credo in ecclesiam*'? For me, to accept Bultmann's

[46] *Christusbotschaft*, p. 26, n. 80.

interpretation would be to transgress the limits drawn by the Reformation; it would be to surrender the possibility of adopting a posture of radical criticism in the face of ecclesiastical tradition. For, since the time of primitive Christian apocalyptic, what ecclesiastical phenonenon has *not* been passed off as an eschatological happening, so that criticism has become necessary? Whence, then, am I to derive the criteria for such criticism? If *credo in ecclesiam* does *not* mean the institution in which I was baptized, through which I have received the Scripture and heard the preached Word, have I any alternative other than to do my own defining and thus set up a self-chosen object of faith? How am I then to escape the danger of becoming the lord of my own faith? How can there then be any solidarity of faith other than in the form of schools of thought and societies of like-minded people?

But it is the last sentence of Bultmann's note which shocks me most: 'It is a scandal in exactly the same way as the Cross is a scandal.' There cannot be any real doubt that 'in exactly the same way' is seriously meant, when Bultmann is prepared to make the Church the object of faith and to say not only that it 'represents' the historical Jesus, but that, as the bearer of the kerygma, it is the medium of the presence of Christ. Once again, 'in exactly the same sense' is still absolutely unacceptable theologically, as far as I am concerned. That Church and Christians may, and indeed must, become a scandal is not a matter of dispute. But this befalls them 'for the sake of the Word of the Cross and for the sake of the Cross itself'. Here every syllable counts. For the Cross creates the Church, and the Church represents, and does not replace, the Cross. Nor can the Church put itself on the same plane as the Cross. It is therefore this note which compels me to oppose Bultmann all along the line and, I am sorry to say, to oppose him in no uncertain terms. Obviously, for me this is the crucial point, exactly as it is for Bultmann, and if my teacher has not been able to convince me that he is right in regard to it, he has nevertheless shown me just how crucial it is and thus helped me to clear my mind as to where I stand.

From our analysis of these modes of expression the totality of the issue at stake emerges yet again – evident, acute, inescapable. What is at stake is the answer to the question 'What has the primacy over faith in the sense that faith derives its criteria from it?' Bultmann and I would agree on the question: we should also agree on the form of the answer; 'It is the Word, the kerygma, the Gospel, which has primacy over faith in this sense.' But this Word neither falls from heaven on the one hand, nor is it simply a matter of choice on the other. It can have no earthly guarantee; and it is made known only in differing words and in multiformity of proclamation, such as we see already in the Scriptures. If, therefore, the concepts of primacy and criteria are to be used for anything more than mere shadow-boxing, there must be a more exact definition of the Word as Gospel. It is in the process of trying to reach such a definition that Bultmann comes to speak of the Church. Admittedly, there is no question of 'Church' signifying primarily an institution, otherwise the Gospel would be reduced to a specific confessional tradition. 'Church' as an eschatological happening certainly means a community of believers which is passing on the kerygma. Because such transmission carries no infallible guarantee, it operates from one point of view as a perpetually renewed act of decision, from another as miracle. This last motif is so strong that it is possible to use an expression like 'Christ is raised up into the kerygma', which obviously picks up a Johannine theme, even if there is probably some exaggeration present. Yet it is fair to say that there are other parts of the New Testament where proclamation takes place and does its work in the power of the Resurrection. When we remember that theology must always be moving towards a culminating antithesis if it is not merely to tilt at windmills and is thus always a dangerous undertaking because of its built-in tendency to one-sided statements and dialectical systems, perhaps there is nothing particularly objectionable about these assertions. The case is altered, however, if they are absolutized.

The individual believer and the community of believers are indeed dialectically related, when the fellowship is thought of purely eschatologically and therefore without institutional traits. The individual is orientated towards fellow believers who, when they take form as real people, either hold different views from his, unite with him in a fellowship of thought or of sentiment, influence him, or, conversely, are determined by him. In this connection terms like 'primacy' and 'criteria' can only be relative, having no common allegiance to a higher authority. But if the community is not thought of in concrete terms, it disappears altogether; it becomes the mere projection of the individual believer, fashioned by him in his own image, or a selection made by him according to the dictates of this image. To put it in a nutshell, the Corinthian community represents the first possibility, the historical writing in Acts the other. It is clear that we cannot simply let either of these tendencies go unchecked. It is true that we are now very near the point at which anthropology undergoes a sudden change into ecclesiology; this transformation can also happen at any time on the basis of the Protestant conception of the Church as the community of believers. But the criteria of faith are not to be found by looking from the individual believer to the collectivity of believers. Or, at least, it is not possible to be certain of them because the believers never exist without there being also a community of anti-faith. The question as to what is prior to faith in the sense that it supplies the criteria of faith can in the last resort only be answered christologically; and answered in such a way as to keep christology distinct from ecclesiology and anthropology and in no circumstances to substitute either for it. Christ alone is the Ground, the Lord and the Judge of faith, of the individual Christian as of the whole community. The kerygma which is worthy of the name does not, then, simply make Christ present; it creates at the same time a proper distance between him and the hearer. This is most true at the very points where the expression 'in Christ' occurs, as we see by Gal. 2.20; the present Christ is yet so separated from me that in believing I become a stranger to myself and from then on can no longer lead my own life. If you are prepared, therefore, to make use of the hyperbole 'Christ rises again into the kerygma', you must at least add that, at the same time, within it he is exalted above us and removed from any manipulation by us. He may awake eschatological self-understanding and the common life of the believers, but in so doing he is not absorbed into either, but challenges them to discipleship and service.

The present Christ does not do this in the same way as the historical Jesus. For he does not operate as an individual among other individuals. It is not accidental that mythological elements begin to appear in Christology after Easter, in Jewish Christianity as much as in the Hellenistic community. The variations and differentiations among christological statements are not to be viewed merely as adaptation to the prevailing images of the contemporary world. This they doubtless are; but they are also and equally declarations that the community does not now – or, at least, not primarily – understand the exalted Lord as a historical figure, as one among many. It seeks to make him stand out from others by conferring upon him all the highest titles of dignity available and, in so doing, lands itself in a fatal impasse; at this higher level it now has to find other comparisons with other saviours. The final conclusion of this process is the God-predicate – a logical 'stop'; in the face of it, all other predications gradually pale into insignificance, as they were bound to do, and the paradox 'God and Man' trumpets forth, without possibility of retreat. We are exposed to the same pressures. For, little though I am inclined to agree with Braun's proposal to replace an understanding of the relationship in personal terms by one in terms of dynamics, the concept of personality itself in this connection is certainly no less questionable in so far as it isolates its subject and is employed to the exclusion of other concepts. The history of dogma in the early Church bears the marks of this experience. As a statement about the constitution of the Risen Lord's being, it is unusable, because no statement of this kind is possible. As a relational concept, it fails to say the decisive thing – namely, that Christ is Lord. The Kyrios of Pauline theology, the mediator of the creation in the post-Pauline writings, John's creator figure, even the Son of Man who is also universal Judge, as in the most primitive Christian apocalyptic – each of these reveals personal traits, but is yet not adequately understood as 'a person', just as the separation of person and work in Christology rends asunder what the New Testament joins. Thus the process of rationalizing Christ which necessarily follows from the use of the category of personality leads to difficulties, whose existence in turn demonstrates the relative justification of mythology within primitive Christianity. What can the creature say about the Creator which goes beyond the acknowledgment of its creatureliness? What else can the servant say about the Lord, except words which express gratitude and indebtedness? The community of the time immediately following Easter, the community which speaks in the New Testament, developed its Christology only within the framework of soteriology, even if its doxologies came later to be interpreted in other and more far reaching modes. It is also true and, in terms of the present debate, almost more important to establish, that its soteriology was christologically based and welded. The nature of its faith is determined solely by the identity of its Lord. This is the way in which it puts its faith beyond its own power to manipulate.

Not the least of the services Bultmann has rendered us is to have broken wide open the question as to how the preacher became the object of preaching. Once he had done this, the significance of the Easter event for Christian preaching and theology was laid bare in a way which his critics have over a long period failed to appreciate.

At the same time he has committed himself so far that the way back has become for him, if not impossible, yet by the very nature of his theses more or less unnecessary and certainly theologically dubious. Strangely enough, he seems not to consider the fact that the phenomenon of the preacher who becomes the object of preaching has been repeated in the history of religion right up to the present day, but that the most interesting and theologically important happening in primitive Christianity (measured by these parallels) remains the reversal of the process. By this I mean that in the Gospels we have a certain specific phase in primitive Christianity reviving, with the help of received tradition (authentic or legendary), the picture of the preacher, although as Kyrios, as Son of God, as Mediator in creation, as the Pre-existent One, as the mysterious Cosmocrator, as the promised Judge of the World, he had long been the object of its preaching. This was done as a piece of historicization, however little the Gospels became thereby historical narratives. Bultmann asks why those involved were not satisfied with the account of the earthly Jesus if what was really important was already contained within it. But when we look at the historical location of the Gospels, the period of their creation and the christology which prevails in them, we see that this question has to be reversed. Tradition about the preacher was preserved and supplemented with legendary material – there is no problem here. But this tradition was embodied in the form of Gospels – here we have something which remains unique. It is only within the Christian religion that the Gospel form exists at all. As Bultmann rightly emphasizes, it is determined by the kerygma. But once this is established, a second point has to be made; it is precisely on the basis of the kerygma that we see a reaction setting in against the hitherto dominant Spirit-theology of primitive Christianity and another, more restricted, against the mythological language of christology. This second reaction is all the more astonishing because of the (relative) justification for such mythology. The key to our problem taken as a whole is not the question of the historical Jesus as such and in isolation over against the kerygma, but the kerygmatic reversion to the narrative form *after* enthusiasm, mythological representations and dogmatic reflection had already carried the day to the extent illustrated by the primitive Christian hymns. Correspondingly, in the case of the mysterious Cosmocrator, a dazzling light is reflected back upon him who traverses Palestine as a rabbi. How could they revert from glorifying him who was the object of preaching to telling the story of him who was himself the preacher – and within the framework of the kerygma at that? This question is of pre-eminent significance, both historically and theologically – but Bultmann has not put it. Obviously, he hardly sees it. Yet it is indissolubly bound up with the one which he has raised. It is the source of the problem of the historical Jesus in the form in which we are familiar with it from the tradition of the last century or two, a problem which is actually unavoidable in this context. It is not in the first instance historical research which forces us to face it, still less for us, the pupils of Bultmann, is it the search for guarantees of faith – it is the kerygma itself. I have attempted to give plausible historical and theological reasons why this is so, and can only repeat them in summary form: as, at the time in question, the Corinthian enthusiasts demonstrate, not only history but also the Spirit is being bent and manipulated by men. The reversion to the form of the Gospel narrative, to the story of the Palestinian preacher, to the 'once upon a time' as against the 'once-for-all', to a historicizing presentation within the framework of the kerygma and, last but not least, to Jesus as he wandered through Palestine; all this occurred as a reaction – theologically relevant and therefore initiated and maintained by the Church – directed towards restoring the autonomy of the Christ, of the Spirit and of faith itself. The presence of Christ and of the Spirit in the community may not be so abused that both evaporate into the eschatological self-understanding of the believers. The primacy of the Lord over his community and his Christians can and must be expressed in terms of chronological priority as well. Present eschatology without this reference back to the past of salvation is delivered over defenceless to enthusiasm and is unable to distinguish anthropology and ecclesiology from christology – or, should the occasion demand, from each other.

We thus arrive finally at what is certainly for us today a very paradoxical-sounding thesis: the very thing which Bultmann can only see as an objectification, and therefore separates sharply from the existential encounter, served in primitive Christianity to demonstrate the autonomy of salvation, the priority of Christ in relation to his own, the '*extra nos*' of the Gospel message, the necessary exodus of the believer from his self-centredness. The earthly Jesus had to keep the preached Christ from dissolving into the projection of an eschatological self-consciousness and becoming the object of a religious ideology. History acquired an eschatological function. The past gave to the present the criteria for discerning the spirits. We see in Luke how dangerous this undertaking was. But theological undertakings are always dangerous whether they are oriented towards apocalyptic, salvation history or existential encounter. They become most dangerous of all when they are absolutized. This is precisely what the New Testament refrains from doing. It does not only contain apocalypses or letters or Gospels. It is determined equally by present and future eschatology and holds both up to the light of the past. This dialectic is theologically relevant. It does not give us the right to appropriate at will just what we like. But it does make it possible for us to protect ourselves from ourselves, from making the correctness of our insights the exclusive law of the community and inflating the theological school or the denomination into the measure and the taskmaster of Christianity. It leaves room for the unprecedented decisions which sometimes have to be taken and frees us from the compulsion to set some particular structure in the place of the Word, to withdraw from pilgrimage back into the established camp.

It will not do to object to this view on the grounds that the past with which the Gospels are concerned can be demonstrated by scientific methods to be largely inauthentic and that the true history is overlaid by the kerygma. In fact the Evangelists did not know this. But in the Gospels as we have them there are decisive pivotal points which allow continuity to be established; Bultmann concedes this much to the existentialist interpretation. These pivotal points do not first occur within the existential encounter. They are grouped round Jesus' message of the gracious God, his critique – conditioned by this message and expressed both in word and work – of the law of Moses and its interpretation, his radical demand for obedience and love, and his death as the logical culmination of his ministry. They are not capable of being used as components in a reconstructed biography of Jesus; but they do give to the '*that* of the coming of Jesus' certain unmistakable traits of his individuality. They do not as such constitute the Gospel; but they do make it possible for the Gospel to 'recall' him and so to incapsulate his history into the Gospel. Even Paul and John themselves do this, though in the most abbreviated form imaginable. A preaching which no longer did this in some measure, or considered it unnecessary, could, in the nature of things, only be docetic in nature and would eventually lead to enthusiasm or legalism. The function of recalling the historical Jesus is thus, within the framework of the Gospel, a permanent necessity.

It is because I begin from this assumption that I evince that comparative lack of interest in the existential interpretation of the passage in question, which Bultmann in fact detects. I had no need of this particular motivation because my sights and my framing of the issues were not directed towards a personal construction but towards a thorough appraisal of the fundamental facts on which any individual interpretation must be based. I do not dispute that the Gospels, as well as Paul and John, both challenge and encourage us to adopt the existential interpretation of the Jesus material. What I do deny is that this interpretation is seen by the Gospels as the *only* bridge to the understanding of the relevance of this material. If their primary object in their setting-out of this material and its legendary penumbra was really the establishment of the criteria of the kerygma, we have first to discuss these perspectives, their premisses and logical implications in order to make possible any firmly-based specific understanding. I have protested in many different places against the practice of calling this process 'objectifying'. If we do so, in my view we are undeniably labelling the existentialist interpretation as subjectivist, and I think that the concrete interpretation of the Jesus tradition in our time shows the justification for this fear from evidence which cuts across all party lines. Methodology by itself is not sufficient to guarantee the correctness of interpretation and this is true even of the existentialist methodology. I cannot go any further into this issue here; it would demand a fresh and comprehensive analysis.

Certainly there is point in raising historico-critical questions without looking first to see how the findings will directly affect oneself; in other words, in the kind of factual way which does not exclude personal involvement but which tries, within the realm of the possible, to discern history as it *actually* happened. The term 'objectification' discredits such efforts unfairly, and recoils on those who use it for this purpose by delivering them over to a systematic theology in which history is discerned only, as, according to them, it *must have* happened. In any interpretation the historical and the material can diverge. But I cannot myself go on from this to argue that we must therefore distinguish and separate the two *a priori*. It seems to me that to maintain this is to adopt a presupposition which poses a threat to the very existence of historical reality or, at the least, certainly does not help us to interpret it.

III

SENTENCES OF HOLY LAW IN THE NEW TESTAMENT*

THE PROBLEM OF law in the New Testament, which has been the subject of such long and violent controversy, seems to me to have been approached in an unfruitful way for the following reason: the partners in this dialogue have believed that it was possible to presuppose for primitive Christianity completely modern views and conditions, without establishing whether or not these actually existed. But in the last resort the heart of this problem is not accessible in terms of the questions which are now being asked. Or at least, that is what I conclude from the debate which in Germany centred principally on the theses of Rudolf Sohm; his work appeared in 1892 but is still stimulating and fascinating today.[1] The New Testament itself offers us a different starting-point. For it contains in its most diverse parts utterances, the structure of which are particularly worthy of notice and which provisionally and in the most general way possible I shall call sentences of holy law. I shall go over stage by stage what prompts me to adopt this term and what I understand it to express. The whole problem of law in the New Testament can admittedly not be properly dealt with in a short lecture. The sole task I have set myself is to provide in our investigation a sound exegetical foundation for a new line of attack and to show clearly the conclusions to which this line would lead in systematic theology.

I begin with the saying in I Cor. 3.17:

εἴ τις τὸν ναὸν τοῦ θεοῦ φθείρει, φθερεῖ τοῦτον ὁ θεός.

If anyone destroys God's temple, God will destroy him.

* 'Sätze Heiligen Rechtes im Neuen Testament', a lecture given at the ninth General Assembly of the Studiorum Novi Testamenti Societas in Marburg, 8 September 1954, and subsequently published in *NTS* 1, 1954/5, pp. 248–60.

[1] R. Sohm, *Kirchenrecht* (Systematisches Handbuch der deutschen Rechtswissenschaft 8), 1892.

The curious structure of this sentence, exactly like the parallels which will shortly be mentioned, has hardly received any attention, even though it ought to have leapt to the eye. The same verb describes in the chiasmus of the protasis and apodosis both human guilt and divine judgment, in order to characterize by this method both the precise correspondence of the two in content and their indissoluble and harsh logical connection. It is evident that the *jus talionis* is being promulgated here: destruction to the destroyer. And at the same time God is being defined with unsurpassable brevity and clarity as the God who rewards every man according to his works.

Talion and chiasmus are also paired outside the New Testament. Gen. 9.6 reads: 'Whoever sheds the blood of man, by man shall his blood be shed.' We find a similar formation in Aeschylus, *Choephori* 312f:

> ἀντὶ δὲ πληγῆς φονίας φονίαν
> πληγὴν τιέτω.
> For murderous stroke let murderous stroke be paid.

A further link with I Cor. 3.17 is provided by the unmistakable use in both passages of legal style. For there too it is equally a case not only of parenetic warning or prophetic threat. While both are certainly present, equally certainly our saying is clearly distinct from other warnings and threats not solely by reason of the talion motif, but also by reason of its form, which introduces the protasis with the casuistic legal expression εἴ τις (interchangeable with ἐάν τις or ὅς δ'ἄν) in the sense of 'in the case of' and then finishes with a statement of the punishment laid down. We might very well feel reminded of the tablet prohibiting Gentiles from the forecourt of Herod's temple, which ends with the words: 'Whoever is caught is alone responsible for the death [-penalty] which follows.'[2] We might see our sentence in the light of a pendant to it, that is, an inscription over the new divine sanctuary. It is distinguished from the parallels we have mentioned solely by the fact that the law which is here proclaimed is not executed by men but is the law of the divine action of the Last Day. The *jus talionis* is, as the future tense of the apodosis shows, located on the eschatological level; and this is possible because, according to the view which lies behind the saying, the Last Day is immediately imminent. Because the transgression touches God's own work, the one who is attacked in this way is no longer merely the source and the guardian of earthly

[2] K. Galling, *Textbuch zur Geschichte Israels*, 1950, pp. 80f. Illustration and English translation in G. E. Wright, *Biblical Archaeology*, 1957, pp. 224f.

justice, but the one who himself vindicates his own honour and makes good his own justice in the immediately imminent judgment of the world. Men serve him in this only in so far as they are already proclaiming in the earthly present the criterion of his ἐκδίκησις. Admittedly, this is only possible for those who, being endowed with charisma, have knowledge of this criterion and are therefore able to proclaim it with prophetic authority. In so doing, they are not merely testifying to the approach of an ineluctable Nemesis. For while the judgment which they announce applies to the whole world, it is yet addressed most immediately to those who, as members of the Christian community, know themselves to be determined by such a future and, precisely for this reason, to be standing today 'before the face of Christ' as the Judge of all. The proclamation of the law, according to which God will act in his Day, means for them that they will not be able at some future time to exculpate themselves. They are from this time forward burdened with their guilt. The proclamation of the judgment is therefore more than a threat. In it a process of being judged is already under way. The word of the one who is endowed with charisma, who discloses within the community the criterion of the divine action, anticipates the verdict of the ultimate Judge. The context of our passage indicates, however, that this process has a peculiar dialectic of its own. For it is not that the tribunal of the Last Day is staged on earth and God's own action rendered superfluous. The prophet's sole task is to open up the vista towards this tribunal and thereby to set the guilty man in the place of decision and face him with the possibility of escaping the eternal judgment. The man who allows himself to be judged here and now will not be subject to the final judgment. The judgment which is exercised through the charismatic proclamation still stands in the service of grace, is one pole of the offer of grace and, precisely by announcing God's justice on earth, is directed towards the conversion and salvation of the guilty and the preservation of the community.

The theological analysis will have to be taken up again in a minute and carried further. But, more immediately, it is important to show that it has not read too much into the passage which we have used as a starting point but rests actually on a broader basis of central primitive Christian proclamation. To begin by remaining with Paul, the saying in I Cor. 14.38, εἰ δέ τις ἀγνοεῖ, ἀγνοεῖται ('if a man does not recognize this, he is not recognized'), unmistakably belongs within our frame of reference. The original nature of this text seems to me impossible to doubt. Like ἀγνοεῖτε in D, ἀγνοείτω in P[46] B K sy is an understandable emendation. The sense of the curious passive voice was no longer clear. It was therefore weakened in a parenetic direction, i.e. assimilated to the jussive of the preceding sentence. But this passive denotes in good Semitic fashion the divine action in its effect on men. He who does not acknowledge it, is not acknowledged by God, that is, he is rejected. Once again talion is indicated; the punishment corresponds exactly with the guilt. Once again, Paul, as one endowed with charisma, bears witness to the law of the ultimate Judge before a community which stands in danger of wounding the honour of its Lord and destroying the Spirit-determined harmony of divine worship. Once again, there is more than a warning here. Paul has been laying down in I Cor. 14 nothing less than the outlines of an order of worship. In so doing he has appealed to the Spirit and to his own character as a Spirit-filled man, but in that jussive style which is later to become characteristic of the language of ecclesiastical ordinances. It is now a matter of recognizing and acknowledging that it is precisely the Spirit who creates such an ordinance and makes possible in the Church authoritative action and the erection of definite law. The true Spirit-filled man must recognize this and he only has the capacity to do so. He who does not do so is, by this very indication, shown to be not Spirit-filled and not a partaker of that election which announces itself in the possession of the Spirit. In the authoritative character of the Spirit-filled man, then, yet another decision is pronounced, wherein spirits are separated and blessing and curse come over men's horizon. The ἀγνοεῖται conveys, in its double function as threat and proclamation, the reality of the curse and, as addressed to the individual, pre-empts something of this reality. In these circumstances, the appearance of the present here instead of the eschatological future is not accidental. The ὀργὴ θεου of the Last Day is exhibited by the apostle here, as in Rom. 1.18ff., as the power which is already determining the present and putting disobedience in question.

The rightness of such an interpretation becomes clear when we make it our starting point for the consideration of I Cor. 16.22: 'If a man has no love for the Lord, let him be accursed. Our Lord, come!' Lietzmann[3] and Bornkamm[4] have taught us to understand this

[3] *Messe und Herrenmahl*, 1926, p. 229; ET, *Mass and Lord's Supper*, Leiden, 1954ff., p. 186.

[4] 'Das Anathema in der urchristlichen Abendmahlsliturgie', *TLZ* 75, 1950, cols. 227–30.

sentence as a staple part of the eucharistic liturgy at the beginning of which the community is summoned to self-examination. Its character as law derives not merely from the acclamation which follows and the preceding action of the kiss of peace but equally from the formulation of the protasis, which is constructed along casuistical lines and the curse with which it ends. Curse and blessing are, for men of antiquity, actions which pass beyond the bounds of private 'space', which determine life totally and publicly and, in the New Testament, anticipate the eschatological judgment. Therein lies the difference between this passage and those we have so far discussed. The apodosis speaks yet again of God's judgmental action and of the recompense he metes out. But talion is now expressed no longer by the correspondence of the verb but directly through the curse. As I Cor. 14.38 opened our eyes to such a possibility, so it also made the sense of a variant of this kind evident. The charismatic does not merely warn, but proclaims the already present power of the Judge, the anticipation of which before the Last Day stands in the service of grace, that is, grants space for repentance. Almost the identical content is seen in Gal. 1.9:

> If anyone is preaching to you a gospel contrary to that which you received, let him be accursed.

Only it emerges even more starkly here that the apostle, as representative of his heavenly Lord, possesses the authoritative power of blessing and cursing and understands it as the function of a specific law, that is, the law which belongs to Christ as lawgiver over against his community. But what is the significance of this alleged law?

I should like to explain this in the light of I Cor. 5.3ff. It cannot be disputed that we are here concerned with a legal process which the apostle at once marshals and anticipates. The themes of the tribunal, the prosecution, the punishment – its logic and its meaning – are thus treated in as precise a fashion as anyone could wish for. Admittedly, this procedure is a very long way from what we call law today. The assembling of the community is certainly described by the term συνάγεσθαι, which technically expresses the calling and coming together of the *demos*. But since this act of assembly takes place in the context of the celebration of Christian worship, it is only in a very limited sense that the community can be called the bearer of the process. In the passage we are considering, after first failing in its duty, the community has obviously no alternative but to carry out the apostolic injunction. As the community, it would, however, even if those in authority within it had seized the initiative, possess only the right of assent. For Paul is now assuming the role which otherwise would presumably have fallen to the prophets. But even he does not take independent action. The very fact that it is in no way necessary for him to be present in person is highly characteristic. What is essential is this: through the co-operation of the apostle and the community the Spirit – and that means the present Lord – himself takes action. His judgments are unambiguous and need neither discussion nor ratification, so that from this standpoint the personal absence of the apostle becomes irrelevant and all that remains to the community is the act of assent. The only thing that matters is that the voice of the Spirit through prophet or apostle should somehow be heard and ratified by the community through its act of assent. Correspondingly, no considerations are raised on the subject of the appropriate penalty. There is only one punishment, i.e. the delivery of the guilty party over to Satan – which is identical with exclusion from the community. But we should miss the whole point if we saw in all this nothing but withdrawal from the sinner. In the view which is expressed in our passage, this punishment obviously entails the death of the guilty. The sentence which is being carried out here is precisely *not* spiritual in our modern sense; it is not merely aimed at the inner life. It does not stand in contrast to a physical judgment but incorporates this in its effects. Such a thing is only comprehensible when we perceive that delivery over to Satan as being 'severed from Christ' (Gal. 5.4) is the antithesis of baptism, which, according to Col. 1.13, on its part denaturalizes from the realm of darkness. Satan has the power of death (Heb. 2.14) as, conversely, the Spirit is the power of the Resurrection and even today is creating the new being and summoning men to obedience in the body. Paul cannot possibly come to terms with the idealistic antithesis between spiritual and physical. What we call spiritual is for him expressed in bodily form. Incorporation into the kingdom of Christ is therefore naturalization into the realm of bodily resurrection; and to be delivered over into the kingdom of Satan results in bodily death. Finally, the end of our passage is bound to seem very curious indeed to us. While delivery over to Satan certainly means exclusion from the community, it does *not* mean that the sinner is simply left to himself. In being handed over to Satan, he is only falling in another mode than hitherto into the hands of his Lord, i.e. into the realm of the ὀργὴ θεοῦ and this, very paradoxically, to the end that thus he may yet be saved. For the man who has experienced judgment in this mode can, if he is thereby brought to repentance, remain exempt from the eternal judgment. The community excommunicates from the body of Christ as from the realm of the grace of God. But it cannot annul the event of baptism, nor place limitations on the right of its Lord over one whom that Lord has claimed as his own in baptism – that must surely be what Paul means when he speaks of πνεῦμα. On the contrary, when it anticipates by its own action the decisive action of the universal Judge, the community makes free space for the *Deus absconditus* to complete the work he has begun. Exclusion from the body of Christ is directed always to the service of salvation, which is revealed as grace in the very action of judgment.

To characterize our passage simply as a piece of documentation for the apostle's magical world-view is too easy a solution. Quite regardless of whether it is so or not, the passage is not in any event to be disregarded as unimportant for Pauline theology. For here, if anywhere, it becomes transparently clear that the apostle does not share our antithesis of spirit and body, judgment and grace, the heavenly Christ and the Lord active on earth through his Spirit and that Spirit's instruments; above all, he does not share our antithesis of spirit and law. There exists for him in very real terms a law which has to be observed within the community, although it has almost nothing to do with the forms of law which we assume and administer. There is also undoubtedly a basic difference from what we observe in late antiquity and Judaism, in that very early Christianity possesses no law of membership, no administrative or disciplinary law and that there cannot be within it even the mention of any canon law. To have demonstrated this is the achievement – never to be underestimated – of Sohm whose only mistake was to draw the false conclusion that primitive Christianity possessed no law at all and that its charismatic order must therefore be set in contradiction to any order based on law. So long as we ask the same questions as he asked and share the assumptions on which they were based, we cannot contradict him. This is why the conclusions of his adversaries have remained so thin and unsatisfying. If we want to specify the law which we undoubtedly encounter in I Cor. 5, we must think in other categories than those of canon law and church discipline; more accurately, in categories which are familiar to us in the comparative study of religion from the sphere of the ordeal. We are concerned here with a divine law in which God himself remains the agent and which, inasmuch as God makes it to be promulgated and executed by charismatic men, may be called charismatic law. But what is characteristic of primitive Christianity is the correlation with the Last Day, i.e. its eschatological orientation. The Judge of all the world who stands at the door is the founder and the foundation of the law in question and of its peculiar mode of existence: it thus becomes a function of the Spirit. One of the most momentous errors of Liberalism was its separation of spirit and law. Since Paul integrated the one with the other, to start from this premiss was to alter the whole character of Pauline theology. In any event, we are now in a position to organize within a wider framework the idiosyncratic jussive sentence from which we began. The eschatological law of God, mediated through charismatic men, is also determined by the fact that on earth it is bound to the exclusive medium of the Word and is fulfilled solely in the proclamation of this Word. Thus, conversely, the Word is lifted out of the sphere of mere information, and the elaborate stylization which we have observed (and of which the legally phrased introduction is a special feature) is explained. To hear this Word is to be thereby condemned or pardoned and always at the same time to become the object of the power of God operative within it.

It might be objected, even if our findings so far are accepted, that the group of utterances we have analysed is so small as to approach vanishing-point, and that to overemphasize it in this way is to produce a false understanding of the whole. The weight of this objection cannot in fact be lessened simply by adding a few more examples to those we have already mentioned. It is true that we find:

> He who sows sparingly will also reap sparingly, and he who sows bountifully will also reap bountifully (II Cor. 9.6).
>
> All who have sinned without the law will also perish without the law (Rom. 2.12).

But these passages only assume importance for us because in them the pattern of the jussive sentence now appears in modified form as part of a parenetic argument. The first saying certainly contains all the individual marks of the pattern but, taken as a whole and in its context, is merely an ordinary indicative sentence. This is even more true of the second, inasmuch as there the chiasmus has a purely rhetorical connection and no longer denotes genuine talion. At the same time, it is not without significance that elements of the original jussive sentence are taken over into the parenesis. This is a proclamation that the claim here made upon man receives its depth and range through that Lord whose grace stands under the sign of the vindication of his justice upon earth and therefore finds its reciprocal in Christian obedience and in no way excludes, but on the contrary establishes and makes possible, that reward according to works on which Paul lays such frequent stress. Sohm's formula 'The obligation of love, not of law' is shown to be absolutely inadequate and misleading.

This emerges with particular clarity in the sphere of the apostle's ordering of the community, of which such sentences as I Cor. 14.13, 28, 30, 35, 37 may be called characteristic. Here there is no longer any talk of guilt and punishment, but some contingency which may occur in the course of worship is set out (introduced by ἐάν or some equivalent participle) and there follows the Pauline ruling on the case expressed in the decretal jussive. The eschatological aspect thus loses its prominence. Nevertheless, it would not be correct to say that it is absent. I Cor. 14.38 shows in fact that it is just those decisions of the Apostle which are pronounced here which are put under the sanction of the divine law. It is precisely of them that it is said: he who does not recognize this is rejected. The preservation of that condition which we call order, and which Paul – not accidentally – designates instead εἰρήνη, is a matter with which the Last Day will concern itself. The good estate and the efficacy of the body of Christ is at stake. The apostle pronounces his decisions concerning the life of the community in the perspective of the eschatological law. Of them, too, it could be said in the words of Acts 15.28: 'It has seemed good to the Holy Spirit and to us.' Paul expresses the same thought in I Cor. 14.37:

> If anyone thinks that he is a prophet, or spiritual, he should acknowledge that what I am writing to you is a command of the Lord.

The Spirit does not gives free rein to arbitrary will but posits firmly established order as the effect and the constituent of holy law. Granted he does not do this by creating an inviolable organization articulated according to some ruling concept; for then man would be the slave of the institution. What the Spirit does do is to give insight into the exigencies of the particular situation and at the same time, by the establishment of the νόμος Χριστοῦ, to set for individuality a limit which it must not transgress. The ordinances of the apostle thus do not possess validity and compelling force in virtue of a system of given and objective values by which life is to be regulated, but neither are they simply commended to the good will of the hearer so that love becomes solely the boundary fence of arbitrary choice. There is a dialectic here: an appeal is made to the discernment of the community and, at the same time, the curse is pronounced on disobedience. A real edict of the Holy Spirit is being promulgated. The discernment of the hearers is not the presupposition and the limit of obedience. And yet these decrees are not issued on the basis of formal legal power. Not only obedience, but discernment of the necessity for it, is demanded and the price of folly is the curse. God does not leave it to man to do what seems good to him, he binds hearts more tightly than any lawgiver has ever done. He does not, however, bind them to a programme and a system and will not be satisfied with an obedience which is merely physical and external; but where he commands, he lays claim to us as men called to understanding and love. His law decrees the total surrender of free men: it is justice and law in that it places resistance under the curse and it is spirit, in that it makes obedience possible for those who see. His decrees are sacrosanct and cannot be questioned. But only understanding love can really fulfil them. Therefore love is here not a substitute for law, but the radicalization of it. It appropriates for itself, as well as the body, the judgment and the heart.

Because this is so, it is not in the last resort as a lawgiver that the apostle approaches his churches, as I Cor. itself shows in the clearest possible way. It was the Pastorals which proceeded to make this form of apostolic activity normative. In them Paul's role has been almost reduced to that of the man who, in virtue of his authority, establishes order within the community and sets up a new system of ecclesiastical law. The order thus promulgated is admittedly still traced back to the Spirit and Paul is understood to be the charismatic instrument of this Spirit. But the Spirit is now the power of the holy and apostolic tradition and is to be obeyed as such, while for Paul himself he was the power of the Christ who stands over against the community as Lord and Judge. But this means that the mark of his appropriation is different in the two cases. Paul, too, requires unconditional obedience, just as, conversely, the Pastorals presuppose the necessary discernment. But this discernment of theirs is the acknowledgment of the tradition which governed the adherence of the Christian to the community and to which he has therefore to subject himself; it is knowing about the obligatory givenness of the ecclesiastical institution and its organization. We have now arrived at the beginnings of ecclesiastical administrative and disciplinary law, the mark of which is the fading of the eschatological orientation, the replacement of the presence of Christ by the tradition about Christ and thus a total shift in the relationship of contemporary situation and historical continuity. Conversely, this new ecclesiastical law is rooted unmistakably in the sacred law of primitive times and thus plays its own part in confirming the nature of that law. Law has now taken on another form of articulation, another system of co-ordinates, if you like. Law is no longer a function of the Spirit, but the Spirit is the guarantee and the sanction, the teeth of the law.

But let our brief and sketchy outline of subsequent developments stop there. There is a question which is more important for us: who smoothed the path by which Paul arrived at his views? Rev. 22.18f. provides a first answer. Here the apocalyptist is harking back to the familiar Jewish formula for canonizing a book, which depends on Deut. 4.2 and prohibits the slightest addition or subtraction. The legal character of our passage is therefore beyond question. Nor is the curse attached to such procedure in the apodosis anything new. Judaism was by this time well acquainted with it. But of course our text is differentiated from its Jewish parallel by its formulation of this curse in the manner – seen for the first time in I Cor. 3.17 – of an eschatological *jus talionis*:

> If any one adds to them, God will add to him the plagues described in this book, and if any one takes away from the words of the book of this prophecy, God will take away his share in the tree of life.

Here we see that it is prophetic proclamation which is the original *Sitz im Leben* for sentences of this kind. It is from this quarry that Paul has mined it, as in other contexts he employs the apparatus of the teacher or the apocalyptist. This thesis is capable of even more precise statement if we complete it by showing that this mode of expression imitated and carried over the form of certain specific Old Testament utterances. We can find sufficient evidence for this if we recall the following passages:

No one who believes in him will be put to shame (Rom. 10.11).
Every one who calls upon the name of the Lord will be saved (Rom. 10.13).
He who does them shall live by them (Gal. 3.12).

Here it becomes evident that holy Scripture provided the primitive Christian prophets with the stylistic form in which to clothe their sentences of holy law. This came all the more easily because they believed God himself to have declared his own law to them in this book.

Our findings so far are strengthened still further by material from the Synoptists. The precise structure which has occupied our attention so far is stamped also on Mark 8.38:

> Whoever is ashamed of me and of my words . . ., of him will the Son of man also be ashamed.

Matthew is so anxious to underline the fact that this is not merely a matter of threat or warning but of the proclamation of the law of the Last Day – i.e., a matter less of instruction than of blessing and curse – that, in his corresponding passage 16.27, he bears testimony to the coming of the Son of Man and the message of recompense according to works. His variant is necessary because he himself has already used the logion as part of an ingenious antithesis in 10.32f., i.e., in a context of prophetically determined proclamation:

> So every one who acknowledges me before me, I also will acknowledge before my Father who is in heaven; but who ever denies me before men, I also will deny before my Father who is in heaven.

In any event this Matthean form is more original than the Marcan, because the verb ἐπαισχύνεσιαι ('be ashamed') in Mark represents a refined, perhaps a post-Pauline, modification of the Semitic ὁμολογεῖν and ἀρνεῖσθαι ('acknowledge' and 'deny'), and the decision in face of the Son of Man is presumably older than that in face of the Gospel. Conversely, and for the same reason, the I-saying of Matthew in the apodosis is to be held secondary over against the Son of Man predication of Mark. It is already apparent from modifications that the saying cannot go back in its present form, either Marcan or Matthean, to Jesus himself; proof of this is to be found both in the content, where the confession of Christ is estimated to be the standard of judgment at the Last Day, and also in the form of the sentence. Prophecy proclaims blessing and curse on those members of the community who confess and those who deny by establishing within it the eschatological *jus talionis*. This is exactly what is done in the words of Matt. 6.14f., where our forgiveness is bound to our willingness to forgive; in Mark 4.24, according to which we ourselves prepare for ourselves the measure of the divine judgment; and, most characteristic of all, in Matt. 5.19 where to abrogate the least of the commandments is to be threatened with the position of least in the kingdom of God. Admittedly, the yield of sentences which are constructed strictly according to the model we have discovered is less than might at first be expected. This fact I shall bear in mind and explain.

If our analysis so far is a just one, we have to do here with very primitive material. It belongs to a stage of development which by the time our Gospels were composed lies already far behind; to be more specific, it belongs to the community of the time immediately after Easter, with its apocalyptic expectation of an imminent end and its prophet-leaders. Only at this point in history was it possible to do without the formation of a law of Church organization in the sense of administrative, disciplinary and canon law in order that rewards and punishments might be left solely to the universal Judge himself; only at this point did the Church see in Jesus the returning Son of Man; only at this point did a battle rage round the continuing validity of the Mosaic law in all its parts. In the measure in which the organization of the Church grew more fixed and the expectation of an imminent end lost its burning inspiration, the ground was cut from under the feet of that eschatological divine law of which we have been speaking. Only such fragments were retained as could be used for parenetic purposes, whether dogmatic or ethical. Hence it is not to be wondered at that the stylistic form we have been considering as good as disappeared from the later New Testament writings. Even Matthew is not an exception. He is characterized by an anti-enthusiastic temper which causes the teacher and Christian rabbi rather to conceal than to expose to view the activity of primitive Christian prophecy. The ecclesiastical ordinances which he has assembled and preserved are therefore conditioned by the fact that they regulate casuistically a wide range of difficulties which are arising. We always find that not only does good order within the community possess disproportionately great weight with him but that also the sentences directed to this purpose are determined by an introduction in casuistical jussive style and by a consequent promise or threat in the eschatological future. To enter into a detailed analysis at this point would be to overstep by far too long the time which remains to me. So I merely call attention to the fact as such and remark that I find in it proof that the heir of the prophets has here been taken over and altered in character by the Christian rabbi. The eschatological divine law proclaimed by charismatic men characterized the primitive community in the strongest possible fashion and became the point of departure for all subsequent Church order and for ecclesiastical law itself.

The remaining historical problem concerns the peculiar connection between prophecy and law. How did this arise? Here, too, I must be content to pin-point the question rather than to work out a satisfactory answer to it. But it seems to me certain that prophecy, which in Palestine (as later on Gentile Christian soil) very quickly became separated from the teaching office, did more than take over the task of keeping the hope of the Parousia alive in the community and – precisely by this means – of strengthening the Christians exposed to persecution. Prophecy had also to remind those who were beset by temptation of the demands of their calling, to admonish, to warn and to punish them. This it did by proclaiming God's recompensing action on the Last Day. The stylistic form in which prophecy found it possible to express this message was offered by the Old Testament, i.e., by those sayings in which the fulfilment of some condition on earth was to be followed in the eschatological future by promise or threat, blessing or curse. This kind of statement is clearly recognizable in the Apocalypse of John and the stylistic means used to express it are, so to speak, exemplified in the 'He that overcometh' sayings in the letters to the churches. It is therefore prophecy's function of leadership in the community which finds expression in the sentences of holy law. Such leadership, on the other hand, would scarcely have been able to develop in Jerusalem since the strong community there necessitated very early on a tighter organization under the apostles and a presbyterate. Prophecy can only have possessed a leadership function within the small communities of Palestine, where the oppressed faithful needed to gather round a charismatic man. Lohmeyer's dichotomy between Jerusalem and Galilee could therefore, when thus modified and with a different approach, take on renewed significance. However that may be, the proper *Sitz im Leben* for our eschatological divine law is the situation in which primitive Christian prophecy 'judges' the messianic people of God, as once the old prophets 'judged' Israel.

I cannot conclude without evaluating the historical result from the point of view of systematic theology. However many points in my analysis may still seem problematical, the presence of sentences of holy law in the New Testament can hardly be disputed. But this means the collapse of a basic tenet of Liberalism: in the very early days of the Christian religion Spirit and Law are *not* separated. At this point the Spirit creates law, and the fact that he does so is the constituent element of his being. The Spirit is the power which proclaims God's law on earth in the preached word, grounds it in the action of the universal Judge on the Last Day and gives it reality in the new obedience of the Christian. More than once, it is sharply emphasized that we have to do here with a law of a particular kind which is bound to appear alien to our modern conception of law. But it is a prejudice and an error if we are only prepared to acknowledge as law whatever can be subsumed under this modern conception. The comparative study of religion and especially the exegesis of the Old Testament point to the existence of a divine law which in the form of the ordeal was for a long time a feature of European history. It has its place in the New Testament also, before it is replaced even this early by the beginnings of the law of the institutional Church.

But what is the significance of the fact that we must recognize this law to be the determining factor in primitive Christianity? Surely this, that God, or Christ, as the Revealer, guides and judges the community. By so doing, he demonstrates his righteousness. For God vindicates his righteousness on earth through the medium of his law. We must therefore speak of a polarity between grace and law. Grace is the power of God, which creates salvation and in such a way that God remains Lord and Judge and maintains law. Law is the power of him who sets up his kingdom among rebels and the expression of the fact that God does not create salvation without at the same time giving reality to his lordship. The fact that God remains God even when he becomes gracious to us and all grace brings us to obedience – this fact moved primitive Christianity to connect Spirit and law. Conversely, it did not separate law from God's saving action. Even his judgment stands in the service of his grace as once again John's Apocalypse expressly testifies. For the fact that God is Lord and wills to become Lord is not to be separated from his calling of us to be his children. His wrath, too, manifests the will of him who has not given us up.

The difference between this holy law in the New Testament and the later Church law is that primitive Christianity understood the law that was authoritative within it to be the foundation of obedience. The object of the law is not order as such, and in the formal sense, but the order – determined by its own content – of the right relationship between Creator and creature; it is therefore in I Cor. 14.33 called *εἰρήνη* and set over against *ἀκαταστασία*. Therefore this law is oriented towards the Last Day and grounded in it. Therefore, again, men may be its instruments but not its executors. What we call Church law originates in a process of impoverishment in which anthropological depth is overshadowed by sociological extension. Now law is formed only by life in the fellowship and therefore takes its standards from a conception of order which is directed towards the good estate of the fellowship. Obviously this community law was further understood as divine law. But for all that, there had been a shift of perspective. The Spirit is now only the power of obedience inasmuch as he creates order in the community. And the community guards this its order; it no longer merely proclaims the word but at the same time regulates the common life of its members in a pedagogical and disciplinary temper which requires a new casuistry, managed by experts. The realm of holy law is thus abandoned. The beginnings of this kind of development are already to be observed in the New Testament and it is a rewarding exercise to set them out more circumstantially. But it was the object of this lecture to do no more than plot the point of departure.

IV

THE BEGINNINGS OF CHRISTIAN THEOLOGY*

BEGINNINGS ARE for the most part hidden. This applies also to the beginnings of Christianity after Easter. The very small amount of information of unquestioned reliability given us by Acts rather emphasizes than illumines the darkness which we encounter there. The historian will certainly not remain satisfied with twilight over a *terra incognita*. He cannot be persuaded that beginnings do not determine what is to follow, and contain, in however veiled and strange a form, the law of the future. He will therefore try to penetrate by continually renewed assaults into that which is hidden and not allow himself to be discouraged but only more vigorously goaded on by the disappointments he encounters, particularly as these form part of his daily bread. In so far as he does not actually need to throw in his hand completely at this point even before he has begun, he owes it to Gospel criticism and especially to the work of the form critics. Certainly, both make it possible for us to ascribe a considerable part of the Synoptic tradition to the proclamation of the community after Easter. Nevertheless, it must be admitted that even their findings have so far been unsatisfying to anyone who is looking for the beginnings of Christian theology. They may and do provide us with a wealth of historical and theological detail which can be assembled rather like a mosaic with many blank spaces; but even comprehensive outlines remain problematic while we are unable to produce even a moderately convincing methodological mode of entry into the heart of the history and theology we are seeking. In what follows I shall be concerned with this mode of entry and with it alone. Scientific knowledge always begins with self-limitations and only the inquirer who, in pursuing this question, gives himself reso-

* First published in: *ZTK* 57, 1960, pp. 162–85. A lecture given to the annual meeting of the editorial board of the *ZTK* in Sindlingen on 23 April, 1960, repeated before the Theological Faculty at Basle on the 18 May and that at Erlangen on 27 May, 1960.

lutely to this one most important task, can hope from this starting point to arrive finally at the wide open spaces not only of further possibilities, but of historical reality.

I am going to underpin this argument with certain observations in the area of form-criticism referring almost exclusively to the Gospel of Matthew. If it is true that the two other Synoptists are unable to give us any particular help here, at least that shows that we have a real problem, causing us to differentiate between the Synoptists – a problem which would be rewarding to investigate even if it bore no fruit so far as our specific question is concerned. Matthew, located somewhere on the borders of Palestine and Syria, writing apparently for Gentile Christians yet out of a wide knowledge of Jewish-Christian tradition, might well be nearer, in the material peculiar to him, to primitive tradition than others, as C. F. Burney maintains in his book *The Poetry of our Lord*,[1] which is based on researches along the lines of form-criticism. I must say with all the emphasis I can command that what is being attempted here is a reconstruction. Anyone who is not prepared to enter on risky experiments deserves our respect for his solid principles. But, conversely, perhaps he will concede to us that historical work cannot live without reconstructions and that, if I see things rightly, even the thinking of systematic theology by no means eschews them.

In an opening section which is designed, as it were propadaeutically, to show the logical necessity of the approach I have chosen, I propose to illustrate by the help of a few examples the way in which the history lying behind our Gospels was filled with very severe theological tensions; how it contains the experience of something very like a confessional controversy; and how the opposing camps both boasted of their own possession of the Spirit and also measured the adversary (and found him wanting) by certain criteria of the Spirit. Matt. 7.22–23 is uncommonly instructive:

> On that day many will say to me, 'Lord, Lord, did we not prophesy in your name, and cast out demons in your name, and do many mighty works in your name?' And then will I declare to them, 'I never knew you; depart from me, ye evildoers.'

It is not fortuitous that Matthew uses this polemic, which, according to v. 15, is directed against false prophets, as his conclusion to the concrete injunctions of the Sermon on the Mount. It is a warning to

[1] *Op. cit.*, 1925, p. 87.

the community that it is in the most grievous danger. Strikingly enough, this menace does not stem from Pharisaism, the adversary with which Matthew is elsewhere particularly concerned and to which he has already opposed the 'better righteousness' in the antitheses of ch. 5; it stems from an enthusiastic piety which conceives of itself as the bearer of wonder-working powers – prophecy, exorcism and even miraculous healing. But this means that Matthew is aiming at a quite specific group among the early community – a group which knows itself to have an endowment from the exalted Christ and – exactly like the community in Corinth – boasts of representing and administering on earth, as the plenipotentiary of Christ, the energies of the Spirit which has been bestowed upon it eschatologically. The parallels in Luke 6.46 and 13.26f. have characteristically expunged this pointed and concrete reference and merely warn the faithful in a timeless kind of way about unfruitful discipleship. It emerges all the more clearly in Matthew – and here there is agreement with the narrative of Acts – that there was an enthusiastic movement not only in Gentile Christendom but on the very soil of Palestine itself and rooted, what is more, in the Easter experiences. But it is no less clear that Matthew himself will have none of this enthusiasm. He does not consider it necessary to establish this in detail and to expose any concrete errors of his opponents. A. Schlatter[2] has rightly described him as an ethical rigorist and as the representative of an incipient Christian rabbinate. He pronounces over all piety which is not determined by the criterion 'doing the will of my heavenly Father' the condemnatory formula 'I never knew you'. This is presented as a solemn and binding declaration by the use of the legal term *ὁμολογεῖν* and is confirmed in its character as a formal curse by the quotation from Ps. 6.9.

If we have here come upon a contradiction between the Evangelist and an already existent practice and doctrine of primitive Christian history, then this earlier stage in the life of the community after Easter acquires sharper contours from Matt. 23.8–10:

> But you are not to be called rabbi, for you have one teacher, and you are all brethren. And call no man your father on earth, for you have one Father, who is in heaven. Neither be called masters, for you have one master, the Christ.

An 'edifying' interpretation of this passage, as if it were directed

[2] *Der Evangelist Matthäus*. 2nd ed., 1933.

against love of titles in general, would be out of place, even if Matthew himself already understood it in this sense. What would emerge along this line would be a polemic against the evolution of a Church order which was taking the form of a Christian rabbinate. For 'teacher', 'father', 'master' are the titles which are bestowed on the rabbi. If such titles, which belong solely to God (or to the Christ), are claimed and allowed on earth, then, according to the viewpoint expressed in this saying, the total congregation of Christ is being devalued and the priesthood of all believers damaged. A protest of this kind, made simultaneously in the name of the sole lordship of Christ and of the eschatological freedom of the individual Christian, can certainly only be made by those possessed of the Spirit; and it can only be directed against a Judaistic government of the community which, on its side, derives authority both in general and in particular from the full power of the Spirit over the community and therefore locates it in the teaching office and nowhere else. Thus, in this controversy over titles which have been taken over from Judaism and which emphasize the dignity of the teacher, what is at stake in the last resort is a proper understanding both of the lordship of Christ and of the manifestation and truth of the Spirit.

We are set in the midst of the same controversy, admittedly from the opposite side, by the hotly debated yet basically quite unambiguous introduction to the antitheses in 5.17–20, which prescribes the keeping of the whole Torah to the last jot. Matthew has obviously taken over the core of the saying from elsewhere. As a member of a church which is already engaged in mission to the Gentiles and is in consequence already detached from the cultic law, he is unable to understand it in the literal sense in which it was originally intended. His own comment is therefore in the sense of the radical commandment of love. Perhaps 18d, 'until everything has happened',[3] is already an addition of his; this certainly applies to v. 20, which demands the 'better righteousness' over against the requirements of the scribes and Pharisees. He can, however, with the proviso signified by these parentheses, hand on the tradition (modified yet again in Luke 16.17) which dictates v. 19:

> Whoever then relaxes one of the least of these commandments and teaches men so, shall be called least in the kingdom of heaven; but he who does them and teaches them shall be called great in the kingdom of heaven.

[3] Thus E. Schweizer, 'Mt. 5. 17–20. Anmerkung zum Gesetzesverständnis des Matthäus,' *TLZ* 77, 1952, cols. 480f.

The very form of the sentence is particularly important. It corresponds exactly with the scheme which I have analysed in my investigation into 'Sentences of Holy Law in the New Testament'[4] and which I have attempted to show to be characteristic of prophetic proclamation: protasis and apodosis express a relation of guilt and punishment or duty and reward. In this scheme the protasis – sometimes a relative construction, sometimes a conditional, sometimes a participial – echoes the introduction of a statement of legal casuistry, while the apodosis is organized in the style of apodictic divine law. The differences between casuistic and apodictic law evidently disappeared in late Judaism, just as the rabbinate in the practice of its jurisdiction no longer distinguishes secular law sharply from religious law. Similarly also, the reward is a heavenly reward, and, while the punishment may be proclaimed by men, it is no longer executed by them, but deferred until the Parousia of the God who will appear to judge the world. The community can dispense with any earthly carrying-out of the sentence because it awaits the imminent End. Its tribunal operates under the shadow of the universal Judge, who announces himself ineluctably in the word of prophecy in such a way as to proclaim the eschatological *jus talionis* and thus at the same time the promise to those who hear and the curse to those who disobey. This is exactly what is happening here.

It is striking that the message of judgment is not directed only against perverted practice. Rather, there is bound up with this practice, and forming the basis of it, a false doctrine. The tradition which Matthew is preserving – that of an obviously and strictly legalistic Jewish Christianity – is condemning with eschatological seriousness and with the knowledge of the criteria and objectives of the divine wrath a different Christian proclamation which on its part is declaring the Law to be wholly or partially abrogated. We are therefore watching the progress of what can only be called a confessional controversy in primitive Christianity. The question has frequently been asked whether Paul himself may not be the target of this condemnation. Well, of course he is, factually speaking, one of the targets, even though the age of our saying precludes his being the immediate object. We should be nearer to the mark if we said that the Hellenist group were here under attack: more precisely, Stephen and his following, who seem actually to have regarded Temple and Torah alike as superseded for the disciples of Jesus from the first Easter, on-

[4] See pp. 66–81 above.

wards, on the grounds of the manifestation of the Spirit, and who in any event disregarded the cultic law in favour of the Gentile Mission upon which they themselves had embarked. Both parties no doubt appealed to their Spirit-given insight, so that here for the first time in Church history spirit is being set against spirit. Hence the severity which does not shrink from the application of Holy Law. Certainly here, as elsewhere in similar contexts, God's sovereignty and freedom is preserved by suspending communion with the adversary on earth while yet not breaking it irretrievably for all eternity. Even if the most minute breach of the Torah prevents the transgressor from attaining anything more than the lowest place in the kingdom of heaven, yet no one dares to pronounce him deprived of this place at any rate. It is not permissible totally to deny the other man's right to the name and estate of Christian. Admittedly, the obvious and intense reluctance with which this limitation is made itself makes clear the stark opposition of the two positions, at least in their earthly relationship.

An equally good illustration of the same point from a different perspective is Matt. 10.5f.:

> Go nowhere among the Gentiles, and enter no town of the Samaritans, but go rather to the lost sheep of the house of Israel.

It is sufficiently astonishing that Matthew has preserved this injunction at all, missing as it is in the other Synoptists. He probably intended it to refer to the time of the earthly Jesus and interpreted it as being abrogated by the mission charge of the Risen Lord in 28.18ff. Yet this way out is barred by Matthew's own portrait of the attitude of Jesus. What we are really hearing in this saying, too, is the voice of the strictest form of Jewish Christianity. Indeed, as late as Acts we can tell that this school strove on principle, if in vain, against any mission going beyond the borders of Israel. The appendix to that book, which is not intended to apply merely for a limited period, says this as clearly as anyone could wish. The injunction only acquires its full weight when it is understood that the object of the polemic here is a mission among the Samaritans and Gentiles – a mission not merely planned and debated, but already begun, as the context requires. It was certainly not the fear of hostile involvement with Judaism which lay behind the command; no one who confessed the crucified Messiah, Jesus, could permanently escape this. It is equally incredible both that strict Jewish Christianity did not take this confession seriously and that, expressing its rejoicing and its hope as it did in its cry of Maranatha, it had given up seeing Jesus the Messiah exalted before and above all things. But in that case the only course left is to interpret the command on the basis of the apocalyptic conception – already represented in the Old Testament – which combines the streaming of the Gentiles to worship on Mount Zion with the eschatological triumph of Israel as the latter's most visible sign. If the Gentile mission (to use this not wholly correct expression) is the proper and eschatological work of God himself, then any human attempt to anticipate it is seen as an arrogant invasion of a right God has reserved for himself. It follows that all that can be done in the earthly present is to lead the lost sheep of the house of Israel back into the unity of the messianic people of the twelve tribes for the precise purpose of enabling the Parousia to come to pass. Paul himself employs the same conception in Rom. 11.25ff., even if in his case it has undergone some modification. Admittedly he does not there entertain the argument which the opposite side, undoubtedly on its own authority, has put up: namely, that with Easter and the Pentecostal endowment of the Church, the end of the world has dawned and the Gentile mission thus bears to this extent the character of an eschatological token and has been launched by God's own action.

This means that a difference of eschatology divides from each other the two groups which we have been considering in primitive Christianity. The one remains within the continuity of the Jewish hopes – the other passes beyond the eschatological tradition of the fathers (as in the question of the Torah and the ordering of the community) through the events of Easter and the receipt of the Spirit, driven on by enthusiasm along a new route. Of course, it is important to be clear-sighted here: it is not enthusiasm as such which separates the two groups. This is common to both (at least to begin with). It kindles the hope of the messianic restoration of Israel just as much as the decision to embark on the Gentile mission in the earthly present. In neither camp is the community prepared to dispense with the voice of the Spirit to whom it knows itself to be subject: and it is prophecy which renders this voice audible to it, whether calling it to missionary work as in Acts 13.2, or commanding it to keep this work within the boundaries of Israel (Matt. 10.5). Common, too, to both groups is the fervent sense of expectation which particularly distinguishes this primitive, Easter-inspired enthusiasm, where the hope is expressed (Mark 9.1; Matt. 16.28; 24.34) that at least a part of the original community may live to experience the Parousia and where the Eucharist is celebrated as the anticipation of the imminent heavenly banquet. It is not enthusiasm as such, but the stamp of different theologies, which is already dividing primitive Christianity into opposing confessional camps with a degree of sharpness that is not to be minimized. Both groups are fundamentally and totally determined by their theology, they stand and fall with it. Hence the adherents of each at the time of writing must be kept to the beaten track by sentences of holy law; hence, again we are moving in the eschatological sphere of promise and curse, where prophecy finds expression as the operative sanction which in this situation directs the community.

These are the historical presuppositions on which we now proceed to base the further investigation of our problem. We are now in a position to delimit and to define it. For we do not propose in what follows to pursue our two groups along every line their history may have taken. We are to some extent informed, through the medium of Acts, of the development of that freedom movement which centred round the Seven. It was, at least in part, driven out of Jerusalem into Antioch, there to prepare the work of the Pauline apostolate and to be dissolved into it. In broad outline we know, too, the fate of that strict Jewish Christianity which gathered around Jerusalem as its meeting-point. It was driven ever more strongly on to the defensive, simply by the mere fact of the irresistible growth of the Gentile Church, until it finally degenerated into a sect. We may easily pass a false judgment on its reaction against this situation, because it seems to have taken the offensive specifically against the work of Paul and his fellows. Whatever Jewish Christianity may have done in detail, its real purpose was to make a despairing effort to keep faith with its ancestral inheritance and not to lose its sense of mission in the face of overwhelming Gentile Christian superiority. The effect was to replace Peter by James and to substitute legalism for the enthusiasm which was setting in – because almost always in the heart of a confessional battle the point of difference becomes the point of decision and those who are fighting for freedom allow themselves to be pressured into narrowness.

But we have still to enquire what became of that Jewish Christianity which did not immediately submit to the gradually growing leadership and authority of Jerusalem in the early days. It may eventually have been forced into the camp of the legalists and ultimately of Jerusalem by the persecution of the Hellenists or equally by the processes which led up to the Jewish War. After all, we do not have to assume that the enthusiastic movement here died out immediately after the martyrdoms of Stephen and James the son of Zebedee, or with the departure of Peter from Jerusalem – or even with the beginning of the Jewish War. Had it done so, it would be impossible to explain how traces of this enthusiasm came to be retained in the Gospels and how indeed the Fourth Gospel, which was far from being rooted in Jewish Christian legalism, came to be written at all.

The problem is a difficult one and, as far as I can see, has hardly been attacked by anybody in a way that is convincing,[5] at least methodologically. Conversely, I derive the logical necessity of the question which has been raised from the unusually significant words in Matt. 10.41:

> He who receives a prophet because he is a prophet shall receive a prophet's reward, and he who receives a righteous man because he is a righteous man shall receive a righteous man's reward.

Matthew is here inserting a piece of tradition peculiar to his own source into a connection of parallel content, which has already been used in Q at the end of the section to emphasize the full authority of the disciple in his mission; according to rabbinic principles, the disciple is the plenipotentiary of the one who sends him and, as the disciple of Jesus, has therefore an eschatological function and dignity. A Jewish saying, according to which the Shekinah is encountered in the person of the rabbi, may well underlie this Matthean saying. Even if this were the case, the peculiar form of the utterance would place it in quite a different perspective. Once again there is an absolutely exact correspondence between protasis and apodosis; the latter is in the eschatological future tense, proclaiming here not punishment but reward. The eschatological *jus talionis* is promulgated afresh. The point of the saying is that the universal Judge takes note of what has been happening on earth because Christ himself is present in the servant of the Gospel and therefore the eschatological event has begun to come to pass. But at the moment I find the strange differentiation between prophet and righteous man even more significant. The excellent hypothesis of E. Meyer[6] (quoted by

[5] The best attempt is by E. Lohmeyer, *Galiläa und Jerusalem* (FRLANT, 52), 1936, although in another context and by other arguments which, to my mind, ultimately fail in their objective.

[6] *Ursprung und Anfänge des Christentums* I, 1921, p. 143 n. 1. Admittedly, Meyer speaks of the 'organization and articulation of the developed Christian com-

Klostermann),[7] suggesting that we have here the reflection of an ancient distinction within the community, seems to me to be immediately enlightening. Forgotten so far as the remainder of the New Testament is concerned, this distinction does at any rate characterize the gnostic sects assailed in Revelation: the community consists of the prophets who obviously exercise leadership in it and the righteous, as the general body of members call themselves, carrying on the Jewish nomenclature.

The same combination[8] has been preserved in the beatitude in Matt. 13.16f.:

> Blessed are your eyes, for they see, and your ears, for they hear! Truly I say to you, many prophets and righteous men longed to see what you see, and did not see it, and to hear what you hear, and did not hear it.

In no sense are we to find here an expression of the distinction between clergy and laity. The prophets only bring into the clear light of day the determining force of the whole community – the Spirit of prophecy himself who governs this community and therefore guides it by means of the instruments he considers appropriate. This is why 5.12 can read: 'For so men persecuted the prophets which were before you.' Because it is marked out by inspiration, the whole community stands in the succession of the Old Testament prophets and therefore suffers of necessity their martyr lot. Correspondingly, we have in 10.19f. the word of comfort for those who are set before the tribunal: the Spirit of the Father will tell them what to say in their defence and how to say it; that is, the Spirit will help them

---

munity' and thus does not take the antithesis seriously: next to the twelve or the apostles (as in I Cor. 12.28) the prophets occupy the most eminent position, followed by the 'righteous' as the tried and trusted among the disciples and the 'little ones' as those who are not distinguished by any particular gifts. Verses 41–42 are therefore seen as an original unity, now divided into three. But 10.40–42 is obviously a composition of the Evangelist's own. I should myself dispute any original combination of vv. 41 and 42 on grounds both of form and content, but this I shall say more about later. There is an absolute identification of the 'little ones' with the disciples in v. 42 and the antithesis of v. 41 is thereby dissolved. Thus Meyer does not recognize the real problem of v. 41 and, for this reason, he reads later viewpoints into it.

[7] *Das Matthäusevangelium*, 3rd ed., 1938, p. 93.

[8] Of course, it is the Old Testament Jewish community which the Evangelist has in mind here.

through by the power of prophecy. In characteristic fashion (and obviously influenced by his anti-enthusiastic attitude) Matthew has preserved only these few reminiscences of what was originally assumed to be a general endowment of the Spirit; and, also characteristically, only in the context of pronouncements about sufferings to come. The early date of the conception is equally revealed by the fact that Luke substitutes in 10.24 the combination 'prophets and kings' for the original 'prophets and righteous men', thus clearly losing the real sense of the latter. If we ask where this hypothetical church order might have prevailed, Jerusalem is eliminated, because there the leadership of the community was exercised first by the Twelve and then, very soon, whether before or after James, also by a presbyterate. The only possibility lies in the little congregations on the borders of Palestine and Syria in which any other form of organization other than leadership by a charismatic man was out of the question because of the small number of their members. Perhaps, too, one peripatetic prophet looked after a chain of such congregations. The promise contained in our saying would then make particularly good sense: such prophets were thrown upon the resources of this divinely pledged, but obviously chancy, hospitality.

The conclusion of this process of reasoning, almost self-evident in itself, yet illuminates in striking fashion the history of primitive Christianity: prophecy (and the prophet-directed community) was the vehicle of enthusiasm in Jewish Christianity after Easter, as it was to be in later Gentile Christianity. What gives this community its particular stamp is that, seeing in the possession of the Spirit the pledge of the imminent Parousia and the ambassadorial authority for its mission, it therefore combines logically within itself enthusiasm and apocalyptic theology. But this conclusion needs to be demonstrated. I turn now in the second part of my lecture to this task, mindful of the brevity imposed on me and not attempting to be exhaustive. I shall analyse first certain forms of the prophetic proclamation and then, in conclusion, the main points of its content.

More significant than any other form, in my opinion, are the sentences of holy law bearing the construction of an eschatological *jus talionis*. Nowhere is there a clearer expression of the viewpoint which reckons with the imminent invasion of the Parousia, professing to know the criteria with which the universal Judge operates and deriving this knowledge from its own inspiration by the Spirit. These sentences belong within the wider framework of what R. Bultmann has designated 'church rules';[9] they are, however, distinguished in content by their combination of a basically apocalyptic outlook with an enthusiasm stemming from prophetic inspiration, in form by the eschatological future of the promise or the curse which follows in the apodosis on the frequently juristic formulations of the conditional sentences.

Matthew has an unmistakable love for this stylistic device which rarely occurs in the other Synoptists. He – I see him as well on the way to a Christian rabbinate – was particularly interested in just these questions of order and therefore combined, without being a legalist, Gospel and divine Law in the closest possible alliance and manifested this by the use of utterances in legal form. It is even worth considering that he may himself have, if not created this literary form of sentences of holy law, at least provided it for the first time with its full weight. That would jeopardize my fundamental thesis, according to which it is the earliest post-Easter community which is expressing itself in these sentences. But we have to set against this hypothesis the fact that both apocalyptic expectation and enthusiasm are equally uncharacteristic of Matthew personally, and that the premises of the sentences in question are therefore lacking in his case when he was in a good position to exploit their schematic construction in the interest of his concern with the divine Law. Further, we find the stylistic form with which we are concerned to be already somewhat diluted in the tradition quoted by Matthew and this would correspond with a later stage of development.

Two examples may clarify this. Matt. 19.28f. runs:

> Truly, I say to you, in the new world, when the Son of man shall sit on his glorious throne, you who have followed me will also sit on twelve thrones, judging the twelve tribes of Israel. And everyone who has left houses or brothers or sisters or father or mother or children or lands, for my name's sake, will receive a hundredfold, and inherit eternal life.

The evangelist has first combined the sayings and then, as a comparison with the other Synoptists demonstrates, altered them in detail as well. In the second logion, for the motif 'for the sake of the kingdom of God', retained in Luke, he substitutes the christological twist 'for my name's sake'. Because it offended his rigorism or his sober cast of mind to look forward to recompense and reward while still

[9] *Die Geschichte der synoptischen Tradition*, 2nd ed., 1931, pp. 138ff.; ET, *The History of the Synoptic Tradition*, 1963, pp. 130ff.

on earth, he erased the antithesis (which is certainly original) 'will receive manifold more in this time, and in the age to come eternal life'. It is impossible to say whether he or his source converted the introduction to the first saying, which was clearly intended as a conditional, into a characteristic of the Twelve. Reference to the Marcan parallel shows, however, that the expression 'will receive a hundredfold' is to be reckoned – even at so early a date – as an abbreviation of Q; the latter was apparently unwilling to allow what had been lost on earth to appear in isolation in the apodosis, even though this would have been the only way of depicting the divine talion in scrupulously exact form.

The same dilution of the stylistic form can be observed in the variation between Matt. 10.41 and 42. Verse 42 runs:

> And whoever gives to one of these little ones even a cup of cold water because he is a disciple, truly, I say to you, he shall not lose his reward.

The introduction is an exact parallel with v. 41. The apodosis still contains the juristic εἰς ὄνομα, the formula of protestation which has almost the form of a solemn oath, and the reward motif, which corresponds to the pedantic conditional of the protasis. But the eschatological future of promise is replaced by the declaration, which, however, admittedly does itself refer to divine action. It is no longer possible to decide whether the prophet or the teacher is speaking here. Similarly, the comprehensive predication μαθηταί and the correlative expression of humility μικροί has further displaced the unique differentiation of prophets and righteous men.

The utterance in Matt. 10.13f. is even more emphatically remote from the stylistic form of the sentence of eschatological law. Here, too, it is a question of the reception accorded to the Christian missionary who brings with him the peace of his Lord but who, if turned away, leaves behind him the curse effected by the shaking off of the dust from his feet. While the protasis in these pronouncements retains traces of the legal style, it has in view now not a concrete act but an abstract norm whenever reference is made to the appropriate or inappropriate behaviour of those to whom the missionaries came; there follows in the apodosis a jussive which is didactic in the sense that here the community is instructing its messengers. This community is looking back on its manifold experiences and providing for different eventualities which may occur in the practice of its mission. Matthew assumes this situation and the modifications of the oral tradition which are bound up with it. He cannot, therefore, be the real author and principal propagator of these sentences of holy law which primitive Christianity has preserved independently of him.

Certainly these sentences are by no means the sole determinant of the prophetic proclamation of the enthusiasm of the period after Easter. There are in addition very characteristic pronouncements, equally couched in the eschatological future. I take as an example v. 15 from the above-mentioned passage, Matt. 10.13ff.:

> Truly, I say to you, it shall be more tolerable on the day of judgment for the land of Sodom and Gomorrha than for that town.

We cannot fail to notice that the same pronouncement, only very slightly modified, occurs again in the lament over the Galilean towns in 11.22, 24. This shows that fixed forms of speech are being used to bring to the hearers' consciousness the terrors of the last judgment, like the saying concerning wailing and gnashing of teeth in Gehenna,[10] although we note the latter only in passing. Furthermore, 11.22ff. proves that such pronouncements are being employed in a particular context, rather like a refrain; Matt. 6.4, 6, 18, where the eschatological *jus talionis* is again proclaimed, provides additional verification: 'Your Father, who sees in secret, will reward you.' As a concluding example, the superiority to the Old Testament type has the ring of a refrain in Matt. 12.41f.:

> The men of Nineveh will arise at the judgment with this generation and condemn it; for they repented at the preaching of Jonah, and behold, something greater than Jonah is here. The queen of the South will arise at the judgment with this generation and condemn it; for she came from the ends of the earth to hear the wisdom of Solomon, and behold, something greater than Solomon is here.

The artificial construction of the two sayings, with their complete parallelism, is clear to see. Only a false conception of inspiration as resulting in an uncontrolled outburst of feeling can enter this in evidence against the presence of prophecy here.[11] Primitive Christianity, as

[10] Matt. 8.12; 13.42, 50; 22.13; 24.51.

[11] A good example of this is to be found in Burney, The *Poetry of Our Lord*, pp. 100f. It is true that 'wonderful powers of poetical improvisation' are ascribed to the prophets. Yet their characteristic quality is 'sudden inspiration'. Later working over of their sayings, especially in regard to the rhythm, is alleged to have given these artistic form. From the point of view of the New Testament, even the use of the concept 'poetical' is thoroughly inappropriate. G. D. Kilpatrick, *The Origins of the Gospel according to St Matthew*, 1946, pp. 77f., speaks more congruously of the

is shown both in its hymns and in the 'He who overcomes' sayings in Revelation, did in fact ascribe to the Spirit this precise capacity of combining concentrated content and artistic form. More important still, however, is the reference back to the Old Testament, which brings our passage into line with others (5.12; 7.23; 10.15; 11.22ff.), and brings about a confrontation between the two generations characterized by the presence of the message of salvation. This procedure is based on the apocalyptic principle, which is formulated more clearly in 24.37: 'As it happened in the days of Noah, so it will happen at the Parousia of the Son of Man.' End and Beginning correspond and, seen from the perspective of the End, the Beginning is mirrored in the Old Testament history. By the use of late Jewish tradition, the Old Testament itself receives an apocalyptic interpretation.

The procedure is so significant that I must insert a brief excursus here. We are encountering at this point the earliest Christian understanding of history, on which all its successors have been dependent. It is the conception of the parallel, even if antithetically ordered, course of salvation history and the history of disaster; a course which finds its judgment and its objective in the Parousia of the Son of Man, Jesus. The mythical character of such a view of history cannot well be contested. But it is certainly too facile simply to try to replace it on this account by the modern insight into the historical nature of existence; this viewpoint, taken in isolation, dissolves historical connection into a series of more or less unrelated situations, reduces God's future to men's futurity, sees the present primarily in the light of the demand it makes upon ourselves and, finally, interprets the past as a background to a mock-up of the decision which we have to face. It is very problematical how far this kind of ethical view of history can preserve history's eschatological character. Conversely, it is true that it was apocalyptic which first made historical thinking possible within Christendom. Since for apocalyptic the world has a definite beginning and a definite end, the course of history therefore takes a definite direction and is irrevocable, articulated into a series of epochs clearly distinguishable from each other. In this scheme the individual being receives its firmly established place, its particularity

liturgical or catechetical character of the material that is being dealt with here. We can see clearly in the Revelation of John that prophetic inspiration, as the New Testament understands it, is not properly synonymous with poetic inspiration in a sense similarly obsolete today.

and co-ordinates, to which historical thinking appeals. Hence also the necessity for the kerygma of Jesus not merely to be proclaimed, but to be narrated. Thus it becomes possible to arrive at the construction of the incomparable literary form of the Gospels, which – in spite of all the quite proper objections which have been made *ad nauseam* to understanding them as biography – yet present us in a highly unique fashion with something like the life of a man, from an eschatological perspective and according to an eschatological interpretation. As the Jewish Passover Haggada shows, apocalyptic cannot dispense with the remembrance of salvation and catastrophe in past history if it is to keep hope and warning alive in the present. Neither can it content itself with a one-for-one interpretation of the Gospels, because it is bound always to be narrating the sacred history in terms of a new situation and out of a new experience. The Gospel cannot maintain its identity without the Gospels. The kerygmatic proclamation becomes the proclamation of an idea only, unless it is narration as well: and unless it is always being grasped afresh in the very process of narration, it becomes a document of mere history. Prophetic proof-texts and typology are the oldest testimonies to this narrative which is rooted in apocalyptic; as such, they determine on their side the proto-gospel of the Passion and, just as much, the genealogy and preface of Matthew, which, though late in their literary form, are nevertheless very early in the context of the tradition from which they came. But we have also to set within this context the sayings which begin 'I am come', which look back over and sum up the finished work of Jesus and which cannot therefore originate with the earthly Jesus but make the voice of the exalted Lord heard through a prophetic mouth. We have already found in our encounter with Matt. 5.17 that in these sayings it is not just a matter of establishing for later generations what was once actually the case but of extracting from the commission and work of Jesus a criterion by which to decide what can properly be called Christian. And this may be confirmed by an analysis of Matt. 9.13; 10.34; 18.11; 20.28; Luke 12.49. The interests of the kerygma thus create in these sayings, the home of which is in the prophetic realm, something not unlike the first summaries of the Gospel; and these summaries in turn form a basis for the development of the narrative element in the Gospel tradition, a development shaped by the kerygma itself. When the Gospel of John delights to make the motif 'I have come' as the expression of the mission of Jesus one central point of its message it is drawing on this tradition. The Gospel history, like the prophetic proclamation, is a fruit of the apocalyptic of the period after Easter.

But I now return after this digression to the theme of the forms of prophetic speech. Their wide variety is to be explained by the many different functions of primitive Christian prophecy, with whom orinally the responsibility for the whole direction of the community lay. Prophecy had not only to admonish and warn but also to comfort and to hold out promises. It calls the disciples of Jesus to obedience by holding up to them the standards of the Last Judgment. But at the same time, it also puts these disciples in a state of gratitude and joy by recalling to them the accomplished acts of God. Gospel and Law are here bound up together in the closest possible way, because the community has to be directed, on the basis of what has already been done of the divine will to that which remains to be done and before which it must bow. Parenesis in the post-Easter community was founded primarily on apocalyptic. That becomes particularly clear where aphoristic material is incorporated, but at the same time reshaped into an eschatological utterance.

That is probably what is happening in Matt. 7.2: 'For with the judgment, with which you judge, you yourselves will be judged, and the measure which you mete out will be meted out to you.' What is universally true and valid is being formulated here stylistically in the form of holy law and, in content, as a criterion of the divine *jus talionis*. When Matt. 13.12 says: 'To each one that already has, shall be given and he will have abundance. But from him who has not, even what he has will be taken away', the variations of the form in which the saying occurs show that it is the expression of a piece of tradition which was capable of different applications. The decisive new factor, however, is this: as the context of 25.29 indicates there has been a transition here from the gnomic future to the eschatological. The same is true of 23.12: 'Whoever exalts himself will be humbled, and whoever humbles himself will be exalted.' Here the eschatological law of the correspondence of deed and recompense is replaced by the other law of the reversal of the earthly state of affairs. The uniqueness of the phenomena with which we are dealing stands out most sharply against the background of the other Synoptists who do not take up this reshaping of the gnomic future into the eschatological: in other words, they reverse the process which has visibly begun in Matthew. Thus Luke in 8.18; 9.24; 12.48; 18.14; 19.26; 20.18 has cited words which, according to their form, could well be interpreted as sentences of holy law with an eschatological future in the apodosis: but he has cited them as aphorisms with a gnomic future and has correspondingly in 6.37f. brought in the tradition of Matt. 7.2 as a considerably extended gnomic utterance. In exactly the same way, Mark has dismembered the original stylistic form in 3.29, 35 and 10.15, and transformed it in a gnomic sense in 4.24f. and 8.35. According to my understanding of the course of history of primitive Christianity, nothing else was to be expected. To the degree that prophecy after Easter gives up its function of directing the community and the expectation of an imminent end recedes, there are bound to be changes in the stylistic forms; even although, out of the whole complex of content with which we are concerned, there remain only the most exiguous relics as evidence anywhere except on the border between Palestine and Syria; namely Mark 8.38; 13.13b; 16.16; Luke 9.26; 12.8–10. Obviously, it was not possible to modify either the form or the sense of these few sayings because of their intrinsic importance. The situation is characteristically quite otherwise with the *Didache*, but I cannot now go into that.

I should be unwilling, however, to omit to call attention to one paradoxical reshaping of an aphorism which seems to me to be equally characteristic of prophetic speech. I refer to what has happened to Matt. 10.26: 'For nothing is covered that will not be revealed, or hidden that will not be known.' The proposition that this saying (like our 'No thread of ours so finely spun that it evades the searching sun') was originally a warning against exposing oneself to the curiosity of a stranger, is only partially satisfactory. We have to explain how the original warning could possibly be made, by means of the continuation in v. 27, into the call: 'What I tell you in the dark, utter in the light; and what you hear whispered, proclaim upon the house-tops.' But that only becomes comprehensible in the light of the apocalyptic law of the transvaluation of all values in the time of the End, the law which Paul exemplifies in I Cor. 1.25ff. With fascinating rashness, prophecy turns the insights of prudence into their opposite: eschatologically speaking, it is a matter of doing the precise thing which otherwise we are most painfully anxious to avoid. Here silence is no longer permissible; the danger must be sought out and recognized for what it is. Divine will nails over the behaviour pattern of the disciple the proclamation: 'It will be revealed and judged.' 10.39 and 16.25 says paradoxically and in the same style of the eschatological law that this behaviour pattern so far as earthly life is concerned, leads straight to death: 'He who finds his life will lose it, and he who loses his life for my sake will find it.' Mark and Luke understood this saying in a gnomic sense, while Matthew, as the connection of 16.24 with the following verse clearly shows, once again gave the future tense an eschatological slant. In so doing, he intended that the mystery of the kingdom of God should be proclaimed, as, according to Mark 4.11, the parables of Jesus proclaim it.

Finally, curse and blessing are also to be counted among the forms of prophetic proclamation. The Revelation of John demonstrates this. I am under obligation to establish, at least by the use of an example, the grounds on which I feel bound to view the Synoptists in the same light, and therefore cannot ascribe the corresponding logia to Jesus. The woes over the Galilean towns in Matt. 11.20–24 bear some typical marks of primitive Christian prophecy and fit without being forced into my analysis so far; I have already discussed the refrain-like sentence in vv. 22 and 24. The reference to the many mighty works which have been done in these towns recalls 7.22f., and the failure which was nevertheless experienced there justifies a saying so clearly in the prophetic vein as 8.11f., according to which many are to come from east and west and assemble themselves to Abraham, Isaac and Jacob in the kingdom of God, while the sons of the kingdom are to be exiled into the outermost darkness. Evidently, Chorazin and Bethsaida (neither of them mentioned anywhere else in the Gospels) were also objectives of early Christian mission in Galilee which successfully resisted capture. Consistent with this line of thought, too, is the typological recourse to the Old Testament in v. 23, where in grandiose hyperbole the threat against Nebuchadnezzar from Isa. 14.13ff. is transferred to Capernaum: the presence of salvation has exalted it to heaven, the rejection of salvation casts it down into Hades. This is genuine apocalyptic which, without throwing any doubt on the seriousness with which Jesus himself preached judgment, we ought nevertheless to ascribe rather to the community after Easter.

As for the beatitudes, the older parallels in Luke's sermon on the plain show that the sermon on the mount represents a filling-out of their original form. To what other source than prophecy could we possibly ascribe the balance of this material, which Matthew has certainly taken over from somewhere but which does not occur in Q? Yet there are weighty reasons for assigning the beatitudes wholly to primitive Christian prophecy. Obviously the beatitude in Matt. 5.11, with its address in the second person, not only does not belong to the same stratum as the previous ones which are all in the third person but also looks back to persecutions already suffered by the community and explicitly promises apocalyptic reward in return. Further, the beatitudes in the Lucan version are combined with woes, which are more correctly designated curses; and I should call that a typical mark of prophetic speech. Finally on this point, the differences of order in Matthew and Luke have always made difficulties for the exegetes, difficulties which can only be met with anything like simplicity if there is no necessity to trace back the original form of both series to Jesus and therefore no necessity to concede priority in content to either. In this case both combine in complementary fashion to comfort not just any group of anonymous hearers but the primitive Christian community in its interior and exterior tribulation. This community is at once the congregation of those who wait and who as such are called to be watchful and of those who are suffering the hardships of this present age; and it is the combination of these rôles which produces their particular ordeal. But in the immediate context of my investigation it makes little difference whether you assent to this reasoning or not, as curse and blessing may be considered without controversy to be a form of prophetic proclamation, and the only real problem is whether Jesus himself had already employed this form.

It is true that the historian cannot be indifferent to this question of authenticity, because he must seek to establish as precisely as possible the central point and the scope of the message of Jesus. Neither can the theologian, because he has had, at least since Albert Schweitzer, the problem of apocalyptic, its necessity, its meaning and its limits, cast disquietingly in his path. Schweitzer and his school identified their task but got in their own way by trying to turn the whole question into a problem of research into the life of the historical Jesus and to explain the very early history of dogma in terms of the delay of the Parousia. On both occasions, they landed up in a cul-de-sac. The situation was this: Jesus admittedly made the apocalyptically determined message of John his point of departure; his own preaching, however, did not bear a fundamentally apocalyptic stamp but proclaimed the immediacy of the God who was near at hand. I am convinced that no one who took this step can have been prepared to wait for the coming Son of Man, the restoration of the Twelve Tribes in the Messianic kingdom and the dawning of the Parousia (which was tied up with this) in order to experience the near presence of God. To combine the two would be, for me, to cease to make any kind of sense. The historical and hermeneutical problem seems to me to become meaningful and urgent only when we see how Easter and the reception of the Spirit caused primitive Christianity to respond to the preaching of Jesus about the God at hand and, in a certain sense, to replace it with a new apocalyptic. For even if my general reconstruction were found to contain some holes, the phenomenon of sentences of an eschatological *jus talionis* to which I have called attention would still require evaluation and would still demonstrate the apocalyptic mind of the community after Easter. To make light of the tasks which face exegesis and systematic theology in this situation simply will not do. Apocalyptic was the mother of all Christian theology – since we cannot really class the preaching of Jesus as theology. Even if the validity of this judgment were challenged and it was desired to associate Jesus more closely with the beginning of Christian theology than seems to me justifiable, those who took this view would still have to recognize in post-Easter apocalyptic a new theological start; they would then have to give some reasonable account of a situation in which dogmatics no longer begins with the problem of eschatology but, according to the traditional pattern, makes apocalyptic the subject of the last chapter.

But now I have already insinuated myself into the concluding part of my lecture, in which I propose, very summarily, to say something about one or two characteristic apocalyptic themes as forming the real beginning of primitive Christian theology. I start from the saying in Matt. 12.32, which again is formulated in the style of a sentence of holy law: 'He who speaks a word against the Son of Man will be forgiven. But he who speaks a word against the Holy Spirit will not be forgiven, either in this age or in that which is coming.' The sense of this much puzzled-over saying is quite clear: the primitive Christian mission is coming up against resistance which, precisely because it knows itself to be determined by the Spirit, it sees as directed against the Spirit and can only interpret as a sign of malice and stubbornness. We might perhaps have expected that other reaction described by Paul in I Cor. 14.24f.:

> But if all prophesy, and an unbeliever or outsider enters, he is convicted by all, he is called to account by all, the secrets of his heart are disclosed; and so, falling on his face, he will worship God and declare that God is really among you.

In prophecy, divine epiphany on earth comes to perfection with an eschatological glory which outshines that appertaining to the earthly Jesus. The latter's life, as judged in the light of the Easter experience, remained still in the shadow of a hiddenness which rendered misunderstanding, doubt and unbelief understandable and forgivable. But to set oneself against the unveiled epiphany of God expressed in the prophetic Spirit is the one absolutely unforgivable sin. In this epiphany it becomes clear that the manifestation of the Antichrist accompanies that of the Christ, and that it is the prophetic message which brings the kingdom of Christ and the kingdom of Satan to the parting of the ways. The same problem which determines all New Testament theology is being raised – namely, that of the relation of the proclamation about Jesus to the message of Jesus; and the answer arrived at here is precisely that the earthly Jesus and the *ipsissima verba* do not come out on top. We only need to substitute Gospel for prophecy and, *mutatis mutandis*, we are with Paul or John. Both proclaim determination by preaching, to which they ascribe revelational character as being the word of the exalted Lord. If in Paul the word of the earthly Jesus recedes into the background in comparison, then, similarly, John 5.20 and 14.12 speak expressly and relevantly of the 'greater works' which are to follow those of the earthly Jesus and refer obviously to the revelation of the Paraclete.

The portrait in Matt. 10.13f., upon which I should now like to cast a backward look, belongs to the same complex. In the missionary the epiphany of salvation appears; he is, so to speak, personally the bearer and embodiment of this salvation, in his capacity as the emissary of his Lord. We must be quite clear that it was only possible for primitive Christianity to transfer this motif of θεῖος ἀνήρ and bearer of 'mana' to the herald of the exalted Lord because it saw this herald's whole character as qualified by his peculiar commission. We have good reason to consider very critically this assimilation into the scheme prescribed by the comparative study of religion; on the other hand, we ought not to regard as finally decisive the conception of the miracle-worker which emerges into prominence from time to time. At bottom, it is a question of portraying the power of the Gospel in and over its servant who, as such, does not remain what he was before and indeed as the organ of his Lord cannot remain so. Neither, indeed, does he become the instrument of an impersonal supernatural force, although the danger of this kind of interpretation is never far away and even finds a place in the New Testament in passages where the category of mana-bearer is all too naively applied to the missionary.

Impersonal power is precisely what the Gospel is *not*: it is the miraculous power of the Christ who gives authority to his messengers and makes them personally responsible. The whole history of primitive Christianity from its beginning to its issue in early Catholicism is one long struggle to formulate adequately the indissoluble and yet always precarious connection between the Spirit on the one hand and the Gospel and Christology on the other. According as this attempt succeeds or fails, the community remains Christian or lapses into Judaism and heathenism, is competent or incompetent to speak adequately of miracle and the ministerial office. Again, when Paul and John identify apostolate and proclamation of the Gospel; when they teach the universal priesthood of all believers; when they understand the Church not as an institution exercising independence over against its Founder but as the place of the non-manipulable epiphany of Jesus the Kyrios; when they see the coming age already present in Christian preaching and therefore derive miracle from the power of the Gospel; then, in all this, they are standing on ground prepared by the enthusiasm of the time after Easter. For it was this enthusiasm which first, by a far-reaching decision affecting all subsequent Church history, made the messenger of the Gospel as such into the bearer of the Spirit of Christ and the mediator of that salvation which in miraculous fashion is still breaking through into the sphere of human corporeality. The message is here seen as the taking of power by the Lord who makes men responsible; and, as such, it is to be distinguished equally from an abstract doctrine about the relationship between God and man and from an incantation, and at the same time to be preserved from dissolving into some pietistic or ecclesiastical self-consciousness. The great theologians of the New Testament are much less original than the romantic movement of the last century in its bondage to the cult of personality assumed. Their principal service is rather to have warded off the dangers of enthusiastic congregational piety from the theological inheritance handed down to them. To do so, they needed only to pick up elements present in their own tradition. This can be illustrated from the significant saying in Matt. 10.32:

> Everyone who acknowledges me before men, I also will acknowledge before my heavenly Father; but whoever denies me before men, I also will deny before my Father who is in heaven.

The *jus talionis* of the Last Day is here not only making reward and punishment correspond to what has been done on earth but seeing them anticipated in earthly happenings, so that promise and threat can carry a reference to them. Salvation and catastrophe, though they certainly determine the ultimate future, are yet already embraced in the decision men make over against promise and threat. In this eschatological *jus talionis* it is certainly not just a question of rewarding the good and punishing the evil – as is generally maintained about apocalyptic. Not even Jewish apocalyptic is capable of being brought so neatly under this denominator, which, however, if you are interested, may be seen as the basis of Chinese representations of the judgment of the dead. The heart of primitive Christian apocalyptic, according to the Revelation and the Synoptists alike, is the accession to the throne of heaven by God and by his Christ as the eschatological Son of Man – an event which can also be characterized as proof of the righteousness of God. It is this for which those referred to by the fourth beatitude have been hungering and thirsting – for the realization of the divine justice on and to our earth. But exactly the same thing seems to me to be happening in the Pauline doctrine of God's righteousness and our justification – which I therefore derive, so far as the history of religion is concerned, from apocalyptic. This can have been the only possible reason why primitive Christian parenesis was primarily grounded in apocalyptic. God's justice done on and to our earth is here no longer a matter for the remote future, although it will not be universally revealed until the Parousia. But it is already being realized in the obedience of those who are waiting for this moment, who hear and accept the prophetic proclamation of the standards of the Last Judgment and pass it on through the whole world. John's saying to the effect that the judgment is already taking place in the present is already foreshadowed in essence within the community after Easter, even though, analysed from the standpoint of the history of religion, the Fourth Gospel expresses it in different forms.

More important still, the call to confess the Christ as the coming Son of Man embraces here in Matt. 10 the call to die as a follower of the Crucified and thus once again anticipates the central message of the whole New Testament. Prophecy after Easter preached from its beginning *theologia viatorum* and *theologia crucis* and based this procedure on the eschatological interpretation of the Old Testament. According to 10.21f., the community knows that the *odium generis humani* is in store for it, together with the cosmic terrors depicted later by Revelation. Here lies the point of deepest difference between the enthusiasm of the community after Easter and that of the Corinthians who say that they have overcome the ultimate trial, boast of having attained the angelic state and express this in many different forms in their practice. For the Corinthians the end of history has already arrived. The very earliest prophecy, however, proclaims that the time of the end of history has now begun and looks both in the Old Testament and in the life of its earthly Lord for guidance for this time and this generation. We must discriminate between enthusiasms as between spirits; we must set up a *cordon sanitaire* between the Corinthian illusionists and the apocalyptic rigorism which knows no salvation without earthly testing (and then only for those who undergo the ultimate ordeal in their earthly life) and which therefore proclaims, according to Matt. 10.22; 24.13, the eschatological law: 'He who endures till the end will be saved.' Here encouragement and summons are indissolubly bound up with each other, endurance of hardship is proof of future salvation, and this salvation is understood not as a gift to be claimed from the Son of Man but as this Son of Man himself with his demanding Lordship and his bestowal of glory. The theology which is being followed here is revealed as evangelical comfort for the sorely tried; it points them along the road to victory.

It has to be admitted that this kind of comfort is dispensed from a vantage point which looks out on the End as imminent. This is why Matt. 10.23 can say, very correctly:

> When they persecute you in this town, flee to the next; for truly, I say to you, you will not have gone through all the towns of Israel before the Son of man comes.

We have to state clearly and without evasion that this hope proved to be a delusion and that with it there collapsed at the same time the whole theological framework of apocalyptic of the time after Easter, at the heart of which was the restoration of the Twelve Tribes but which also fought for the Mosaic Torah and against the practice of the Gentile mission. There is also that way which leads from Easter to the theology, first of a Jewish Christian minority and later to that of a sect within the Great Church and then finally, leaving only literary traces behind it, disappears for good. There is no clearer illustration of this than the famous word to Peter in Matt. 16.19 which again contains all the marks of the prophetically proclaimed eschatological *jus talionis*: 'I will give you the keys of the kingdom of heaven, and whatever you bind on earth shall be bound in heaven, and whatever you loose on earth shall be loosed in heaven.' A story of confusion and misunderstanding is connected with this saying ominously enough from the very beginning, in that a Petrine party was already confining to their leader in his role of first witness of the Resurrection the plenary authority promised to the whole community corporately in Matt. 18.18; in so doing, they were declaring themselves to be a sect. They thought to be able to defy the gates of hell in the name of their master; but they were unable to resist the sands of time which buried them. Dare we say that in this very episode primitive Christian apocalyptic may be seen as the archetype of what is always happening in the history of the Church? Or has there ever been a theological system which has not collapsed? Have we been promised that we should know ourselves to be in possession of a *theologia perennis*? The protagonists who battle with each other in the pages of the New Testament – they, at any rate, with, and indeed because of, their theological maps, went down into oblivion. Only certain fundamental themes in the proclamation are carried on from one generation to the next and thus preserve the continuity of the history of theology.

But, seeing this and being conscious of it, we ought not to oversimplify and find the central theme of apocalyptic after Easter in a doctrine of recompense which we then profess to discover everywhere. The New Testament owes too much to this apocalyptic to allow us to treat it in this cavalier fashion. This central motive was in fact the hope of the manifestation of the Son of Man on his way to his enthronement; and we have to ask ourselves whether Christian theology can ever survive in any legitimate form without this theme, which sprang from the Easter experience and determined the Easter faith.

V

ON THE SUBJECT OF PRIMITIVE CHRISTIAN APOCALYPTIC*

PRIMITIVE CHRISTIAN Apocalyptic[1] seems to be an unfashionable theme[2] in the eyes of the generality of specialist theologians. Kierkegaard's nice picture[3] of the oarsmen turning their back on their goal is a justified warning to Christianity against forgetting its present task and getting lost in anxieties and dreams.

* 'Zum Thema der christlichen Apokalyptik', Guest Lecture before the Theological Faculty of the University of Oslo, 18/19 September, 1962; first published in *ZTK* 59, 1962, pp. 257–84. The articles by G. Ebeling, 'Der Grund christlicher Theologie', *ZTK* 58, 1961, pp. 227–44, and E. Fuchs, 'Über die Aufgabe einer christlichen Theologie', *ibid.* pp. 245–67, obliged me to rethink, expand and develop my essentially purely historical analysis, 'The Beginnings of Christian Theology' (see above, pp. 82–107). The differences in our formulations of the subject show that our exchanges extend over different levels of discourse. That is also quite justifiable because the systematic question cannot and should not be separated from the historical. If I nevertheless begin by continuing the historical analysis, I do so for two reasons. It seems to me that we have before us here a field which in recent times has remained uncleared and, secondly, I do not agree with Fuchs (p. 248) that the present is in itself the revelation of God. Indeed, I should never use the term 'a source of revelation'. This would not be because I wished to dispute that revelation happens in the present. But the procedure of a sermon bound to a text makes it clear that this happens only by the taking up of past revelation. The theological relevance of the historical, always acknowledged by the Christian Church, is not abrogated by any thesis, however arbitrary in its exaggerated one-sidedness, however problematic in its formulation. This theological relevance may primarily consist in our seeing ourselves confronted by questions which we have to answer anew. But for me it is important that questions were put to us before we began to ask and that these questions ought to guide our own. We do not find ourselves carrying out a perpetual spring-cleaning in order to be able to begin again from the very beginning. My judgment in this matter coheres with my extensive disagreement with Fuchs, p. 254; I cannot abstract from the Easter faith nor, consequently, from the history of the Church. Otherwise, as the 'quest of the Historical Jesus' and Fuchs himself demonstrate, concern with the historical Jesus leads to our becoming prophets instead of theologians. In the face of this possibility, I agree with Fuchs (p. 251) that 'I cannot possibly value prophecy thus highly.' There must at least still be room for the theologian who conducts a debate

But the picture he draws certainly implicates the coxswain who gazes ahead and has the job of preventing the crew from taking a wrong course or even from catching a crab. Is it possible to dispense solutions

---

not only with himself (so Fuchs, p. 255) but with the fathers, and then his debate with himself may in this proper context receive its modest place, its relative justification and, above all, the necessary clarity within the theological field. I hope I may therefore be forgiven if my main concern is once again 'the beginnings' and if I only cast more or less open or concealed glances in passing at 'Basis' and 'Task'. Not everyone can do everything; amid the present flood of 'interpretation', some have to dedicate themselves to administering the literary estate of the historians with the object of preventing the interpreters from settling down too comfortably.

[1] Ebeling (*op. cit.*, pp. 230f.) rightly requires me to define the word 'apocalyptic' in precise terms. Since eschatology and the doctrine of history became almost identical in Germany, we have been embarrassed by no longer having any specific term for the particular kind of eschatology which attempts to talk about ultimate history. It is not in dispute that 'apocalyptic' is ambiguous. But of what term is that not true? It emerges from the context that almost throughout I speak of primitive Christian apocalyptic to denote the expectation of an imminent Parousia. Where this is changed in apocalyptic literature to the expectation of something far distant in time, the change occurs because of disappointed hopes and consequent caution in prophecy, without being able to conceal the original phenomenon. We can understand well enough why apocalyptic seldom enjoyed the good will of the dominant Church or theology. For this reason it is all the more important to define the limits of the problem which is presented by the fact that the beginnings both of Church and theology were conditioned by 'imminent' expectation. Because, in my view, primitive Christian apocalyptic in this sense was released on the Church by the experience of the Spirit in the time after Easter, preserved as a living phenomenon by those endowed with the Spirit, nourished theologically from the tradition of Jewish apocalyptic, and finally accompanied by enthusiastic hopes and manifestations, I see in it the first phase of advancing post-Easter enthusiasm.

[2] The history of the theology of the last two generations shows that the rediscovery of primitive Christian apocalyptic in its significance for the New Testament, for which we are indebted especially to Kabisch, Johannes Weiss and Albert Schweitzer, provided discoverers and contemporaries alike with such a shock as we are hardly able to imagine. Weiss retreated with all speed into the liberal conception of Jesus, Schweitzer proceeded boldly to draw the logical consequences from his theses about the historical Jesus – which, to make things worse, were themselves untenable – and, for the rest, there was zealous study of the realms of the comparative study of religions, of cultic devotion and of mysticism. Barth's *Epistle to the Romans* brought 'thoroughgoing eschatology' back out of its existence among the shades and made it into the keynote of New Testament interpretation in Germany, of course in a multiplicity of very disparate versions. The general trend is admittedly in the same direction and can hardly be summed up better than by a quotation from P. Althaus, *Die Letzten Dinge, Lehrbuch der Eschatologie*, 7th ed., 1957, p. 272: 'In principle the world comes to an end with the judgment, with the kingdom, with Christ. In this sense every historical time, like history in its totality, is the time of the End, because individually and as a totality these times lap like waves on the shores of eternity, each exposed directly to its judgment and its redemption. To this extent all the hours in history are one and the same last hour.' It is the achievement of M. Werner in his controversial book *Die Entstehung des*

for today without taking into account the possibilities of the imminent morrow or of the distant future? To encourage the Christian community to contemplate its own navel is certainly to render it no service at all. That exodus from established positions which characterizes the Church in its true being has never taken place without apocalyptic hope and warning. Conversely, the necessary step into the freedom of the coming moment at a given point in history has been dictated as often by hope as by despair; moreover, the challenge has often been not specifically Christian but one proceeding from humanity as such. There are historical matters of fact which, though we may shrink from them in the name of a modern dogmatic theology, can only be ignored at our peril, when they ought to be driving us to critical reappraisal. This is exactly the position of our theme. It is not only in New Testament theology that this question, which was put

---

christlichen Dogmas (1941; ET, *The Formation of Christian Dogma*, 1957) that he recalled us to the unsettled problem, more or less industriously eliminated or pushed away to the outer fringe of our awareness, of primitive Christian apocalyptic, although it is true that he failed to get New Testament scholars in any respect beyond the theses of Schweitzer.

This state of affairs arouses the suspicion that history and interpretation have been secretly exchanging their proper roles; to be more specific, interpretation is no longer the servant of the history which has to be illumined, but is making the latter into a quarry for its own arbitrarily constructed buildings for homeless contemporaries. Ultimate hermeneutical problems raise their heads here, as the exchanges between Ebeling, Fuchs and myself have already shown. For example, it seems to me a thoroughly inappropriate mode of categorization, unjustifiably carried over from classical natural science into the historical field, which can encourage us to talk of the happenings of the past as being objectively there and at our disposal. That can be maintained equally well and equally perversely of the present. The errors of the historians and interpreters and the misunderstanding of what is closest at hand belong without any doubt together and arise in no way out of sheer stupidity; they prove that we fall victims to a short circuit if we make the element of strangeness, whether in present or past history, into something objective which is manageable by us. I believe the confusion of understanding and decision to be no less ominous. The supposed compulsion always to take up a position immediately, instead of first listening and waiting for what is being given or taken away by the 'other', is mostly the death of understanding, the stifling of the real question, the missed opportunity to learn and, learning, to grow. How many of our students today grasp the truth that understanding is always in addition a process of personal growth and therefore demands time and patience right up to the limits of self-forgetfulness; that he who does not himself mature in the historian's trade will shake nothing but unripe fruit from the tree of knowledge? The principal virtue of the historian and the beginning of all meaningful hermeneutics so far as I am concerned is the cultivation of the listening faculty, which is prepared to take seriously what is historically alien and does not think that violence is the basic form of engagement.

[3] Cf. Ebeling, *op. cit.*, pp. 241ff.

to us afresh two generations ago, is being reinterpreted before it has been seriously heard. This is unworthy both of the scholarship and the content involved. My purpose is to show this by setting out, necessarily in sketchy fashion, the origin, significance, phases and vicissitudes of apocalyptic from after Easter up to, and including Paul.

I. JESUS AND JEWISH CHRISTIAN APOCALYPTIC AFTER EASTER

What is probably the most difficult problem of all presents itself at the very outset. When did Christian apocalyptic in the strict sense really begin? Hardly any New Testament scholar will now be left who agrees with Schweitzer's answer – namely, that Jesus, inspired by a burning expectation of the End, sent his disciples out on a hasty mission to Palestine and himself proclaimed an 'interim ethic'; then, finally, when his hopes proved ill-founded, sought to force divine intervention by his journey to Jerusalem and so perished. In general the problem is now being reduced, as, for example, by W. G. Kümmel,[4] to the question whether, and how far, Jesus combined and equated present and future eschatology. On the side of the latter are the message of the *basileia* (especially prominent in the parables), the sayings about the coming Son of Man, the decisive example of which is Mark 8.38 and parallels, and perhaps the journey to Jerusalem. However, it seems to me that we really have no certainty about the intentions and expectations of Jesus regarding this last journey. The peculiar style of the logion in Mark 8.38 leads me to believe that it is, from beginning to end, a primitive Christian prophecy,[5] proclaiming eschatological law. Only the *basileia* sayings which go back to Jesus himself remain uncontested. It can hardly be disputed that God's lordship is for the most part regarded in them as yet to come into force. Characteristically, however, the way in which this is expressed in the more certainly authentic material does not emphasize the apocalyptic element very strongly, and herein lies the distinctive

[4] *Verheissung und Erfüllung*, 2nd ed., 1953; ET, *Promise and Fulfilment* (SBT 23), 1957.

[5] Has Fuchs considered that his words on pp. 251f., 'not the forms but the points of view expressed in the content', will be interpreted as a general renunciation of all form criticism? He also passes an untenable judgment on my analysis of the sentences of sacred law: 'He thus starts out from a stylistic apocalyptic archetype, from what might be called a hypothetical apocalyptic principle of sacred law.'

difference between it and the preaching of the Baptist. We have good reason not to forget that the baptism of Jesus by John belongs to the indubitable happenings of the life of the historical Jesus. For its significance is that Jesus began with the same burning expectation of the End as the Baptist, and that he therefore had himself 'sealed' from the imminent judgment of wrath and incorporated into the holy remnant of the people of God. It is very difficult not to see the way of Jesus in act and word as being in contradiction to this beginning. It is not fortuitous that the Gospels depict Jesus as healing in the power of the Spirit, as driving out demons and as using no particular ascetical discipline – all these in antithesis to the Baptist and his sect. There are other relevant considerations. He speaks of God as a child speaks of his father, he combines with the prayer for the doing of the eschatological will of God (still traceable in the liturgical formulation we call 'the Lord's Prayer') the other prayer that the needy may be helped: he addresses himself by preference rather to sinners and publicans than to the pious, he expounds the Torah solely from the standpoint of the kind of obedience which embraces love, he gathers round him no community governed by a rigid discipline. All this leads compellingly to the conclusion that the Baptist's message concerning the remote God who is about to come as Judge is receding strangely into the background, that the rigorism in matters of the Law practised by the Pharisees and the men of Qumran, directed as it was towards exclusiveness, is broken through and that the final apocalyptic dreams of the holy war must now seem completely absurd. Jesus is obviously speaking of the coming of the *basileia* in a sense different from that of the Baptist and of contemporary Judaism; his reference is not only or primarily to an end of the world which can in principle be dated within chronological time. This means, however, that the alternative – so useful in other contexts – of a present or a future eschatology becomes, ultimately and in the strict sense, useless when applied to the message of Jesus just as the question of the Messianic self-consciousness is uselesss unless the designation 'Son of Man' can be ascribed to Jesus himself. It is my conviction that it is just the historian who is obliged to speak of a unique secret in Jesus. It consists in the fact that we find ourselves unable to make a just estimate of him within the limits of established categories: that a battle fought in terms of these remains both hopeless and embittered and every attempt to evaluate him according to the criteria of the comparative study of religions ends up in a blind alley. I put this forward as a remarkable historical phenomenon, not as an axiom from which we might perhaps deduce the absolute nature of Christianity. Yet much would be gained if, looking back on two hundred years of tough and violent controversy, radical criticism were at least to ask itself whether it was not precisely because of the unquestioned acceptance of universal categories that the endless travail of the scholars failed to bring them success. This is in no way to imply that scepticism and irrationalism, such as haunt the celebrated conclusion of Schweitzer's *Quest of the Historical Jesus*,[6] are inevitable. Bultmann himself, in his book *Jesus and the Word*,[7] began a breakthrough which has only just begun to be recognized and is still not valued at its true worth: but Liberalism, too, saw a point of cardinal importance when it emphasized the immediacy of the relation of Jesus to God as Father. On the other hand, Schweitzer's apocalyptic approach obscured rather than illuminated the true state of affairs. For every departure from historical criticism, distinguishing as it does between authentic material and what dates from after Easter, prevents a proper interpretation. Obviously, in the mind of Jesus there is no separation between the God who is near and the God who is far off, because Creator and Judge cannot be separated without doing injury to the Godhead of God. It is just the giving, forgiving, helping, comforting God who is withdrawn from our selfish presumption and claim, and therefore far off. But in resisting our alleged rights over against him and all the privileges we base upon them, he is yet present for us in his Godhead, as all Old Testament piety which remained undistorted by legalism had always proclaimed. The weight of the preaching of Jesus lies here. At the decisive point it reverses the message of the Baptist by orientating the repentance which it, too, requires, not towards wrath but towards grace; consequently it calls man to the service of God in his daily life as if no shadow lay upon the world and God were not inaccessible. This service of God is then coupled with love of one's brother man as if there were no necessary distinction of cultus and ethic, and creation remained yet undisturbed. Love of one's brother, however, actually includes the far-off unknown and the enemy as if there were no world-renouncing piety required as the sign of the ineluctable will of God and no one could flee from this will. Though man may be in flight from God,

[6] *Von Reimarus zu Wrede: eine Geschichte der Leben-Jesu-Forschung*, 1906; ET, *The Quest of the Historical Jesus*, 1910, 3rd ed., 1954.

[7] See p. 55 n. 43.

yet God has never withdrawn himself from man. No 'works' are therefore required to call him back, just as there is no assurance in the face of his judgment. On the basis of this remarkable 'eschatology', which views all life as lived 'before God', it is easy to understand how Jesus, so far as we can see, did not baptize, built up no community as a holy remnant and as the nucleus of the messianic people of God and recognized no sharpening of the Torah other than the demand for obedience and love.

If these findings outline the boundaries which separate Jesus from his Jewish environment, they also provide the background against which the message of the Jewish Christian community after Easter stands out in sharp relief. My second task is to demonstrate this. Once again I begin from a fundamental postulate, and characterize the attitude of the primitive community by the label 'post-Easter enthusiasm'. This is expressed in the Jewish Christianity of the period immediately following Easter as expectation of an imminent Parousia. It may well have already been such expectation which brought the fugitive disciples back from Galilee to Jerusalem, although any other place clearly offered better protection to the adherents of the crucified Nazarene. But the primitive community could settle nowhere else, because it was in Jerusalem that the Jewish people already expected the epiphany of the Messiah. The return of Jesus in the role of the heavenly Son of Man is indeed the central hope which the original disciples derived directly from the Easter experience and constitutes, as such, their own peculiar Easter faith. Thus it was that the Easter happening came only at a relatively late date to be restricted to Jesus himself; originally, however, it had been understood as the dawn of the general resurrection and therefore interpreted apocalyptically and not as an isolated wonder. We bar our own access to the primitive Easter kerygma if we ignore its apocalyptic context. It is not just concerned with the re-animation of the dead. Neither is the Easter faith without support in the life of Jesus in this particular regard. The mighty acts, without which that life is unthinkable, had already been interpreted by Jesus himself as heralding the breaking-in of the *basileia* and as being something to which the disciples could look back after Easter. Admittedly, this does not mean that the Easter faith can be grounded in the message of Jesus. That is ruled out, because the crucifixion, as the Gospel tradition still shows, shook the expectations of the disciples to their foundations; more, it utterly destroyed them. But Easter does not merely signify a fresh start along the old way after a temporary interruption. With the application to Jesus of the title 'Son of Man', which (it seems to me) is anchored in the primitive material firmly to prophetic tradition, there begins that development in the history of theology which culminates in the confession of the divinity of Jesus.[8] From this point onwards the earthly life of Jesus and his resurrection are seen in terms of the dialectic 'without confusion, without division', which is the Chalcedonian formula for the solution of the Christological problem and any rupture of which, on one side or the other, has always to be paid for with theological or ecclesiastical degeneration. The Son of Man is, as the exalted one, above all the bearer of the Last Judgment; in his epiphany the earthly Jesus returns for this purpose with heavenly glory and with a universal and divine function to which the correlate on the human side is the general resurrection. That means that now, with the name of Jesus, the final act of the governance of the world (and, consequentially, the course of history as a totality) is bound up in an eschatological whole. A Christology which transcends[9] the significance of the person of Jesus in relation to the summons to decision which he brings is therefore now

[8] I agree in all essentials with what Ebeling has to say (pp. 228f.) about the concept of theology, and also that this one kerygma beyond all interpretations never identifiably existed and never can. But we are also agreed that nevertheless there is this one kerygma, which I should call the Gospel, at once the heart and the criterion of all the variations of preaching and interpretation; thus certain forms of preaching and theological statement can be shown to be particularly adequate, others to be thoroughly inappropriate. I am also convinced that we can and must bring to light from among the wealth of variants something like a historical sequence, which does not necessarily denote priority of content. My own contention tends to be that apocalyptic of the time after Easter designates the earliest variant and interpretation of the kerygma. Admittedly, we can then no longer ask the question whether it was more help or more hindrance in getting a grip on the necessary theological task. Certainly it was the first to acknowledge and attack the task. It cannot be disputed that the theology of the Church has to a large extent seen its task as consisting in the vanquishing of apocalyptic. Are the early Fathers therefore the first theologians? Is classical Greece the godparent of Christian theology? The New Testament scholar may be permitted to ask what price we should have to pay and what gamble we should embark upon if, as theologians, we were to become heirs of Greek thinking in our systematics. One does not conquer apocalyptic and escape scot-free.

[9] It goes without saying that it has never been my intention to talk of any apocalyptic other than that (to use the words of Ebeling, p. 234) 'modified by faith in Jesus'. The critique exercised on Jewish apocalyptic by this faith is quite evident from a comparative study. But theological advances will become rare if they are undertaken only under the safe cover of text-books. I am satisfied if I can get as far as articles and then hope for my flank to be guarded by good friends and well-disposed readers.

in occupation. For Jesus never ascribed cosmic authority to his preaching, even if he did understand it eschatologically. With this new Christology, and corresponding to the changed conditions it creates, goes a new self-understanding on the part of the disciples. This, too, comprehensibly enough, is orientated towards the patterns and motifs already given in Judaism and it is not at all strange that now, when the eschatological function of the Church has to be described, we find a particularly close similarity to the Qumran community: the Christian society, united in a common hope by the Easter experience, regards itself as the holy remnant, which mediates the continuity of the Old Covenant with the people of the twelve tribes in its reconstituted character and already represents on earth the eschatological New Covenant. The 'signs' – ecstasy and healing – now taking place within the Christian community it ascribes to the Spirit which has been promised for the time of the End, and they confirm for it its understanding of itself. The Old Testament idea of the people of God thus forms the model for the earliest ecclesiology. The miracle-working Spirit, who has been received since Easter, gives to the present time, however, the character not merely of historical effect but of eschatological completion of the Old Testament covenant, as the dawning, already visible and yet still hidden, of the reign of God on earth.[10] Hence the churches are now governed, in accordance with the dictates of heavenly law, by apostles, who count as the pillars of the heavenly city of God, and newly arisen prophets. These execute their office by proclaiming the will of God in terms of the Last Day, whether as a return to Old Testament injunctions or in antithesis to the Jewish Law and to rabbinic interpretation; thus the divine will is preserved within the messianic covenant.

These facts explain the absence from this earliest stratum of tradition of any independent and explicit anthropology. The individual Christian is what he is simply and solely as a member of the people of God. Even the outpourings of the individual at prayer, such as we

[10] As against Ebeling (p. 233), I should not describe the presence of the Spirit as the complement but as the ground of the expectation of the time after Easter. In Qumran, at least, the two are similarly combined. I have to confess that I cannot go along with the idea of the resurrection of the dead as a third member in this doctrinal structure; Ebeling is principally interested in the structure as such while I am more concerned with the historical phenomenon. Otherwise I should no longer find it necessary to talk of primitive Christian apocalyptic (see pp. 228f. below).

meet in the Thanksgiving Psalms of Qumran or the Odes of Solomon, are still totally lacking. If their place is taken by beatitudes and woes, this indicates that anything in the nature of anthropology only becomes possible in the context of parenesis. Here, too, there is as yet (once again in contradistinction to Qumran) no sign of technical vocabulary. Yet the message of salvation, unlike myth, cannot be indifferent to the fact that the eschatological people of God is still subject, so far as its earthly existence is concerned, to the 'Woes of the Messiah' and that temptation is the locus of faith. The individual Christian must therefore be preserved from apostasy and maintained in fidelity to the Covenant by means of comfort, warning, admonition and judgment. Soteriology properly so-called, on the other hand, is determined almost exclusively by the idea of the people of God which thus gives a foundation and an object to parenesis. Christian theology is thus in its origins very far from being anthropology.[11] The latter is in no way an independent expression of theology but only the parenetic concretion and application of ecclesiology. This means that the earliest Christian theology cannot adequately be interpreted from an existentialist starting-point, if decisive weight is to be given to its fundamental understanding of itself.

We have to be grateful to Ernst Fuchs[12] for putting in precise terms the question as to what then the central task of theological reflection in the community immediately after Easter really was. He himself answers it in terms no less precise by saying that it had become necessary to think out a new relationship to the Law, in order to do justice to the activity of Jesus that had preceded it. But the discernible history does not justify this answer; it does not even lend it the hypothetical value of a plausible conjecture. For the problem of what to do with the Law did not arise for the early Christian community out of its concern with the preaching and activity of Jesus, but out of a reality which suddenly overtook them – the reality of the Gentile

[11] Fuchs (p. 256) has quite correctly remarked: 'He refuses to concede that theology is always at the same time – legitimately – anthropology and a particular understanding of time.' At least, he is correct if anthropology means, as with him it obviously does, anthropology oriented towards the individual. On the other hand, I think he is doing me an injustice when he maintains that I identify proclamation and theology. It is true that in practice the two cannot be forcibly separated; but they must, as I learned from Bultmann, be distinguished in principle.

[12] *Art. cit.*, pp. 248ff. To maintain that the crucifixion of Jesus led to a conflict with the Law and a permanent attitude of *credo quia absurdum* seems to me to be to overlook the fact that, for primitive Christinanity, Easter overcame the offence of the Cross.

mission and its unpredictable success, driving Jewish Christianity more and more into a corner. The latter had as yet – however strange this may seem to us – seen no problem at all here, and thus had not offered the slightest offence to Judaism at this point. It might well have remained a special fellowship within the total Jewish religious connection. The first persecution was aimed solely at the Hellenist Christians and, further, according to the accusation directed against Stephen, took place on account of a usage which was interpreted as a break with Law and cultus and indeed probably was. The possibility considered by Fuchs did therefore exist in fact. It was already present in that the post-Easter community was drawn mainly from the class designated by the rabbis as *'am-ha-aretz* and was thus bound to clash with the piety of the Pharisees. Indeed, we can only speak of a sharpening of the Torah among them in the sense that the requirement of love provided the Mosaic law and the tradition of the fathers with a core of content and thus radicalized it.[13] But this is not to say that the Torah as such had become problematic. Practice is not always logical. If after Easter the community had turned away from the law of Moses or questioned it in principle, the claim to be the messianic people of God and the mission among the Jews which was bound up with this claim would both have been robbed of all credibility. On the other hand, it could not receive into its ranks the 'lost sheep of the house of Israel' if, like Pharisaism and Qumran, it were to adopt a policy of exclusivism and to insist on a rigorous observance of the whole Torah. In a strangely unaffected and unconsidered fashion the community followed in the tracks of its Master between the two extremes by interpreting the commandment of love as the summary of the Law and as the better righteousness. It was the inauguration of the Gentile mission by outsiders which first compelled it to take up a definitive attitude to the question of the ceremonial and ritual Law and to clarify to itself how far it was still (or no longer) Jewish. In the course of a stormy development the scales began to turn ever more decisively in favour of Judaism. That, too, shows that at the very beginning it was not a thought-out policy which urged the community along an increasingly narrow road. The

[13] It would be my view, as against Fuchs (p. 249) that Matthew himself already belongs to the era of an anti-enthusiastic teaching ministry, is totally unfamiliar with the letter/Spirit antithesis and therefore cannot possibly have the objective of 'melting the judgmental ice of the letter in the warm current of the liberating Spirit'.

thesis put forward by Fuchs fails to recognize the slowness of this far from straightforward process and also its characteristic trend which led back towards legalism instead of liberating the community progressively from it, as logic demanded. One could only venture to put forward this thesis of Fuchs if one were prepared as a matter of course to treat the problem of the community after Easter anthropologically, i.e. from the angle of the life of the Christian individual. Such a methodology would require historical sketches and thus contain within itself a *reductio ad absurdum.*

The task which the community actually took up after Easter followed from its understanding of itself as the people of God in the messianic age which, as the holy remnant, is waiting for the restoration of the twelve tribes of Israel. The task here is neither more nor less than mission, to which each member of the community has to contribute according to his potentialities. The self-understanding and the hope which is rooted in it also determine the character of the mission: it cannot reach out beyond the borders of Palestine and has thus a limited objective – the eschatological renewal of the Covenant. This is not to be read in any sense as particularism. The opposite to this would be universalism, expressing itself in the expectation of the Son of Man and of the general resurrection. But universalism does not necessarily lead to a Gentile mission, because, according to ancient prophetic tradition, the restoration of Zion is to draw the nations in and to cause them to submit to the rule of God. For the primitive Jewish Christian community, then, the Gentile mission is God's concern which indeed cannot enter the arena before the restoration of Israel has taken place. To this every Christian is called in terms of his total life, as the actual verification of his faith and hope, so that mission is not something additional but the energy of faith and hope themselves. Thus we have here the root of the doctrine of the universal priesthood of all believers. From this standpoint, too, we are to understand the new role of baptism: it is now the seal of membership in the eschatological people of God. Perhaps also a question which has hitherto been open may find its solution in this area – the problem of the original *Sitz im Leben* of Q. While we continue to think in terms of the mutual edification of the community or of Christian instruction, it remains absolutely inexplicable why what is undoubtedly the most important element for all time – the narrative of Passiontide and Easter – was omitted. On the other hand, it is clear that the expeditionary force of the heavenly Son of Man receives injunctions for its discipleship and provision for its mission[14] in the authentic or alleged sayings of its earthly master; we see examples of this in Matt. 10 or in the earliest working-over of the parable material. Indeed, this material reveals something which for a long time has received insufficient attention – namely, that guidance for mission was sought precisely in the tradition about Jesus and that thus considerable areas of primitive prophetic material were taken up and preserved. Finally, changed circumstances demanded new kinds of regulation so that the continuity of a permanent interest led to the amalgamation of material very disparate both in its date and in its content.

When we define the circumstances of the community before and after Easter solely or even mainly in terms of the concept 'faith', we run the risk of abstracting[15] from the breakthrough to the eschatological (Gentile) mission so decisive for Christian history and also from the minting of a first Christian theology constructed with distinctively apocalyptic themes. Of course we both can and must speak of faith in Jesus before as well as after Easter. But in any case it is necessary to differentiate here. It is not without significance that faith before Easter appears as essentially personal, as the hearing of the Word and as discipleship, whereas after Easter it appears primarily as the appropriation of 'acts of salvation' such as the Cross, the Resurrection, forgiveness, New Covenant etc., and presupposes a developed eschatology, christology and ecclesiology. Nothing is gained here by levelling and formalizing everything under the banner of 'faith'. To do this is merely to cover up the fact that even faith is not extra-temporal and that there is no such thing as a situation without unique historical contours. Furthermore it seems to me inadmissible to make faith's framework of reference pre-eminently the existential condition of its bearer instead of its object or its con-

[14] Here I take up in my own way the problem which has been posed in all its ultimate severity by H. E. Tödt, *Der Menschensohn in der synoptischen Überlieferung*, 1959, pp. 244ff.; ET, *The Son of Man in the Synoptic Tradition*, 1965, pp. 246ff.

[15] The impoverishment of an idealistic or anti-idealistic existentialist theology, trapped in individualism, is shown by the fact that talk of mission is almost everywhere confined to institutes for missiology or social ethics; elsewhere the schema faith/love reigns supreme. It would be possible in this connection to speak of mission under the general heading 'love', provided that it was the common task which was meant, and not merely the ethical I-Thou relationship which was envisaged. From Fuch's definition of theology (pp. 254f.), 'Not the promulgation of propositional truths and, to this extent, not the explication of revelation either, but, on the contrary, that hermeneutical procedure which destroys the identification of revelation with propositional truths', I can only dissociate myself.

tent, for this is to subject *fides quae creditur* to *fides qua creditur* and then to reduce the former to the imitation of Jesus.[16] The fact that after Easter mythological modes of speech are characteristic determinants, of the 'language of faith' – as they were not before Easter – must however, be explained in terms of content and not only in terms of the comparative study of religion as assimilation to the religious environment or in terms of pedagogical method. But such explanation is only possible if we postulate the break effected by Easter in primitive Christian history and if our understanding of the sudden advent of powerful new factors makes this break, rather than the historical Jesus, its point of departure. Bultmann is absolutely right when he distinguishes the proclamation of Jesus sharply from the primitive Christian kerygma; and primitive Christianity itself saw the existence of the believers before and after Easter in quite different lights. Not until we have reached the point of no return here can we meaningfully ask whether the break in question signifies complete disintegration or indicates a transformation which may be interpreted as continuity within discontinuity.

It is this last question which I must now begin to examine more closely.[17] By designating Jesus as its Lord and as the Son of Man who was to come and by its consciousness of itself as sent 'in his name', the primitive community was laying claim to a continuity of history and of content. But this can only mean that after Easter eschatology, christology and ecclesiology were and are bound up with the message and activity of Jesus. It seems to me that it is precisely the historian who is in no position to reject the propriety of this claim out of hand, provided that he has previously clarified for himself what it entails. As Bultmann said in a celebrated utterance: 'The preaching of Jesus already contains an implicit christology.' Admittedly we have to guard against a kenotic interpretation of this judgment; such a

[16] This problem, which is the real nub of the controversy between us, must certainly be reserved for a more comprehensive process of dialogue. Does Fuchs mean the same as Jeremias, for example, when he uses the expressions 'perspicuous first-fruits of the Spirit in the historical existence of Jesus', 'God's Word which has become perspicuous in Jesus', 'perspicuity of revelation and of the person' (pp. 260f.) What is the implication here for the Reformation doctrine of the revelation of the *deus absconditus* in the Cross? Does this self-evidence exist – if we may relate it to the 'seeing' of the Fourth Gospel – apart from Easter and otherwise than in hearing and believing? Is there, in other words, immediate historical access? If so, what is the meaning of II Cor. 5.16? My own feeling is that to deal with so crucial an issue by aphorisms is intolerable.

[17] Here I am trying, honestly and, let it be understood, in the superficiality of a first probe, to answer Ebeling's questions on his p. 236.

judgment, taken dialectically, might produce the conclusion that this implicit christology had nothing in common with that developed by later dogma and that therefore the claim of Jesus to absolute authority had been just one such claim among many. In actual fact it is not comprehended fully and unambiguously in terms of any christological predication of sovereignty; but it makes the application of such predicates easy to understand. For, even though, because of their previous history, they are bound to give a stereotyped impression, yet their general trend is towards asserting the uniqueness of him who is bringing salvation; and it is precisely this uniqueness which, in my view, the historian cannot help but establish. Jesus is concerned with the imminent *basileia* not in the same way as the prophets in their message but, rather, in the mode of the Baptist or of Qumran. But Jesus combines his call to decision with healings and exorcisms in a way which distinguishes him from the Baptist or the Teacher of Righteousness in Qumran or the rabbinic workers of prayer miracles. This means that for him the call does not precede the promise but, on the contrary, the promise is the basis of the call; and, to clinch the matter, the sole content of the call is that we should accept and hold fast the promise of the God who is at hand. Only when we remind ourselves that Jesus began his ministry in the context of the Baptist's message can we measure the full weight of this fact: Jesus regarded it as his task and as the grace given to him to witness to the gracious God as present and as breaking into the world. His approach to his task resembled that of the Old Testament prophets: he interpreted his own message and his personal advent as the beginning of the divine activity, just as, according to Matt. 11.12, the proclamation of the *basileia* at hand is itself the proximity of this *basileia*. Thus he enters on his proclamatory function as, so to speak, the incarnation of the divine promise; he can no longer be subsumed, as can the Baptist, under the category of forerunner but, if a category of some sort must be used, only under that of mediator who brings in the eschatological age by the act of announcing it. This is once again reflected in the call he gives which validates the Torah simply and solely on the basis of obedience and love, and therefore in fact reduces it to these; thus, in principle, repealing it as the Torah of Moses with its multiplicity of obligations. He knows the will of God with a knowledge not mediated to him by the Torah. The Torah and the tradition of the fathers are no longer, so far as he is concerned, the 'boundary fence of Israel'. A second element enters into the situation at this point, very closely bound up with the first: here we have a member of the Jewish people interpreting, reducing and, so far as its traditional indivisibility is concerned, repealing the Torah in such a way as to shatter the fundamental structure of Judaism without the formal exterior act of leaving it – and all with a most remarkable lack of embarrassment. There is no irrefragable testimony that Jesus ever extended his purview beyond the limits of Palestine and, as later Christendom was to maintain, initiated the Gentile mission. On the other hand, there is equally little irrefragable evidence that he remained within the boundaries of the idea of the people of God or of the conception of the holy remnant, even though the community immediately assumed this. He did not purport to renew the privileges of Israel, he did not, like the Pharisees and Qumran, seek to make the pious more pious still. Zealots and tax collectors gather round him. His radicalization of the Torah extends the scope of grace instead of narrowing it. But he still comes into conflict with the devout. He destroys for them the religious illusions, on the basis of which they play off against God their privileges and works and reject the condition of those who wait, hunger and trust. They treat God as though he were remote by putting the Law and the tradition in his place, by demanding blind obedience, by refusing to treat their fellow human beings as the sphere of the authentic service of God and, in so doing, separating the Creator from his creature and the creature from his neighbour. Certainly, we have to pray for God's coming: but we do not need to have anxiety about it, because God is always, and in spite of everything, at the door. Our concern must be not to leave our station as God's creatures nor to deprive others of it. Otherwise the God who is at hand becomes the judging God, who is thus in actual fact the God who is remote. If the Baptist proclaimed him who was coming to judgment, then Jesus understood and embodied God's gracious approach as judgment on those who are under the illusion that they can interpose law, piety and theology between God and themselves. He orients himself in teaching and in act towards the Creator and his creature. Thus in practice the Torah comes to pieces in his hands and his message implies universality in that it is addressed to the Jew not as a Jew but as a human being and creature of God.

Here, however, he is actually pointing away beyond his own earthly reality into a future the freedom of which he respects. He expresses this by refraining from founding a church and keeping it in being, yet finding and teaching disciples who can become a church. His own peculiar secret is this: he is open, when his whole environment is hostile to openness. He is open to the God who is at hand and the fellowman who is at hand and to the present moment, but open also to the suffering, without which such openness cannot be, and therefore he is incomprehensible to his disciples both before and after the Cross and infuriating to his enemies; he is not concerned with theological formulations, nor can he be pinned down by them, but in the totality of his being he is an enigma, a question, a promise, demanding fulfilment and response. You might also say that he becomes Lord even on earth by his power to translate men into the freedom of the children of God and to embody this freedom in himself. At Easter this comes home to his disciples at a depth clearly unknown before and the only response possible to them is in terms of apocalyptic. Provided we do not attempt to father upon them modern thought-forms and conceptions, we shall even regard their apocalyptic as the appropriate response to the fact that in Jesus the ultimate promise of the world is encountered. For those disciples the ultimate in authority must be also the ultimate in time, the lordship of the Free Man could become visible only in the destruction of the power of death, their teacher and helper could only have abiding and universal significance if he were bringing in the age of freedom which the earthly people of God had been so long awaiting. Their theology and their mission are the modes in which they submit to this freedom, and make it comprehensible to themselves and accessible to others. Easter points to the kingdom of freedom in the continuity of the freedom of Jesus.

2. HELLENISTIC ENTHUSIASM AND PAUL

Before the end of the New Testament era, apocalyptic was already firmly fixed within the penumbra of the messianic Judaism of Palestinian provenance. The fact that it has from time to time reappeared in Church history is simply evidence that the Church, both historically and in regard to the content of its message, has always remained a Church composed both of Jews and Gentiles and even on Gentile Christian soil has not been able to separate itself without further ado from its Jewish heritage. There are limits set to its capacity for transformation. But in so far as the Jewish heritage did undergo a transformation on Greek soil, it becomes plain that the Church is neither a Christian synagogue nor a Jewish temple with a 'Court of the Gentiles'. We may not simply eliminate here: we have to differentiate. Inheritance and mutation have to be thought of together. Again, it is necessary to look for the continuity within the discontinuity without reducing the element of discontinuity within the continuity. The paradigm case for the discussion on which we are now entering is the information we have about the church at Corinth. For here we have an undoubtedly eschatological enthusiasm unambiguously distinct not only from apocalyptic expectation of an imminent End but also from any theologically relevant future hope. Today we may take it for granted that the dominant group in Corinth believed themselves to have reached the goal of salvation already – in the shape of baptism – and Christian existence here on earth meant for them solely the temporal representation of heavenly being. For that the resurrection of the dead has already happened was not only the slogan of the heretical teachers of II Tim. 2.18; it was the basic assumption of the whole of that Christianity which, moving in circles where the writ of Hellenism ran, understood the Christian religion as a mystery religion. We encounter this outlook in the New Testament primarily in the fragments of hymns and confessions of faith such as Eph. 2.5; 5.14; Col. 2.12f. As participants in the Cross of Christ, the baptized are at the same time participants in his Resurrection and Enthronement, liberated from the old aeon of death and the powers and translated into the new aeon of the Kingdom of Christ. Of course, this conception is scarcely to be found preserved anywhere in the New Testament in its pure state, i.e. free from metaphor or hyperbole. Thus the willingness to use fragments of hymns in the deutero-Pauline writings shows that it was possible to come to terms with the traditional Jewish eschatology. For the letters themselves contain a future hope which is already somewhat muted. The Fourth Gospel goes further still; in it, apart from a few editorial additions, present eschatology reigns supreme. Here, too, however the original very crudely realistic concept has been corrected in that the transformation of the Christian's existence is no longer effected by the Sacrament, but by the quickening Word of Jesus. In Romans 6, Paul has even separated present participation in the Cross from future participation in the Resurrection; he discerns the reality of the new life solely in the *nova oboedientia*. These corrections of emphasis all bear an anti-enthusiastic stamp and, for that very reason, point back to a previous stage of Christian thought marked by enthusiasm.

Further witness is borne to the existence of this period by II Tim. 2.18 and especially by I Cor. 15. Here it is not indeed Hellenistic 'enlightenment' which is denying the corporeal resurrection yet to come, but a sacramental realism which sees complete redemption to have already been effected, in that by baptism a heavenly spiritual body has been conferred and the earthly body has been degraded to an insubstantial, transitory veil. This is the root of all that has gone wrong in Corinth; the contempt for discipline and decency, the want of consideration for the weaker brother at the Lord's Supper and in daily life; the rise of women ecstatically gifted and the over-valuing of glossolalia and sexual asceticism, which are being regarded as the outward expressions of angelic status. Those who are endowed with *pneuma* are exempt from the laws of those who have nothing but *psyche*. Indeed, they are exempt from the power of destiny and represent heavenly freedom in the world. What comes to the surface here in anthropological form has, however, its origins in Christology. In the mirror of humanity we behold the destiny of the redeemer in whose train and company the believers have been swept along. Those hymns to Christ which have been preserved for us show us what is at issue. There is no doubt that they are either wholly (like Phil. 2.6ff.), or, at least in their main themes, of liturgical origin and this attests not merely their wide circulation but their very early date. They are documents of a nascent Christianity on Hellenistic soil. They centre on the exaltation of Christ understood as an enthronement, over against which the incarnation is represented as a humiliation and sometimes the pre-existence as the point of departure for the way of salvation. Redemptive happening is therefore here unfolded in the manner of a mystery drama with changing phases, and thus both a presumption of, and a foundation for, a salvation history is provided. This implies, however, that at the decisive points we have to demonstrate not only contact with apocalyptic conceptions but also dependence on them. The different horizon and the different arrangement of the themes should not lead us to make any mistake. In the atmosphere of which the mystery religions were a characteristic expression, what had previously been seen primarily as the turn of the ages was translated into a statement about man, and what had originally been a temporal and teleological assertion was transformed into a timeless Idealism. There was a concern, therefore, to demonstrate anew the significance of the Resurrection of Christ, by then regarded as the starting-point of all theology. Apocalyptic had already associated it with the Ascension of Jesus, which made the Christ exalted at the right hand of God into the hidden Lord of the World, known only to his Church. The Hellenistic Christian community, as Bousset's *Kyrios Christos*[18] rightly and lastingly showed, orients all its theological assertions round this theologoumenon of the exalted Kyrios. This is done in opposition to apocalyptic with the one, all-important qualification which necessitates 'present eschatology' in the strict sense: into the place of the hidden and, to tell the truth, at this point no more than designated Lord of the World, whose return in glory to seize earthly power the community is now awaiting, steps the one who already rules[19] over the principalities and powers and so over the world hitherto dominated by them. The task of the community is to proclaim (as it does, for example, in I Tim. 3.16) the transformation of the world which has been accomplished by this assumption of sovereignty and which is central to its worship. The gift of the Spirit is the pledge of the reality of the eschatological happening, and enthusiasm remains the characteristic expression of the young Christian religion. This Christianity sees itself transported into a world of miracles and heavenly existence and indeed cannot help so doing when the new Cosmocrator has entered upon his sovereignty by resurrection and exaltation, has dethroned the former rulers of this world, has compassed in battle the end of fate and the demons and brought into being the kingdom of eternal peace and universal reconciliation. Just as a message like this had points of contact with the Wisdom myth, which had already become so fruitfully associated in the synagogue of the Diaspora with Greek speculation about the Logos, so it also fulfilled the expectations of that Hellenism which finds expression in sublimated form in the Fourth Eclogue of Virgil. The background against which this transformation scene is played out, and the situation which justifies it, is the success of the Gentile mission. An authentic theology certainly never comes into existence as an intellectual construction in a vacuum. Thus the scheme we are considering could rightly claim that it had the support of experience.[20]

[18] See p. 44 n. 25.

[19] This is my answer to the question put by Fuchs (p. 247). In my view, it was the Hellenistic Church which first taught that the already completed enthronement of Christ entailed the subordination to him of powers and principalities. Rev. 11.15; 12.10; 19.6 still refer in their acclamations to the enthronement as an element in the future judgment.

[20] From this point of view, the strictures passed by Ebeling (p. 235) on 'apocalyptic fantasies' seem very modern and not at all perceptive.

Men saw daily with their own eyes how the outreach of Christ's Kingdom was extending over the whole world and those who had been slaves of the demons were becoming liberated men. It must have been believed from then on that Jesus was Ruler of all. But it seemed obvious that he was no longer merely the hidden Son of Man whose entry into his kingdom was still in the future, and this new insight had therefore to be formulated theologically. The immediate conclusion to be drawn is that there was no thought of giving up cosmology even if anthropology was now coming to the fore. Of this period it might be said in some sense that anthropology is still in the shadow both of Christology and cosmology, and thus the continuity with apocalyptic is maintained. The believer who is swept along as a participant in the destiny of the Christ is the representative of a new world, and his membership in the Church *is* membership in this divine new world. The theme – which may well go back behind Paul – of the Church as the body of Christ is a precise expression of a relevant theology for the very reason that it emphasizes better than any other conception of the Church the world-wide nature of a Christianity which is breaking through to the Gentile mission and the universality of the redemptive happening which this breakthrough indicates. No less does it correspond to the newly gained christological position: the community which is Christ's must have a universal reference and appear in the light of a new creation if indeed Christ is really the Ruler of the world. Nor is it any contradiction to say that, in spite of all this, anthropology is now acquiring a significance for soteriology which cannot be established as having existed previously; indeed, this phenomenon corresponds to the kind of understanding of the salvation event which we have postulated. Even the most radical enthusiasm cannot ignore the fact that there is still a world not yet subjected by Christ to himself, the reality of unbelief and of hostility to faith, the area of mission. For the Hellenistic Church, therefore, Christ's dethroning of the principalities and powers is primarily a heavenly event which has not yet become known everywhere on earth, not yet been everywhere verified, still awaits completion and, for this reason, obligates the earthly community to mission. The actual situation, in spite of all the missionary successes of the Hellenist community, is not basically different from the situation on Palestinian soil. This community must therefore, like Jewish Christianity, answer the question as to what earthly reality corresponds to their message of redemption; indeed the more strongly it brings forward a present eschatology, the more urgent the question becomes. Jewish Christianity answered it by referring back to the Old Testament promise and interpreting the gift of the Spirit as the fulfilment of this promise: we are the holy remnant and, as such, the first-fruits of the messianic people of God which is to find renewal in the time of the End. But the concept of the people of God ceased to be viable once the Gentile mission had in principle been embarked upon; more so, once the Church had actually become overwhelmingly a Church of Gentile Christians. The idea of the people of God could now only be used figuratively and clearly no longer as an argument for a continuity which could be historically demonstrated but solely for the continuity of grace which could only be believed. For those who received the promise no longer coincided exactly with those who received the fulfilment. This is where anthropology moves rapidly into the breach which is opening – an anthropology clothed in the garments of myth, reaching out beyond the visible limits of salvation history and only using it as a quarry for archetypes. The sequence and contrast of the first and the second Adams occur at this point, the sowing of the earthly and the heavenly seed, those who live according to the flesh and those who live according to the Spirit, those who are subject to the cosmic powers and those who are called to the God-given endowment of freedom. It was possible to express this antithesis by the image of the two peoples so that the concept of the people of God was retained as a metaphor; it was equally possible to attach to the apocalyptic motif that of the succeeding aeons, especially as in Judaism the temporal perspective of the chronological succession of these aeons was already associated with the spatial perspective of the two worlds set over against each other. The inheritance of apocalyptic thus extends its influence: but it is transformed by being integrated into a metaphysical dualism, which itself then finds concretion and contemporary force in a doctrine of man. The question of the reality of the saving event can now be answered in a new way by starting from this anthropology. There are those who call themselves the redeemed and elevate themselves above the unredeemed world. The gifts of the Spirit, i.e. miracles and ecstasy, show that a new, heavenly creation has taken root. Because the heavenly as such is the peculiar character of this new creation, no essential differences can any longer subsist within it. The characteristic slogan of this Hellenistic community runs, thus: 'Neither Jew nor Greek, neither slave nor freedman, neither male nor female.' The formula is historically as well as materially interesting, because in it we have the key to the starting-point, the continuation and the ultimate concern of a Christianity which is entering upon world mission under this sign. Neither Jew nor Greek – this is how it began, as the circle of the Seven and their following, whose designation as Hellenists cannot be fortuitous, separated themselves off from the Hebrews, as Acts already narrates. The glory of the Son of Man in his exaltation at the right hand of God outshone that of the Jewish cultus and Law and made a reality of that mission which was becoming an exodus out of the Jewish religious community and must therefore inevitably burst the bounds of the theology of apocalyptic after Easter.[21] This exodus appeared to those who achieved it as a step out of a freedom already received into one yet to be verified, while those who remained behind discerned in it only the break with the past and the gamble with the future and were thus driven to take up ever more strongly reactionary attitudes. In this newly acquired room for manoeuvre freedom becomes the all-embracing watchword and its expression in action the peculiar content and the permanent task of the Christian life. But freedom brings with it at the same time the problems of a voluntary association in which there are strong and weak, men and women, masters and slaves. Is freedom not straitened and hidden from view when men have to compound with such given realities as these? Does the order of earthly creation set limits to heavenly reality? To agree to this proposition would be to confess oneself no true 'spiritual man'. Thus the logical consequence of this exodus from Judaism is emancipation, producing a drive towards equality and a longing to be done with every form of subordination within the community. But the ideal which is hovering in the atmosphere here is not an equality of social rights but the angelic state which, once again, apocalyptic promised to the redeemed. This state is considered by the whole ancient world to be demonstrated primarily by the abrogation of sexual differentiation and is anticipated by asceticism or even, according to I Cor. 7.36ff., by the phenomenon of the *subintroductae*, so that it can be quite seriously said: neither man nor woman. This is Hellenistic enthusiasm's radical

[21] I am dealing here with Ebeling's questions in his second note on p. 229. Whenever anything important about the historical Jesus comes to light in the Hellenistic Christian writers, then it is hardly in historical continuity but, as sometimes in Paul and John, in similarity of content. For everything that we know about them points to an enthusiastic and ecstatic circle not going back behind apocalyptic, but developing beyond it.

interpretation of the baptismal statement that the redeemed are risen with Christ and enthroned with him in the heavenly state. Expectation of an imminent Parousia thus ceases to be meaningful because everything which apocalyptic still hopes for has already been realized. What is really important to notice, however, is that a large-scale process of transformation is going on here, in which present eschatology is linked directly with Jewish Christian apocalyptic of the time after Easter.

Now for the first time we are in a position to ask about Paul's place and significance within this whole context. Bultmann's fascinating interpretation of Paul is determined by its resolute placing of the apostle's present eschatology at the controlling centre of his thought. There is no reason not to admit that this interpretation is not merely tenable, but enables vital elements of Pauline theology to be unforgettably impressed on the mind. But we shall then have to regard the apostle as a representative – an extremely important one, no doubt – of the Hellenistic Church, just as radical historical criticism since Baur has actually done; the most impressive version of this view is undoubtedly Bousset's. In this case, Paul's particular contribution may be seen as his systematic development of anthropology. It certainly cannot be present eschatology, because this had already been developed by Hellenistic Christianity before his day. Seen in this light, what is the significance of the relics of apocalyptic theology which are to be found everywhere in the Pauline epistles? Indeed, is it permissible to use the phrase 'relics', unless we shut our eyes to the fact that Paul's apostolic self-consciousness is only comprehensible on the basis of his apocalyptic,[22] and that the same is true of the method and the goal of his mission? But his individual line, especially when seen against the background of the Hellenistic Church, appears much more sharply defined when we find that he did not tread the road of the enthusiasts, but neither did he tread the road of Johannine theology which led to the more or less fundamental setting-aside of future eschatology. Yet if we do not wish to do violence to the texts of his letters as we now have them, we are bound to say that there is in them a compromise between present and future eschatology. But this, too, is not the whole story. The Reformation exegesis of Paul compels us to see the apostle's pre-eminent self-revelation in the debate in which he takes, through his doctrines of the Law and of

[22] In spite of many exaggerations, G. Sass has correctly argued this in his *Apostelamt und Kirche*, 1939.

justification, the anti-Judaistic side.[23] The service which the comparative study of religion has rendered is to have set the anti-enthusiastic front alongside the other. But in the last resort and at bottom, the anti-enthusiastic battle waged by the apostle is fought under the sign of apocalyptic.[24] If we try to see the things through the eyes of his adversaries, we shall have to describe the Pauline theology as a retarding, more, a reactionary stage of development. This can be illustrated from various angles. In this paper, where there can be no question of trying to give a complete and well-rounded picture, it may well prove the most stimulating course to begin from that which anthropology presents. The systematic development of anthropology is indeed without any doubt the particular personal contribution of the apostle, which still causes him to stand out from among his pupils, for they succeed in preserving only a few pitiful fragments of his terminology and practically nothing of his grand design. Paul expounds a richly differentiated anthropology, of which no slightest element is taken up in the rest of the New Testament (nor does it ever reappear elsewhere): this is sufficient evidence that he is not in agreement with the one found among the enthusiasts. He finds himself unable to adopt their basic premise that the Christian participates not only in the Cross, but also in the Resurrection, of his Lord. It is not that he is not acquainted with this assertion, as emerges above all from his modification of it in Rom. 6.4f.: for him, too, baptism effects participation in the destiny of the Redeemer and therefore plunges him into the death of Christ. It even conveys participation in the heavenly life by making possible the *nova oboedientia*, which demonstrates the working of the power of the Risen Lord upon us. Nothing would be easier than to go on to say that we therefore and to this extent participate in the resurrection life of Christ. Yet Paul refused to follow his predecessors in taking this step. He does, admittedly, associate sharing in the Cross with sharing in the Resurrection: but in so doing, he builds in a remarkable caveat in the shape of an eschatological reservation. Participation in the Resurrection is spoken of not in the perfect tense, but in the future. Baptism equips for it, calls to it, but does not itself convey this gift. If baptism makes the *nova oboedientia* possible, yet this is still only an anticipatory

[23] Thus Fuchs, p. 250.

[24] Contrary to Ebeling's assumption (p. 234), Paul is the classical witness for a struggle against enthusiasm under the banner of primitive Christian apocalyptic, the evidence extending far beyond I Cor. This statement I shall now try to verify.

hint of what, in the temporal sense, is undoubtedly in the future. Christ alone is risen, we have in the Spirit the reversionary expectation of the Resurrection and proclaim this by the new obedience of our lives. Further than this Paul, unlike the enthusiasts or even his own pupils, is not prepared to go. This is evidently not merely a matter of using different language. I Cor. 15 shows that what is at stake is a fundamentally different theological conception which enables Paul to remain true at this point to the apocalyptic tradition. Without it, his whole anti-enthusiastic argument would lose its heart and its meaning. I should like, if I may, to illumine this statement by referring to I Cor. 15.20–28, a passage which, in my opinion, lays bare as no other does the dominant motif of Paul's theology of the Resurrection.[25] The apostle is here proclaiming the certainty of our resurrection, but he does it noticeably in such a way as to set the anthropological hope from the very beginning in a wider context. The content of the Resurrection is primarily not anthropological at all, but christological. It is the work of the Second Adam and therefore its meaning is not immediately and primarily our re-animation, but the lordship of Christ. 'Christ *must* reign': that is the nerve centre of the design and the firm ground which gives us confidence concerning our own destiny. But Paul is not content with this. In a way which is more than strange, he immediately adds to this first assertion a second – that the lordship of Christ is limited and passing. The only goal it serves is to give way to the sole lordship of God. Christ is God's representative over against a world which is not yet fully subject to God, although its eschatological subordination is in train since Easter and its end is in sight. No perspective could be more apocalyptic. With the greatest clarity it emerges here that Paul is absolutely unable and unwilling to speak of any end to history which has already come to pass, but, he does, however, discern that the day of the End-time has already broken. This is the case since the Resurrection of Christ, because since then the subjection of the cosmic powers has been taking place. The present eschatology of the enthusiasts is therefore picked up but apocalyptically anchored and delimited as it is not with them. For Paul, it is not an alternative to, but a component of, a future eschatology – to express the position in terms of slogans.[26] Its realm is called the *basileia Christi*. Paul obviously borrowed this formula from tradition; equally of apocalyptic origin is

[25] Here I take up the challenge of Fuchs (p. 246).

[26] Cf. my essay 'The righteousness of God in Paul', pp. 168–82 below.

the outlook which sees in the Kyrios not the lord of a cult, but the exalted Ruler of the Universe. This is the point at which the correctness of my reconstruction, which derives the theology of the Exaltation from apocalyptic, is confirmed: it is not the heavenly Son of Man in his hiddenness who is the Lord of the World, but the Christ exalted to God's right hand, and the extent of his lordship – this is the sense of the Hellenistic hymns to Christ – is the extent to which the world-powers have been put in subjection. There remains only the end of the lordship of death upon earth, which is identical with the end of history. The Resurrection of Christ is therefore, even while it counts as the beginning of the general resurrection, still for the time being the great exception, in which we can participate by hope alone. The *regnum Christi* is distinguished precisely by this very state of affairs: death has no more dominion over him, but it has over us. It (the *regnum*) is therefore defined by the two poles, his Resurrection and ours, and must be described materially as the realm of the power of the Resurrection in a world which has fallen a prey to death, and thus to the other cosmic powers. But how is this assertion to be combined with the other one (taken over from enthusiasm) according to which the powers have already surrendered to Christ? We have to give a twofold answer. In the first place, Paul distinguishes sharply between the Church as the redeemed and the world as the unredeemed creation and thus modifies the apocalyptic scheme of the two aeons. For the Church is for him as for enthusiasm an entity similar to the world: it is the world in obedience to God. In the Church the powers, except death – note the eschatological reservation which is made even here – have lost the lordship to Christ, whereas they still reign in the world which surrounds the Church. But to what extent is this really true of the Church, which is visibly exposed to the same sufferings and temptations and dangers that beset the rest of the world? At this point, for the first time, anthropology comes into play. For Paul defines the Church as the company of the obedient who, as such, stand in the succession of the obedient Adam. But in the obedience of the Christians the Church manifests itself as the new creation which is now restored to the state from which Adam fell. In her obedience it is seen that the power of the Resurrection governs her and that the powers of the world – other than death – no longer reign in her. Once again we must ask how far this is actually true. The answer to this question must begin from the premise that the apostle, with unmistakable emphasis, demands obedience in the body and has transposed the Christian service of God into the daily life of the world. This naturally does not mean that heart and disposition do not enter into it and that the service of prayer or of the assembled community is without significance. Only, for Paul it is all-important that the Christian life is not limited to interior piety and cultic acts. One of the most remarkable, and at the same time one of the least known sentences of the Apostle runs (I Cor. 6.13): 'The body belongs to the Lord and the Lord to the body.' The first half of the sentence is not so striking as the second. We can only understand the latter if we are quite clear that 'body' for Paul does not mean, as Bultmann would have us believe, man's relation to himself, but that piece of world which we ourselves are and for which we bear responsibility because it was the earliest gift of our Creator to us. 'Body' is not primarily to be regarded and interpreted from the standpoint of the individual. For the apostle, it signifies man in his worldliness and therefore in his ability to communicate. Christ's mission and presence was not, and is not, first and foremost to individuals. That would have been an unthinkable idea for Paul, however often it has recurred over the long history of the Church. Because Christ came into the world and wills its existence for himself as God's representative, he is therefore present for the body as the reality of our being in the world and, indeed, the possibility of our having fellowship in our humanity. In the bodily obedience of the Christian, carried out as the service of God in the world of everyday, the lordship of Christ finds visible expression and only when this visible expression takes personal shape in us does the whole thing become credible as Gospel message. But this rounds off the curve which enables the bodily obedience of the Christian to be described at once as an abiding in the power of the Resurrection, as the manifestation of the new life, and as the reversionary expectation of the reality of the Resurrection. We saw indeed from I Cor. 15.20–28 that resurrection for Paul is not primarily oriented towards the reanimation of the dead or any such thing, but towards the reign of Christ. Because Christ must reign, he cannot leave his own in the grip of death. Conversely, his own are already engaged today in delivering over to Christ by their bodily obedience the piece of world which they themselves are; and in so doing they bear witness to his lordship as that of the Cosmocrator and thus anticipate the ultimate future of the reality of the Resurrection and of the untrammelled reign of Christ. The apocalyptic question 'To whom does the sovereignty of the world belong?' stands behind the Resurrection theology of the apostle, as behind his parenesis which centres round the call to obedience in the body. Apocalyptic even underlies the particular shape of Pauline anthropology. For the technical terms 'spirit' and 'flesh' do not signify, any more than the term 'body' does, the individuation of the individual human being, but primarily that reality which, as the power either of the heavenly or the earthly, determines him from outside, takes possession of him and thereby decides into which of the two dualistically opposed spheres he is to be integrated. Man for Paul is never just on his own. He is always a specific piece of world and therefore becomes what in the last resort he is by determination from outside, i.e. by the power which takes possession of him and the lordship to which he surrenders himself. His life is from the beginning a stake in the confrontation between God and the principalities of this world. In other words, it mirrors the cosmic contention for the lordship of the world and is its concretion. As such, man's life can only be understood apocalyptically. Thus, what is described as the dialectic in Paul between the indicative and the imperative, between the state of having been redeemed and ultimate salvation which lies yet ahead, is nothing else but the projection into the human condition of the Christian of the relationship of the lordship of Christ to the subjection of all cosmic principalities. Here we have the answer to the crucial question why Paul did not take over the present eschatology of the enthusiasts but set over against it eschatological reserve and apocalyptic. He is unable to assent to the statement that the Christian has only to demonstrate his heavenly freedom because the powers and principalities have already become subject to the Christ. According to Rom. 8.18ff., he knows that not only does the creation cry out for the glorious freedom of the children of God, but the Church, too, joins in this cry, even in her worship, because her perfection has still to be accomplished. He knows, we can now say more directly, the tempted condition of the believer who is still living through the pangs of the Messiah, free because he has been called once and for all into sonship but menaced by the last enemy which is death and therefore by the cosmic principalities; these are continually striving to wrench him away from sonship and freedom, and so he is compelled continually to be re-established in the *nova oboedientia*.[27] Present eschatology by itself, and not comprehended within a future eschatology – that would be for

[27] I cannot therefore concede to Fuchs (p. 258) that it is the Law which appears in and with the Pauline imperative.

the Christian pure glorying in the flesh, such as enthusiasm has certainly sufficiently demonstrated in every epoch. It would be illusion and not reality. It is precisely the apocalyptic of the apostle which renders to reality its due and resists pious illusion. The Christian Church possesses the reality of sonship only in the freedom of those under temptation – the freedom which points forward to the resurrection of the dead as the truth and the completion of the reign of Christ.

This is a suitable point at which to break off my hasty progress through primitive Christian history as far as Paul. I hope I have made it clear why I describe apocalyptic as the mother of Christian theology. I have been asked[28] if, in this case, there is anything else left to preach. I would answer this simply by repeating the themes which have, one after the other, come to light in our investigation of primitive Christian apocalyptic: mission, the freedom of the Christian community, faith under fire – these are the different aspects of the reign of Christ.

[28] Fuchs, pp. 247, 254.

VI

THE STRUCTURE AND PURPOSE OF THE PROLOGUE TO JOHN'S GOSPEL*

It cannot be maintained that the problem of the prologue to John's Gospel has been solved, however many investigations have been devoted to it since Harnack wrote his essay on the relation of the prologue to the Fourth Gospel to the whole work[1] nearly sixty-five years ago. He asked:

> What is the aim of the Gospel, what is the aim of the Prologue? Are these aims simply identical or is the Prologue really an introduction, an introduction to the Gospel? Does the Gospel take on where the Prologue leaves off or is the Prologue the proleptic quintessence of the Gospel?[2]

His answer ran thus:

> The Prologue is not the key to the understanding of the Gospel but is designed to prepare its Hellenistic readers for the Gospel.[3]

In more recent times the question has for the most part not been either so clearly posed or so clearly answered. All the same, C. H. Dodd managed to find himself near enough to Harnack's position all over again.

> The Logos doctrine is placed first, because, addressing a public nurtured in the higher religion of Hellenism, the writer wishes to offer the Logos-idea as the appropriate approach, for them, to the central purport of the Gospel, through which he may lead them to the historical actuality of its story, rooted as it is in Jewish tradition.[4]

* 'Aufbau und Anliegen des johanneischen Prologs', first published in *Libertas Christiana, Festschrift für F. Delekat*, 1957, pp. 75–99.

[1] A. von Harnack, 'Über das Verhältnis des Prologs des vierten Evangeliums zum ganzen Werk', *ZTK* 2, 1892, pp. 189ff.

[2] *Art. cit.*, p. 191. [3] *Ibid.*, p. 230.

[4] C. H. Dodd, *The Interpretation of the Fourth Gospel*, 1953, p. 296.

E. C. Hoskyns had sharply contested this thesis: 'The Prologue . . . is not so much a preface to the Gospel as a summary of it.'[5] He was thus looking back to an approach which Belser[6] had claimed as never having been lost – at least theoretically – on the Catholic side and had proceeded further to sharpen it: the Prologue is designed to announce the programme of the Gospel in the manner of a thesis, the Gospel follows on with illustration, verification and confirmation. Today, it is true, we are generally content to point to the close affiliation in terminology and themes and to characterize the Prologue as an overture to the Gospel; and, in so doing, we obscure rather than help on the real question.

The structure of the Prologue is at present a matter of more vigorous debate than its purpose. An analysis meriting particular attention is that of R. Bultmann, which appeared originally in his essay on the religious background of the Prologue to St John's Gospel,[7] and after that in his commentary.[8] According to Bultmann, the basis of the Prologue is a hymn of the Baptist community, originally composed in Aramaic, deployed by the Evangelist (with the help of prose insertions in vv. 6–8 and 15) against the veneration of the Baptist as Messiah and provided by him with exegetical observations, as the further use of prose style in vv. 12c–13, 17–18 indicates. Two lines, each with two stressed words, dovetail regularly in the hymn whether as complements, parallels or antitheses; an intricate and chain-like construction results in the conclusion of the first line being often taken up in the second, or in the next verse. According to Bultmann, when the Evangelist began to work on the original, i.e. to translate it into Greek, this artistic construction was disturbed in a number of places. In the text we have today vv. 9, 10, 12 and 14 certainly break out of the assumed scheme of couplets. Bultmann helps himself out by eliminating the clarificatory *ἄνθρωπον* in v. 9, which he treats as an unnecessary doublet of the current rabbinic designation of man 'having come into the world', and also the equally superfluous *ἐξουσίαν* in 12b. In v. 10, either one line of the couplet has been lost or else 10a is to be ascribed to the Evangelist. Similarly, in v. 14 he postulates the disappearance of one line or, better, an original combination

[5] E. C. Hoskyns, *The Fourth Gospel*, 1947, p. 137.

[6] J. E. Belser, 'Der Prolog des Johannesevangeliums', *Theologische Quartalschrift* 85, 1903, p. 517.

[7] 'Der religionsgeschichtliche Hintergrund des Prologs zum Johannesevangelium', *Eucharisterion für H. Gunkel* (FRLANT 36.2), 1923, pp. 1–26.

[8] *Das Evangelium des Johannes*, 1941.

of 14e and 16a.[9] In this last case, 16b would fulfil the function – which we know to occur elsewhere – of the concluding sentence of a hymn, extra to the metre. The repetition of 1b in v. 2 Bultmann regards as a construction of the Evangelist's; this accounts for the fact that v. 2, with its three accented syllables, diverges from the scheme of the two stressed words and must eventually have displaced a mythological sentence which was in the source. The Prologue is divided into two sections: vv. 1–4 with the theme 'The Pre-existence of the Logos', and vv. 5–18 under the title 'The Logos as Revealer within History'. This is the way in which Bultmann answers the question – already a matter of discussion in the early Church – as to the point at which reference to the historical Christ begins, but he does so, admittedly, only in the Evangelist's own terms. The unmistakable interpolation in v. 14 indicates, says Bultmann, that it was in this Baptist hymn that reference was first made to the epiphany of the Revealer. In his earlier work Bultmann took the present tense in v. 5, which stood in the way of an interpretation of this kind, to be a 'timeless' present, exactly like *φωτίζει* in v. 9; but in his commentary he would see in it an emendation of an original imperfect.

We may well admire the precision and logic of these postulates and, equally, the neat result of the analysis. But, on the other hand, we shall not ignore the fact that the solution is built up on a wealth of hypotheses and thus vulnerable on several different fronts. As everything depends here on the most extreme precision, we have to clarify this judgment in detail. About the most assured finding of modern Johannine research is, or is alleged to be, that the Evangelist is writing in an Aramaicizing style. But it remains very questionable whether he has used an Aramaic original, say, of the sermons of the Baptist[10] or of Jesus[11] and indeed this hypothesis has recently been refuted on good grounds by C. K. Barrett.[12] I cannot see that the case is other and better in respect to the Prologue. Black himself exercises the greatest reserve over against the argument of C. F. Burney's book, *The Aramaic Origin of the Fourth Gospel*, and even subjects it to severe criticism, while Bultmann has found it equally unsatisfactory as a basis for his own argument. For even if he, too, regards the ἦν which

[9] Bultmann is here taking up a thesis which has often been put forward and can be supported from e.g. Belser, *op. cit.*, pp. 501, 510f., and J. Wellhausen, *Das Evangelium Johannis*, 1908, p. 8.

[10] So M. Black, *An Aramaic Approach to the Gospels and Acts*, 2nd ed., 1954.

[11] So Bultmann in his commentary.

[12] C. K. Barrett, *The Gospel according to St John*, 1955.

introduces v. 9 as the reproduction of a *hū'*, he does not, however, reckon it to be a misunderstanding of the Evangelist who perhaps misread *hu'* as *hᵃuā*,[13] because he sees that v. 9 could not, after vv. 6–8, begin with οὗτος ἦν.[14] But when he, with Burney,[15] derives ἴδιοι and ἴδια in v. 11 from a common *dīlēh*,[16] it is difficult to see why the translator should not have translated the same word in his original with the same equivalent. In both cases we can manage with the hypothesis of virtual translation, without having to die in the last ditch for the thesis of actual translation.[17] While Black[18] would prefer to follow Burney[19] in making the ὅτι which originally belonged to 14e and is now in 16a, a mistaken translation of a relative ·ד – 'of whose fullness we have all received' –, the Greek is nevertheless comprehensible without this postulate.[20] It is certainly not possible to call the argument for an Aramaic original decisive, and in any event it will not stand up under the weight of the further hypotheses which some would build upon it. This finding affects Bultmann's analysis to this degree, that it makes us question the validity of the judgment that the words ἄνθρωπον in v. 9b and ἐξουσίαν in v. 12b are additions made by the translator. They are obviously not essential to the content. On the other hand, there is no doubt that they clarify, in the Greek, the tenor of the text. It is only possible to maintain that they have been inserted by a translator, if we are already convinced of the existence of the Aramaic original. But even the probability of this has not been established by the arguments we have been examining.

Bultmann's chief concern at these points is obviously his reconstruction of the pattern of the couplet which, according to him, governs the hymn. To presuppose an Aramaic original makes it possible for him to cling on to this pattern. But if we find ourselves unable to go on sharing the presupposition, we shall have to dispute, on the evidence of vv. 9 and 12, the exclusive use of the couplet. In so doing, we shall be picking up again where E. Ruckstuhl[21] left off in the unusually careful criticism he raised against the hypothesis. This criticism tries to show that we cannot speak of a uniform rhythmical

[13] So Burney, *op. cit.*, 1922, p. 33. [14] Commentary, p. 31 n. 6.
[15] *Op. cit.*, p. 33. [16] Commentary, p. 34 n. 7.
[17] According to Burney, the translator was concerned with key-words.
[18] *Op. cit.*, p. 56. [19] *Op. cit.*, p. 39.
[20] Bultmann, commentary, p. 51 n. 4.
[21] E. Ruckstuhl, *Die literarische Einheit des Johannesevangeliums* (Studia Friburgensia NF 3), 1951.

pattern in the Gospel, that the rhythm as such is not really the decisive criterion used in Bultmann's own source criticism and that the ascription of various sayings to the so-called Sermon-source is subject to all kinds of subjective evaluation;[22] but all this need not shake our faith in the possibility of reconstructing the hymn within the Prologue. For the deliberate construction of this passage and the sharp relief in which it stands out over against the rest of the Gospel are so very obvious that these qualities in themselves stress most starkly the difficulties of the attempt to discover a source of revelation in the Sermons and reveal the questionable nature of the attempt itself.[23] But against this, there is another criticism which may not be so easily disposed of: even after Bultmann's emendations the verse-lines 9b, 12b and 16a are still too long, the hypothesis of the disappearance, even the displacement, of a line of some sort in vv. 2, 10 and 14 is quite arbitrary and the text we have today gives us undoubted triplets in vv. 9, 10 and 12, and equally in vv. 6 and 7.[24] Bultmann's reasoning at these points simply will not do. What would the Evangelist have been correcting in v. 2, when he took no offence at the content of v. 18b, than which there could scarcely be anything more mythologically formulated? Are we not therefore bound, if the emphatic repetition of 1b in 2 really stems from the Evangelist, to reckon with a triplet? In v. 10 the weight of the present text rests without question on the first and third lines, while the second merely echoes v. 3 and does not even go well with vv. 5 and 9. Does not the verse lose its own peculiar force if 10a, of all verses, is struck out simply to preserve the couplet pattern? Are we in a position to strike out anything at all until we can assume with some degree of certainty an Aramaic original and are therefore not bound to retain yet another triplet in v. 9 and a line that is at least over-long in 12b? In view of these difficulties, should we not do well to let this postulate (already erected by Burney[25]) of a consistent couplet pattern go by the board, and the textual changes it necessitates can go with it? It may be conceded that the couplet dominates as far as v. 12. But it seems to me that to maintain on this basis the existence of a rigid scheme is to cross the frontier which separates an acceptable reconstruction from thoroughly dubious hypotheses.

[22] *Ibid.*, pp. 43ff.

[23] Cf. my discussion of Bultmann's commentary in *Verkündigung und Forschung*, 1942/46, pp. 187f.

[24] Ruckstuhl, pp. 50f., 67f.   [25] *Op. cit.*, pp. 40ff.

On the other hand, we are very greatly in Bultmann's debt for having emphasized with such energy the parallelism between vv. 5 and 9ff. and for having gone on to draw the inescapable conclusions and, in particular, the conclusion that the first section of the Prologue ends at v. 4.[26] The view that the second section does not begin until v. 6 is certainly almost universally held.[27] The confusion of theological interpretations which inevitably results from articulating the passage in this way ought to alert us to the fact that such a division cannot possibly be right. Its immediate attraction stems naturally from the feeling that the words about the Baptist mark a transition which, christologically speaking, separates the being and activity of the pre-existent Christ from the incarnate. But if we allow this, it is then scarcely possible to make any sense of v. 5. Protestant theology today will be at the very least unwilling to accept Ruckstuhl's interpretation,[28] tolerable still to Idealism, that the Logos is the light of all men 'inasmuch as their life of reason and will, i.e. all their natural spiritual activities, are produced by his working'. This interpretation is bound, even apart from everything else, to be seriously embarrassed at least in dealing with v. 5b, which speaks not only of not apprehending but of not comprehending. Harnack[29] has given us the facile solution and interpretation:

> The most apt solution seems to me to be this, that, in so far as the Evangelist is thinking of the illuminative activity of the Logos, he certainly has the activity of the human spirit in mind, but is regarding it *sub specie aeternitatis*.

Pluperfect, perfect and present are thus bound together. There is no question here of a movement in the temporal sense, but of a movement towards the concrete and specific.'[30] In the face of this edifying device

[26] So too H. Schlier, 'Im Anfang war der Wort', *Die Zeit der Kirche*, 1956, pp. 276ff.; A. Wikenhauser, *Das Evangelium des Johannes* (Regensburger NT), 1954, p. 38.

[27] So Harnack (see n. 1), p. 218; Belser (see n. 6), p. 485; A. Loisy, *Le quatrième Evangile*, 1903, pp. 151f.; F. Overbeck, *Das Johannesevangelium*, 1911, p. 431; B. Weiss, *Das Johannesevangelium als einheitliches Werk*, 1912, p. 2; W. Heitmüller, *Das Johannesevangelium* (Die Schriften des NT 4), 3rd ed., 1918, pp. 40f.; T. Zahn, *Das Evangelium des Johannes*, 5th and 6th eds., 1921, p. 64; M. Goguel, *Introduction au Nouveau Testament* 2, 1924, p. 183; M. J. Lagrange, *Evangile selon Saint Jean*, 1925, p. 1; R. Tillmann, *Das Johannesevangelium*, 4th ed., 1931, p. 46; W. Bauer, *Das Johannesevangelium*, 3rd ed., 1933, p. 15; Hoskyns (see n. 5), p. 140; Ruckstuhl (see n. 21), p. 71; H. Strathmann, *Das Evangelium nach Johannes* (NTD), 1951, p. 29; Barrett (see n. 12), p. 125.

[28] *Op. cit.*, p. 79. [29] *Op. cit.*, p. 218.

[30] Similarly Loisy, p. 184: from the abstract to the concrete; Barrett, p. 133: from the eternal to the temporal and particular.

which treats the problem as though it did not exist, there is something refreshing about the untroubled way in which W. Baldensperger could write, in his still fascinating study.

> It is only a pity that the dawn of history, proclaimed here, is unable to break through completely in the next section (9–10), which is again covered by a network of metaphysical clouds.[31]

He cuts the Gordian knot by not making the 'new thing' of the Incarnation begin until v. 14.[32] Dodd is the most recent writer to agree with this view, although admittedly in the extremely dialectical fashion which is so characteristic of him. In his view, the Evangelist is very fond of ambiguity and has so expressed himself that the Hellenistic reader can think of the λόγος ἄσαρκος up to v. 13, while the Christian can understand everything from v. 4 on as referring to the Incarnation.[33]

The state of this discussion is not a happy one. Theories or – even worse – nice formulae obstruct precise answers to precise questions. In my opinion, it was Bultmann who first decided the problem clearly and cogently. Since the parallelism of v. 5 and vv. 9–11 cannot be disputed, the phrase 'his own' in v. 11 ought no longer to be understood as referring to Israel as the people of special possession.[34] The cosmological slant is not characteristic merely of the introductory verses, but of the whole Prologue, which is once again in complete agreement with the Gospel here. And the parallelism between vv. 10 and 11 is unmistakable. Opposition to the Revealer therefore coincides with unbelief towards the Jesus who has appeared in history, as 12c also expresses it. If, however, 12c is really a gloss of the Evangelist, the point is made with equal force in 12b: to be the child of God is, according to the whole New Testament, an eschatological gift bound to the manifestation of Jesus Christ. The parallelism between v. 5 and vv. 9ff. implies, accordingly, that the portrayal of Jesus Christ as appearing in history begins at v. 5. Verses 6–8 are also only comprehensible on this basis. It is true that Baldensperger[35]

[31] W. Baldensperger, *Der Prolog des vierten Evangeliums*, 1898, p. 2.

[32] *Ibid.*, p. 30. [33] *Interpretation of the Fourth Gospel*, pp. 282ff.

[34] So Harnack, p. 220; Baldensperger, p. 13; Overbeck, p. 395; B. Weiss, pp. 7f.; Tillmann, p. 59; Zahn, p. 72; Goguel, p. 184; Hoskyns, p. 146; Dodd, p. 270; Strathmann, p. 35; Barrett, p. 136. On the other side, Loisy, p. 173; Schlatter, *Der Evangelist Johannes*, 1930, pp. 5 and 17; Lagrange, p. 13; W. Bauer, p. 21; Wikenhauser, p. 40; Schlier, p. 281.

[35] Baldensperger, p. 11.

passionately attacked the view that these verses were an excursus. 'No one has yet made it clear why this alleged parenthesis should be interpolated at this point.' Well, if that were true before him, it was certainly due to him that a breach was made here. The dignity of the sole Lord Jesus Christ must be defended even against the claims of the Baptist community, which is proclaiming its Master as Messiah. Baldensperger may rightly be given credit today as a pioneer for having proposed to make this insight the key to the whole Prologue, more especially as he found no one to follow him along this line. The 'polemic-apologetic' utterance in vv. 6–8 was not the motive power and the heart of the Prologue. It remains in reality a parenthesis, in which the exaltation of Jesus Christ even over against the proclamation of the Baptist community is being justified. It is thoroughly understandable that this should happen at this point and no other: the advent and activity of the Baptist is similarly seen throughout the whole New Testament as eschatological, that is, as bound to the advent and activity of Jesus Christ. The 'polemic-apologetic' digression of the Evangelist follows therefore immediately upon the mention of the manifestation of Jesus Christ. Neither ought Bultmann's judgment that we have here an interpolation into the hymn to be disputed. The fact that it is nevertheless still being disputed at the present time ties up with the further fact that, unfortunately, the methods and findings of form criticism have not won universal acceptance. What are we to say when Barrett[36] denies the 'poetic' structure of the Prologue on the grounds that Burney and J. Weiss have proposed different reconstructions? Yet both are agreed in recognizing that the whole bears a hymnic form. Barrett's own dividing-up process,[37] by which vv. 1–5 describe the cosmological significance of the Logos, vv. 6–8 the witness of the Baptist, vv. 9–13 the manifestation of the Light, vv. 14–18 the plan of salvation is by no means any more convincing. It offers no systematic unity, it does not take into account the problem of the relationship between vv. 5–9 and vv. 14–18, it does not explain the difference of style in vv. 6–8 and v. 15 against the total context; equally, we have to say that cosmic significance is attached to the Logos throughout the Gospel and that vv. 14–18 certainly do not develop a plan of salvation. Ruckstuhl's analysis is in no better case. True, he does not close his eyes to the prosaic and sober character of vv. 6–8, but he explains it with more depth than clarity by saying that the being and work of the Baptist were not played out on the

[36] Barrett (see n. 12), p. 126. [37] *Ibid.*, pp. 125ff.

same level as those of the Logos. As if we were not concerned in both cases with the earthly milieu rather than the eschatological divine act! Even if we allow that these verses have a rhythmical character and claim 6–7 as a triplet,[38] we still cannot well ignore the difference in rhythm, style and general tenor between them and the surrounding verses. Finally, Ruckstuhl maintains that the whole Prologue presents us with narrative-type discourse and not a hymn, which is why 'the outward signs of inner feeling, warmth and sympathy' are absent.[39] But this is to import the standards of a particular kind of modern poetry-making into primitive Christian hymnody. A glance at I Tim. 3.16 cannot but demonstrate that we have there the same austerity of presentation and that primitive Christianity was quite capable of expressing manifest devotion and praise in the actual recital of God's mighty act. I hope this criticism has confirmed the finding that what the Evangelist has actually done is to take a hymn as the basis of his Prologue and to interpolate into it vv. 6–8. Whereas the first four verses were intended to speak of the pre-existent Logos, vv. 5 and 9ff. are concerned with the revelation of Jesus in history.

But this finding certainly places us in a most embarrassing situation. For we must now answer the question as to the kind of relationship which exists between vv. 5 and 9ff. on the one hand and vv. 14ff. on the other. Of course, those exegetes who consider that the Incarnation does not come into the picture until vv. 9ff. have the same question to answer. Only Baldensperger is exempt from this particular worry; according to him, the Prologue up to v. 13 refers to the pre-Christian revelation, v. 10 specifically to the heathen world and v. 11 to Israel.[40] The difficulty of this has always been felt. The very fact that v. 11 has so often been understood as referring to the divine epiphany to Israel serves to emphasize the contrast with vv. 14ff. Here again, Harnack produces the interpretation which seems likely to be fruitful:

> Thirdly, what has long been tacitly presupposed now finds explicit utterance. He who is known as the Logos has been characterized according to his nature and operation: now he is to be defined according to his appearance in history which has been hovering before the writer's eyes from the beginning.[41]

[38] Ruckstuhl (see n. 21), p. 78. [39] *Ibid.*, p. 70.
[40] Baldensperger (see n. 31), p. 13. [41] Harnack (see n. 1), p. 220.

Verse 14, on this view, is not seen as the transition from the λόγος ἄσαρκος to the λόγος ἔνσαρκος but

> this historical event which, in its effects, was taken into account as early as v. 5 is now brought into particular prominence.[42]

We have met this solution of the problem before: from the abstract or the universal to the concrete or the temporal. But is this not yet another case of impressive words doing duty for rigorous analysis? Is what is being said from v. 3 onwards really abstract and, conversely is the validity of vv. 14ff., because it is of cosmic range, not universal also? With what enviable clarity, over against doubts such as these, does the statement of Baldensperger ring out, unacceptable as it now is:

> The whole section 9–13 . . . is obviously intended to bring to the awareness of the readers in what wide fields and for how long a stretch of time the Logos has been operating, long before the advent of the Baptist.[43]

But there still remains Bultmann's solution, espoused before him by Heitmüller[44] and after him by Lagrange,[45] Strathmann,[46] Wikenhauser[47] and Schlier,[48] viz. that vv. 5–13 give a picture which directs attention forward to the advent of Jesus Christ. What we have here is obviously intended primarily as a slight emendation of Harnack's expedient. It receives its particular stamp from being combined with the other thesis that the Evangelist has applied to the manifestation of Jesus language which in the pre-Christian hymn referred to the time before the coming of the actual Revealer. This certainly explains the parallelism between vv. 5, 9ff. and 14ff. which is the central problem of our passage, but does it thereby do away with all our difficulties? In particular, can Bultmann's premisses bear the weight of his reconstruction? The critical observations on the question of the Aramaic original and of the couplet scheme make us sympathetic to W. Bauer's hesitations[49] in classing Bultmann's finding as completely assured. But these hesitations have to be taken further. Within the framework of this investigation of mine, I am prepared to let the comparative side of the problem stand over, although there are questions here which remain to be settled. It is solely the Logos-predication of the Revealer in the sense in which Bultmann expounds

[42] *Ibid.*, p. 221. [43] Baldensperger, p. 30. [44] Heitmüller (see n. 27), p. 44.
[45] Lagrange (see n. 27), p. 19. [46] Strathmann (see n. 27), p. 37.
[47] Wikenhauser (see n. 26), p. 41. [48] Schlier (see n. 26), p. 281.
[49] Bauer (see n. 27), p. 14.

it which enables serious consideration to be given to the idea of a pre-Christian origin for the hymn. It is a thoroughly reasonable hypothesis, on the other hand, that a Hellenistic Christianity plucked this title out of its own intellectual atmosphere, especially as Philo had already identified Logos with Sophia. Such a possibility becomes even more likely if we are doubtful, or feel bound at any rate to regard it as highly problematic, whether a community which honoured the Baptist as Messiah would have maintained his pre-existence – as a divine being, no less – and have counted on his manifestation under changing appearances. However illuminating Bultmann's analysis in the field of comparative studies may be, his exaggeration of it in his thesis of an orginal hymn of the Baptist community appears precarious and even forced to the same degree. But for our purpose, a test of Bultmann's analysis in terms of form criticism might well be more fruitful and therefore more important. Its basic presupposition is the parallelism between vv. 5ff. and 14ff. How has this parallelism come about? Is the sole answer to be that the Evangelist misunderstood the point his source was making, so far as vv. 5ff were concerned? If that were really the case, the Evangelist must obviously not have felt the pressure of the difficulty which gives his interpreters so much trouble. Neither the historical explanation of the parallelism between vv. 5ff. and 14ff. nor the postulate of a certain development in thought from the evocative picture to the new departure in v. 14 can conceal the fact that the point of the alleged hymn is lost in v. 14 through the Evangelist's lack of understanding. It is this which leads Baldensperger to reflect, not wholly without reason:

> What a great step forward the Evangelist would then have been taking and what a violent set-back the reader would then have felt the beginning of v.14 to be.[50]

A second and perhaps a more adequate avenue of explanation is opened up when we observe that the chain-like interweaving of lines and verses finishes at v. 12. Indeed, the theme of sonship to God is not further pursued. Rather, the other motif of becoming flesh sets in abruptly at v. 14. This poor connection of v. 14 with vv. 12f. was felt to be a problem by Loisy[51] and Hoskyns[52] also. Both hit upon the same way out of the dilemma, although they diverge on some details: Loisy accepts the reading of v. 13 – frequently preserved by the Latin

[50] Baldensperger (see n. 31), p. 26. [51] Loisy (see n. 27), pp. 184ff.
[52] Hoskyns (see n. 5), p. 164.

Fathers – which has the verb in the singular, and thus refers to Christ. Hoskyns conjectures an association of ideas on the part of the Evangelist, which has carried him on from the children of God to the Son of God. Both are wide of the mark. The variant in v. 13 is rightly regarded almost universally[53] as being secondary. Even if we leave the poor quality of the testimony to it out of account, it would be almost impossible to understand why it should have been corrected in the *textus receptus*, while its origin can be ascribed to the wish to produce a Johannine witness for the Virgin Birth. Against Hoskyns, on the other hand, it has to be said that the parallelism between the children of God and the Son of God is precisely what is *not* established; rather, the reference is to the Logos which is becoming flesh. The only virtue of these two hypotheses is that they bring out in sharp relief the fact of the missing connection. This chain-like interweaving, however, is not to be found again in what follows. For if we really wanted to connect v. 16a with 14e and could legitimately do so, even then we should only get a word association which we could not proceed without further ado to identify with the other stylistic form at the beginning of the Prologue. This procedure produces no less of a change in style; 14d-e and 16b suddenly introduce a number of phrases in apposition instead of co-ordinate principal sentences. Bultmann's reconstruction of the hymn offers no parallel to this. If, however, we leave v. 9 as a triplet, we certainly get a clause in apposition in 9c.[54] But can that really be compared with v. 14, where three short sentences attract two lines of phrases in apposition? Shall we not rather look for a parallel in v. 6, a prose sentence from the hand of the Evangelist? We shall have to deal later with the fact that the third person singular of the hymn is abruptly replaced in v. 14 by the first person plural of the confession of faith; but here we must at least note it in passing. Finally, there is a question of content which has to be raised in connection with these critical observations on matters of style. When Bultmann claims v. 14 for his gnostic Baptist source, he is necessarily ascribing to it not only the tenet of the pre-existence of the Baptist, but also that of the

[53] On the other side I include for the sake of completeness (although I do not think he makes his case) F. M. Braun, 'Qui ex Deo natus est', in *Aux sources de la tradition chrétienne: mélanges offerts à Maurice Goguel*, 1950, pp. 11–31.

[54] Ruckstuhl, pp. 76f., has once again defended the view that the participle and the verb are here being combined periphrastically. However much my own argument might gain from putting this construction on v. 9, I can find equally little justification for doing so: the predicate would be torn apart by the relative clause and the current anthropological usage of the rabinnate ignored.

incarnation of the Revealer. But is a pre-Christian use of the theme of becoming flesh in its Johannine formulation and intention really credible? The motif as such, as W. Bauer[55] has thoroughly demonstrated, is Greek. But the emphasis of the Hellenistic epiphany narratives is less on the moment of the Incarnation than on the veiling of the descending divinity. In pure Judaism the Messiah, once he has appeared, cannot conceivably be the object of proclamation, and, as far as gnosticism is concerned, parallels to the Johannine formulation and paradoxical statement would certainly need to be produced. Is not the logical conclusion from this that the stress on the Incarnation as the medium of revelation is a special characteristic of Christianity? This in turn would mean that the contention that we have here a pre-Christian hymn would, at least as far as v. 14 is concerned, become even more insecurely based. But is it permissible to content ourselves with a statement of this kind? Do not our critical observations of the style of these verses lead to the more radical implication that from v. 14 onwards it is definitely not the hymn but the Evangelist himself giving utterance? W. Bauer has already remarked:

> With reference to the last part of the Prologue, i.e. vv. 14–18, in my opinion it is no longer possible to conjecture with any degree of security about original material which has been taken over.[56]

Ruckstuhl[57] characterizes this section as the conclusion drawn by the Evangelist from the first two, and Bultmann himself considered, as early as 1923, that 'a source is used only in vv. 1–13 and the Evangelist's own composition begins at v. 14'.[58]

In my view this conjecture attains the status of an established certainty when we look back to the original problem of the parallelism between vv. 5–13 and 14–18. There is absolutely no convincing argument for the view that vv. 5–13 ever referred to anything save the historical manifestation of the Revealer. The pre-Christian character of the hymn is more than problematical, the Aramaic original incredible, the alleged Baptist hymn a pure hypothesis. Those who maintain that vv. 5–13 present a proleptic picture of the appearance of the Revealer in history do so out of the necessity of distinguishing sharply this part of the Prologue from vv. 14–18. In fact, the section contains all the expressions which belong to the portrayal of an epiphany. The verb in v. 5 is not 'timeless'[59] but, like the excellent parallel in

[55] Bauer, p. 23. [56] *Ibid.*, p. 22. [57] Ruckstuhl, p. 97.
[58] *Eucharisterion*, p. 24. [59] Against Bultmann, *ibid.*, p. 5 n. 1.

I John 2.8, has a present 'sound'.[60] The idea of a rhetorical change of tense[61] is superfluous; the conjecture that the Evangelist has changed an imperfect into a present is as desperate an expedient as the explanation that he is here reaching back into the catechetical tradition.[62] Verses 9–11 speak of the presence of the Revealer in the world,[63] of the opposition he finds and of the faith with which he is met. Verse 12 specifies the gift which is his to bestow and the goal of his redeeming effectiveness. The establishment of sonship to God through the Son of God is the eschatological end of all God's dealings with the world, the goal of the Creator and the Creation. Verse 12 is therefore preeminently suitable to serve as the conclusion of a Christian hymn. The whole of salvation history is here recited, the second creation likewise emerges as the recapitulation and the completion of the first; this thought is familiar to us from the hymn Col. 1.15ff. Correspondingly, two strophes stand, clearly articulated, over against each other. The first includes vv. 1–4 (without v. 2?), the second vv. 5 and 9–12. My own inclination is to understand v. 13 as a note of the Evangelist's, because of its prose style. The second section is longer than the first because the weight falls on it, so far as the sense is concerned. We could, however, reasonably ask whether v. 9, too, ought not to be ascribed to the Evangelist. It is at least stylistically striking that the main sentence has attached to it, first a relative clause, then a phrase in apposition. The rabbinic twist in 9c indicates prose. Governed perhaps by an accurate intuition, Bultmann tried to make the last line a piece of rewriting by the Evangelist.[64] The determining adjective of 9a, *ἀληθινόν*, is, more than anything else, typical of the Evangelist.[65] Verse 10 links excellently with v. 5. The insertion of v. 9 is easy to understand in view of the necessity to link up again with the hymn after the words about the Baptist. Verse 10 could certainly not follow v. 8 without some connecting link. On this point Baldensperger was very definite:

The whole content of v. 9 contrasts as clearly as anyone could wish with v. 8 and yet at the same time serves as its completion, so that there is

[60] Bauer, p. 14. [61] *Loc. cit.* [62] Ruckstuhl, p. 93.

[63] For this is what the following section is primarily about – not the advent, which Ruckstuhl (pp. 76f., 86f.) emphasizes so strongly and which he draws out of his hypothetical periphrastic constructions in v. 9. Thus the 'came' in 11a is in parallelism with 'was' in 10a and delimits the phenomenon of the coming.

[64] *Eucharisterion*, p. 19 n. 4.

[65] Ruckstuhl, pp. 80f., naturally disputes this but has to concede the antithetical character of the adjective.

absolutely no justification for separating the verses or for the hypothesis that a new section begins at v. 9.[66]

Ruckstuhl's verdict is similar: he emphasizes strongly the epexegetic character of the relative clause as well, and concludes with the biting comment that, if the text had actually been handed down in the sequence 5, 9, 10, 11, 'Bultmann would undoubtedly single out v. 9 as the unhappy interpolation of a redactor.'[67] There are therefore, in spite of everything, very weighty reasons on the side of this proposal. If we allow it to stand, the first part of the hymn contains seven (eight) lines. The second, up to the end of v. 11, would also contain seven lines. Verse 12 could then be regarded as the culmination of the whole. In it is summed up, as a resumé, what was achieved by the manifestation of the Revealer. The length of the verse, too, becomes comprehensible if seen in this light. I cannot myself quite see how the last line can be ascribed to the Evangelist's redaction. Its appositional character is the sole evidence for this suggestion. In any case its content offers no difficulties within the context of a Christian hymn. The addition of the explanatory comment of v. 13 would even be easier to understand if 12c belonged to the original source. It is as if those who composed the hymn are stepping forward and saying together that there is one condition to be fulfilled, and one only, if men desire to participate in sonship to God: it is granted only to those who have faith in his Name.

I have now reached the first objective of my analysis, having attempted to illuminate in my own fashion the structure and the genesis of the Prologue; I must now turn to my second task, namely the exposition of the Evangelist's purpose in the composition of the Prologue. The methodological key to this operation I find in an evaluation of the fact that the Evangelist provided the hymn which he had before him with an epilogue – i.e. vv. 14–18. His purpose should become plain in this epilogue, if anywhere. From now on, therefore, we must concern ourselves with the analysis of these verses. Once again, in so doing, we shall have to come to terms with Bultmann's argument and interpretation which not only reach their culmination at this point but also radiate a magnetic power which could not but exercise the strongest possible influence on subsequent Johannine scholarship. Once again, too, I take as my starting-point a relatively compact

[66] Baldensperger, pp. 9f. [67] Ruckstuhl, p. 81.

summary of Bultmann's theses. Its characteristic mark is to be found in the fact that it makes v. 14a the fulcrum of its exegesis.[68] In so doing, it is undoubtedly swimming with the stream of the prevailing tradition and thus it is no accident that the first words are:

> As with the *incarnatus est* of the Mass, a new tone sets in here.

Certainly, it takes its unmistakable shape from the radicalism which is expressed by the sentence which immediately follows:

> The event of revelation is a question-mark, a scandal. This is what the *ὁ λόγος σὰρξ ἐγένετο* is saying, and nothing else.[69]

The foundation for this judgment is laid by the statements:

> The Revealer is nothing other than a man. . . . The Logos is now present as he who has become flesh and as no one else. . . . In his humanity pure and simple he is the Revealer.[70]

Of course, Bultmann has then to put to himself the question as to what is the significance of the fact that the Evangelist continues: 'We saw his glory.' His answer runs thus:

> If the glory had not been there, there could be no talk of revelation. But this is precisely the paradox, which runs through the whole Gospel; the *doxa* is not to be seen alongside the *sarx* or through it, as through something which is transparent, yet it is to be seen nowhere else than in the *sarx* and our regard must continually and firmly be fixed on the *sarx* and never allow itself to be drawn away, if its desire is to see the *doxa*. Revelation is therefore present in a peculiar hiddenness.[71]

This theme is developed in antithesis to the gnostic view of revelation as a natural process within the cosmos, in which redemption does not really apply to the individual but, basically, only to the species; in antithesis also to the view of the Revealer as the mediator of a gnosis, the reception of which in effect makes the Revealer himself superfluous; finally, in antithesis to the 'pietistic misunderstanding'. This last understands the humanity of the Revealer

> not as offence and paradox, but as an act of condescension which makes the Revealer immediately perceptible . . ., relieves the man who encounters him of his anxiety and opens up to him a human and personal relationship to the Revealer. The humanity of the Revealer here is his immediate accessibility which causes him to awake trust and to have a moving effect on those who encounter him.

[68] Commentary, pp. 38ff. [69] *Ibid.*, p. 39. [70] *Ibid.*, p. 40. [71] *Ibid.*, p. 41.

Against this view Bultmann writes, with cutting emphasis:

> But it is man and only man who is immediately accessible and not the Logos; that this man is the Logos, I can in any event know only outside of and alongside my knowledge of him as man. But this means that, in any such understanding of the Logos, becoming man is never seen as the decisive event of revelation. Thus the Johannine portrayal of the Revealer who has become flesh has no trace of this immediate accessibility; to meet him is to be faced with a question, not to be persuaded of something.[72]

Equally forceful is the warning against the danger of seeing the Revealer as the mediator of a general truth:

> But in John, to meet with him who has become man is to meet with the Revealer himself; he does not bring teaching which renders him superfluous in himself but, as the one who has become man, he sets every man to face the decisive question as to what that man's attitude to himself is. Thus the Gospel is already preparing its peculiar embarrassment for us, namely, that it does not give us a 'teaching' of Jesus in the proper sense. . . .[73] The intention of this construct becomes quite clear when the 'we saw his glory' is interpreted in the following sense: in the revelation of the glory there is no question of a demonstration visible to the natural eyes whether of the body or of the soul, fascinating and convincing the natural man; *doxa* is not some quality the Revealer has but the Revealer himself, inasmuch as he makes real to believers what he is, and those behold his glory who, as believers, allow him to be for them the one he is.[74]

Such detailed quotation has been necessary, not only to bring out the closed circle character of the interpretation, but also to allow criticism the requisite freedom of manoeuvre. For in so far as these utterances claim to be exegesis, they seem to me to contain a strange mixture of truth and falsehood.

According to my own analysis of the structure of the Prologue, I must first of all say that I can no longer accept Bultmann's interpretation as correctly distributing the stresses. I find myself taking offence at its very first sentence and thereby raising again a question we have already asked. How far is it true that a new tone sets in at 14a? That it does so at the *incarnatus est* in the Mass is beyond question. But the situation is different in the Prologue because in vv. 5–13 there has already been mention of the historical-eschatological manifestation of the Logos. So can ὁ λόγος σὰρξ ἐγένετο mean anything different from the ἐν τῷ κοσμῷ ἦν of 10a, especially as Bultmann describes the

[72] *Ibid.*, p. 43. [73] *Ibid.*, p. 42. [74] *Ibid.*, p. 45.

becoming flesh as the appearance of the Logos in the sphere of the this-worldly and the human, its transience, its helplessness, its nothingness and the seductive power of what lies before the eyes?[75] In other words, is 14a anything more than the mere taking over of what has already been said in the hymn, a phrase of connection and transition which allows the Evangelist to come now to what is really important to himself and to declare the purpose of quoting the hymn? Harnack asked this long ago. He begins by characterizing dialectically the position he intends to dispute:

> The words [sc. 14a] are so powerful that they positively cannot be relegated to a secondary place. It is therefore *a priori* certain that the theology of the Fourth Evangelist is to be understood in the light of them.[76]

But he raises an immediate objection:

> Nowhere does the Fourth Evangelist display anything of the intoxicating impression which posterity was to gain from the ὁ λόγος σὰρξ ἐγένετο; nowhere does he produce a formulation flowing from this statement.

Indeed, the 'coming from above' rather than the becoming flesh is probably the decisive thing for this gospel.[77] He says very astringently:

> A strongly expressed idea does not always take effect in the direction and in the proportion intended by its originator, but according to its own inner logic and its own balance of forces. . . . The idea ὁ λόγος σὰρξ ἐγένετο has had a history which was not that designed for it originally by the Fourth Evangelist.[78]

Overbeck's judgment is more pungent still; he maintains that the historical significance of 14a is due to

> theological reflection which was to discover in this point – so smoothly by-passed by the main stream of the Gospel – an intellectual somersault, and with it the sanctification of all further somersaults of the same kind. The Evangelist certainly had no inkling of the meaning which was later to be attached to his sentence.[79]

Finally, Baldensperger is making the same point when he says:

> In John's original conception, *sarkosis* is only the means by which the *doxa* of the Logos becomes evident to the senses . . . it is for this reason that the Evangelist, after he has announced the historical happening, hastens

[75] *Ibid.*, pp. 39f. [76] *ZTK* 2, p. 227. [77] *Ibid.*, p. 228. [78] *Ibid.*, p. 231.
[79] Overbeck (see n. 27), pp. 376f.

to proclaim the purpose of it (which, in his view, is the main point here) namely, the revelation of the *doxa* of the Logos.[80]

This is characteristic of the whole Gospel, in which the humanity of Christ recedes totally into the background.[81]

Only the *word* σάρξ is pronounced. But where is the actuality? . . .[82] The Prologue never loses sight of the programme laid down for it by the Evangelist – καὶ ἐθεασάμεθα τὴν δόξαν αὐτοῦ, the heavenly glory of him who has become flesh. This presupposes that, according to the original intention of the Evangelist, the becoming flesh does not fit in to the Prologue in the way which the Church soon came, for dogmatic reasons, to assume that it did and which was therefore read back into the text.[83]

We have to keep statements like this in our mind if we are to understand the alignment Bultmann is taking up. Only then can we evaluate the particular stress he lays on 14a and comprehend the content of the new element which, for him, enters in at that point. It finds expression in the following sentence: 'In this sphere the Logos appears, i.e. the Revealer is a man and nothing else.'[84] This might have been put another way: he became a man in weakness, helplessness, nothingness, as a man he was exposed to the seductive power of what lay before his eyes. But Bultmann with cheerful pungency, uses the formula 'a man and nothing else' and speaks immediately afterwards of 'pure and simple humanity'. This is the new tone which vv. 5ff. did not in fact as yet contain. This is the centre and the basis of all Bultmann's subsequent arguments which only make sense if we make this our point of departure. We have not yet reached the question of the dogmatic concern of this interpretation; we are only as far as its exegetical and historical justification. Everything depends on whether it is both possible and legitimate to eliminate from 14a this 'and nothing else', the phrase about 'pure and simple humanity'. We have to return a negative to this question if 14a does nothing more than take up 10a and make a transition to what follows, as I myself should prefer to assume and, as the basis of my analysis of the structure properly may assume.

Admittedly, an immediate objection to this view may be made on the grounds that 14a deliberately does not speak merely of becoming man or of existence in the world, but of becoming flesh.[85] Is it not

[80] Baldensperger (see n. 31), p. 31.
[81] *Ibid.*, p. 32. [82] *Ibid.*, p. 35. [83] *Ibid.*, pp. 36f. [84] Commentary, p. 40.
[85] So B. Weiss, p. 10, and Strathmann, p. 37 (see n. 27).

precisely in the use of the concept σάρξ that Bultmann's 'a man and nothing else', the 'pure and simple humanity' is expressed? This touches on a very difficult problem over which it may now be impossible to reach any agreement. Compared with Paul, John speaks surprisingly little of σάρξ and, when he does so, is obviously moving throughout along traditional lines. Even if we leave the authenticity of 6.51–58 unquestioned, we can still find there nothing more than prefabricated eucharistic terminology. In 3.6 we have an axiom which breathes the atmosphere of Hellenistic dualism and a radicalism which the Evangelist himself certainly does not share. He is concerned with the possibility of rebirth in which flesh does *not* remain flesh but becomes spirit. Only in so far as this possibility is miracle – that is, does not stand within the power of man to compass – is the Evangelist able to take and use this axiom which is so characteristic of his environment. Like the sentence itself, the σάρξ concept it contains is re-interpreted by him and this explains why he does not bring out the antithesis of σάρξ and πνεῦμα as Paul does. In 17.2, 'Thou hast given him power over all flesh', as in 1.13, John has taken over the linguistic usage of the Judaism of the Old Testament in which man is designated 'flesh' in his stance over against God. The equally conventional text 8.15, 'You judge according to the flesh', has the same sense. What is meant is undoubtedly something like 'as men do'. We have left only the verse with which we are now concerned, and 6.63, – 'the flesh is of no avail'; and here we see the real crux of John's use of σάρξ: are we firmly to interpret the first of these texts in the light of the second? I believe that we must certainly answer this question in the negative. 6.63, like 3.6, is also an axiom which has sprung from dualistic soil. The antithesis of flesh and spirit which determines its meaning is *not* characteristic of our Evangelist. It is thus reinterpreted in a certain direction by its context. In the light of the previous verse, the manifestation of the ascending Christ is seen as πνεῦμα, while in the light of the subsequent verse the 'word of life' is seen as a heavenly gift. Once again σάρξ is therefore being understood as the sphere and manifestation of the earthly. Naturally this sharply dualistic mode of expression cannot simply be dismissed as having no significance for our Evangelist. But it presents only a very faint possibility within the framework of a linguistic usage to garner which he has had to range far abroad and to harvest many different fields: this possibility he exploits, as it were, very gingerly and then places his own interpretation upon it. His point of departure, like that of the letters of Ignatius, is the identification of 'flesh' with what is human and earthly. The earthly has a double character; it is either that which, over against the heavenly world, is subordinate, limited and in need of divine help and illumination *or* that which, over against the heavenly world, strives for its autonomy and rejects divine help and illumination. Thus the aspect under which it appears and the verdict which is passed upon it vary. But the burden of creatureliness never fades; it is most distinctly heard where the earthly, according to the Gospel, is able, indeed compelled, to be an intimation of the heavenly, in that the peculiar property of the creation consists in its being oriented towards the Creator. If we take all these findings together we shall at least no longer be able to say with Heitmüller: 'The flesh is the extreme of opposition to all divine existence';[86] we shall agree with Barrett that '*σάρξ* in John is not evil in itself . . ., but stands for humanity over against God.'[87] The implication of this for the exegesis of 1.14 is this: 'flesh as the place where the Word of God is recognized.'[88] What is meant is, quite simply, creatureliness in the whole range of its possibilities. The paradox – and there certainly *is* a paradox – in 1.14a consists in the fact that the Creator enters the world of createdness and in so doing exposes himself to the judgment of the creature, not stopping at complete rejection or at crucifixion. That this is what it is really all about, and nothing else, the continuation *καὶ ἐσκήνενσεν ἐν ἡμῖν* in 14b, shows conclusively. The 'presence of God' on earth is the real goal of the becoming flesh. This 'presence of God' on earth may be combined with the stumbling block to men, but this does not in any way imply that the becoming flesh as such is the stumbling block. It is true that the Jews take offence at the fact that Jesus, whose earthly lineage they think they know, designates himself the Son of God. But this offence is on the same level as that which Pilate feels in the face of the King of Truth. In any event we may say of him that in him the scandal is raised to a higher power. But he is not to be identified with it without remainder, because otherwise the miracles of Jesus, especially the raising of Lazarus, would be bound to rob this scandal of its force; while, according to John, it is the miracles which do in fact constitute the motive for the killing of Jesus. The real scandal to the world represented by the Jews lies here: the Jesus who appears on earth makes himself equal to God and proclaims his unity with the Father, that is, he claims obedience

[86] Heitmüller (see n. 27), p. 44. [87] Barrett (see n. 12), p. 137. [88] *Loc. cit.*

as Creator over against creature. The world refuses to its Creator the obedience which is owed to him and excuses its attitude with every kind of evasion, including the humanity of Jesus and the demand for authentication which arises from it. To the world, however, the scandal is not really the mode of Jesus' claim on the obedience of the creature but the fact of the claim itself; or, more sharply expressed, not the becoming man as such but its function, i.e. that by means of it God moves in to the attack. The world survives by keeping God at a distance even while it is making him a manageable and predictable object of its speculations, as its religious traditions have brought it up to do. Through Jesus this safe distance is annihilated. His becoming flesh is the manifestation of the Creator on earth, as we are meant to conclude both from 14b, with its continuation in 14c, and from the use of *σκηνοῦν* which is taken from the vocabulary of revelation. If this is true, however, then the *σάρξ* concept does not provide a justification of Bultmann's interpretation of 14a. 'Flesh' for the Evangelist here is nothing else but the possibility for the Logos, as the Creator and Revealer, to have communication with men. 14a takes up 10a and makes the transition to what follows. The theme for which this transitional phrase prepares the way, is stated in 14c: 'We beheld his glory.' This theme is at the same time that of the whole Gospel which is concerned exclusively throughout with the presence of God in Christ.

We have now to make this hypothesis secure on several fronts. In settling my account with Bultmann, I have given the appearance of relapsing completely into the position of Harnack, Baldensperger and Overbeck. The dangerous nature of this position, however, becomes clear when Overbeck can produce a formulation of this kind: 'Indeed, he has appeared in this fleshly form so that his heavenly glory may become visible to men.'[89] Or, again, when Baldensperger states that the act of incarnation makes the glory of the Logos more accessible to the senses of man:

> Not until he veiled himself in flesh could the divine Logos come as near to men as was possible to him. While in his previous state he came only infrequently to his own, he came now to dwell permanently among them.[90]

It is evident that the idea of transparence, against which Bultmann contends so passionately, is being employed here.[91] But in so doing

[89] Overbeck, p. 376. [90] Baldensperger, p. 37.

[91] Cf. *ibid.*, p. 38: the *sarx* is no veil 'designed to conceal the glory, but the means

the writer is failing to understand the nature of the peculiar dialectic which determines the Johannine concept of 'seeing'. Man can never see the Creator in the same sense in which he can see a phenomenon within the created world.[92] He can only be seen in reality by those who hear and obey him. If it were otherwise, we might come face to face with a wonder but not with the Lord, who does not expose himself to the neutral observer. It is precisely the Logos predication which should make us heed the fact that we can only discern the Creator in the process of acknowledging his claim and in becoming aware that our existence is oriented towards him. So it is not even true of the exalted Lord, let alone of the incarnate, that he came to dwell permanently among his own. The farewell discourses, which circle round this problem, show that clearly. Though from this point of view Bultmann's polemic against the use of the idea of transparence is wholly justified, conversely it certainly runs the risk of shattering the Johannine dialectic of 'seeing' and 'believing' from the other side and of interpreting the incarnation of the Logos in the sense of the kenosis doctrine; this is proved by the formulations 'a man and nothing else' and 'pure and simple humanity'. We must maintain emphatically that, according to the Fourth Evangelist (and, for that matter, according to the Synoptists) he who has become flesh does not cease to exist as a heavenly being;[93] that he undergoes no 'transformation';[94] and that John, as Schlatter expresses it, did not feel the activity of the Word in his fleshy state to be a humiliation.[95] 'The idea of a God appearing on earth in the form of a man would have nothing incredible about it for the first readers of the Gospel,' states W. Bauer with absolute pertinence.[96] What he is getting at here can also be put this way: as it is only the believer who, according to the Johannine message, really sees, so in Jesus the world acquires something which is always there to see. Bultmann has rightly pointed out with unmistakable force that the Johannine Christ brings with him

---

to display it to the best advantage'. B. Weiss, p. 10: the flesh designates the side of his being by which humanity, orientated towards sensible experience, could recognize him. Tillmann (see n. 27), p. 60: the divine glory shines through the veil of the flesh.

[92] Cf. on this point Bultmann, 'Untersuchungen zum Johannesevangelium', *ZNW* 29, 1930, pp. 169ff.

[93] Loisy (see n. 27), p. 186; Baldensperger, p. 55; W. Bauer (see n. 27), p. 23; Wikenhauser (see n. 26), p. 41; Barrett, p. 138.

[94] Lagrange (see n. 27), p. 20. [95] Schlatter (see n. 34), p. 22.

[96] Bauer, p. 23.

no information about the nature of the heavenly and no specific teaching other than his proclamation of his own person; and that, in the message of Jesus, the *fact* of his mission quite stifles the *mode* of it. Yet it does not seem to me a tenable position to couple this remarkable phenomenon with a second – the alleged fact that pure and simple humanity is at the heart of the Johannine concern. Such a perspective is obliged to operate in abstraction from the mighty works unhesitatingly performed by the Christ of the Fourth Gospel. Indeed, he provides the world with so much to see that the miracles, and in particular the raising of Lazarus, lead to his death. This situation is not altered by the fact that the world takes his miracles as mere wonders and thus renders them unfruitful. Incarnation for John is really epiphany.[97] God does not merely speak, when he becomes man, nor does he call forth mere speech in return. As Bultmann has always very strongly maintained, his revelation is act; not only because it is a summons but also because it is accompanied by miracle and signs. Thus, in a certain sense, John depicts the *mode* of revelation no less than do the other Evangelists. While the discourses direct our attention almost exclusively to the *fact* of the mission of Jesus, this preoccupation cannot possibly be derived from the interest in the pure and simple humanity of Jesus. It is not without reason that two millennia have loved the Fourth Gospel because it portrayed Jesus as the God who walked the earth. But how then is the obviously theologically conditioned reduction of the message of Jesus to his self-proclamation, to the fact of his mission, to be interpreted? The Evangelist answers this question by emphasizing the ambiguous nature of all signs and the world's hunger for wonders. Everything depends on understanding the miracles of Jesus correctly, that is, as pointers to the Creator who is revealing his glory. The gifts may not be isolated from the Giver; for, when that happens, we are back with wonder-working. John does not deny the reality and factual nature of the miracles; he renders to the God who gives (not less but) more glory than the other Evangelists. But, by reducing the content of the message to the fact of the mission of Jesus, he is expressing the truth that it is not the gifts as such but only the Creator – or, more exactly, the presence of the Creator – which is and conveys the salvation of the creature. The 'presence of God' shown forth in the Revealer is more than each gift and deed taken in isolation. It is not only more decisive but the only decisive factor. What is at issue, then,

[97] Loisy, p. 186.

in the theological reductionism of the discourses is not the pure and simple humanity of Jesus but the content of the message; 'one thing is needful', namely, that the Creator should become contemporary and present with his creatures. Only where that is heard and understood can the further assertion be made, that the Creator does not come to meet his creatures with empty hands and does not merely speak to them but manifests himself as Creator in miracles and signs as well as in his word. If this were not so, he would not be the Creator who dispenses the bread and water of life, the wine of perfect joy, salvation from the sickness unto death, light for the blind, the way and the door for those who have gone astray, a home for those who are oppressed and the resurrection of the dead. One is inclined to say that in the Fourth Gospel demonstrations are continually taking place. But they remain empty demonstrations or demonstrations which do nothing but harden those to whom they are addressed, unless they are interpreted as signs of the presence of the Creator on earth, of the 'present Christ'; this is what happens in the discourses with their grandiose and monotonous restriction to a single theme.

The reciprocal of this 'presence of God' on earth is the immediacy of the encounter with the Revealer and so with God himself when man believes and obeys the word of the 'preached Christ'. This is the background against which we must interpret the absence of any conception of an ecclesiastically privileged ministry, an absence which shows up most clearly in the lack of any emphasis on the apostolate and in the way in which the apostles cede pride of place to the 'beloved disciple'. The same is equally true of the relative, or, if with Bultmann we assume editorial insertions at this point – the absolute unimportance of the sacramental element in this Gospel, for which I should contend strongly, even against O. Cullmann's *Early Christian Worship*.[98] If John really does belong to the third Christian generation such reserve over against the sacramental is unheard of. It only becomes comprehensible when we assume here also an attitude of deliberate antithesis: over against early catholicism, proclaiming as it does the mediation of truth and grace through Church, ministry and sacrament, John declares that salvation lies only in an immediate encounter with the Revealer and that such an encounter arises only out of the preached Word. It is obvious that the complex of problems demarcated by Dodd in his formula 'realized escha-

[98] O. Cullmann, *Urchristentum und Gottesdienst*, 2nd ed., 1950; ET *Early Christian Worship* (SBT 10), 1953.

tology' and by Bultmann in his formula 'present eschatology' can equally well be interpreted from this angle; where the immediacy of the encounter with the Revealer is at issue, primitive Christian apocalyptic, even if it does not completely disappear, is bound to recede into the remote background. Then, conversely, the problems of 'first- and second-hand disciples' as in 4.35ff., and of the distance between the believer and his exalted Lord become acute and unavoidable. The strict theological consistency of the Evangelist is manifested here: he makes no attempt to escape these problems and even imports his own viewpoint into the narrative material by portraying the ideal disciple in the person of 'the disciple whom Jesus loved'. In this disciple, lying as he does on the bosom of Jesus, there is reflected the direct relation of the Son to the Father, for, according to 1.18, Jesus is for ever in the bosom of the Father.

In this last section of our discussion we have been employing the Gospel as a kind of commentary to help us to make out the sense of the phrase 'We saw his glory'. The justification for this procedure was that we ascribed vv. 14–18 to the pen of the Evangelist. It became quite clear that 14a was to be regarded as the premiss of what followed. As certainly as it is the believers who say 'We saw', equally certainly the content of their seeing is the godhead of Jesus as the Revealer who brings eschatological salvation to the world. It is precisely this which is the concern of the last verses of the Prologue also. As the Baptist has borne witness to the pre-existence of him who is the Creator, so the Christian community – 'we all' – bears witness to the eschatological manifestation of heavenly fullness and divine salvation in him. Here we must disagree, on critical grounds, with Schlier. He, too, states that in Jesus we encounter, 'that ground of the world which creates and illumines life', and continues:

> But if, in our encounter with the incarnate Word Jesus Christ, all these themes of creation are repeated on a higher plane, this means that in the processes of faith we have to do with phenomena that are not primarily psychological and moral, but ontological.

Schlier puts on his words the further gloss that 'life on the basis of reality' is here opening up.[99] This is what German Idealism was thinking and saying, in Fichte's advice on the happy life for example, although Schlier naturally does not intend to be understood in the Idealistic sense. But he will be hard put to it to prevent anyone who

[99] Schlier (see n. 26), p. 286.

is unable to share his catholic outlook from relapsing into Idealism if they adopt his premisses. Where the Johannine Prologue is approached from the viewpoint of an ontology, this is not only possible but logically necessary. I hardly need to observe expressly that, on the basis of my own analysis, I am bound to protest against such an interpretation. But I can easily comprehend the logic of this once one accepts Schlier's analysis, which rests on Augustine and which finds the principal concern of the Prologue in two propositions: the first, one which 'is also acknowledged by the philosopher, that of the originating Word as the ground of existence' and the second 'which is for him incomprehensibly foolish, that of the incarnation of the Word in the Person of Jesus Christ'.[100] It is easy to show that Schlier is here echoing in his own way the prevailing view of the purpose of the Prologue. Almost always the balance of interpretation tends towards setting christology in the centre of the Prologue. Even Bultmann has, as we saw, not been able to eschew this tendency, however much his interpretation may differ from others. But it seems to me thoroughly questionable whether it is really the intention of the Prologue 'to say as expressly and succinctly as possible who it is with whom we have to do in the historical figure of Jesus Christ'.[101] The concern of the hymn is, in any event, unequivocally and exclusively soteriological. The mythological language in vv. 1–2 only serves to remove the Logos from the realm of createdness and to prepare the Creator-predication in v. 3. The conclusion of the hymn, in which the fruit of the saving work is set out, makes it clear beyond a peradventure that the door is not being opened to any ontology. But the Evangelist allows the weight of his propositions to fall not on 14a but on 14c. He has no ontological interest here either. What then is he really trying to do?

We have paid some attention to the change from the 'he' to the 'we' form of expression in v. 14, introducing as it does a confession of faith. What is happening here is *not* (as Harnack thought) that

> the statements about the Person which in the first half were brought forward as propositions are now being reiterated on the basis of subjective impression and spiritual achievement.[102]

Nevertheless he is right in pointing us to the experience theme, which is being expressed in these verses and was even more clearly detected

[100] *Ibid.*, pp. 284f. [101] Strathmann (see n. 27), p. 28.
[102] Harnack (see n. 1), p. 222.

by Overbeck,[103] B. Weiss[104] and Strathmann.[105] Schlier formulates this theme in conclusive terms: 'Now it is the turn of those who have received him and therefore recognized him to put their experience into words.'[106] Here we have the real concern of the Prologue brought before us. Our immediate task now is to see that the proclamation of the Evangelist is rescued from the isolation which seems to inhere in every proclamation associated with an individual and which in the case of the Fourth Evangelist is greater than usual. Behind him and his message, which can so easily be understood as the expression of an idiosyncratic and aberrant theology, there stands the witness of the community. But this statement is not sufficient in itself. The 'we saw' of 14c and 'we have all received' of 16a have too strong a tone. The Gospel which now follows could be regarded, as I am convinced Luke is to be regarded, as historically an introduction to 'the time of the Church'. The Evangelist sets his 'we saw' over against any such conception. In this Gospel we are to be concerned not with a past happening in history but with the 'presence of Christ'. What is reported in what follows, according to the testimony of the community (which is not restricted here to eye-witnesses in the historical sense), is the eschatological presence of salvation. '*Tua res agitur*': that is the sense of the footnote with which the Evangelist provides the hymn, and the real reason for prefacing it with a Prologue at all. It is in the interests of this total conception that the Baptist is introduced as early as the Prologue; the mention of him (at least, according to v. 15) is in no way designed to have an exclusively polemic or apologetic character. The Gospel does not exist without the confessing community, whose first representative John the Baptist was. This community prevents an historicizing misunderstanding of the testimony about Jesus. The Prologue is therefore neither a summary of the Gospel nor a pedagogic introduction for the Hellenistic reader. It must, like the Gospel, itself be theologically understood: it bears witness to the presence of the Christ, whose earthly history lies now nineteen hundred years in the past, as the Creator of eschatological sonship to God and of the new world.[107]

[103] Overbeck (see n. 27), p. 431. [104] B. Weiss (see n. 27), p. 16.
[105] Strathmann, p. 29. [106] Schlier, p. 281.
[107] I must take at least brief note here of E. Haenchen's essay 'Probleme des johanneischen Prologs', *ZTK* 60, 1963, pp. 305–34, which has appeared since my own article first appeared. Together with R. Schnackenburg's 'Logoshymnus und johanneischer Prolog', *BZ*, NF 1, 1957, pp. 69–109, I regard it as the most important recent contribution to the discussion. But while it would be necessary to

make a comprehensive and detailed treatment of Schnackenburg, certain of Haenchen's basic findings and decisions provoke me to immediate contradiction. We are agreed on the stylistic question: there is no strict symmetry to be found in the verse structure here. But this assessment should not lead us to view with a jaundiced eye *every* hypothesis of a construction by strophes. I find it incomprehensible, for instance, when Phil. 2.6ff. is *not* divided up into two strophes. I Cor. 13, however, is certainly not a hymn but a prose composition in the language of the Wisdom literature, and thus cannot be used here for purposes of comparison. But if Haenchen is going to maintain that the verses even after v. 12 are deliberately interlinked, he ought not to dismiss as lightly as he does the difference between his version and Bultmann's outline of the verse structure in 1–5 and 10–12b. We are rather deeper into the business of primitive Christian hymns than Haenchen makes it appear or is prepared to admit. It is obvious that he cannot very well speak of strophes if the verses before v. 14 refer only to the *Logos asarkos*. But it is a principle which obtains today far beyond the field of theology that stylistic research has to precede the historical question and the interpretation of content and must, as far as is possible, be kept separate from them. For my part, I can find absolutely no further reference to the *Logos asarkos* after v. 5. Whether in the last resort what is said has its roots in the mythological concept of the truth which has nowhere to lay its head is, in any event, not the decisive factor in the meaning of our verses. I cannot myself interpret such statements as that the light shines in the darkness, was in the world, created division, in a timeless sense. That can only be maintained at all if we treat v. 12 as not original, and I cannot agree to do this. The relationship between protasis and apodosis, which Haenchen feels to be a problem, reflects, admittedly in modified form, the relationship of summons and promise. Sonship to God is not something which we take for ourselves. It is something which is granted to us. Above all, Haenchen does not seem to me to have considered the point that such an emphatic and detailed utterance about the *Logos asarkos* would set up a violent tension with v. 18. On his logic, it would not be possible to say 'No man has seen God'. I am only outlining my thesis here, as otherwise I should have (as in regard to Schnackenburg) to rewrite my whole essay, without expressing differently anything of real importance. I am therefore contenting myself with indicating the different direction in which I should set the points. The reader may then see for himself which position he must choose.

My analysis certainly entails one conclusion which does not square with that of Haenchen, to the effect that we have here the 'proper beginning' of the Gospel, 'the primal origin of Christian salvation history and revelation' (p. 308). This is totally consistent with the logic of his analysis: the circles contract until the incarnation is reached. Such a conclusion is to a great extent not only what we have to expect from an interpretation but also what is left over after it has been made. That does not seem to me to be inconsiderable. We have no complete monopoly of truth, whereas clarity is being demanded of us. If we bear this fact in mind, Haenchen's criticism of his partners in dialogue on p. 307 is hard by any standards. He, too, in his own way 'has aimed at settling all the problems at one blow' and, indeed, *has* so settled them – not, to my mind, without violence: to ascribe vv. 6–8, 12–13 and 15 to the redactor and not to the Evangelist seems to me to be violence and, on my presuppositions, unnecessary violence at that, and we have to ask ourselves yet again whether this does not expose the problematical nature of the whole thesis. The lines of reasoning which lead to the thesis I hope confidently to be able to refute completely. They stem from the particular total understanding of the Johannine theology and of what was possible for the Evangelist. But that takes us into so wide a field that I am not prepared to begin upon it within the framework of a supplementary note, especially as it fell to me to discuss very thoroughly the essay 'The Father who sent me', *NTS* 9, 1962–3, pp. 208–16, and, furthermore, I would want to portray the Johannine christology in very different terms.

Here and now I should like simply to point out that the 'beginning' in vv. 1–18 does not simply continue in vv. 19ff. A deep gulf separates the style even more than the pericopae. That beginning loses more and more as it goes on the narrative character – if it ever had it – which Haenchen's thesis obliges him to postulate for it. From v. 14 at the very least, it has quite unequivocally the character of a confession of faith. But to say that is to affect the whole and its relationship to what follows. Confession is, in the last resort, quite distinct from narrative and is thus not merely a 'beginning', which can be continued in historical or historicizing fashion. I agree with Haenchen in refusing to understand the Prologue as either a summary or an introduction for the Hellenistic reader. I disagree with him in understanding it not as the beginning of a salvation history, but as an indication of direction for the Gospel and the readers for whom it is meant, which really anticipates the conclusion: 'It is with the story of the Son of God that we have to do' (20.31).

VII

'THE RIGHTEOUSNESS OF GOD' IN PAUL*

THE EPISTLE TO THE ROMANS subsumes the whole of the preaching and theology of Paul under the one head – the self-revealing righteousness of God. In so doing, it undoubtedly gives to the unique Pauline message a nucleus and a name which bring its own peculiar nature into the sharpest possible relief against the background of the rest of the New Testament. Conversely, the central problem of Pauline theology is concentrated in this theme, as I shall remind you briefly in my first section. For only if we keep this problem and its centrality clearly in front of our eyes have we any

* 'Gottesgerechtigkeit bei Paulus', a short lecture delivered at the Oxford Congress on 'The New Testament Today' on 14 September, 1961, and first published in *ZTK* 58, 1961, pp. 367–78. The exegetical and systematic disputation with other interpretations which would normally take place on such an occasion could not be carried out in detail within this framework. For this reason also, the logical consequences of my own understanding of the matter are indicated rather than developed. But I should like to refer specifically to the criticism by Bultmann in his article '*Δικαιοσύνη θεοῦ*', *JBL* 83, 1964, pp. 12–16. I have to say that this criticism once again isolates the problem which, by the use of numerous analogies and passages with related content within the Pauline theology, I here set against a wider horizon; and that it does not touch upon the relationship of this concept to the outlook of the Thanksgiving Psalms of Qumran, where I myself find the eschatological 'Now' and the Jewish formula disputed by Bultmann to be very clearly expressed. I also lay the strongest possible emphasis on the fact that the dominating sense of the divine righteousness in Paul is that of a gift; thus, Bultmann's reiterated proof of this point is otiose. Similarly, I do *not* maintain that the concept 'must have the same meaning throughout the Pauline corpus'. On the contrary, my essay begins from the premiss that this is not the case. Only when this premiss is laid down, do I go on to try to show that, so far as tradition goes, the sense 'the power which brings salvation' continues to occur here, is met only rarely in Paul in the direct usage, but qualifies throughout the sense 'divine gift', so that gift and Giver remain inseparable. In brief, the issue is whether the context and Pauline theology as a whole permit us to absolutize the meaning 'gift', which, from a merely superficial examination of the various concepts involved, certainly does present itself to us as primary; and in so doing to explain all passages which do not fit in with this view as rhetorical. Bultmann does not explicitly discuss this question, but implicitly dismisses it.

chance of attaining that precision in interpretation which is so necessary at just this point and which, as I see it, has not, in spite of very various attempts, yet been satisfactorily achieved.

Our difficulties begin immediately, with the question as to whether the genitive construction δικαιοσύνη θεοῦ is to be construed as subjective or objective, as the righteousness which belongs to God and proceeds from him or as the righteousness which is acceptable in God's eyes and bestowed by him upon us. It is beyond dispute that the general tenor of the Pauline utterances on the subject, like that of the Reformation tradition which determines our attitude, tells in favour of the objective genitive. Phil. 3.9 emphatically and, as has been said, with an air of authentic interpretation, sets the δικαιοσύνη ἐκ θεοῦ over against Paul's own righteousness. According to Rom. 2.13, our status παρὰ τῷ θεῷ is characterized by δικαιοῦσθαι and its cognates. The fundamental either/or of righteousness by or through faith and righteousness by works is only comprehensible from this perspective, and Rom. 5.17 speaks expressly in the same sense of the δωρεὰ τῆς δικαιοσύνης. Nevertheless, we ought not to be too hastily satisfied with these very impressive arguments. Is there really no special reason why Paul should speak so emphatically of God's righteousness and not of the divine righteousness bestowed upon us, imputed to us, justifying us? Is it permissible to disregard the fact that the δικαιοσύνη θεοῦ appears in Rom. 1.17; 10.3ff. in personified form as Power and that it can therefore be identified with Christ in I Cor. 1.30 (a quotation from a Christian hymn), the further fact that in II Cor. 5.21 it is used to describe the reality of the redeemed community and, finally, the undisputed subjective genitive in Rom. 3.5, 25f., for here at least it certainly characterizes God's own activity and nature?[1] Have we here simply an expression of the Apostle's inconsistency, in which case the causes of this inconsistency have still to be brought out into the open? Or does the tension displayed here reveal the existence of a fundamental issue, the right understanding

[1] Bultmann (p. 13) cannot understand these passages except in the light of distributive justice; as I see it, here in essence is the whole problem which is at issue between us. He bases his case on ἄδικος in v. 5, and, in so doing, overlooks the parallelism between the 'righteousness' and the 'faithfulness' of God, of which vv. 4 and 25 both speak; for this reason he has to connect the activation of God's wrath in v. 5 with forgiveness in v. 25 under the master concept 'judicial righteousness'. The context, however, seems to me to show quite unambiguously that in both cases Paul is speaking of the triumphant saving faithfulness of God, which maintains the Covenant against those who transgress it and in so doing remains, and expresses his nature as, true=consistent.

of which is a necessary preliminary to making a positive or negative judgment about any more comprehensive interpretation?

The question must remain open for the time being. It is well known that there are sizable difficulties of interpretation in the 'gift' aspect of God's righteousness, and these must be taken into consideration at the very beginning. Once again I shall start from an incontrovertible fact: almost throughout, this gift is received by us as already present, is described as effective in us and through us, and II Cor. 9.9f.; Phil. 1.11 even name its fruit. It is all the more striking that Gal. 5.5 regards it as possessed only by hope and its ultimate realization as lying still in the future. In pursuing our theme we thus encounter the phenomenon usually designated, not altogether happily, as Paul's double eschatology. Even the righteousness of God is seen in this double aspect; salvation and the things which salvation brings appear sometimes as already present by faith and baptism, sometimes as only to be realized at the End through the Parousia. Further, this dialectic of having and not quite having is here projected on to the very condition of being a Christian. For *λογίζεσθαι εἰς δικαιοσύνην*, used as a technical formula in Rom. 4 and Gal. 3.6, certainly means that righteousness is only to be had on earth as a pledged gift, always subject to attack, always to be authenticated in practice – a matter of promise and expectation. Paul exemplifies in himself the meaning of Phil. 3.12:

> Not that I have already obtained this, or am already perfect, but I press on to make it my own, because Christ Jesus has made me his own.

Thus, even the gift of the divine righteousness does not bring us to the goal, but only sets our feet upon the road. It is given to us in such a manner that it lies always before us and has to be continually appropriated anew. Or, we can formulate it in terms of Rom. 5.6–10: the divine righteousness possesses us before we grasp it, and we retain it only as long as it holds us fast. The gift itself has thus the character of power. The meaning of this in concrete terms is quite clear. Paul knows no gift of God which does not convey both the obligation and the capacity to serve. A gift which is not authenticated in practice and passed on to others loses its specific content. Obviously, therefore, the breakthrough into the unceasingly renewed future of receiving and appropriating, and the consequent transformation of gift into service, is to be understood, in the light of Gal. 5.5, as the reflection of the fact that the ultimate righteousness of God is still to be realized.

We have admittedly not yet clearly established the extent to which these statements follow necessarily from the very nature of the divine gift. In no circumstances is it permissible to make the idealistic answer – namely, that this gift is, in the last resort, the principle of our vocation which we have perpetually to renew and to realize concretely by our action. For this would be to misunderstand the gift and to turn it into law, and then righteousness through works would inevitably replace righteousness through faith. But neither can support be found in the relevant passages, as has sometimes been thought, for distinguishing between the righteousness of the beginning and the righteousness of the end, between righteousness of faith and righteousness of life. Rather, this distinction, exactly like the one which former generations attempted to make between the ethical and juridical and the mystical and sacramental approaches, only reveals the logical embarrassment into which the apostle here precipitates his modern readers. The same Paul who, in Rom. 4, undoubtedly describes God's δικαιοῦν as a forensic act of declaring righteous, says with equal decision in Rom. 5.19 that the state (i.e. of justification) is founded on righteousness. He has characterized this state with particular clarity in the hymnic and liturgical passages Rom. 8.30 and I Cor. 6.11 as the reality of the transformed existence conveyed in the baptismal event, and – in accordance with the whole structure of Romans – has based on it the *nova oboedientia* of the Christian. Neither are justification and sanctification to be separated. The Christian service of God in everyday life, portrayed parenetically in Rom. 6. 11ff. and Rom. 12–14, dissolving as it does all cultus, whether Jewish or heathen, is the manifestation of God's righteousness on earth – that δουλεία τῆς δικαιοσύνης which can be properly rendered only by those to whom God has given the gift of such service and whom he has counted among his liberated children. Perhaps it may be sufficient at this point to make a brief analysis of the argument so far. My primary intention was simply to remind you and myself of the tensions associated with the Pauline doctrine of justification and with the theological dialectic which it reveals. This dialectic may rightly be explained in terms of the apostle's war on two fronts – against legalism on the one hand and enthusiasm on the other – and of his not infrequent stratagem of combating the one with the terminology and the motivation of the other. But our particular problem is to identify the unitary centre from which he managed to combine present and future eschatology, 'declare righteous' and 'make righteous', gift and service, freedom and obedience, forensic, sacramental and ethical approaches. Only after we have answered this question with the necessary clarity can we say whether it is possible – and perhaps obligatory – for us to pursue this same dialectic in our own day. In trying to establish this, we cannot be content with partial solutions even when they are correct; if particular aspects of the question are made into absolutes, as has frequently happened, the Pauline dialectic is destroyed.

I begin my own attempt to interpret the facts by stating categorically that the expression *δικαιοσύνη θεοῦ* was not invented by Paul. It appears independently in Matt. 6.33 and James 1.20 and can be traced back in the Old Testament to Deut. 33.21. Two quotations may serve to show that it persisted in late Judaism. The original text[2] of the Testament of Dan. 6.10 runs: *ἀπόστητε οὖν ἀπο πάσης ἀδικίας καὶ κολλήθητε τῇ δικαιοσύνη τοῦ θεοῦ*, and similarly, in the Rule of Qumran 11.12: 'If I stumble by reason of the wickedness of my flesh, my justification lies in the righteousness of God.' The significance of this statement is for the most part not perceived; certainly, it has not had the attention it merits. The methodological implication of Paul's adoption of a ready-made formulation is that the righteousness of God, as he uses the term, is not to be subsumed under the general concept *δικαιοσύνη* and thus deprived of its peculiar force. It is of course extremely significant that the apostle describes God's saving activity as righteousness, and we must conclude by investigating the history which lies behind this fact. From the outset it will be noticed that in the field of the Old Testament and of Judaism in general, righteousness does not convey primarily the sense of a personal, ethical quality, but of a relationship; originally signifying trustworthiness in regard to the community, it came to mean the rehabilitated standing of a member of the community who had been acquitted of an offence against it.[3] Any interpretation which begins from the general concept and its specifically juridical application is bound to centre on the character of righteousness as gift and, in practice, on anthropology. But the formulation which Paul has taken over speaks primarily of God's saving activity, which is present in his gift as a precipitate without being completely dissolved into it. Obviously, if righteousness through faith and righteousness through works are to

[2] Cf. A. Oepke, '*Δικαιοσύνη θεοῦ* bei Paulus in neuer Beleuchtung', *TLZ* 78, 1953, cols. 260ff.

[3] Cf. R. Bultmann, *Theologie des Neuen Testaments*, 1948–53, pp. 268ff.; ET, *Theology of the New Testament* I, 1952, pp. 270ff.

be sharply contrasted, the whole emphasis will fall on the gift. Only, it should not be forgotten that the expression 'the righteousness of God' runs parallel to the other similar expressions, the 'energy', the 'love', the 'peace', the 'wrath' of God and that these, equally, can be used in personified form and can connote divine power. Thus Rom. 1.17 and 3.21 speak of this righteousness revealed in an earthly epiphany,[4] Rom. 10.6 portrays it as itself speaking and acting; while it appears in I Cor. 1.30 as the direct manifestation of the Christ, and in II Cor. 5.21 as that of the community. Rom. 5.21 treats of the *βασιλεύειν* of grace through righteousness, Rom. 6.13 and II Cor. 6.7 of the weapons of righteousness, Rom. 6.18f. of the *δουλεία* of righteousness, II Cor. 3.9 of the *διακονία* of righteousness; none of this is fortuitous, and it is all summed up in the characteristic expression in Rom. 10.3 'submit to God's righteousness'. We see here that Paul has kept to the aspect of righteousness as power, implicit in the formulation itself and supported by the various parallel expressions. God's power becomes God's gift when it takes possession of us and, so to speak, enters into us, so that it can be said in Gal. 2.20, 'It is no longer I who live, but Christ who lives in me.' This gives

[4] The problem of interpretation, which is the real issue here appears once again in sharp relief when Bultmann ('*Δικαιοσύνη θεου*', *JBL* 83, p. 14 n. 5) attacks my translation of *δύναμις* by *Macht* as onesided and not in correspondence with general usage, saying that he himself would almost always prefer '*Kraft*' – which I should myself accept in principle without any argument. [In English the corresponding shade of difference might be that between 'power' and 'energy'. – Tr.] We reach the nub of the matter, however, when, following on from this, Rom. 1.16 is understood as saying 'The possibility of salvation is the Gospel.' As a free paraphrase, I would even be prepared to let this go. But as it is intended as a strict translation and set in polemical opposition to the idea of *Macht*, there has to be a decision about the sense of the verse. Characteristically, Bultmann chooses the translation which substitutes for the motif of the God who acts and creates and who prevails in the Gospel the quite different motif of an alleged anthropological 'given'. Giver and gift stand naturally in a causal relationship. God is the 'auctor'. But for me everything depends on the Gospel's being the manifestation of this God, in which he himself enters the lists in his sovereignty and prevailing power. Like Bultmann, and indeed because of his exaggeration of the facts, I, too, am bound to make a question of translation into a theological decision. At this point philology and the history of ideas prove broken reeds because, if we confine ourselves to the insights they provide, both solutions appear acceptable. The whole of the apostle's theology has now to be subpoenaed in order to reach the correct translation of a single word and, conversely, the correct translation of this one word determines, as I see it, the whole of the apostle's theology. But an example of this kind also demonstrates that, methodologically, the historical is not simply that which can be shown to be what actually happened, but the field on which the self-understanding of the interpreter is either confirmed or shattered, or else triumphs by violence. We ourselves are at risk here.

us a proper understanding of the double bearing of the genitive construction: the gift which is being bestowed here is never at any time separable from its Giver. It partakes of the character of power, in so far as God himself enters the arena and remains in the arena with it. Thus personal address, obligation and service are indissolubly bound up with the gift. When God enters the arena, our experience is, that he maintains his lordship even in his giving; indeed, it is his gifts which are the very means by which he subordinates us to his lordship and makes us responsible beings. The widely-held view that God's righteousness is simply a property of the divine nature can now be rejected as misleading. It derives from Greek theology, which speculates about such properties; it contradicts the basic sense of 'righteousness' within the tradition of the Old Testament and later Judaism – namely, faithfulness in the context of the community; and it proves ultimately inadequate because it postulates what cannot be convincingly intellectualized – namely, the making-over to a human being of a property of the divine nature. *Δικαιοσύνη θεοῦ* is for Paul, as it is for the Old Testament and Judaism in general, a phrase expressing divine activity, treating not of the self-subsistent, but of the self-revealing God.

We take the decisive step along the road to the proper understanding of Paul when, and only when, we grasp the indissoluble connection of power and gift within the conception of the divine righteousness; having done so, we wonder why this finding has not long ago come to be taken for granted. A fundamental phenomenon of the whole Pauline theology is at stake here. One or two examples may illustrate the wide range of variations within the one essential content. Just as, according to II Cor. 12.9 and 13.3.f., the power of God is at the same time active as a gift within us, so the Spirit who effects the resurrection of the dead is at the same time the *πνεῦμα ἐν ἡμῖν*, so, too, Christ, whom Paul already hails as Lord of the world, not only gives himself *for* us but also dwells and lives *in* us. While *χάρις* means primarily the power of grace, nothing could be more concrete than its individuation in the *χάρισμα* bestowed upon each of us. The *agape* of God in Rom. 8.39 is the power from which nothing can separate us; in Rom. 5.5 it is the gift poured out into our hearts. The Gospel appears in I Cor. 9.19 as *ananke* controlling the apostle and in II Cor. 2.14ff. as the power of life or death, so that Rom. 1.16 expressly calls it *δύναμις θεοῦ*: yet in the kerygma we become partakers of it and Paul can speak of 'his' Gospel. The eucharistic element *σῶμα χριστοῦ* incorporates us, according to I Cor. 10.16, into that body of Christ which is the Church. The key to this whole Pauline viewpoint is that power is always seeking to realize itself in action and must indeed do so. It does this with the greatest effect when it no longer remains external to us but enters into us and, as the apostle says, makes us its members. Now it may well be that what continues to be called the 'mystical' conception of the Christ or the Spirit dwelling within us does in fact owe the outward linguistic form in which it is expressed to analogies drawn from the ideas and formulae of Hellenistic mysticism. But, so far as content goes, it is not in any kind of contradiction with the other conception of the Christ *extra nos* and indeed it is a more radical form of it: for the total realization of a lordship over us occurs when such lordship acquires power over our hearts and enlists us in its service. Conversely, every gift of God which has ceased to be seen as the presence of the Giver and has therefore lost its character as personal address, is grace misused and working to our destruction. Justification and sanctification must therefore coincide, provided that by justification we mean that Christ takes power over our life. But at the same time the understanding we have now gained excludes the possibility of righteousness by works and of boasting of one's own moral achievement. The same Lord who calls us to his service enables us for it and requires us to render it in such a way as to ensure that his gift is passed on. As an instrument of grace, one cannot reasonably go on talking of one's own achievements. The watchword must always be 'If anyone wants to boast, let him boast of the Lord.' In these circumstances there is no longer any real tension between sacraments and ethics. The Lord whom we receive in and with our baptism as the Giver of the Spirit, that is, as the Power who establishes his lordship, this very Lord urges us on to break through to a service which is perpetually being renewed and to a future which is always open. We no longer exist simply for ourselves and cannot therefore simply dig in behind what we have received. Only so long as we keep on the pilgrim way and allow ourselves to be recalled daily to the allegiance of Christ, can we abide in the gift which we have received and can it abide, living and powerful, in us. In many quarters today we hear the relationship between indicative and imperative in Paul described in terms of the formula 'Become what you are'; while this is certainly not wrong, it is yet, in view of the origin of the formula in idealism, not without its dangers. Paul was not primarily concerned with the Christian in some purely notional individual capacity, much less with the Christian personality. To say that a man only believes as an individual is simply to say that here, as in the case of ministry in the world, he cannot shrug off responsibility. But I find myself totally unable to assent to the view that Paul's theology and his philosophy of history are orientated towards the individual.[5] To understand the righteousness of God exclusively in terms of gift is to ask for trouble: the inevitable result is that the Pauline anthropology is sucked under by the pull of an individualistic outlook. The sense of the parenetic imperative as the logical implication and the verification of the indicative is much better described in terms of the formula 'Abide by the Lord who has been given to you and by his lordship', which constitutes the core of the conception of 'abiding' in the Johannine farewell discourses. This is the way in which the Christian really does become what he is. For Paul sees our existence as determined at any given time by the Lord whom we are serving. If a transformation of our existence is really effected in baptism and if God's Word does posit a new creation, this cannot help but mean a change of lordship. The new Lord cuts us off from what we were before and never allows us to remain what we are at any given time, for otherwise he might be the First Cause but he would not be our Lord in the true sense. In this particular theological context, man is never seen as free in the sense of autonomous. But he does receive – eschatologically – the possibility of choosing between the kingdom of Christ and the kingdom of Satan, and the ordeal of temptation, like the call sounded in preaching, is for ever demanding that the Christian should make this choice anew; thus the Christian life may rightly be seen as a perpetual return to baptism.

We are now in a position to resolve the tension in the relationship of 'declare righteous' and 'make righteous'. If we see in the divine righteousness only a gift which is an entity in itself, it is bound to look either as if God were in principle imputing to us something which we ourselves had first to realize, or as if he were changing our existence in a naturalistic way. In both cases the Pauline dialectic remains unintelligible. On the other hand, the situation is quite different when proper consideration is given to the character of the gift as power and the lordship of Christ is recognized as its peculiar content. According to I Cor. 12.2f, God's power, in contrast to the power of the false gods, is not silent but bound up with the Word. It speaks to us in love and judgment so that we experience the pressure of its will,

[5] As against R. Bultmann, *History and Eschatology*, 1957, pp. 43ff.

and, by means of the Gospel, sets us in the posture (which it alone determines) 'before the face of Christ'. It is in this condition, which can never be attained except through the Gospel, that the righteousness bestowed by God consists. This righteousness is the possibility of access to God, in which we have peace (Rom. 5.1) and are reconciled with God (II Cor. 5.19ff.). But a Lord is no assured possession and not subordinated to our arbitrary disposal. His existence for us is experienced only according to the mode of promise and can only ever be verified by faith which puts its trust in the promise and which is properly described in terms of παρ' ἐλπίδα ἐπ ἐλπίδι (Rom. 4.18). On the other hand, however, the status of a Christian under such lordship is no fantasy or ideological programme. According to Rom. 10.6ff., the righteousness which comes from faith – in contradistinction to the Law – proclaims the nearness and the presence of grace, and the *nova oboedientia* proves that, when the promise is heard and appropriated, faith is right hearing. Thus the divine promise posits reality. But whether or not this remains a living reality and whether or not the Christian status in the eyes of God (Paul calls it indifferently 'in the face of Christ' and 'in Christ') is preserved by obedience – these things are bound up with the actualization of the promise.

I have so far by-passed the question as to why Paul describes the eschatological saving action of God by this particular word δικαιοσύνη and does not always keep to ἀγάπη θεοῦ, which he also uses. It cannot be disputed that in so doing he stands within the tradition of the Old Testament and of later Judaism; but this only gives the very faintest clue as to the direction in which an explanation may be sought. Very frequently the problem is not even raised, and the righteousness of God is left to be defined simply as saving action and as salvation. But Paul's theology is always carefully thought out: the last adjective one could apply to it would be 'naive'. We get a little further when we discover that in Rom. 3.25f. the apostle, quoting a fragment of a Jewish-Christian confession,[6] can speak of the δικαιοσύνη θεοῦ as God's covenant-faithfulness. If we ask why this does not happen more often and why the quotation is even corrected or at least glossed in v. 26, the answer is that Paul, unlike the community of the days immediately after Easter, does not base his thinking on the conception of the renewed covenant and the holy remnant, or at least only does so rarely and as a makeshift expedient. For him Christ is definitely not,

[6] Cf. my article 'Zum Verständnis von Römer 3.24–26', *Exegetische Versuche und Besinnungen* I, 1960, pp. 96–100 (not included in ET).

as for instance, in Matthew's Nativity story, the second Moses; he is the second Adam and, in this role, brings in the new covenant and the new creation. In so far as this is so, God's righteousness cannot now for Paul be primarily the divine covenant-faithfulness towards Israel. Conversely, however, he can pick up the Jewish–Christian quotation in Rom. 3.25 and employ καινὴ κτίσις and καινὴ διαθήκη as parallel expressions. For him, too, God's righteousness remains – and in the juridical sense[7] – ἔνδειξις of the divine faithfulness to the holy community, although admittedly this refers not merely to Israel but to the whole creation.

In general, the Pauline doctrine of justification is distinguished from the Jewish by the fact that in it the antithesis of faith and works is associated with the other antithesis between present justification and justification which is still to come (or even, still in the balance). There is no shadow of doubt that Paul lays the strongest emphasis on the present nature of salvation. Rom. 1.16 and 3.21 by themselves would prove this. Nevertheless, it is by no means adequate just to establish the bare fact. For just as the apostle can speak in Gal. 5.5 of righteousness yet to come, so the Thanksgiving Psalms from Qumran show very clearly that the present manifestation of the divine righteousness was already being stressed in apocalyptic Judaism in precisely the same way as can be detected in Paul. 'Realized eschatology', if we are prepared even to use the slogan at all, is in no sense the exclusive mark of primitive Christian proclamation and in so far as it is a characteristic of Paul, he still stands basically wholly within the possibilities and realities at least of one particular stream of Jewish apocalyptic. Naturally, it is the christological orientation which distinguishes his theology from this Jewish tradition. Only, everything now depends on clarifying the content of this observation, and it seems to me that, with the knowledge we now have of the Thanksgiving Psalms, we can no longer do this satisfactorily in terms of an understanding of the self and of history determined solely, or even primarily, by present eschatology. It was not merely Christian enthusiasts who experienced the presence of the Spirit, but also Jewish apocalyptists. What distinguishes the Pauline theology from both is rather the unprecedented radicalization and universalization of the promise in the doctrine of the justification of the ungodly. The message in the Damascus Document 20.20 'that salvation and righteousness are arising for those who fear God' is Jewish, and even

[7] Cf. W. G. Kümmel, 'παρεσις und ἔνδειξις', *ZTK* 49, 1952, pp. 154–67.

the Thanksgiving Psalms can be seen to remain true to the thinking of the Covenant pattern. Paul's interpretative amplifications, when he speaks of the righteousness of God and of its revelation *χωρὶς νόμου*, are the sign-manual of his theology. It is certainly not by chance that in the context of Rom. 3.22 and 8.29 Paul clearly thinks of the *δόξα θεοῦ* of which all men have been deprived through the Fall, as being given back together with the righteousness of God; nor that, according to II Cor. 3.18 and 4.6 this *δοξα* now streams into the world from within the *διακονία τῆς δικαιοσύνης* It is part of the same design when, in Rom. 1.18–3.20, he sees the world before and outside Christ *not* under the goodness and long-suffering of God, but under the judgment of the wrath – the judgment which expresses itself in the heaping-up of guilt, hardness of heart and rejection, which strikes Jews and Gentiles alike and is revealed simultaneously with the Gospel.

Only within such a framework can Paul speak in Rom. 9–11 of God's righteousness towards Israel. Doubtless, Israel presents a special case, in that it is the people of the promise and of the experiences of grace, and, for this very reason, the archetype of the religious man in general. It is a matter for discussion whether God's relationship with this people and, by implication, with the religious man, differs from his relationship with the rest of the world[8] and whether his faithfulness in this area is maintained by means of some immanent continuity. These chapters show that this is not the case. On the contrary, they recapitulate the course of the whole epistle, exhibiting the freedom of God, accusing the guilty and asserting their rejection, and proclaiming finally the apocalyptic promise. 11.32 sums up in almost triumphal tones: 'God has consigned all men to disobedience, that he may have mercy upon all.' In any event, therefore, Israel is not a special case in the sense that the working out of God's righteousness upon Israel is any different from its working out elsewhere. Rather, we have here, in the clearest and most penetrating terms possible, an open declaration that the way of salvation passes invariably through the justification of the ungodly. The attempt to secure for oneself status before God and a righteousness of one's own in virtue of good works and an appeal to the fathers is even more characteristic of the will of the flesh than is the idol-worship of the heathen: for this will of flesh looks for independence over against the Lord who lays claim totally and unremittingly to our whole self, and it therefore becomes subject to the wrath of God. For in these

[8] Cf. my article 'Paul and Israel', pp. 183–87 below.

circumstances God does not remain God nor man man – that is, the man who is subordinate to the power of God and wholly thrown upon God's grace. To undertake to preserve independence over against God is the root sin, in whatever concrete form it may express itself, and such an undertaking invariably receives an answer in the form of the διὸ παρέδωκεν αὐτούς of Rom. 1.24ff. The eschatological salvation thus begins with the revelation of the Godhead of God and the necessity of man's becoming human. In the new creation, there is a reference back to creation *ex nihilo* and a reference forward to the resurrection of the dead. The καινὴ διαθήκη is no longer just the Sinai covenant renewed and extended; and πίστις is its sign, not νόμος.

But equally God continues in that faithfulness which is called *ṣ^e^dākā* in the Old Testament and is there, as in Judaism in general, bound up with the Covenant; the same faithfulness is very powerfully recalled in Rom. 9.4. Through thick and thin, Paul holds to the view that God activates his righteousness not in a renewed, but in a totally new Covenant, and the apostle can thus legitimately transfer the motif of the people of God on to the Christians as the eschatological Israel. He is thinking here of that faithfulness with which the Creator persists in his work of creation in spite of, and beyond, the falling away of his creatures and with which he preserves his creation and gives it a new foundation. Thus δικαιοσύνη θεοῦ and πίστις θεοῦ are associated in Rom. 3.3–5, which contain the burden of this faithfulness, and it emerges at the same time that the righteousness of God is precisely what, as the power of the justification of the ungodly, it must be – God's victory amid the opposition of the world. By it, all human self-righteousness and insubordination come to destruction, while that which does not exist is called into being and the dead are made alive. Christ is the new Adam, because, as the bearer of human destiny, he brings in the world of obedience. All that we have been saying amounts to this: δικαιοσύνη θεοῦ is for Paul God's sovereignty over the world revealing itself eschatologically in Jesus. And, remembering the Greek root, we may also say that it is the rightful power with which God makes his cause to triumph in the world which has fallen away from him and which yet, as creation, is his inviolable possession.

If this is correct, the righteousness of God does not, in Paul's understanding, refer primarily to the individual and is not to be understood exclusively in the context of the doctrine of man; but it is impossible to avoid doing these two things if its character as gift is given first priority. It is true that Paul does, for the purpose of his mordant polemic against the Jewish motif of the 'covenant people', portray the believer, and him alone, as the recipient of salvation. But the emergent category of the individual human being is to be seen here in immediate relation to the divine will for salvation, now directed towards the whole world and no longer limited by the confines of the Law. Equally, it is characteristic of the Pauline theology that it alone in the New Testament presents us with a fully worked-out anthropology, the distinctive nature of which we cannot grasp without taking this fact into account from the outset as central. Conversely, however, this doctrine of man is only one part of Pauline theology and, as such, has its specific function within the whole. It demonstrates the present reality of the divine action directed towards the new creation as this reality is manifested in the pressure of earthly temptation. The faithful *are* the world as it has been recalled to the sovereignty of God, the company of those who live under the eschatological justice of God, in which company, according to II Cor. 5.21, God's righteousness becomes manifest on earth. Yet to content ourselves with this statement as it stands is to foreshorten the theological perspective and to misinterpret Pauline anthropology as a whole. It is precisely the apostle's doctrine of justification which shows that God's action in Christ, as in the creation of the world, prevails and that the Pauline dialectic of present and future eschatology encroaches on Christian existence as it is actually lived out; but this doctrine is not essentially concerned with anthropology. Consciously, and under a sense of apocalyptic pressure, Paul conceived his task to be the universalization of the Church's mission. Any interpretation which loses sight of this fails to give historicity its due and therefore minimizes the theological problems with which Paul faces us. The apostle's present eschatology cannot be taken out of its context of future eschatology, any more than the gift of justification can be isolated from the context in which the righteousness of God is spoken of as a power which brings salvation to pass. Even when he became a Christian, Paul remained an apocalyptist.[9] His doctrine of the

[9] I am here proceeding further along the lines of my essay 'The Beginnings of Christian Theology' (pp. 82–107 above), and going over to the counter-offensive against the criticism expressed by my friends Ernst Fuchs (Über die Aufgabe einer christlichen Theologie', *ZTK* 58, 1961, pp. 245–67) and Gerhard Ebeling ('Der Grund christlicher Theologie', *ibid.*, pp. 227–44).

For the present I cannot afford to be on the defensive. Not only would the time have to be available, we should have to be able to spare it. The problem I have

δικαιοσύνη θεοῦ demonstrates this: God's power reaches out for the world, and the world's salvation lies in its being recaptured for the sovereignty of God. For this very reason it is the gift of God and also the salvation of the individual human being when we become obedient to the divine righteousness.

---

attacked here is at least just as important as that of the historical Jesus, and ought perhaps even to take precedence over it. It would help our theological situation if the fire that has been kindled were not extinguished too quickly. Whether it is a funeral pyre or not will be revealed in due course – there are also such things as Easter fires. [An allusion to a German custom of having bonfires on Easter Eve. Tr.]

VIII

PAUL AND ISRAEL*

THE ANTI-SEMITISM of the ancient world, sharpened in a Christian sense, occurs for the first time in the New Testament in the earliest of Paul's letters, I Thess. 2.15f.:

> [They] killed both the Lord Jesus and the prophets, and drove us out and displease God and oppose all men by hindering us from speaking to the Gentiles that they may be saved – so as always to fill up the measure of their sins. But God's wrath has come upon them at last!

It is the problem of our theme that the same Paul, in Romans 11, with equal passion sees as the whole object of his activity the winning of Israel for Christ, and binds up all Christian hope with the achievement of this object. For Israel, according to Rom. 9.1–5 is particularly the bearer of the promise:

> I am speaking the truth in Christ, I am not lying; my conscience bears me witness in the Holy Spirit, that I have great sorrow and unceasing anguish in my heart. For I could wish that I myself were cut off from Christ for the sake of my brethren, my kinsmen by race. They are Israelites, and to them belong the sonship, the glory, the covenants, the giving of the law, the worship, and the promises; to them belong the patriarchs, and of their race, according to the flesh, is the Christ.

The antitheses of these two passages may be neither played down or played off against each other. Psychology which interprets them as respectively the beginning and the end of a process of development does not really get us any further; neither do historical analyses which see Paul as the representative now of Jewish thinking, now of Hellenistic syncretism or, again, as the precursor of ecclesiastical dogma. The element of justice in these appraisals does no more than set the Apostle within the field of forces out of which the whole New Testament emerges, and the various interpretations exhibit in the last

* 'Paulus und Israel', a broadcast talk, first published in *Juden, Christen, Deutsche*, ed. H. J. Schultz, 1961, pp. 307–11.

resort a theology governed by a paradox. For the unchangeable mark and the unifying centre of this theology which alone makes sense of Paul's relationship with Israel is the experience of the justification of the ungodly. Phil. 3.4–9 demonstrates this:

> If any other man thinks he has reason for confidence in the flesh, I have more: circumcised on the eighth day, of the people of Israel, of the tribe of Benjamin, a Hebrew born of Hebrews; as to the law a Pharisee, as to zeal a persecutor of the church, as to righteousness under the law blameless. But whatever gain I had, I counted as loss for the sake of Christ. Indeed I count everything as loss because of the surpassing worth of knowing Christ Jesus my Lord. For his sake I have suffered the loss of all things, and count them as refuse, in order that I may gain Christ and be found in him, not having a righteousness of my own, based on law, but that which is through faith in Christ, the righteousness from God that depends on faith.

Paul is here setting a boundary between himself and his own past – as the past of a devout Jew.

Taking his guidance from the law, he had been pursuing a righteousness of his own, only to find the pursuit rendered pointless when Christ revealed to him quite another righteousness as being God's will and salvation. But that is precisely how Rom. 10.2–4 describes Israel's destiny:

> I bear them witness that they have a zeal for God, but it is not enlightened. For, being ignorant of the righteousness that comes from God, and seeking to establish their own, they did not submit to God's righteousness. For Christ is the end of the law, that everyone who has faith may be justified.

That means: the apostle's real adversary is the devout Jew, not only as the mirror-image of his own past – though that, too – but as the reality of the religious man. For man, whether he knows it and acts correspondingly or not, is the being who is set before God: and this fact the devout Jew acknowledges. Certainly such a profession is no protection from illusion. In fact, religion always provides man with his most thorough-going possibility of confusing an illusion with God. Paul sees this possibility realized in the devout Jew: inasmuch as the announcement of God's will in the law is here misunderstood as a summons to human achievement and therefore as a means to a righteousness of one's own. But that is for him the root sin, because now an image is set in the place of God; man, in despairing presumption, erects his own work into the criterion of the universal judgment and God becomes an approving spectator of our doings.

Who really *is* God? That is the central concern of Paul's theology, as also of his relationship with Israel. The break in his life came when he learned that such a question could only be answered from the Cross of the risen Jesus: the real God is the enemy and judge of every human illusion – especially every pious illusion – which professes to exhibit to God saving works, to make claims, to glory in one's own achievement and to take comfort in one's own righteousness. The Old Testament, newly interpreted in the light of the Cross of Jesus, confirms for the apostle the truth that before God no man is righteous in himself. The only ground of glorying is that God has been merciful. This is the point where the apostle comes into conflict with Israel – a conflict which is in fact a dispute about the nature of true righteousness before God. This righteousness may not be connected with religious achievement any more than with a demonstrable possession – shall we say, circumcision as the token of the Covenant? – or with an appeal to a specific past – shall we say, the past of the patriarchs? It remains bound to the God who acts, to whom, as the poor named in the first beatitude, we stretch out our arms, for whose sake we, with Abraham and the people of the wilderness, must be forever abandoning our prepared positions. Right and righteousness can only be ours in so far as God gives them to us anew every day – i.e. in faith. It is not that his gifts guarantee continuity, says I Cor. 10.1–13; their importance is rather that they direct us back to the Giver.

It is therefore the sovereign and gracious God, and not any distinction he may previously have conferred upon us, who is the sole ground of our hope. This is why Paul does not speak, as did the Jewish Christians before him of a *renewed*, but of a *new*, convenant; this is why he calls the heavenly Jerusalem, and not the earthly, the mother of us all. Moses is for him the antitype, not, like Abraham, the prototype of Christ as the fulfiller of the promise. His hope for Israel is not, as in the Qumran texts, built squarely on the idea of the holy remnant, and the idea of the people of God is used by him in a different sense and much more loosely. For since Easter it has become clear that God's dealings are with all people and that Israel's election in days of yore points forward beyond Israel into that comprehensive history which began with Adam. There is no privilege in the face of God's omnipotence. God's grace shows its strength always and only in the weak. God's kingdom is always built out of material which is, in itself, unusable. God's righteousness appears as creation out of nothing and as the resurrection of the dead; and, indeed, in opposition to everything which pretends to be self-made and self-sufficient. Only the godless are ever justified. So long as this lesson has not been learned at the foot of the Cross of Jesus, the godhead of God is not truly acknowledged and honoured: and in consequence man has not yet become human.

What has been said makes it clear that Paul is obliged to destroy those claims of Israel which are grounded in its own history in exactly the same way as those of the individual religious man. The express fashion in which he does this shows that Israel has exemplary significance for him; in and with Israel he strikes at the hidden Jew in all of us, at the man who validates rights and demands over against God on the basis of God's past dealings with him and to this extent is serving not God but an illusion. It is not therefore fortuitous that the three long chapters Romans 9–11 repeat the argument of the whole letter: guilt is impeached, the wrath of God is proclaimed as leading to blindness and rejection, the Old Testament is cited as prophetic witness to the judgment which has broken in. Is the apostle contradicting himself when he nevertheless ends ch. 11 with the promise of salvation for the whole people of Israel? Have we here the voice of the Jewish patriot, the man Paul, the biblical theologian, breaking through at last? It seems to me that only the exemplary significance of Israel can explain and demand such an otherwise incomprehensible reversal: if real salvation comes only from the Judge of our illusions, then there can be authentic promise only for the broken, for those who have been thrown back on to the true human condition of guilt, of waiting and of suffering. It is just this that Paul finds illustrated in the Old Testament; this is what is stamped on the covenant-history which is there rehearsed and which thus preserves the character of the history of promise pointing the way to the Cross of Jesus and yet at the same time pointing beyond the Old Covenant to God's dealings with all people. For, according to Rom. 3.29–30, God is one, and for this very reason the God not only of the Jews but of the Gentiles, just as Abraham in Rom. 4.12 is called the father of those who believe among circumcision and uncircumcision alike. This does not prevent Paul from conceding to Israel the rights of the first-born. In his election of Israel God has sketched out his way with all his creatures and therefore the confirmation of this election is to Paul the closing act of history. The problem of Israel receives its exemplary significance for Paul through his assumption that in it the whole question of God's relationship with devout men is here thematically posed and then solved in a way visible to all men. The question is: What is the promise to devout men who were once marked out by the divine calling, leading and blessing? Paul answers: Precisely the same as the promise to the Gentiles. On earth it can only ever be (Rom. 4.18) against hope to believe in hope. For the promise does not develop out of the continuity of human history. On the contrary, in that history it shines only upon our failure, our guilt and our graves. The only kind of promise there is, even for the devout man, is that which was born at Easter and comes from Easter; that God remains true to himself and does not throw up his work once begun even if the ungodly reject it. As the Lord of the world he proclaims in the Cross of Jesus his judging, and yet abiding, solidarity with the ungodly as his creatures. But this solidarity with the ungodly unites Israel after the flesh with the Gentiles, who before were not God's people. Thus the justification of the ungodly, which is also the resurrection from the dead, is the only hope both of the world in general and also of Israel. For, according to Rom. 11.32, God has shut up all, Jews and Gentiles alike, under disobedience, in order that he may have mercy upon all in the establishment of the obedience of faith.

IX

WORSHIP AND EVERYDAY LIFE*

A note on Romans 12

THE CONTEXT OF parenetic tradition in the New Testament was not originally determined either by the laws of logic or by those of systematic theology. This insight we owe to the self-sacrificing and passionate care for detail with which Martin Dibelius pursued his life-long study of the problems of New Testament parenesis. Many and diverse streams of tradition mingle to make up the material which the community, whose Christianity is in parts only skin-deep, selects and passes on, often in traditional form and sequence, perhaps superficially connected by some common key word. When this material is taken up into the Gospels and Epistles, we have of course arrived at literary compositions with a ruling theme. But, even at this stage, detail which is either out of context, or can only be integrated into the passage by forcing the meaning, not infrequently betrays the fact that the thematic connection was created as an afterthought and often for worse rather than for better. Such an historical insight already shows in what small degree the New Testament possesses an 'ethic' in our sense, i.e. a system of morality developing logically out of a single nucleus. This fact has not been recognized clearly enough nor been satisfactorily evaluated, and indeed we must admit that we shall not have grasped its full implications until we have also taken into account its converse: there is no mass of individual casuistical injunctions which might take the place of a system, although doubtless there have been incursions of casuistry stemming from Jewish influence. Otherwise the 'ethic' of the New Testament would necessarily govern our moral action in all its situations and possibilities in a legalistic way, whereas in fact these

* First published in *Judentum, Urchristentum, Kirche: Festschrift für J. Jeremias*, ed. W. Eltester (BZNW 26), 1960, pp. 165–71.

are only very partially comprehended and scarcely ever really under control. What is here required is neither a universal – good conduct in general – nor a particular – the observance of an all-embracing order; although I Cor. 14.33 is aware that God is not a God of confusion. The concept of order is, on the contrary, quite naturally heightened by the eschatological concept of peace, the correlative of which is the commandment of love. Love, however, does not content itself with what is demanded by a precept or moral usage but serves *this* actual neighbour in his present need. It does not, therefore, persist in blind obedience to an established norm but acts with open eyes and decisive common sense, its gaze fixed on something which has urgently to be done *now* and will not recur. Individual injunctions can, then, only serve as reminders that Christian behaviour is a matter of discovering the demand of the present moment and that God as Lord of the world wills to be acknowledged in man's interior life.

Only if we start from these presuppositions in the field of New Testament parenesis are we enabled to see that Romans 12 introduces a new stage in Christian 'ethics'. Certainly this is not yet true of the formal structure:[1] an exact articulation of the passage is not easy, and the individual injunctions (at least from v. 9 on) are connected not logically, but at best within a framework of juxtaposed fragments of tradition. The significance of this is that as yet no foundation has been laid for an ethical system which might, or, more correctly, would demand to be abstracted from the letter as a whole and would have as its original intention a general coverage of all the relevant departments of life. Nevertheless everything in the passage is oriented round a theme on which emphasis is placed as early as vv. 1f. It embraces the total action both of the individual Christian and of the Christian community and sets the parenesis within a firm theological framework: the theme of 'spiritual worship' through the offering-up of the bodies of the Christians describes what it means to stand under the righteousness of God[2] with that simplicity which is the mark of the truly great conception. The brevity with which this is done ought not to blind us to the width of the horizon which is taken in and the depth and originality of the approach. On the other hand we should

[1] A. Nygren, *Commentary on Romans*, ET, 1952, p. 412, thinks indeed that we can speak, at least as regards the inner construction, of a 'definite structural plan'. But for the argument against this I need only refer to O. Michel, *Der Brief an die Römer*, 1955, pp. 269f.

[2] Cf. Michel, *op. cit.*, pp. 257f.

note the peculiar openness which sets the concrete individual injunctions in juxtaposition without deriving them from a single material principle, and yet does not arrange them in casuistical form. Fundamental decisions within a field of systematic thought are not sufficient for the erection of a system, and the individual exhortations remain simply pointers towards the worship which at that time was necessarily something new which had to be recognized as such and then practised.

Just because Paul is conscious of the significance of this particular part of the letter, there is a certain solemnity in the way in which the theme is brought into relief by a series of more detailed qualifications. The key phrase 'spiritual worship'[3] originally played a leading part in the polemic of the Hellenistic enlightenment against the 'irrational' cultic offerings of the folk religions; it was then modified in a spiritualizing sense by Hellenistic mysticism in order to qualify the *oratio infusa* of the praise rendered to the Godhead as true divine worship by the man endowed with *pneuma* as representative of the whole creation. Paul can properly take up this key phrase because in his thought also only the man endowed with *pneuma* is in a position to offer spiritual worship. This is why he utters his exhortation in the exact language of adjuration: 'by the mercy of God'.[4] The condition (which is now to be described) of standing under the divine righteousness is only made possible by this mercy and is only maintained so long as we cleave to this righteousness and our action is borne along by it.[5] Thus at the same time Paul takes up a polemic stance over against every other form of divine worship in the world – the stance which belongs to the key phrase by reason of its origins, although modified yet again as v. 2 shows. His own reckoning with the current doctrine of sacrifice is no longer settled from the standpoint of spiritualizing mysticism.[6] The apostle designates as spiritual that divine worship which, in contrast to all this-worldly existence, takes place eschatologically in the power of and in response to the claim of

[3] Cf. O. Casel, 'Die λογικὴ θυσία der antiken Mystik in christlich-liturgischer Umdeutung', *Jahrbuch für Liturgiewissenschaft*, 1924, pp. 237ff.; P. Seidensticker, *Lebendiges Opfer* (Neutestamentliche Abhandlungen 20), 1954.

[4] Cf. with this H. Schlier, 'Vom Wesen der apostolischen Ermahnung', *Die Zeit der Kirche*, 2nd ed., 1958, pp. 178ff.

[5] No distinction need be drawn between λογική and πνευματικὴ θυσία, cf. I Peter 2.5 and the parallels cited by the commentaries.

[6] So also Schlier, *op. cit.*, p. 86; Michel, *op. cit.*, p. 261. But the variation is not to be played off against the continuity of the tradition, as in G. Dehn, *Vom christlichen Leben* (Biblische Studien 6/7,), 1854, p. 17.

the new age; which therefore presupposes a transformed existence and authenticates itself by an unrelenting critical distinction between the divine will and every earthly will. In no sense is this to be interpreted simply as inner life and ethical sentiment. For the eschatological happening consists precisely in this, that God has begun to reclaim for himself the world which belongs to him. Christian existence would not deserve its name if it did not bear witness to this. Spiritual worship is only the realization of God's eschatological work when, seemingly in most paradoxical fashion, it consists and takes place in the offering up of our bodies.[7] Naturally, that implies the surrender of the whole man. But the Pauline conception of the body is not a matter exclusively or primarily of the personality of man but, at least in the passages of greatest theological significance, of his capacity for communication and the reality of his incorporation within a world which limits him.[8] God lays claim to our corporeality because he is no longer leaving the world to itself, and our bodily obedience expresses the fact that, in and with us, he has recalled to his service the world of which we are a part.

At the same time, where the worship of Christians takes the form of their bodily obedience, there is in principle an abandonment of the cultic sacred place which is characteristically a place of divine worship for the ancient world, where it has not been affected by the Enlightenment. Sacred times and places are superseded by the eschatological public activity of those who at all times and in all places stand 'before the face of Christ' and from this position before God make the everyday round of so-called secular life into the arena of the unlimited and unceasing glorification of the divine will. At this point the doctrines of worship and Christian 'ethics' converge. This shows conclusively that the total Christian community with all its members is the bearer of this worship and that not only sacred functions but also cultically privileged persons lose their right to exist. The universal priesthood of all believers, called forth and manifested in the whole range of its activity, now appears as the eschatological worship of God which puts an end to every other cultus. The harshness of this finding certainly seems to contradict the fact that in this

[7] So K. Barth, as early as *Der Römerbrief*, 4th ed., 1924, pp. 415f. (ET, *The Epistle to the Romans*, 1933, pp. 429f.); A. Schlatter, *Gottes Gerechtigkeit*, 1935, p. 332; P. Althaus, *Der Brief an die Römer* (NTD 6), 9th ed., 1959, pp. 112f.

[8] At this point R. Bultmann's analysis in his *Theologie des Neuen Testaments*, 1948–53, pp. 189ff. (ET, *Theology of the New Testament* I, 1952, pp. 192ff.), seems to me to stand in need of correction.

passage Paul deliberately and in no way fortuitously employs cultic terminology and, in particular, the language of sacrifice.[9] But in reality it is precisely this which demonstrates the radical nature of the shift which has taken place here; so far from there being any room left for cultic thinking, the use of cultic terminology becomes itself the means of making clear, through a paradox, the extent of the upheaval. In the eschatological age there is no longer anything 'profane',[10] except what man himself renders profane or demonic: but similarly there is nothing holy in the cultic sense except the community of the holy people and their self-abandonment in the service of the Lord to whom the world and all its dominions belong.

We may rightly conclude on the basis of vv. 3–5 that the text has not been forced nor even had a subjective gloss put upon it. Obviously the actual parenesis begins here, as is shown by the new paragraph with its reference to Paul's apostolic authority and its concrete warning against conceit. Conversely, the theological foundation in v. 4 makes it manifest that his intention is to give the admonition of v. 3 particular weight.[11] It could be said that everything which follows stands under the watchword 'Do not be conceited'. An essential element of the authentic worship of God in the world is the right 'measure'. In this connection the taking up here of σωφρονεῖν,[12] a key word of popular philosophy, indicates that this concept, like that of 'spiritual worship', is not completely unknown even to Gentiles, although the apostle has to give it a specific Christian point and direction – the right measure is not the integration of the self-sufficient human being which enables him to adjust socially to his given environment,[13] but participation in faith as the estate of the Christian man, which God has given specifically to each as a grant-in-aid of grace, i.e. as *charisma*.[14] For *charisma* signifies technically in Paul the specific participation of the individual Christian in grace, in the Spirit or, as here, in faith – a participation which as such expresses itself correspondingly in a specific πρᾶξις of the member in and for the body of Christ. Grace is just not received in a package deal and

[9] So at least Michel, *op. cit.*, p. 261. [10] Rom. 14.14.

[11] So too Schlatter, *op. cit.*, p. 336. W. Lütgert, *Der Römerbrief als historisches Problem* (BFCT 17.2), 1913, pp. 98f., has already raised the question as to the reason for this emphasis.

[12] Cf. Dehn, *op. cit.*, p. 29; Michel, *op. cit.*, p. 264.

[13] Cf. A. Dihle, *RAC* III, cols. 738f.

[14] So too R. Bultmann, *Theologie*, p. 321 (ET, vol. I, p. 324), and, as early as 1924, 'Das Problem der Ethik bei Paulus', *ZNW* 23, p. 140.

without differentiation'[15] but apportioned correctly in the form of a *charisma*, i.e. an individuation of the power of grace. It is not ours as an inalienable possession or as a property of our inner life but only as the energy of service[16] and as calling,[17] so that Karl Barth can very rightly speak of the 'only ethical possibility'.[18] Gift and task are never separable in Paul, because the Giver is at the same time the Lord, and with his gift invariably unites his claim upon us. All existence, according to the apostle, is to be understood from the perspective of the activity of the giving and forgiving God. Precisely for this reason Christian existence is based on baptism as the event of the new creation; it must therefore (in its character as existence before God) prove itself by obedience to be true worship and, so far as its corporeality makes it a constituent element of the world in which it is set, to be also the service of love. Membership in the body of Christ can thus in the last resort only be described as that participation in the universal priesthood of all believers which is posited by baptism.[19] Finally, there is also given to the individual Christian in his *charisma*, along with his gift and his task, his limitations and his 'measure'; so that at the same time conceit is seen as being of its very nature an act of rebellion against the Creator who endows each one with concrete and specific gifts, and the way is opened to mutual service on the part of those who need each other.[20] Over the community, in which each possesses his own 'measure' and all have the same Lord (so that no one can either dominate or be passive), the peace of Christ as the eschatological sharpening of earthly order reigns supreme.

This leads us to take up a problem which has aroused astonishingly infrequent interest and to which hitherto no really satisfying solution has been offered. We have to ask what is the relationship between the activity of the prophets, deacons, teachers, ethical instructors, distributors of alms, those who 'preside' and perhaps[21] of those who tend the sick, and what is sometimes found quite senselessly lumped together in our Bibles under the general heading of 'Christian duties'.[22]

[15] Michel, *op. cit.*, p. 265. Schlatter, *op. cit.*, pp. 336f., has a justifiable polemic against any supposed ideal of equality in Paul.

[16] I Cor. 12.5f. [17] Rom. 11.29. [18] *Römerbrief*, pp. 432f. (ET, pp. 447f.).

[19] Michel, *op. cit.*, pp. 261f., and Nygren, *op. cit.*, p. 415, both point pertinently to the baptismal terminology of the text.

[20] I Cor. 12.12ff. E. Brunner, *Der Römerbrief* (Bibelhilfe für die Gemeinde, Neutestamentliche Reihe 9), 1948, p. 86.

[21] So Dehn, *op. cit.*, p. 40.

[22] M. J. Lagrange, *Saint Paul, Épitre aux Romains*, 6th ed., 1950, p. 291, speaks

Though the accumulating participles of the first group may well indicate that the reference here is not to officially installed office-bearers,[23] there can be no doubt that nevertheless representative functions of the Christian community are being described here.[24] What kind of unity is there between them and the private virtues enumerated in vv. 9ff.? But such a question is to impose on the passage modern categories which make its drift unintelligible. For if the Christian, because he exists 'before the face of Christ' as of the Lord and Judge of the world, stands with his whole being exposed to the light of eschatological day, for him there can no longer be any realm of 'private life' such as we are in the habit of conceding to the individual.[25] Correspondingly, the concept of virtue as used in our morality is fundamentally inapplicable to him. For he who walks 'in Christ' or 'in the Spirit' lives by the power of grace and his activity is a manifestation of it. Even his 'ethical' existence is understood eschatologically in Paul and the concept of *charisma* is intended to demonstrate this as clearly as possible. That means that, while the functions of the members within the body of Christ can be distinguished by differences in scope and importance, they can nevertheless not be divided into private and public, 'functional' and 'official'. Each Christian has his own particular service to render in his calling and also in his 'office'. From the perspective applied here either the conception of office is wholly untenable because it presupposes the differentiation of the private and the public sphere or it is valid for every Christian activity because the *charisma* of the individual being is at all times and in all places a duty owed to the Lord of the world; and conversely, there is no office within the Church other than that which is constituted by a charismatic gift and calling.[26] But this

---

of the *duties* of the Christian and therefore disputes the view that there is any mention in vv. 6ff. of specific functions in the strict sense.

[23] So E. Kühl, *Der Brief des Paulus an die Römer*, 1913, p. 428; E. Brunner, *op. cit.*, p. 87.

[24] A. Jülicher, *Der Brief an die Römer* (Die Schriften des Neuen Testaments, 3rd ed., II), 1917, p. 312, established that there was at least a transition here from the 'Spirit-possessed' to the 'faithful', cf. Michel, *op. cit.*, p. 257.

[25] A. B. Macdonald, *Christian Worship in the Primitive Church*, 1935, p. 18, did not see this clearly enough when he took the view that vv. 3–8 were speaking of the assembly for worship and the following verses of the daily life of the community, without any clear line of demarcation between.

[26] The same formula describes the apostolate and every other Christian function in v. 3 and v. 6.

means that the admittedly smooth transition from vv. 6–8 to vv. 9ff. carries us on, from the *charismata* which give leadership to the community and are most striking in terms of its internal life, to those charismatic modes of life which characterize Christian existence both in the community and in the world. It would be incorrect to include both under the same heading of love;[27] indeed, vv. 6–8 do not expressly speak of love. For, just as love in I Corinthians 13 is the determining and unifying force of all *charismata*, the point here – made with exactly the same degree of emphasis – is that every activity of the Christian community is to be characterized as charismatic, because in this total activity the 'spiritual worship' becomes real in the world. The whole community and each of its members is here being called to the universal priesthood of all believers and in such a manner as to address each one along the line of what is possible, because commanded, to *him*; that is, of the maintenance of his situation in and under grace.[28]

It is true that no system of Christian 'ethics' is being propounded here; but for the first time in the history of the Church the total activity of the community and its members is being looked at from a unified perspective. It is theologically defined as the response of faith in the everyday life of the world to the call of the grace by which that world is being grasped and held.

[27] So Dehn, *op. cit.*, p. 457; Nygren, *op. cit.*, pp. 412f.; Michel, *op. cit.*, p. 257.
[28] Cf. C. K. Barrett, *A Commentary on the Epistle to the Romans*, 1957, p. 237.

PRINCIPLES OF THE INTERPRETATION OF ROMANS 13*

MY CONCERN IN this lecture is exclusively to initiate a discussion of this passage which has suddenly become so relevant to our contemporary situation. I shall therefore begin by saying something about the problem of Pauline parenesis in general – a matter which is of particular importance for us of all people; I shall then repeat briefly the questions and insights, the formulation of which lay at the root of my article on 'Römer 13.1–7 in unserer Generation';[1] and I shall conclude with the interpretation of those textual problems which are decisive ones for our theme.

I. THE UNDERSTANDING OF PAULINE PARENESIS

Over and over again we find difficulties in the way of our understanding of Pauline parenesis simply because we are unable for the most part to discern distinctly its historical and factual presuppositions. Two things above all must be brought out into the clear light of day: just as the New Testament is not the first Christian 'Dogmatic Theology', but (apart from the Gospels) a collection of occasional writings and individual theological tracts, similarly it contains no 'ethic' in our sense, i.e. no logically articulated system designed to be normative for Christian behaviour. It is true that in the New Testament all activity of the Christian is described and evaluated from the perspective of eschatology, as and because the total proclamation is here eschatologically determined. But this does not mean that this activity can be deduced and developed from a master principle.

* First published in *Unter der Herrschaft Christi*, ed. E. Wolf (Beiträge zur evangelischen Theologie 32), 1961, pp. 37–55.

[1] *ZTK* 56, 1959, pp. 316–76.

This in turn is shown by the fact that the 'ethic' of the New Testament puts forward without any hesitation single injunctions in almost casuistic fashion. And if these single injunctions may sometimes be comprised in the command to love or included with the summons to obedience, the significance of this is that the whole man is at all times under obligation both to God and to his neighbour and that he cannot be quit of an obligation of this kind by a merely partial commitment. If elsewhere they are brought under the denominator of the good, the decent and the useful which is laid upon us, this is a way of marking out our daily round as the field of our service; and if, finally, the call to the imitation of Christ is heard, it is no ideal that is being set before us but we are being pointed to that reality in which a necessary element in all action is enduring, suffering and dying in personal union with the Master. In brief, the whole thing is a matter of the ability to stand outside oneself in the presence of God as the reality of Christian existence, towards which all the possibilities inherent in individual actions are directed. But this is no principle which could be made into the foundation of a system: equally, it provides no basis for a casuistry. For this ability may be realized in the specific action but it is not patient of manipulation, as any system of casuistry presupposes; it cannot be plotted within the system of co-ordinates on which any one of our plans may be based, nor can it be logically calculated and theoretically contemplated. It is the possibility and the reality of that grace which does not allow itself to be deduced, limited and manipulated. If in the New Testament this ability makes its claim cogent through the medium of countless single injunctions, this is as much as to say that it is taking us into its service, just as we are, with all our relationships and all our capacities: us with our world and our world with us.

If all this is true, we have already established indirectly a second point. In the course of a long development and employing the key principle of scriptural interpretation – the mutual relation of Gospel and Law – we have evolved as it were a mode of dividing up the content in which it seemed obvious that the parenesis should be allotted to the Law. There was, too, a stretching of the concept of law which gave to the divine law the sense of an absolute norm. Parenesis appeared from this standpoint to be the description of moral duties. If an ethical system is really being substituted here for the New Testament exhortations, the error of such a conception emerges with special clarity in the light of Paul's understanding of all activity of the Christian as charismatic, i.e. as the concrete manifestation of self-differentiating *charis*.[2] As grace endows us, so it puts us also at its disposal by making us willing and able to enter its service – we might say, using the full complex sense of the word, it empowers [German ermächtigt] us to serve it. Grace and service do not permit themselves to be forcibly divorced. There is no other possible way to preserve grace and to make it real except by persevering in its service. Thus Christian action does not stand under the slogan 'I must and I shall', but under the quite different one 'I may and I can', and for this reason it is looked upon in the Fourth Gospel as the outward expression of eternal life. No categorical imperative dictates it, but the voice of child-like freedom and rejoicing is heard in it. And because this is so, Rom. 12 begins: 'I appeal to you . . . by the compassion of God.' God's compassion is the power which calls us to the service of Christian men; it is God's compassion which wills to show its strength through this service; it is God's compassion which both empowers it and is glorified in it. In all this it must not be forgotten that the New Testament never proclaims cheap grace. God's compassion comes to meet us from the Cross of Christ, and cannot continue to be what it is where the ταπεινοφροσύνη, the suffering and dying with Christ, does not continue to be the distinguishing mark of those who are its recipients. If we begin here, even the conception of sacrifice can be used acceptably, as in Rom. 12.1: the service of Christian men is the only sacrifice in which God still takes pleasure. Admittedly, everything depends on whether, as Schlatter once expressed it, we are really offering here the sacrifice of thanksgiving garlanded with joy. In any service which is wrung reluctantly out of us and rendered with sighs God's compassion cannot be glorified nor the freedom of his children demonstrated.

This, then, is the connection in which Rom. 13.1–7, too, stands and demands to be treated. It has been frequently maintained that this section does not possess the eschatological ring which normally dominates the Pauline parenesis; and laborious attempts have therefore been made to exhibit connections with the immediate context. These attempts to relieve our verses of the character of a foreign body by clamping them more firmly in their frame have in general not

[2] I have tried to establish this in some detail in my essay 'Amt und Gemeinde im Neuen Testament', *Exegetische Versuche und Besinnungen* I, 1960, pp. 109–34; ET., 'Ministry and Community in the New Testament', *Essays on New Testament Themes* (SBT 41), 1964, pp. 63–94.

succeeded because of their obviously forced nature. They fail to recognize that the structure of the Pauline parenesis in its detail is built up by co-ordination and not by subordination and deduction, by association of ideas and not by logic. Rom. 13.1–7 is in fact a self-contained passage which as such cannot be directly associated either with the command to love one's enemy in 12.20f. or with the epitomizing demand for love in 13.8–10 or with the eschatological conclusion of the general exhortation in 13.11ff.; much less can it be said to receive its relevance and its theme from any of these. The political authority is neither the adversary of love nor its object. It has to be obeyed, no more and no less, precisely because it is a symbol of the transitory world – a symbol which as such does not in any way point beyond itself to the End. This is the first exegetical acknowledgment, and the premiss of any which may follow, that there can be here no premature connection made between passages which are externally juxtaposed. It is true, however, that our text, and with it the whole parenetical section of this chapter, stands under the sign of the introductory verses 12.1f. – the call to the spiritual worship of God in the everyday life of the world – and is also controlled by the key theme (promulgated in 12.3–6) of charismatic activity. This second indispensable insight for any adequate understanding of the section should also be extremely important for the present analysis: even obedience to earthly authority is regarded by Paul as a fragment of the Christian's worship of God in the secularity of the world and exhibited as having the character of charismatic action. Naturally non-Christians also may render this service in like fashion, grudgingly or enthusiastically or in sober objectivity. Christians are not distinguished from them because they live in another world or because there is any question of their having different tasks laid upon them or of their coming nearer to perfection. But if they are obedient to authority and serve God in this way, they are led and reformed by the grace which leaves no earthly sphere and no ramification of man's inner life without a claim and blessing upon it. In the last resort, therefore, it is not the categorical imperative, a norm, a law or even an obligation which is sovereign over Christians, though even under the rule of grace it is not impossible for the divine word to be 'you must be subject'. In Christ, and concretely in baptism, grace decides our destiny but, according to I Cor. 9.14ff., enables us freely to embrace it. Christians manifest by their doings that the earth, and all that therein is, belongs to the Lord, is not abandoned by him and is blessed in the form in which blessing always and invariably takes under the sovereignty of Christ, i.e. in the form of that free and joyful service of the children of God which is the victorious ensign of the new age planted high in this transitory world.

2. A CRITIQUE OF TYPICAL ATTEMPTS AT INTERPRETATION

I am now repeating in summary and schematic form the thesis of my earlier essay which was exhaustively set out and discussed there. Almost all the history of the interpretation of our passage, which in essence is divided into four representative types, suffers from its conception of the real problem as lying not in the content of the exhortation as such but in the basis on which it is made – to be specific, in the concept of the divine authorization of the present 'powers that be'. This is naturally seen to be a premiss from which very important conclusions can be drawn; I propose to speak about it at length in due course. We may in no wise underplay or trivialize the fact that Paul is here providing a foundation for parenesis and is doing it in the precise manner indicated in the text. At the same time, I believe it to be an error to make this the pivot of the whole thing. I therefore formulate my third fundamental decision: the tenor of the passage is not didactic as if the parenesis were a conclusion from a thesis. The stresses must not be incorrectly interchanged; otherwise we shall almost inevitably find ourselves on a path which does not correspond to the emphasis of the passage. It is just this fact which demonstrates clearly and sometimes even grotesquely the course taken by the history of its interpretation.

The traditional catholic construction has continued to influence Protestant exegesis right up to the present. With the intention of providing a foundation for the parenesis, it finds in Romans 13 a doctrine of the State which can more accurately be called a metaphysic of the State. The State, as part of a structure of being comprehending heaven and earth, represents that order of creation, of natural law, which empowers and gives direction to man's earthly being and (as the expression or profile of the 'eternal law') at the same time points him beyond himself and the earthly order to that supernatural order already realized by anticipation in the Church. Correspondingly, the obedience which is due to the State has only one boundary, i.e. the good estate and the authority of the Church.

Apart from the fact that the parenesis which determines the text is here being overshadowed by a theological system, there are three kinds of criticism to be levelled against this interpretation. To assume so cavalierly that Paul's main purpose here is to speak of the State is to reduce what he is trying to say to an abstraction. It is certainly true that Paul is dealing with the political powers that be and, because he is concerned with the authority they bear, can talk summarily as if *exousia* and political authority were interchangeable terms. But he has his eye on the circumstances of his own time when he takes as his starting-point the plurality of powers and then speaks personally of the rulers and the ministers of God. He is obviously not thinking primarily or exclusively of the Roman *imperium*, but of all who possess power *de facto* – perhaps therefore of the magistrature also; he is looking not at the nature but at the function of these authorities, i.e. the jurisdiction to which they lay claim and which they exercise. It is a matter of giving them their due respect whenever we encounter them even if it is only in the person of the inspector of taxes. Unlike his later interpreters, the apostle is most at home in the realm of concrete, everyday reality in which there are policemen, writ-servers, magistrates, governors and ultimately, of course, the emperor. It is therefore not necessary for him to theorize as he would have to do if he were propounding a doctrine of the State; he contents himself with the call to obedience and the basis of it, without ranging round the firmament. Thus he goes on to speak not of heavenly and earthly order but of the divine ordinance, the ordaining will of God and not of the 'orders', the immediate concern of metaphysics. Finally, to set up a relation of analogy or a polarizing harmony between the heavenly and the earthly is just what our text does not do. Necessary political obedience is not understood as a sign pointing beyond itself to a completed transaction elsewhere. Rather, it is a piece of Christian worship in this world, justified and fulfilled in itself and needing no sanctioning by a theory which regards it as training for salvation.

A variant of the catholic interpretation is that of conservative Lutheranism. In the succession of Reformation idealism, this variant speaks mostly of the 'magistrate' rather than of the State, and this would be thoroughly in accord with the tenor of the text if we were not far too ready to associate with such a conception the whole burden of legality. Paul is not, however, reflecting on the process by which those powers that be of which he speaks in v. 1b came into existence.

For him the man who has asserted himself politically has a God-bestowed function and authority simply as the possessor of power *de facto*. This is why I translate the Greek word *exousia* and its derivatives by power [German *Gewalt*], powers, holders of power: I want to include tyranny and despotism, which in any event reigned supreme over wide stretches of the Roman Empire. It is characteristic of the Lutheran position that it develops on the basis of the Pauline parenesis a theology of 'orders' which speaks now of orders of creation, now of so-called orders of preservation and orders of wrath; and the bearers of political power appear in this scheme of things as the pre-eminent representatives of these orders. If such a view is taken further by speculation, the Catholic metaphysic of the relation of nature and super-nature is apt to be replaced by a theology of history which frequently develops into a salvation history. Support can be found in the mistaken assumption that the predications 'minister, servant of God' were originally sacral terms and have sacral significance in our text also. It is not surprising if, as a logical conclusion, an eschatological function is then ascribed to the political powers that be: they keep the forces of chaos at least within certain definite bounds, thus fulfilling the intention of the divine law, and in both these operations they point beyond themselves to the divine kingdom of perfection, even when they show themselves to be its enemies by overstepping earthly limits. A further immediate critical objection to this kind of interpretation is that the text does not speak of 'orders' but of the 'ordinances' of the divine will and does not move beyond the field of inter-personal relationships into any cosmic dimension. At best then, it provides a springboard for a systematic scheme such as we have outlined but does not reveal it simply by inspection. Whatever may or may not be the theological justification for such a scheme, the exegete as such cannot take on any share of the responsibility for it. On the contrary, he must immediately call attention to further dangers which, as appeared in the Church struggle, are liable to become sinister: this whole approach almost always presupposes the conception of the constitutional State. Now doubtless Paul has in mind the legal function of the possessors of power when he speaks of the punishments and rewards they mete out. But in the same breath he mentions rates and taxes, thus indicating that his interest is really in the concrete and obvious forms of political power. There is no question of a generalizing, abstract meditation on its essential nature. Despotism, in modern terms the police state, is in no way excluded by what is said in the text. It is even more dangerous to set up an eschatological horizon behind these verses. The only place in the New Testament where this happens is in the Revelation, and here political power appears as the might of Antichrist. There is no kind of evidence for giving it a positive significance in salvation history. On the contrary, any glorification of political power is conspicuous by its absence, as is for the most part any attempt at making it into a mythology or a demonic force. The pathos, which systematic theology tends to develop at this point is altogether lacking in the New Testament texts, apart from the Revelation. Political power in them has, in general, nothing to do with the forces of chaos but with the individual Christian to whose advantage it functions and with the individual transgressor of its order, whom it punishes. Above all, it is not the representative in the political sphere of the divine law: it cannot possibly be this, because the divine law is administered solely by the proclamation of the divine work. Rather, it falls wholly and exclusively into that category of the contingent in which there is also eating and drinking, marriage and slavery and, like these other functions and relationships, becomes the proper object of parenesis. For the contingent is not of no importance for the Christian. It is precisely in everyday life, which is determined by contingency, that his service to God has to be rendered.

Undoubtedly we find it very difficult to do justice and to remain faithful to this kind of demythologization of the contingent, to the sobriety and objectivity on this point which arises out of primitive Christian eschatology. Evidence of this is provided by the sort of interpretation which reads an angelology or demonology into our text, maltreated as it is often enough without this. It proceeds on the assumption that it is possible for Paul's understanding of *exousiai* to include the angelic powers, and maintains that this is always the case when mention is made in a theological context of 'every authority' and of the powers. The final conclusion drawn from this is that our text regards earthly political authority as the instrument of the angelic powers, as the Jewish doctrine of the angels of the nations was still doing at the time. It was not accidental that this thesis played a prominent part in the Church Struggle. At that time men came up against what appeared to be the apostle's overwhelmingly positive valuation of political authority which accorded ill with their own experiences. The comparative study of religion and the outlook it engendered deprived the passage of its sting. An earlier generation, still uninfluenced by the theology of dialectic, would have denied without further ado that it had any theological relevance. As it was no longer possible to do this so lightly, the next move was to bring forward the peculiar ambivalence of the powers: originally bound to the service of God, they have a perpetual tendency towards revolt, and then they become the inspiration behind earthly rebellion. On this view of things Paul has, as it were, only shown us one side of the phenomenon whose obverse is revealed by the Revelation. The interpreter who takes account of both can and indeed must provide a solution in terms of theological dialectic. The question must surely arise as to whether anything is gained by this except an escape road, which may and will lead to a relativization of Scripture in both directions. It seems to me that a dialectical theology argued in this way with the help of a mythology and a theology extracted from a concordance does little credit to its initiators and proves only that it is possible to defend oneself by ingenious harmonization against the ultimate challenge of the text without ever having given this challenge its full weight. But such fruit, plucked unripe from the tree of knowledge, was not bitter enough even yet. The thesis expounded above was patient of being combined with the outlook of the primitive Christian hymns, according to which the heavenly and demonic powers have been subjected to the exalted Christ. By adding the further interpretation that these powers had been made the servants of Christ, these theologians arrived ultimately at the so-called christological foundation of the State. The to-and-fro of argument and counter-argument in the debate, pursued as it was with great passion on all sides, does not need to be repeated yet again. In my opinion the exegetical battle in this matter came to a decisive end when A. Strobel, in his article on Rom. 13,[3] showed conclusively that the Jewish doctrine of the angels of the nations is not to be imported into our text and that, all along the line, the terminology we encounter here has its origin in the vocabulary of secular government in the Hellenistic world. We might say that Paul was the first to revive the importance of the usage and phraseology customary in Hellenistic officialdom, by employing them in the service of his theology. This coheres excellently with our other findings: the background here is that of everyday life in the Hellenistic world and this life finds exact verbal expression in the terminology used. For instance, the rationale of the parenesis finds its closest parallel in the sentence in Josephus:

[3] 'Zum Verständnis vom Röm, 13', *ZNW* 47, 1956, pp. 67–93.

'Sovereignty comes to no man, unless God so orders matters.'[4] If we isolate our own passage, the only voice which echoes in it is that of the synagogue of the Diaspora and its environment. This also explains why eschatology plays no part in it; why what it has to say is based much more on a doctrine of creation. It takes on a Christian imprint solely from its connection with the introduction to the whole parenetic section in 12.1–6.

The only other attempt at interpretation about which I am going to particularize is that represented by Karl Barth and his school. While it is a fact that the theory of angelic powers standing behind the earthly authorities has had some influence on this interpretation its centre of gravity does not lie there. The concern of Barth and his disciples is with the present lordship of Christ over all the world as it is directly and powerfully proclaimed in the primitive Christian hymns. Even the State and the political authorities in general are for the faithful, since the exaltation of Christ, not simply brought into subjection to an abstract divine Creator and Preserver. They are located in the area of christology: admittedly not in the innermost circle in which the community operates, but still in the wider one indicated by the proclamation of Jesus as the Cosmocrator. They, too, must in their special fashion and, even against their will, serve the Christ and those that are his. Conversely, having knowledge of this mystery, those who believe are enabled to assume political responsibility in an unprejudiced, sober and critical spirit – in short, as servants – and thus carry out what may not be the most important part of their service of God in the world, but is nevertheless an indispensable one. Barth's concern is that this is precisely what should happen. Everything else is of interest only as ministering to the necessity and possibility of such a task. The Pauline parenesis is treated as the heart of the passage; and from this standpoint it is heavily underlined and expounded at length with the exegete's eye on the conditions obtaining in contemporary democracies. In New Testament times political responsibility was only a live option for the Christian in rare and exceptional cases and in areas of subordinate jurisdiction. If Paul limits his scope to the requirement of obedience, this corresponds with reality; there was normally no other means of political expression for the stratum of society out of which early Christianity arose. For this reason it is impossible simply to transpose our passage into our modern situation. The fact that this has nevertheless been

[4] Josephus, *Jewish War* II 8.7.

done in Protestantism for at least a century contributed to the phenomenon of 'passive obedience' and the catastrophes it conjured up. It is a dangerous factor in biblicism, which guards the letter and neglects prophecy, the actualization of the message. None of this should be forgotten when interpreting Romans 13. Exegesis can only be an auxiliary here; it cannot be a substitute for real interpretation, i.e. a translation into contemporary modes of understanding. I am certainly not saying that free course should be given to a systematic theology which has been arbitrarily imposed on the text, as must inevitably be the case when Barth and his followers give the present passage a christological orientation. It is characteristic of our chapter that any christological, as well as any eschatological, patterning is found wanting. To ignore this is to build castles in the air and to betray oneself in so doing by the christology and cosmology one employs. It is true that the primitive Christian hymns proclaimed that the lordship of Christ had already broken in on the world and the cosmic powers had been brought into subjection. But these hymns originated in the enthusiastic religious life of the community and to this extent it is no accident that they base their message on the myth of the world saviour familiar to us from Vergil's *Fourth Eclogue*. Paul, however, had to fight a life-long battle not only against Judaism but also against enthusiasm. Some fruits of this battle can be seen in his replacement of the pattern of the Incarnation and Exaltation of Christ by the other pattern of the Cross and Resurrection; in his ascription to Christians of a present participation in the Cross but not immediately in the glory of the Resurrection; and in his treatment of the statement that the kingdom and powers of this world have been subjected to Christ, a statement which in I Cor. 15.28 he transposes from the perfect or the present to the future tense, thus refraining from ascribing to Jesus the title of Cosmocrator. These are all ways of fending off enthusiasm. This is not to say that Jesus is not for Paul also the exalted one, and the Kyrios not of the Church only, but also of the world. He is Kyrios, however, in a peculiar hiddenness, so that the assault of grace upon the world is borne forward by the gospel concerning him and by the servanthood of the community, and no corner of our earth is left free from the demand and the promise of that same grace. To speak of Christ's universal sovereignty otherwise than in this relation to the word of preaching and the servanthood of the community can only be to come once again under the spell of enthusiasm and to fall a prey to the same mythology in which primitive Christian enthusiasm found for itself a means of expression. In my view, Barth and his followers do not protect themselves sufficiently against this danger. Earthly institutions and authorities cannot be grounded in christology – only the community of believers and Christian activity.

I have set out in this section the most important types of interpretation of Rom. 13, but have so far not touched upon what is really the latest development. This can best be described by saying that all the positions outlined above are being more or less criticized from within their own camp, and it is becoming clear that modifications and reductions in their claims have to be made. This is happening, under the influence of an exegesis which, here as elsewhere, is pushing back systematic theology. Admittedly, it is not quite so obvious as it might appear that we should applaud this process. For, while on the one hand certain specific fundamental historical findings are gaining general acceptance, on the other, sharp theological contours are becoming blurred. It is becoming continually more difficult to know what is really happening in the guerilla warfare of the specialists, in which there are so many shots fired and so few targets hit, so many issues confused and so few decided. I am not going to develop this point further, but shall attempt in conclusion, only touching lightly on what has been said already, myself to reach something like an interpretation of the most important problems of the text.

3. NECESSITY AND FREEDOM IN CHRISTIAN OBEDIENCE

What does *ἀνάγκη ὑποτάσσεσθαι* mean? What is the real aim of the apostolic argument for it? Is there any limit to the obedience which is here being demanded? These are the decisive questions thrown up by our text. We may profitably begin with the verb, placed as it is at the beginning of the sentence in a manner which we cannot possibly ignore. Why does Paul not use *ὑπακούειν* instead? The many and varied derivatives of the root *τασσ-* which we encounter in our passage must at least have been intended to make it clear that this is no arbitrary choice. *ὑπεταγή* is the obedience which we owe because it is inherent in some specific *τάγμα*, i.e. it arises out of given earthly relationships, while *ὑπακοή* simply designates obedience as an achievement. Paul looks out on a world in which superiors and subordinates exist and intends his readers to come to terms with this reality. Just for this reason he can also demand that obedience should be rendered to the subordinate political authorities. Actually our text does offer at this point some foothold for the different variations of that theology of 'the orders' which I delineated above. To dispute this would be to lose the right to criticize this theology from the standpoint of the text. Any serious attempt at interpretation must take up some posture towards the problem even if only to emphasize at once that this approach is not necessarily patient of further development. For Paul himself is not immediately saying any more than that God has so arranged the world from the beginning – at the creation, by all means, if you like – as to make it possible to render him service within it; and this is why he created superiors and subordinates. The questions which arise out of this situation for us, with our demythologized world-view and our prevailing image of political democracy, are not yet felt as questions. Two examples make this clear: the apostle takes the system of slavery in the ancient world for granted and even affirms it on occasions, even though slave revolts were already taking place in his time and, as hinted at in the letter to Philemon, there were in existence armies of runaway slaves and even the theological question as to the relationship of Christian slaves to their Christian masters was already being raised. Paul has so little interest in all this, at least so far as erecting this last case into the sign of a new and better social order is concerned, that, according to the *prima facie* understanding of I Cor. 7.21, he can recommend a slave not to take advantage of a possible release; let alone to strive for it. He bases this on what may rightly be called the provocative axiom 'Every one should remain in the state in which he was called'. The same thing happens when the problem of the equality of the sexes has to be faced, at least in respect to the common life in Christ. Paul continually sets forth the subordination of the woman to the man as self-explanatory and God-ordained and thus remains in this regard within the limits of the conventions both of the classical and the Jewish worlds. The self-explanatory and God-ordained nature of this state of affairs was not in fact so ineluctable as the apostolic decision and the biblical words in question seem to some contemporary theologians, and even to many Church governments, to make it. For, according to the first letter to the Corinthians, at least in those congregations which were under the controlling influence of enthusiasm the question was stirring as to whether, with the invasion of the new age and the reception of women into the Church, female partners in a Christian marriage and the female Christians within a congregation ought not to be exempt from obsolete earthly convention. But, in the face of just such questions as these, Paul holds strictly to tradition, so that we can now summarize the results of this part of our investigation in three propositions:

1. Obviously, the injunction to obedience to the political authorities is connected with the injunctions to slaves and women, indeed, more accurately, runs parallel to them.

2. In this area Paul always acts as the representative of the conservative attitudes of a view of existence we must call patriarchal – a view which, historically borrowed from the synagogue of the diaspora, bases social ordinances on theological principles.

3. Where the apostle is not simply and naively reproducing these attitudes, he is having to sharpen them because in his concrete situation he is confronted with an eschatological enthusiasm. The burden of this is, that in Christ the life-forms of the past have been fundamentally recapitulated and should at least be effective signs within the Christian community of the reality of the new heavenly world. For this reason, such enthusiasm keeps as far aloof as possible from the given realities of political conditions. Paul manages in remarkable fashion to relate to his purpose in a renewed form the opposing positions he captures, even in the context of such a raw encounter with their deep-rooted theological premisses and conclusions. It is in the perspective of this encounter that he propagates the slogan *ὑποταγή*; he seeks to convey thereby that he is harking back to the will of the Creator, acknowledging the reality of superior and subordinate authorities in our world, forcing the Christian to face this reality and designating it the field of his (the Christian's) everyday service of God.

Can we rest content with this historical clarification of the phenomenon? That would mean that the question of the content was irrelevant so far as we were concerned. For while it is quite certain that the Christian community will always from time to time have to reckon with enthusiasm, it is equally certain that it will not, in the circumstances of today, wish to make the field of social order the venue of this confrontation. The Church would be acting in extremely reactionary fashion if she were not to recognize that it is impossible to maintain the apostolic arguments for the subordination of women or for political subjection as they stand, after the argument for slavery has collapsed. Obviously, we can no longer rely solely on the argument from 'my station and its duties' without becoming involved in hopeless contradictions. If the controversy about the Dibelius letter[5] has any theological relevance at all, this is what it has revealed. But is Paul really in the last resort primarily concerned with maintaining respect for existing authorities which doubtless may embody principles of order but may equally preserve principles of disorder or may, in a changed world, become transformed from factors in social order into factors in social injustice? The problem is important enough to justify a digression. I should like to glance here, as I did in my introduction, at I Corinthians, but this time at 11.2ff., where Paul orders that women should be veiled. He makes quite clear the object of this usage, which was probably first introduced by him and was in any case quite foreign to the behaviour pattern of a Greek woman (and for this reason is productive of indignation among the Corinthian enthusiasts); the object is to incorporate into worship itself a sign of the God-willed subordination of the woman to the man. Basically it is a matter not of the custom as such, which could hardly be made the subject of a passionate theological disputation by the two sides; it is more a matter of the problem of Christian freedom, so far as it affects the status of the sexes before God which is now a common and indistinguishable status. In worship least of all – so the Christian women of Corinth may well have argued – ought those distinctions to be adopted which might otherwise be tolerated as the convention and perhaps even the continuing necessity of a transitory world. We ought to be struck by the severity with which Paul reacts against this enlightened and indeed theologically well-founded viewpoint as well as by the unmistakable irritation which drives him to juxtapose the most diverse counter-arguments. We encounter first something like a metaphysic of graded emanations, then, secondly, the creation story; this is followed, thirdly, by what is to our notions a superstitious picture of the presence of lustful angels at Christian worship, fourthly by an order of nature constructed more or less *ad hoc* and, finally, the universal custom of the Pauline congregations. Such an accumulation only succeeds in suggesting to the unprejudiced hearer and reader that no single one of the reasons adduced, thrown together as they are in this odd way, is convincing in itself. This is how a man argues when he is on the defensive, and in any case Paul eventually lost this particular battle. All the more remarkable, there-

[5] Bishop Otto Dibelius, 'Obrigkeit? Eine Frage an den 60-jährigen Landesbischof [Lilje], 1959', in *Dokumente zur Frage der Obrigkeit,* ed. Mochalski and Werner, 1960, pp. 21–31.

fore, appears the apostle's determination that he will in no circumstances give up the point of principle lying behind the practical issue on which he is being pressed. It is impossible to maintain that he displays a happy touch here. On the contrary, here, if anywhere, we see that the concrete argumentation behind a piece of Pauline parenesis can be problematical; it may neither have a real theological foundation nor be illuminating in its own right. Not only does it make use of traditional attitudes which have already failed to convince their original hearers: sometimes, it does not scruple to dig back into the arsenal of a dubious world-view, even into that of popular superstition. Not until we look clear-sightedly at all this does the question really become a burning one, as to what Paul is really contending for with such determination and yet at the same time with such poor arguments. For neither of these does the preservation of what is traditionally called the 'orders of creation' provide a sufficient motive. The watch-words of the Corinthian enthusiasts, like the letter as a whole, indicate rather that, so far as the custom which forms the *casus belli* here is concerned, the battle for the 'orders of creation' must be considered only as helping to solve the problematic of Christian freedom by providing a paradigm case. The Corinthian watch-word 'freedom', which, considered both in itself and in connection with the specific case at issue, seems to be more enlightened than the Pauline reaction to it, suffers from the basic defect of enthusiastic piety; it takes account of freedom exclusively as freedom from burdensome compulsion. The apostle, on the other hand, is concerned here, as always, with the freedom which knows itself to be called to serve and it is just this freedom which he sees threatened where enthusiasm is rattling at the doors of the existing order and proclaiming its allegedly just claims in the name of the Spirit. The Christian is determined as Christian by service. Spirit ceases to be Holy Spirit if this criterion of Christian existence in the world is obscured, endangered or superseded. It is for the sake of this determining of Christian existence in the world that Paul sets himself so passionately against the separation of creation and new age. The new age is not suspended in mid-air: it takes root on this our earth to which Christ came down. It does not create for itself there an island of the blessed as the Corinthians believe: it creates the possibility of the kind of service which can no longer be universal and alive if it is not carried out in the midst of the old, passing world, thus declaring God's rightful lordship over this earth; that is, preserving the world as divine creation. According to Paul, it is none other than the Spirit who imposes himself on the everyday life of the world as being the locus of our service of God; while emancipation, even when it appeals to the Spirit, prefers to retreat from this everyday life and the possibilities of service that are given with it, and is thus a perversion of Christian freedom.

Now let us return to Romans 13. It seems to me that it is permissible for us to use the method of appraisal applied above without any hesitation in our consideration of this text also. The argumentation on which the parenesis is based is not quite so problematical as in I Cor. 11.2ff., but cannot be said without further qualification to be illuminating. Its brevity, which indicates that it is dealing with familiar material, is enough to mark it as traditional. This is even more true of a certain optimism about political aims which does not merely see in the existing political authorities the divinely constituted servants of the divine will but goes so far as to declare that they are objects of fear only for evil men. The argument is that of the synagogue of the Diaspora which had every reason to be concerned about the integration of its members into the existing set-up. Paul was able to pick up this precise point in his use of traditional material in I Cor. 11. But Rom. 13.1f. shows that his own purpose goes one layer deeper. Certainly he can look at the given realities of the world and say, 'We must be subject'. He can do this because he sees also in these given realities the will of the Creator at work. But equally, the logic of the total theology of the apostle makes it clear that the real basis and the peculiar centre of his gospel do not lie here. The traditional arguments are, to put it in a nutshell, Paul's emergency aids to call the Christian to take his stand before the true God, the Lord of the earth, and thus to call him to the possibility of genuine service in everyday life. Anyone who prefers to live in isolation from the world and its powers is in practice taking away from the world its character as God's creation and is thereby disqualified from serious service. For Christian service must take place on earth and in earth's everyday life; otherwise it becomes fantasy. We have no need arbitrarily to seek out a field in which to serve. It is just the life of everyday which is for us 'the given'; further, it is the same life to which the political powers that be, and even, in certain circumstances, a dictatorship, belong. To acknowledge the given nature of this everyday life, which may possibly wear the colours of dictatorship or slavery – it is just this that is charismatic activity, the possibility of Christian freedom.

Finally, it is not the given realities in themselves which move the apostle to argue that 'We must be subject' but the necessity to authenticate Christian existence and the Christian's status in the eyes of the Lord, who stakes his claim to the world by facing it continually, in the person of his servants, with the eschatological token of his lordship – the quality of *ταπεινοφροσύνη*.

We can now in conclusion take a look at v. 5. What does 'not only to avoid God's wrath, but also for the sake of conscience' mean? The difficulty lies in finding a just interpretation of the concept *συνείδησις*. Its meaning in Paul is confined to the attitude of the man who recognizes himself to be subject to the demands of a categorical imperative and, to this extent, is endowed with the possibility of self-criticism. The frame of reference here, then, as with *νοῦς*, is the critical awareness, certainly in the measure that the critical faculty is directed back in introspection at the man and his own actions. When Lietzmann paraphrases the verse freely as 'not only because of the wrath, but out of conviction', that is obviously going too far because it is interpolating into our passage the phenomenon of the good conscience. Paul is saying no more than 'in the knowledge of the binding summons of God addressed to you'. I am unable to see any compelling reason for regarding v. 5 as a gloss.[6] It is true that v. 6 follows well on v. 4. But v. 5 and v. 6 run parallel to each other, in so far as, corresponding to the argument of the whole section, testimony is borne to the divine ordinance and authority revealed in the existing political power, before attention is paid to the duties which the Christian does actually fulfil. That he does so without question is seen as proof that he has in fact no reason to fear the bearers of political power. Verse 5 does not therefore bring a double motivation to bear – obedience both out of fear and for conscience' sake – but an alternative: others may have grounds to fear the powers that be, the Christian obeys them as one who knows himself to be confronted in their claim with the divine summons and who in his obedience is rendering service to God. There can then, here or elsewhere, be no question of interpreting Christian obedience in action as slavish passive obedience. Christian obedience is never blind; and, indeed, open-eyed obedience, directed by *συνείδησις*, must even be critical. For him, God does not dissolve into his own immanence to the extent of being identified with it; rather, he remains Lord of the world and as such calls the Christian into the freedom of sonship. An obedience which

[6] R. Bultmann, 'Glossen im Römerbrief', *TLZ* 72, 1947, col. 200.

does not breathe this freedom of sonship does not deserve the designation 'Christian'. The transitory is not here being identified with the ultimate, the earthly is not having divine glory ascribed to it, a human claim is not being equated with the divine will, even if the divine will creates the encounter with the human claim. The significance of this for the individual case cannot be laid down beforehand. He who is called to the service of God in the world has always to make sure what the issue is (Phil. 1.9f.); as well as knowledge he needs *αἴσθησις*, which I should translate as 'the feeling for the actual situation at the time'. We are not exempt from this proviso in our dealings with the political authorities. At this point there opens up before us in principle that whole range of variations of practice exemplified in Acts, which stretches from willing subordination to martyrdom and from the silent endurance of maltreatment to the appeal to Caesar and the axiom that we ought to obey God rather than man. Christian obedience demonstrates its charismatic nature by its very incapacity to be uniform and conformist. There are for specific cases something like models of the particular attitude required. But no one is robbed of his own power of decision, of the use of his own eyes and his own reason, of the *αἴσθησις* of Phil. 1.10; nor is the feeling for tact and moral inevitability, self-respect and dignity in any way circumscribed.

This brings us to our final question for which, although it does not arise directly out of the exegesis of the passage, our interpretation, taken as a whole, must have some satisfactory answer. Is there anything which might rightly be called a limit to the obedience here being demanded of the Christian and, if so, where is it to be drawn? In a nutshell my answer would be: 'Christian obedience comes to an end at the point where further service becomes impossible – and only there.' That happens incontrovertibly when the suggestion is made to the Christian that he should deny his existence as a Christian and abandon his particular Christian task. On the other hand, that is not the same thing as saying that the Christian has to hold fast inflexibly to certain traditional forms of Christian existence, responsibility and community life. The Lord, who brings upon us new historical situations, does not call us to a conservative or even reactionary attitude, and those who are endowed with *charisma* are able to distinguish between tradition and the opportunity of the hour. Martyrdom for the sake of the traditional form of our service is not enjoined upon us, any more than retreat into 'inward religion' and 'private life'. What we have to do is to authenticate the Christ as the hidden Lord of the world in our doing and in our being. The outward form which corresponds to this content of the hidden Lord of the world may be the narrowing down and straitening of the Church's room for manoeuvre even into the compass of a prison cell or a grave. Sometimes the Lord of the world speaks more audibly out of prison cells and graves than out of the life of churches which congratulate themselves on their concordat with the State. The space his lordship occupies is not identical with our space, the fact that we are hemmed in does not annul the breadth of his word, nor does our death annul his possibilities. A place on earth for us and our institutions is not the ultimate criterion about which our deeds and omissions have to be orientated. The boundary of our service is the point at which we cease to acknowledge Christ as Lord of the world, not the point at which the hiddenness of this Lord as such is demonstrated and made sensible to us. On the contrary it is precisely his hiddenness which, paradoxically enough, defines our service. We ourselves are not permitted to plunge into that most profound hiddenness which still characterizes him today as Lord of the world. We have rather so to bear it both as hallmark and as burden that we do not collapse under its weight into a Christian anonymity. Anonymity cannot be combined with conscientious obedience; we have to resist escape into it and pressure towards it. It is possible to soldier on, or to offer resistance, anonymously, but not to serve.

This raises the problem of the possibility of Christian resistance to the existing political power; it raises, that is, the specific question of participation in revolution. It is clear that this possibility could not yet be considered by Paul, because it is a product of modern democracy. It is equally clear that there cannot be a Christian revolution as such. Earthly revolutions are not to be justified simply by using the name of Christ. The sole consideration is whether, within the framework of modern democracy, that is, as a citizen and acting in full political responsibility, the Christian can rightly take part in a revolution and indeed can manifest his conscientious obedience in this very context. Once again, this question is no more capable of being answered in advance and in general than any other question about our relation to earthly reality. Here we have obviously to create for ourselves and each other a fundamental freedom to make different, and sometimes opposite, decisions. But the presupposition of such different, and even opposite, decisions cannot remain open at both ends; and this is because in both cases the individual decision stands under the sign of the Christian service of God in and for the world. The question of the possible participation of the Christian in a revolution is now framed in sharper terms. Is there such a thing as participation in revolution as an authentication of the service of God in the world? When and where can this be possible – not merely for the citizen of a democratic community in the carrying out of his political responsibility, but for the man who being such a citizen, yet wills to be, and to remain, a Christian also? My own personal answer would be, that such a possibility could only exist when the possessors of political power are threatening and destroying in a radical way those ties which hold together a political community as a whole in bonds of mutual service. When it becomes impossible any longer to render whole-hearted service within the total context of a common life, but every concrete act of service within the individual's province takes on the character of participation in a common self-destruction – and in my view this possibility became reality for every man with eyes to see in the Third Reich (at least after Stalingrad) – then it also becomes impossible to deny to the Christian his right as a citizen to take part in revolution. Christian obedience in everyday life takes its significance from the fact that we have both the duty and the privilege of service; for this reason, and in the same way, in the conditions of a democracy, Christian obedience can and must end at the point where, because of the nature of the existing political authority, service, though still possible as an act of the individual, is yet robbed of all meaning within the total context of the life of a given community.

It has been my purpose in making these last points to lay bare the issues in this matter of the Christian's conscientious obedience. If my own answer to the question I have posed has not been misleading in its general drift, it may still have been inadequately formulated. But it seems to me necessary that the question should at least be discerned and posed, if we really want to understand Romans 13 not merely in the light of past and present exegesis but as a piece of guidance for ourselves. In this exercise everything will depend on preserving the paradoxical connection of necessity and freedom at the point of their deepest unity – that free man's service which is the good estate of Christian existence in the world.

XI

A PAULINE VERSION OF THE 'AMOR FATI'*

THE ONLY ROAD by which one can really penetrate to Paul, the integral human being, goes through his theology. For, conversely, this theology is more strongly conditioned than that of any other New Testament writer by the humanity of its author. This interweaving of person and content is displayed at its most attractive when Paul is defending his right to be provided for by his churches and, in the same breath, refusing to exercise it. If I may, I am now going to repeat some previous work of mine and attempt to clarify further by an exegesis of I Cor. 9.14–18 the contradictory attitude of the apostle on this point – gracious, and yet extremely dialectical. The passage runs:

In the same way the Lord commanded that those who preach the Gospel would get their living by the Gospel. But I have never taken advantage of this right; nor am I writing this now, in order to secure any such provision. It would be better[1] for me rather than for – no one should make my boast[2] an empty boast.[3] For if I preach, there is no question of boasting. For necessity lies upon me. I should be miserable if I were to give up preaching. If I did it on my own initiative, I should expect reward; but as I do it under a sense of compulsion, I am, on the other hand, simply discharging a trust.[4] Then what is my reward? The satisfaction of preaching the Gospel

* Inaugural lecture at Tübingen, 3 June 1959, first published in *ZTK* 56, 1959, pp. 138–54.

[1] A fact is being established here, surely, not a wish expressed. Cf. J. C. K. Hofmann, *Die Heilige Schrift Neuen Testaments* II/2, 1874, p. 186. [This passage departs from the RSV and follows the author's own version. Tr.]

[2] Generally applied to the 'matter for boasting'.

[3] It is now generally accepted that the sentence is an anacoluthon. Cf. H. Lietzmann, *An die Korinther* (HNT 9), 4th ed. by W. G. Kümmel, 1949, p. 43.

[4] In accordance with an older hypothesis, Hofmann, *op. cit.*, p. 168, G. Heinrici, *Handbuch über den ersten Brief an die Korinther*, 1888, p. 257f., P. Bachmann, *Der erste Brief des Paulus an die Korinther*, 1921, p. 320f., R. Liechtenhan, *Die urchristliche Mission*, 1946, p. 61 n. 4, all take vv. 17b and 18a together. Kümmel (in Lietzmann, p. 180) admits this to be possible; J. Weiss, *Der erste Korintherbrief*, 1925, pp. 240f., raises some not very convincing objections.

without financial reimbursement, without, that is, taking advantage of my rights as a preacher.[5]

It is very difficult indeed to understand the passionate[6] and breathless nature of these verses revealed in the apparently quite illogical assertions which follow without pause on each other's heels. In particular, the 'obscure structure of ideas'[7] 'in the middle is in striking contrast to the clear articulation in the rest of the chapter in which Paul is illustrating (over against the enthusiasts) by his personal renunciation the principle that love sets bounds to Christian freedom. The first section (vv. 1–14) lays the foundation – by means of numerous examples and the express command of Scripture taken as that of the Lord – of the apostolic right to make claims on the community. The third (vv. 19–23) was reduced in Luther's 'Freedom of a Christian Man' to the neat formula that, in faith, the Christian is a free lord of all things and subject to no one, but that, in love, he is a profitable servant and subject to all men. The fourth (vv. 24–27) closes appropriately with an injunction to self-discipline. Within the framework of this composition our verses seem to be totally superfluous, because the design of the whole is quite clear even without them.[8] Their solemn character appears abruptly. The uncontrolled agitation of the apostle is not only somewhat offensive in itself, but it also obscures the meaning of the statements and the logical progression of ideas. What is the point, for example, of the anacoluthon 'It would be better for me to die than for – no one shall make my boast an empty boast'? Is Paul perhaps taking fright at the rashness with which he has nearly precipitated himself into self-malediction? The conclusion of the sentence does not, in any case, have a palliating effect, but, setting aside with deliberate defiance any second thoughts which may possibly have arisen, goes on 'No one shall make my boast an empty boast.' We cannot ignore the fact that the correlatives 'boast' and 'reward' are in the air here and that the second is used in various different ways. It is true that similar stylistic observations can be made at many points in the Pauline letters. The temperament of the apostle

[5] The verb does not mean 'misuse' (so J. Schniewind, *Die Begriffe Wort und Evangelium bei Paulus*, 1910, p. 99 n. 3) but 'use to the limit', as in 7.31; cf. Hofmann, *op. cit.*, p. 189; R. Cornely, *Prior epistola ad Corinthios*, 1890, p. 255; J. Weiss, *op.cit.*, p. 242.

[6] This quality is perceived by K. Heim, *Die Gemeinde des Auferstandenen*, 1949, p. 117.

[7] Bachmann, *op. cit.*, p. 319.

[8] O. Holtzmann, *Das Neue Testament . . . erklärt*, 1926, p. 537: 'Here Paul has digressed somewhat from his objective.'

is for ever breaking through the ordered pattern of established rules. But it is permissible for the expositor to take comfort in psychology when these embarrassing moments occur? Ought he not rather to enquire whether the particularly remarkable features of a given passage do not indicate the presence of an especially significant statement and perhaps even the core of the whole chapter?[9]

At least we can say that it is only the section with which we are concerned that prevents the text being misunderstood and interpreted as a universal moral truth amounting (allowing for a very secular kind of exaggeration) to 'Noblesse oblige'.[10] Even though our verses do in fact prepare the way for, and indirectly bring home, a call which applies to every Christian, nevertheless Paul is speaking primarily only of that law which determines his own life.[11] Yet the life and activity of the apostle are an eschatological phenomenon; they belong to the realm opened up by the Cross and Resurrection of Jesus, bounded by the expected judgment of the world and characterized in the present by the message of the Gospel. To understand the statements in the passage in the sense of a universal truth of religion or ethics would be not merely to flatten out their specific contours but to deprive them of their peculiar character, i.e. their connection with the Gospel.

This assertion plunges us, of course, deep into the problem which lies at the heart of our passage, so far as its content is concerned; because this claim which it makes to preach the Gospel is highly controversial and, in point of fact, very questionable. In the Gospel, as developed by Paul, the anthropological issue is that man should become truly human. There is therefore bound up indissolubly with this Pauline Gospel a criticism of human presumption, especially in its religious dress – i.e. the fantasy that man can, by his own achievement, acquire security over against God, boast of him as his own possession and claim a reward from him. It is all the more astonishing that the apostle speaks here without any embarrassment of his boast and the reward which is bound up with it. In so doing, surely he is contradicting the rest of his theology and what lies at its heart –

[9] Thus J. Weiss, p. 239, discerns here 'the most intimate motivations'. The point is made circumstantially and clearly by C. Maurer, 'Grund und Grenze apostolischer Freiheit', in *Antwort: Festschrift zum 70. Geburtstag Karl Barths*, 1956, pp. 630ff.

[10] Cf. C. Maurer, p. 631.

[11] Commentators frequently lay stress on the singular from v. 15 on; e.g. Cornely, p. 252; Bachmann, p. 318; J. Weiss, p. 239.

the teaching about justification? Is he preaching to others what he is unable to keep up himself? More alarming still, are we even being shown here that the Reformation doctrine of justification which stressed so strongly 'by faith alone' was wrong in calling upon Paul as its chief witness and, to say the least, had a one-sided picture of his attitude?

In fact, the confessional battle flares up again whenever the question of the exposition of this passage arises. The clearest expression of the interpretation which has prevailed in the history of the Church is to be found in the commentary by the Jesuit Cornely at which, even after seventy years, we cannot but marvel for the precision of its argument. This runs: when Paul describes his preaching as something that is laid upon him and thus not to be looked upon as a service which brings with it a reward, he is, in his own way, picking up the saying of Jesus in Luke 17.10:[12] 'We are unworthy servants; we have only done what was our duty.' If, however, he is not renouncing in principle the ideas of 'boast' and 'expecting reward', then he must offer some sacrificial achievement. This he does in the shape of his refusal to make any claim on the Church. One sentence summarizes this:

> The apostle is really opposing works of supererogation and their reward to those which are done by commandment.[13]

The phrase 'works of supererogation', the religious 'work' which has a special value just because it was not required, has been the more or less accepted concomitant, whether tacitly or implicitly, of the exegesis of our passage from the early Church through Aquinas up to F. C. Baur's essay just mentioned;[14] and even today it has by no means completely died away.[15] In the interests of a searching examination, therefore, it is something rather to be regretted than welcomed that mention of it is now for the most part carefully avoided and that it no longer plays the same part as formerly, even in Catholic

[12] The words of Jesus are recalled at this point by writers of the Early Church as well as, in more recent times, by F. C. Baur, 'Beiträge zur Erklärung der Korintherbriefe', *Theol. Jahrbücher*, 1852, p. 546; F. Godet, *Kommentar zu dem ersten Briefe an die Korinther* II, 1888, p. 31; Heinrici, p. 258; J. Weiss, p. 240.

[13] Cornely, *op. cit.*, p. 234. [14] *Op. cit.*, p. 546.

[15] So, in particular, F. S. Gutjahr, *Die Zwei Briefe an die Korinther*, 1907, p. 240. The pattern of obligation and 'works of supererogation' is stressed by A. Schaefer, *Erklärung der beiden Briefe an die Korinther*, 1903, p. 173; W. Wrede, *Paulus*, 1904, p. 13 (ET, *Paul*, 1907, pp. 15f.); J. Sickenberger, *Die Briefe des heiligen Paulus an die Korinther und Römer*, 1932, p. 43; L. Cerfaux, *L'Eglise des Corinthiens*, 1946, p. 69.

exegesis. On the Protestant side, there is no doubt at all that this silence is due to the ever-increasing disaffiliation of exegesis from dogmatic commitment. But because it was impossible to get rid of the passage itself, it now became necessary to find some explanation in comparative studies or in psychology for what was, from a modern and liberalistic standpoint, seen as dogmatically unacceptable.

If this were true, it was but a short step to the hypothesis that Paul had not totally overcome or broken with the Jewish scheme of 'works' which he had inherited.[16] Rabbinic teaching certainly makes a distinction between the fulfilment of commandments and good works,[17] between what is enjoined and what is voluntary,[18] and thus establishes the possibility that man may use the freedom which is given over to him for activity which is well-pleasing to God and fruitful in the world. Regarded historically, this hypothesis represents an undoubted gain. For, in my opinion, we ought to admit that the apostle shows himself to be intimately acquainted with Jewish tradition and operates with it, at least in his vocabulary – i.e. in his use of 'boast' and 'reward', in his distinction between compulsion and freedom, in his emphasis on renunciation as a personal sacrifice. To deny this is to do both Paul and ourselves a disservice – however excellent the reasons which might lead us to regard such an admission as dangerous to the Pauline message and therefore suspicious in itself. Even an apostle stands within a situation which is conditioned by an historical inheritance and may not be simply interchanged or equated with our own.

The assumption (which today is frequently worked to death) that historical understanding requires the effort to become contemporary with what is to be understood is only meaningful so long as it does not deprive what is past of its historical contour, its uniqueness and the mystery of individuality, with which we have always to reckon. The beginning of all historical knowledge is respect for the strangeness of the other into whose skin we cannot simply slip without further ado. The man who has forgotten how to marvel or to disapprove, who no longer remembers that detachment is the natural point of departure for the historian, has lost the capacity for real hearing and learning. That which is 'other', that which is past, may become for

[16] See particularly Wrede, pp. 13ff. (ET, p. 16); H. Weinel, *Biblische Theologie des Neuen Testamentes*, 1911, p. 309.

[17] Strack-Billerbeck, *Kommentar zum Neuen Testament aus Talmud und Midrasch* IV, 1928, pp. 559ff.

[18] *Ibid.*, III, 1926, p. 400.

him a mirror and an occasion for self-awareness. But a history which is basically narcissistic does violence to anything which does not fall into its lap, which it cannot manipulate in its own interests; it lives, whether in its naive or its fanatical form, on the kind of lack of respect for the particular which fundamentally incapacitates for the recognition of truth. Of course Paul was, and remained, a Jew. The fact that he became the apostle of Jesus Christ does not mean that he can rightly be forced into the scheme of Protestantism, whether orthodox or liberal – on the contrary. It can by no means be taken for granted from the beginning that it was impossible for him to relapse from time to time – and therefore perhaps in this very passage – into the Jewish doctrine of merit. Historical phenomena seldom or never take forms which afford us complete satisfaction; and biblical texts were not written, neither are they intended to be studied, for the purpose of providing proof texts for a personal, or an ecclesiastically obligatory, theology. They have their own right to existence – ultimately, an historical right. Not to see this and acknowledge its validity is to be driven into adopting an illusionary theology – and of these there are, unfortunately, no lack today.

If we have at this point succeeded in marking the horizon of our questioning, or at any rate in making it clear that objectivity (in the sense of the requirement insisted on by the liberals) is demanded in the face of every finding which forces itself upon us, we may now dispute all the more resolutely the view that our passage actually *does* contain the 'works of supererogation' outlook. We have three arguments to marshal. F. C. Baur[19] maintained, as long ago as 1852, that the distinction between *opera imperata* and *opera spontanea*, *mandata divina* and *divina consilia*,[20] is in contradiction both 'to the absolute ground of obligation of the moral consciousness' and equally, to the express teaching of the Gospel, according to which God lays radical claim to us in all our powers and potentialities and thus no room is left for us to perform any 'works of supererogation'. Any argument of the apostle's which did not heed this fact would not be watertight; it would rest on 'a surface appearance of dialectic' and would need to be subjected by us to criticism on grounds of content. Secondly, the alleged viewpoint does not fit with the sequence of ideas and general tenor of the chapter. For the renunciation ascribed to the apostle – a renunciation made with one eye on recompense in heaven and thus made in his own interests – has nothing in common with a renuncia-

[19] *Op. cit.*, pp. 544ff. [20] So Cornely, p. 254.

tion of one's well-founded personal rights in the interests of love. Of course even an apostle can be subject to delusions and confusion of mind. But we shall not impute them to him without investigating further to see whether there may not be some other explanation. In fact, the definition at the end of the passage gives us some help:

Then what is my reward? The satisfaction of preaching the Gospel without financial reimbursement, without, that is, taking advantage of my rights as a preacher.

'Reward' obviously does not mean here the claim to a reward,[21] the 'works' which merit a 'reward which is already on deposit with God,'[22] and certainly not the heavenly, eschatological reward,[23] not even in the sense that eschatological salvation as such is in prospect.[24] Rather, the apostle with his marked preference for paradox is describing his renunciation of his own rights as itself his reward and, in the fine words of James 1.25, is 'blessed in his action'.

It must be admitted that we are only escaping from one embarrassment into another, from the realm of Scylla into that of Charybdis; but Cornely's laconic observation is in no sense a correct demarcation of the danger zones, when he writes: 'All this is not exegesis; this is Protestant prejudice.'[25] This may be clarified by taking a cross-section through modern exegesis in so far as, whether Protestant or Catholic, it centres on the conclusion of our passage. If it was Ritschl[26] who first gave substance to the idea that here we had the apostle 'expressing his self-consciousness', then F. Godet[27] adorns it in edifying detail; 'There is perhaps no other single passage in the apostle's letters where his generous disposition, his deep humility, his noble Christian self-consciousness find expression as they do here.' Heinrici,[28] J. Weiss,[29] O. Holtzmann – 'the strong self-consciousness of the apostle feeds on the true worth of his personality'[30] – hand on the password to Lietzmann who speaks of the

[21] G. Didier, *Désintéressement du Chrétien. La retribution dans la morale de Saint Paul* (Theologie 32), 1955, pp. 66ff.

[22] Gutjahr, p. 239.

[23] As against A. Schlatter, *Paulus, der Bote Jesu*, 1934, p. 278.

[24] As against J. Schniewind, p. 99 n. 3, and G. P. Wetter, *Der Vergeltungsgedanke bei Paulus*, 1912, p. 148.

[25] *Op. cit.*, p. 258.

[26] A. Ritschl, *Die christliche Lehre von der Rechtfertigung und Versöhnung* II, 1889, pp. 367ff.

[27] *Op. cit.*, p. 32. [28] Heinrici (see n. 4), p. 259.

[29] Weiss (see n. 4), p. 239. [30] Holtzmann (see n. 8), p. 537.

'strong feeling of disinterest'.[31] Bousset put it like this: 'He who attempts to pay the apostle for his work deprives him of his most treasured possession, his pride', his 'interior peace'.[32] 'An inner lift of the spirit, an inner joyousness,' says J. Weiss;[33] Löwe sees this personal joy in voluntary service as the nerve of Paul's feeling for life,[34] while the Jesuit, Didier, calls it the noblest pearl of human pride, the meaning of Christian self-respect.[35] The English scholar, Moffatt,[36] the Norwegian Asting[37] and the Dutchman Grosheide[38] take the same line. Schweitzer professed to detect 'in this determined clinging to his material independence . . . something of the mentality of the modern man'.[39] Sickenberger praises the heroic example,[40] as Wrede had already done,[41] Allo 'the noble example and heroic unselfishness',[42] Cerfaux 'the delicacy of the labourer in the Gospel' which erects the renunciation of financial support into a point of honour.[43] One's first impression on hearing the harmony of these voices from different camps, confessions and nations is one of astonishment. Yet what we really have here is an interpretation inspired (or infected) by Liberalism surmounting the discrepancy within the historical phenomenon by treating problems of theological content, which it now finds alien to it, from the side of psychic conditions and experiences and, in so doing, causing them to disintegrate.[44] The spiritual roots of this interpretation become visible when H. Weinel declares:

> Therein is expressed the twofold character of the ideal experienced by the Apostle; it is an 'I must', an 'I can no other', and yet a *summum bonum*, immediately accompanied by the feeling of absolute freedom over against both things and men.[45]

[31] Lietzmann (see n. 3), p. 43.

[32] W. Bousset, *Die Schriften des Neuen Testaments* II, 1917, p. 116.

[33] Weiss, p. 239.

[34] R. Löwe, 'Das Selbstbewusstsein des Apostels Paulus', *Monatschrift für Pastoraltheologie*, 1955, p. 392.

[35] Didier, p. 65.

[36] J. Moffatt, *The First Epistle of Paul to the Corinthians*, 1938, p. 120.

[37] R. Asting, *Die Verkündigung des Wortes im Urchristentum*, 1939, p. 403.

[38] F. W. Grosheide, *Commentary on the First Epistle to the Corinthians*, 1954, p. 209.

[39] A. Schweitzer, *Die Mystik des Apostels Paulus*, 1930, p. 312; ET, *The Mysticism of Paul the Apostle*, 1931, p. 322.

[40] Sickenberger (see n. 15), p. 44. [41] Wrede, *Paulus*, p. 13 (ET, p. 16).

[42] E. B. Allo, *Saint Paul, Première épître aux Corinthiens*, 1956, p. 222.

[43] Cerfaux (see n. 15), p. 69.

[44] C. Maurer's polemic against this procedure (op. cit. [see no. 9], p. 636) is thoroughly justified.

[45] Weinel (see n. 16), pp. 301f.

Here psychology has sharpened the rigorism of an idealistic ethic from which it takes its origin and which it is unwilling to deny. Thus the tone of the dictum 'to be blessed in one's act,' is transposed from that of a divine call into that of an ideal,[46] then into that of representative personality and finally into that of an aspiration. There is thus a certain circular development when the slogan 'selfless love' gains ground[47] as it has done recently. Didier in particular has pursued this theme through all the Pauline epistles and built his findings up into a monograph of which our passage is both the point of departure and the culmination. As he attempts to refute the observation of Moffatt that Paul never in fact poses the subtle question about the possibility of selfless love, he is obliged, as was Allo[48] before him, to guard himself against the suspicion of having been inspired by Kant's ethic. It remains a moot point whether his effort to trace the ancestry of his own exegesis back as far as Augustine[49] is an adequate reply. So far at least as Protestant thought is concerned, the pathos which encourages the cry for disinterested love undoubtedly derives from Kant. That it is possible in Catholic circles to integrate it into other – mystical – contexts is proved by Adrienne von Speyr's commentary, which interprets the passage in the light of the conception of the Imitation of Jesus.[50] I shall have to return to this outlook later; it is also influential in Protestant exegesis.

Now, however, our immediate task is to sum up the findings of this concentrated review in which we have encountered various names and theories in the field of modern exegesis. This is where we shall really come face to face both with the individuality of the apostle and, at the same time, with the way in which content and person are indissolubly interwoven within the Pauline theology. But this means that a hitherto undreamt-of multiplicity of possible interpretations opens up, very greatly increasing the difficulties of adequate exegesis and showing the exegetes to be subject to the changes and chances of the historical consciousness and its prevailing images. The quest for truth is a tragic destiny in this field, too – it is bound up with the necessity of suffering error. Speaking concretely and without denying the correctness of many observations concerning detail, we may

[46] Schaefer (see n. 15), p. 173.

[47] Wetter (see n. 24), p. 133: 'In religion the norm is not justice, but love'; Bachmann (see n. 4), p. 323; Allo, p. 223; M. Meinertz, *Theologie des Neuen Testaments* II, 1950, p. 194.

[48] *Op. cit.*, p. 223. [49] Didier, pp. 17, 69f.

[50] A von Speyer, *Korinther I*, 1956, pp. 259ff.

assert that modern exegesis in general habitually succumbs to the temptations of enthusiasm. It fuses together person and content in the apostle from the angle of vision provided by (non-philosophical) idealism, and ascribes to him goals which were never his. For he did not subscribe to the shibboleth of the self-perfecting free personality nor to the associated ethic of the good for the good's sake and of disinterested love.[51] He is separated from the one by the Cross of Jesus which compels us towards death and unmasks even charismatic gifts as fragmentary; and from the second by the fact that he reckons seriously with that God who speaks the ultimate Word over us by recompensing every man according to his works[52] and remaining not only the Judge of but also the judgment on our ethical conduct.[53]

But what have we then so far gained? Have we perhaps merely been following in the footsteps of that unforgettable genius and *enfant terrible* of the Tübingen school, of theological criticism, D. F. Strauss, who played off supranaturalism and rationalism against each other and in so doing provided a *reductio ad absurdum* of each? Would we wish in so dialectical a manner to nominate legalism and enthusiasm as the two permanent accompaniments and temptations of Protestant interpretation of Scripture? I should not wish to dispute the propriety, indeed, the necessity of such an undertaking. But our own objective was more modest and less dangerous. Exegesis plots its problems by demarcating the field of the reality which it, too, passionately seeks and by separating the historically actual from intellectualized possibilities. In our passage, looked at in this way, we encounter two apparently contradictory statements. The apostle, who elsewhere rejects all boasting of himself as presumption over against God, here defends both his own right, and even the obligation laid upon him, to boast of himself; and, while elsewhere he reserves for God as eschatological Judge the power of reward, he here describes as his own reward his particular mode of rendering his service without pay. Each of these assertions may be paradoxical within the total context of his theology, but both have always been there, although in unrelated juxtaposition until this point. We arrive therefore at the kind of logical absurdity which is characteristic of the exegetical trade: the individual passage cannot be fitted smoothly into the

[51] Rightly emphasized by W. Meyer, *Der Brief an die Korinther* I (Prophezei), 1947, p. 323.

[52] As against Wetter, p. 156.

[53] This is as far as I can go with J. Héring, *La première épître de Saint Paul aux Corinthiens*, 1949, p. 74.

living whole; indeed, it even contradicts it, and threatens to paralyse it.

The real trade of the exegete only begins at the point where this logical absurdity is experienced as inescapable; his raw material is the nuance; his delight is in the process of differentiation, his besetting temptation is the smooth, reductionist formula. Only the courage to set ourselves problems, and the knowledge that we are always bound to raise more problems than we can solve, keeps us alive as exegetes and keeps our text from losing contact with real life. Life pitches us from one problem into another; in the same way, the text loses its character as personal address if we try to force it into the Procrustean bed of any given systematic theology.

At the risk of indulging too freely the urge to differentiate, I should like to declare my disagreement with the thesis, represented particularly by A. Schlatter,[54] R. Bultmann[55] and W. G. Kümmel,[56] of the parallelism between our passage and II Cor. 10.11. It is true that there, as here, Paul describes his renunciation of financial support as his 'boast'. But there he does so, as the controversial nature of II Cor. 10ff. shows, in order to define what distinguishes him from his rivals. It would be easy similarly to refer the apostle's 'boast' in our particular passage to his relationship not with God but with other men, and also to his self-understanding, especially as I Cor. 9 is, on the whole, directed against enthusiasm and vv. 1–6 contain a comparison with the other apostles. But it seems to me that polemic is not detectable in quite the same way in our passage: on the contrary, the connection between the key words 'boast' and 'reward' is such[57] that it would be difficult to talk[58] of the apostle's natural, human feelings and nothing else without denying the real theological significance of the assertion and taking the sting out of the problem implicit in the passage. In any event we cannot reach a final conclusion so long as we confine our attention, as has been the case hitherto, to the beginning and end of our text without making any reference to the highly individual middle section.

[54] *Paulus*, p. 275ff., where, like a true modernizer, he turns the apostle's renunciation into a positive: it is Paul's work with his hands which is his boast in face of the community. Löwe, p. 392, is also concerned with Paul's stance over against the community.

[55] *TWNT* III, p. 652. [56] Lietzmann, ed. Kümmel, p. 180.

[57] A. Ritschl, p. 368, called attention to this.

[58] So O. Kuss, *Die Briefe an die Römer, Korinther und Galater*, 1940, p. 155, who sets Paul over against the other apostles.

One remarkable thing is the lack of embarrassment with which Paul here employs the concept *ananke* – a concept which for our ecclesiastically conditioned sensibility speaks rather shockingly of destiny, of necessity. For it seems to me – although this has been disputed in principle[59] and as good as rejected in practice[60] – that *ananke* has to be translated in this way and in no other. In general, the modern exegesis of this passage is an up-to-date version of the kind of exegesis I have already characterized. First of all, it may be ethical, in that Paul's declared feeling of necessity in the matter of preaching is referred back to the obligation of his calling;[61] or, it may be psychological, in that there is talk of an inner compulsion[62] and, in particular, a recalling of the Damascus road;[63] the exegete then derives from this overpowering call of the persecutor a special apostolate over against that of the Twelve[64] or even a felt necessity of working off a debt of gratitude.[65] Not surprisingly, the passage then begins to be understood as a piece of edification, in which a 'holy must'[66] or the deep, almost exaggerated, humility[67] of the apostle is found to be the central feature. Finally, C. Maurer adopts the linguistic usage of the LXX and of late Judaism which denotes a situation of pressure.[68] It is very remarkable that in all these varying interpretations there is no hint of the logical absurdities which now open up. Yet the difference between the calling of the Twelve and

[59] Schaefer, p. 174; A. Robertson and A. Plummer, *A Critical and Exegetical Commentary on the First Epistle of St Paul to the Corinthians* (ICC), 1929, p. 189; C. Maurer, p. 638.

[60] It is true, however, that Bultmann(*loc. cit.*) speaks without further explanation of the 'divine ἀνάγκη'. W. Lütgert, *Freitheitspredigt und Schwarmgeister in Korinth*, 1908, p. 314, is on the target when he speaks of compulsion by the Spirit. The only writer to apply the concept of destiny without embarrassment or further reflection is K. Heim, pp. 117ff., 124.

[61] Schaefer, p. 174; Sickenberger, p. 43. Bousset, p. 116, speaks of the 'compulsion of the "must" of obligation', H. D. Wendland, *Die Briefe an die Korinther*, 1948, p. 54, of 'the divinely imposed "must" of proclamation', Robertson and Plummer (p. 189) of the special commission, Asting (p. 402) and Löwe (p. 392) of obligation.

[62] Schniewind (p. 99 n. 3) speaks of 'the compulsion of the prophetic Word'. Heim, pp. 117ff., does certainly speak of destiny, but psychologizes the 'Woe'.

[63] F. Godet, p. 29; Schaefer, p. 174; O. Holtzmann, p. 537; Robertson and Plummer, p. 189; Allo, p. 222; Cerfaux, p. 69; Grosheide, p. 209; W. Meyer, p. 321.

[64] Godet, p. 29; Gutjahr, p. 238. Schlatter, p. 276; W. Meyer, p. 319.

[65] Gutjahr, p. 237.

[66] O. Schmitz, *Die Bedeutung des Wortes bei Paulus*, 1927, p. 15; K. Deissner, 'Das Sendungsbewusstsein der Urchristenheit', *ZST* 7, 1929/30, p. 787.

[67] Allo, p. 222. [68] Maurer, p. 638.

that of Paul is not that the former is determined by the free acceptance of discipleship but that it is not the risen Christ who is active in it. For the rest, the accent on both occasions is on the miraculous phenomenon that men, under the compulsion of a mysterious summons, *must* follow Jesus, although it is true that Paul paints the event in more powerful colours. That means at the same time that it is an eschatological happening which is being depicted here and which may not be ethicized with impunity. It is therefore highly inappropriate, though just possible, to speak of the obligation of the apostolic calling. Equally, we should not desire seriously to ascribe to Paul a greater responsibility or a more elevated sense of duty than to the other apostles. In any event, what criterion could we work out for an evaluation of this kind? The antithesis to the other apostles is thus a blind alley. The ethical and psychological interpretations clearly pay no heed to the fact that our passage professes to concern itself with a compulsion exercised on Paul from outside. '*Ananke* lies upon me' is said of destiny which lays hold on a man,[69] not of feelings which animate us, nor of an obligation which we have to satisfy. The recollection of the Damascus experience, however, does serve as an illustration; yet it will not do as a canon of interpretation, because Paul is not looking back on what happened in the past and on its effects, but speaking of his service in the present. In the last resort, it is not just any situation which is calling the apostle to the work, nor is it an emergency. His commission, and the compulsion arising out of it, originate with his Lord. The reigning interpretation displays nothing more than an incapacity for any understanding of the power of grace other than the psychological, i.e. that which begins with human experience. It is true that the voices of Old Testament prophets[70] have not infrequently been recognized as the closest parallels to our Pauline passage; in them, similarly, the commission to preach is described as an ineluctable destiny and the prophet even haggles with God about his fate.[71] If the Old Testament 'Woe is me' stands as an antithesis to the Pauline '*Ananke* lies upon me', this acts as a reminder that 'Woe', both in the Old and New Testaments, can signify a personification of the divine curse and eschatological wrath, in the power of which God executes his judgments.[72] Because of the wide-

[69] Cf. Homer, *Iliad*, VI, 458. [70] Particularly Amos 3.8; Jer. 1.6f.; 20.9.

[71] Schniewind, pp. 69ff.; Moffatt, p. 121; J. Weiss, p. 240; O. Holtzmann, p. 537; Wendland, p. 54; Grundmann, *TWNT* I, p. 350; Maurer, p. 639.

[72] J. Weiss, p. 240, quotes Hosea 9.12; Rev. 9.12.

spread reluctance to admit the concept of destiny, no serious attempt has been made to draw out the logical implications of this relationship.[73] But drawn out they must be, if justice is really to be done to the text. *Ananke* and Woe are personified here to convey the sense that in them the epiphany of divine power is taking place.[74] In precisely the same way Paul finds it possible to ascribe the character of power in action to the grace, love, righteousness, glory or the wrath of God; he is speaking, not of qualities but of manifestations of the God who exhibits himself as powerful. *Ananke* describes here the power of the divine will which radically and successfully challenges man and makes its servant its instrument. This definition, then, makes it clear that, simply in his capacity as a Jew, Paul cannot be speaking, like the Greek with his *ananke* or the Roman with his *fatum*, of an impersonal force of blind ill-omen or chance. He may indeed be making use of the Greek concept, but only in order to delineate the character of the divine power as sovereign, inexorable and ineluctable. He who sets himself against it experiences it as a curse which – in accordance with the outlook of antiquity – smites man like a consuming sickness, penetrates his very being and destroys him from within. It is the ultimate distinguishing mark of this Christian and apostle that he has been both able and compelled to see the Gospel in this light. For *ananke* in this sense has entered his life with the Gospel and taken possession of it. The Gospel itself is for him that power of God,[75] which thus smites man in the manner of a destiny (as Paul himself actually experienced it on the Damascus road) and conscripts him into its service in such a way that the old form of existence is summoned to its death, and of the new it is rightly said: 'It is no longer I who live, but Christ who lives in me';[76] through him 'the world has been crucified to me and I to the world.'[77] The encounter with the Gospel imprints the stigmata, as Paul has expressly stated of himself.[78] Because this is so, he can rightly compare himself with a gladiator in a world-wide arena, he can call himself a spectacle for angels and men or dregs in the eyes of every-

[73] Schniewind, pp. 69ff., comes nearest.

[74] Schniewind, p. 70, speaks of an 'interiorly working power'.

[75] Cf. E. Molland, *Das paulinische Euangelion*, 1934, pp. 48, 53ff.

[76] Gal. 2.20. [77] Gal. 6.14.

[78] Gal. 6.17; cf. J. Hempel, 'Wort Gottes und Schicksal', *Festschrift A. Bertholet*, 1950, pp. 224–32. It is there suggested that, in the Old and New Testaments, the personified divine Word is frequently found where 'in other religious contexts we encounter the idea of *fatum*'. 'The Word of God shapes destiny and itself becomes destiny.'

body,[79] he can recount his sufferings and hardships in a detailed catalogue; and, in the deliberately exaggerated passage in II Cor. 10–13, he can properly depict his apostolate in the sombre colours of the shadow of the Cross. For him, as for classical tragedy, it is the destiny which is the measure of the man. Of course for him it is the Gospel alone which is destiny; to it alone he can attribute eschatological power (power which determines the present and the future), to it alone the decision between eternal life and eternal death, bliss and perdition.[80] This power of God drives him without rest or respite like a slave through the Mediterranean. The external observer cannot really decide whether he is the object of grace or of wrath, whether he is a herald or a demoniac, whether he is to be admired or pitied or shunned and abhorred.

It is only when this background is taken into full consideration that the full significance and logic of the statement '*Ananke* lies upon me' becomes comprehensible. Now it seems to me evident that the depth and radical nature of the self-recollection which the apostle has been carrying out here excludes direct polemic or apologetic. Paul is not now conducting a controversy with the enthusiasts, he is not defining the difference between himself and the rest of the apostles, he is not defending himself against reproaches from members of the community; he is giving account to himself of the truth of his apostolic existence. It belongs to this truth that, as one stamped by the call and the Cross of his Lord, he can make no claim to financial support. He would have a right to such support, if he had taken on the work of his own volition.[81] One can demand no reward from *ananke*, one can only bow to it or rebel against it. Paul himself expresses this in the form of words he uses: 'but as I do it under a sense of compulsion, I am . . . simply discharging a trust.' We should have expected the apodosis to run: 'I cannot rightly expect a reward.' Indeed, in the text we have today protasis and apodosis taken together produce a tautology.[82] The rationale of such a construction can only be to exclude the reward motif altogether and thus, as in the preceding sentence, to bring out the will of the Gospel as the sole motivation in the apostle's work. This gives an even more paradoxical ring to the question that follows: 'Then what is my

[79] I Cor. 4.9ff. [80] Particularly in II Cor. 11.23ff.

[81] In spite of the objections of Baur (p. 543) and Didier (p. 68), cf. also J. Weiss (p. 241), 17a is universally regarded today as an unfulfilled conditional.

[82] Lietzmann, p. 42, destroys this tautology with his paraphrase, 'Thus I am entrusted with nothing but the ministry only.'

reward?'; and the answer itself is bound therefore to sound paradoxical also: 'The satisfaction of preaching the Gospel without financial reimbursement, without, that is, taking advantage of my rights as a preacher.'

We have, in conclusion, to establish the sense in which this last phrase is intended. The exegetical roads we considered and found theoretically possible at an earlier stage are now barred by what has been said since. Paul cannot possibly be speaking of some work of supererogation from which merit might accrue. In face of *ananke* there can be as little question of merit as of reward. But there is no better case for the kind of view which we have inherited from the nineteenth century and which talks of 'the rewarding consciousness of the inner moral worth of an action'[83] or of 'the royal consciousness' of 'the totally self-surrendered soul.'[84] It is admittedly already present in Judaism in words like these:

> Be not like servants who serve their Lord to gain reward, but be like servants who serve their Lord without thought of reward. . . .[85] When thou hast fulfilled much of the Torah, do not indulge in self-congratulation, for this is the purpose for which thou wert created.[86]

But it is not fortuitous that these words lack the Pauline paradoxes and the motif of an *ananke* which characterizes the calling and the ministry of the prophet. The modern view, being principally interested in the self-consciousness of the apostle, tends to throw all the emphasis on the motive of achievement in that it abstracts idealistically from the question of reward and sees the worth of a good action as inhering solely in the action itself. It is thus a variant of the first interpretation, as legalism is always a mutation of enthusiasm. The closing section of the passage cannot ultimately be understood in the context of the Imitation of Jesus or of discipleship. It was just this kind of basis which Paul rejected both for his renunciation and his boast, although it would have been an easy option for him and various ways leading to it were easily accessible.[87] On the contrary,

[83] Baur, p. 544; similarly, Godet, p. 30; J. Weiss, p. 240; Allo, p. 222.

[84] Kuss, p. 155. [85] *Aboth* 1.3.

[86] *Aboth* 2.8. Maurer (p. 635) refers to Strack-Billerbeck I, 1922, pp. 561ff., according to which the rabbis are to transmit the God-given Torah without pay.

[87] It is just this which emerges so clearly from C. Maurer's essay. One certainly quite impossible interpretation is that of W. Meyer, which speaks of the 'continuation of the saving act of Jesus', of 'Christ-like dignity' as 'the true self-fulfilment of man' (p. 320), and culminates in the judgment that Paul 'discovered in a holy

he defended his legitimate right to receive support from the community, by reference to the command of Jesus.[88] It is not the model of the humble earthly Lord that keeps him from exercising this right; it is not the shadow of the Crucified who freely gave himself up; it is not even the concept, so frequently found elsewhere in the apostle's writings, of being 'in Christ', which motivates ministering love as the law of Christ.[89] If anything is remarkable in our passage, it is surely that there is no word of any of this. The attempt to solve the problem by taking a diversion through Christology is therefore impermissible. The ἀνάγκη which comes into being with the Gospel does not derive simply from the way Jesus went, nor it does allow of a simple comparison with him.

We have to remember that the process of thought in our passage goes through three stages: 1. No acceptance of financial support, because otherwise Paul would lose his boast and his reward. 2. Because the Gospel exercises on him a force like that of destiny, he is not a free agent. 3. Nevertheless, he is blessed in his action. The expositors ignore altogether the graduations of this process of argument and, in consequence, jump rapidly from the first stage to the third or else allow the second a merely psychological significance. But this is to mistake the real problem. It consists in the fact that Paul is not addressing himself to the question of disinterested love; otherwise, the second part of the argument would be superfluous. It consists, further, in the fact that Paul is not setting up a Categorical Imperative to which, as a child of his age, he gives a mythological foundation: '*Ananke* compels to service.' If he were doing this, the first section of the passage, which deals with his right to boast, would be quite out of place; but without this section, the connection of the whole chapter would be lost. Its burden is, that he who loves can and must renounce his rights, however well-founded they may be, if he is to go on really loving and serving effectively. Once that is clear, the fundamental problem of our passage can be formulated thus: 'How can the man who experiences the compulsion of the Gospel as that of his destiny at the same time be, and remain, the man who loves?

---

assimilation to the free self-abandonment of Christ his own personal motive for free service over and above the call of duty' (p. 322). When A. von Speyr (p. 260) describes the way of discipleship as leading from the gift of freedom to the compulsion of love, she, too, obviously misunderstands the passage.

[88] See v. 14. [89] Verse 21; Gal. 6.2.

Does not compulsion exclude love, or at least rob it of all significance?' This is precisely what Paul is denying. The state in which he finds himself is the exact opposite of being subjected to a dark fate to which he has to bow even against his will. His destiny brought him at once into obedience and into love, because in and with it the power of grace invaded his life and took it into its service. His destiny is the Gospel, in the service of which is blessedness. If this were not so, if the servant were really not to be distinguished from the slave or the demoniac, the Gospel would no longer be recognizable for what it is. The prophet may yet suffer and sigh under his mission, the apostle is full of joy and gratitude – each blessed in its deed. His destiny is at the same time the object of his love. What is the distinguishing mark of this love? Just this, that it loves and therefore does not insist on its own rights – not out of disinterest, but out of involvement. This mark of love Paul is neither willing nor able to renounce. It would be better for him to die than to lose it. It is his boast and his reward.[90] For it shows that the slave of the Gospel is at the same time seized of the glorious freedom of the children of God, and is called through love to further loving.

Here, then, is the womb of the dialectic which dominates the section that follows. He who in love is the servant of all men can in faith be a free lord of all things, but only because, when he encounters the Gospel, he encounters the love of God as his destiny; and he would be denying his freedom and its grounding in the love of God, if this freedom did not authenticate itself in the joyful sacrifice of the servant. Here Paul seems to be very close to the Stoic, who can also say, 'I am free and the friend of God, so that I may freely obey him.'[91] Yet there is the deepest possible difference between them. For the Stoic assents to his destiny because, although he is the prisoner of cosmic necessity and the plaything of the moods of chance, he can take comfort in his individuality and freedom in the realm of the spirit. Paul did not laud the autonomy of the spirit but the power of the Gospel liberating man for the service of his neighbour and moving him to love because he had been loved. Thus he is here playing his, the evangelical, variation on the theme of the *amor fati*. Paying

[90] Preparatory work for this interpretation has been done by Godet (pp. 29ff.) and Lütgert (pp. 31ff.). They both emphasize the offering of the free will as the apostolic answer to the divine Necessity. At a deeper level, there is Schlatter (*Paulus*, pp. 275ff.; *Erläuterungen zum Neuen Testament* II, 1926, pp. 75ff.); and Maurer (pp. 637ff.) recognizes love, joy and gratitude to be this answer.

[91] Epictetus IV 3.9, quoted by K. Deissner, p. 787.

tribute yet again to the Genius loci, I sum up in some words of A. Schlatter who, though in mutual and long-standing opposition, has been and has remained my teacher:

> But because the sacrifice consists in what God gave us and has about it the crystalline necessity of the divine will, it becomes a business of joy. . . . The sacrifice itself is not carried out with groaning but crowned with joy, and is part of our blessedness. For it is thanksgiving.[92]

[92] *Das Gott wohlgefällige Opfer*, Freizeiten-Verlag Velbert (undated), p. 6.

XII

PAUL AND EARLY CATHOLICISM*

LET ME BEGIN by explaining the expression 'early catholicism' in my subject.[1] Ever since the eschatological understanding of the New Testament replaced the idealistic interpretation, we can and must determine the various phases of earliest Christian history by means of the original imminent expectation of the parousia,

* 'Paulus und der Frühkatholizismus. A lecture delivered to the *Theologische Arbeitsgemeinschaft* in Tübingen on 21 June, 1962, and published in *ZTK*, 60, 1963, pp. 75–89.

[1] The sense and validity of the expression 'early catholicism' are currently the object of lively discussion in connection with the Lucan problem, with strongly opposed points of view. Since I was probably the first to use this expression publicly in the dispute over Lucan theology, I would like to explain at least by way of a footnote how I arrived at this phrase and what causes me to defend its continued use.

In the investigation of the Pauline doctrine of spiritual gifts which I began in 1941–2, I necessarily encountered the completely different view of church organization and its rationale in the Pastorals and in Luke. This problem of two contradictory conceptions of Spirit, Church, office and tradition, already within the New Testament itself, was at first extremely disturbing to me. But the war and the immediate post-war period prevented me from pursuing the literary study of the problem myself, though I was aware that from this insight the history and theology of earliest Christianity required a fundamentally new construction, that the question of the canon became urgent, and that in the future Acts was no longer to be read primarily as history, but as theology.

The problem was immediately radicalized and complicated because it was very soon apparent that it could not be confined to the two strands of Paulinism and the theology of Luke together with the Pastorals: One visible root of the latter reaches back beyond Paul into Jewish Christianity, and Paul's position, on the other hand, is by no means a fixed point in earliest Christian history. This history must therefore be discovered and pondered anew from its beginnings through its development to the last phase indicated in the New Testament. To this final phase I gave the name early catholicism, because where it appears certain basic presuppositions of the ancient church, distinguished from earliest Christianity, are also present.

I admit that a church historian might be inclined, even in this final phase, to emphasize the similarities with earliest Christianity more than those with the ancient Church. Transition periods are especially ambiguous. The use of a catchphrase in an attempt to characterize such periods is of little significance in itself, its modifications and its final extinction. Early catholicism means that transition from earliest Christianity to the so-called ancient Church, which is completed with the disappearance of the imminent expectation. This by no means occurs everywhere at the same time or with the same symptoms and consequences, but nevertheless in the various streams there is a characteristic movement toward that great Church which understands itself as the *Una Sancta Apostolica*.

The current problem to be resolved is where, how extensively and strongly early catholic tendencies are apparent already in the New Testament. The formulation of my subject, in placing Paul and early catholicism in confrontation, corresponds to the current Protestant view of an opposition between the two which leaves open only the question of possible connecting links.

I would like now to discuss the validity of such a viewpoint. I propose to do this in such a way as to bring the person and achievement of the apostle into focus. To start off I propose the thesis, surely

---

so long as there is no agreement on the perspective which it implies and the phenomenon to which it points. The argument makes sense only when it concentrates on the phenomenon which I intended to bring into sharp focus with my expression.

It seems to me that the New Testament scholar has no right to regard earliest Christianity and the boundaries of the New Testament as coextensive. The designation, 'sub-apostolic age,' formerly used for the last phase of the period covered by the New Testament, is inadequate, since all New Testament writings except Paul must be placed in this category. It is also imprecise, in that it provides for no distinction from what follows and no criterion for its actual content. When this difficulty is not felt and the entire New Testament is claimed for earliest Christianity, my differentiation of the various stages leading up to the ancient Church will naturally appear to be mere provocation. In that case, however, it will be impossible to break out of basic unclarity concerning the driving forces and the course of early Christian history.

In any event, the traditional schemata are no longer usable. It is impossible to write a history of earliest Christianity on the basis of our present insights, unless a new schematization is first determined. I can acknowledge as earliest Christianity only that which still has its focus in an eschatology determined by the original imminent expectation in its changing forms. When this focus shifts, a new phase is to be established. That is undoubtedly the case with Luke and the Pastorals. Till now, no designation other than early catholicism has been suggested for this, with the exception of the unsuitable one, the 'sub-apostolic age'. I therefore continue to use it, and the conclusion of the essay will once more demonstrate why I view it as necessary and appropriate, so long as a better suggestion is not offered.

In any case, I cannot give recognition to any criticism which disputes the designation, but offers no better historical and theological characterization of the intended phenomenon, with its impulses and its new goal. Otherwise there will only be levelling where everything depends on differentiation. We still lack a new draft of the Lucan theology, which would undoubtedly radicalize the present debate. Astounding phenomena are as yet scarcely touched.

unusual for a Protestant, that from a purely historical viewpoint, Paul himself was a forerunner of early catholicism. He was a forerunner, directly and indirectly, in accordance with and against his will, at least in the effect which he produced. As a point of departure for our enquiry, it is probably impossible to by-pass the radical antithesis of a simple black and white sketch and the schemata of an oversimplifying view of history, which determine even the Protestant understanding of Paul. Nonetheless, historical reality never coincides with schematic representations and radical antitheses. It is always in twilight, just as our own present. Historical research has perhaps its final and deepest value in the fact that it disillusions. How true this is even and especially of Paul has scarcely received sufficient recognition till now.

Prevailing opinion views the apostle as the pioneer of the Gentile mission and as the classical theologian of earliest Christianity. Was he really either of these? Upon simple reflection, even the first characterization will be recognized as questionable. The pioneers of the Gentile mission were undoubtedly those more or less anonymous men who came to Antioch from Judea in connection with the persecution of the Hellenists. And there were those other completely forgotten men who founded the churches in Damascus, Ephesus and Rome, to mention only examples. They are obscured by the broad shadows which Paul cast over them, primarily through those letters of his which were preserved and through the narrative of Acts. The few reports which we possess concerning Barnabas and Apollos prove that there were significant Gentile missionaries independent of Paul. Also, we must not simply overlook the rivals in Galatia, Corinth and Philippi whom Paul names, not to mention the figures which appear in his greeting lists.

How and when did he achieve his significance and independence? After all, the account of Acts seems to indicate that, after initial failures or at least unproductive attempts at independent missionary work, he was for a considerable time attached to Barnabas and obligated to Antioch an account of spiritual and material aid.[2] It was the break with both which first made him that for which he is remembered. Nevertheless, even at this point we have to guard against overrating, however difficult it be to resist the saint's legend which still flourishes today. Is it not a completely open problem, how long the churches founded by Paul remained faithful to him and

[2] Cf. E. Haenchen, 'Petrus-Probleme', *NTS* 7, 1960–1, pp. 187–97, 193f.

preserved his tradition? Almost all of his letters show that Hellenistic enthusiasm rebelled against the authority of the apostle already in his lifetime; alien missionaries were continually breaking into his field and easily establishing themselves there; rival groups hindered discipline, stability, and Paul's attempt to leave a lasting imprint on his converts. Paul bent every effort to maintain his position in Corinth, but it is unlikely that his influence continued after his death. Not even that much can be said to Galatia. The book of Revelation gives no indication that Asia Minor is indebted to the apostle. Only the letters of Ignatius show that he was still remembered in Syria, if even that is not saying too much. For Matthew, John and the *Didache* betray nothing of this memory.

It could be objected that all these observations are inconclusive, since so few texts have been preserved. Nevertheless, the letters of Paul themselves are eloquent in their witness, and there are enough extant texts to attempt something like circumstantial proof. Finally, we arrive at similarly meagre, for the most part even negative, results, if we enquire into the echo of Pauline theology among his contemporaries and the immediately following generations.

Opponents of Paul in Corinth, apparently with the concurrence of a large fraction of the church, had already characterized the letters of the apostle as not very intelligible, which is indeed correct. About a century later, in the latest document of the New Testament, II Peter 3.16 points up this difficulty and indicates that heretics were taking advantage of the writings of the apostle. It is obvious that his theology of justification and of the cross evoked the opposition of the legalists and the enthusiasts equally. Even the early disciples of Paul moderated the severity of his theology in favour of edification, as in Luke or in the Pastorals. Or they subsumed it under a new theme, as in Ephesians, and in a certain respect paralysed it by the glorification of a church extending from earth into heaven. His doctrine of spiritual gifts has almost always been taken up and given recognition by sectarian extremists right down to the present. I Clement and the epistle of Polycarp transform the message of the apostle into a simple church piety. Otherwise it was for a long time ignored or mute. The great exception, Marcion, confirms the remark in II Peter and shows in which circles the theologian Paul was still esteemed.

I have given a superficial and cursory sketch, though it would be rewarding to go into detail. I was concerned initially only with what I consider to be an indisputable conclusion. Paul, who set out to lay the Mediterranean world at the feet of his Lord, undoubtedly fulfilled the role of a pioneer of early Christianity while it was rapidly and dynamically growing. But the enterprise which he planned did not endure. It was submerged in the broad stream of the early Christian mission, in which even the distinctive voice of his theology died away. The pioneer, martyr and theologian was widely, though not everywhere, held in honoured memory. He survived only because some of his letters were kept and circulated, though in general they were little understood, inasmuch as they transcended common piety.

It seems to me that this has been the lot of Paul down to our own day, except in times of crisis for the Church when his letters have been rediscovered as the voice which called man into divine righteousness and Christian freedom. Otherwise he has been repeatedly and in various ways ecclesiastically domesticated, first as missionary and martyr, later as dogmatician.

This was done already by Luke, his first historian, in such a way that that one cannot but admire the skill of this disciple as well as his love for his hero. I shall call attention only to a few, characteristic things. It is well known that Acts, with a single exception, denies Paul the title of apostle, and instead sees him as the evangelist who carries the message emanating from Jerusalem into the Gentile world. A comparison with Galatians shows how much critical caution must be exercised toward Acts' contributions to Pauline biography. Naturally Luke did not invent his version. He drew it from legends which were circulating. However, he is probably responsible for its inner consistency, which rests on a presupposition which is self-evident for him: Paul must be shielded against the suspicion that he was an individualist and Christian freebooter. There is salvation only within the Church, whose history, thanks to divine guidance, shows a continuous progression, and it is precisely into this history that Paul is drawn.

After Paul was baptized by Ananias, he set out at once on the way to Jerusalem. There he was introduced by Barnabas to the original apostles, and began his mission in Judea with their blessing. Barnabas also brought him later to Antioch. From there, after solemn ordination, they were sent as a delegation to the Gentiles. They therefore rendered account to the church when they returned. Finally, at the apostolic council, their work was again very solemnly approved by the mother church at Jerusalem. Thus one link joins with the next, as is fitting for apostles, and under heavenly guidance it is not expected to be otherwise. On the other hand, not the slightest consideration is given to the fact that Paul himself vehemently asserts and even documents his independence from the Jerusalem church, indeed from men generally. The legends which apparently circulated already during his lifetime outlived him. For they allowed him to be seen in concert with the dogmatic postulates of a later generation, if not in concert with historical realities.

This later generation should not be too hastily condemned. In some ways its image of Paul seems more authentic and credible than the historical reality, as we can recover it from the letters of the apostle. It is characteristic of the letters that the entire mission of Paul is determined by the expectation of the imminent end of the world. We seldom stop to consider what this means concretely, and so I would like to broach its significance with a few indications.

Of the approximately twenty-five years which the apostle had for his work, at least two are to be assigned to his initial efforts. At the apostolic council, which can be dated thirteen years later at the earliest, he is still a partner of Barnabas and probably together with him a spokesman of the Gentile Christian centre of Antioch. Only subsequently does the time come when he can proceed, independently, to realize his own plans. For this work, then, he has barely ten years left. In this period he travelled up and down all of Asia Minor and Greece, with long stays in Ephesus and Corinth. At the end of the decade he considered his task in the east complete and turned toward Spain in the far west, without ever reaching that goal.

In trying to establish a precise relationship between space and plans in this manner, one can hardly escape the impression that here a possessed man is pursuing a feverish dream. This impression is heightened when one notes the goal and hope clearly outlined in Rom. 11.13ff. Paul is completely convinced that Israel will be converted when the full number of the Gentiles is won for Christ. He reverses the prophetic promise, according to which the Gentiles come and worship when Zion is redeemed from earthly humiliation in the endtime. The mission of the apostle is a colossal detour to the salvation of Israel, whereby the first become last. Still, world history cannot end until those first called have also found their way home as the last. On this tour and detour, however, Paul himself is nothing other than John the Baptist claimed to be, namely the forerunner of the end of the world.

It is easy enough to appreciate the fact that a later generation could no longer grasp such a conception, not to speak of passing it on after its failure.[3] The salvation-historical view of a Church that permeates the world in a protracted but steady process and thus wins it back to its Lord, and the view of the apostle as the incomparable champion of this development, must have appeared to be not only the more realistic but also the only viable view. Paul was absorbed into the history of the saints in order that salvation history on earth could proceed and remain comprehensible. The miracle worker was acceptable; the apocalypticist had become intolerable. Indeed, this image of the apostle, which fits him into the early catholic world, has always been affirmed and beloved. Its destruction is still regarded as a sacrilege, even by many historians.

The theme 'Paul and early catholicism' catches sight of only a segment of that radical transformation which led to the ancient Church. However, this segment has paradigmatic significance. Here it becomes apparent that nascent catholicism was the historically necessary outcome of an original Christianity whose apocalyptic expectation had not been fulfilled. It may likewise become clear that – expressed or not – the mark of nascent catholicism is the message about the world-pervading Church as the reality of the kingdom of Christ on earth. We have thus arrived at a perspective relative to the total problem and can now go on to test its accuracy once more in detail.

Against my exposition it will probably be objected that Paul himself already understood the Church as the world-pervading domain of Christ; this understanding did not begin with early catholicism. In itself, such an observation is completely accurate, as is shown by the Pauline motif of the Church as the body of Christ. But I do not agree with the reasoning behind it, which in my opinion isolates the phenomenon instead of locating it historically. I would like to reverse the process: That observation shows that the Pauline concept of the Church paved the way for the early catholic view. Just as the apostle prescribed for his successors the horizon of their mission, so he also presented them with the basic theme of their theology. He was not by any means assimilated into their salvation history solely as a prisoner of their illusions. They did not comprehend his distinctiveness, but they found something in his personal and theological legacy which

[3] H. J. Schoeps, *Paulus*, 1959, p. 291, ET, *Paul*, 1961, p. 273, correctly recognized this. His book at least has the merit that it opposes the current image of Paul and thereby compels fresh reflection.

illuminated their own reality. For the conception of the Church as the body of Christ is the adequate expression for a community which carries on a worldwide mission in the name of Christ. In this respect it far surpasses the other conceptions of the people of God and the family of God. It is not accidental that this conception has been carried over into the doctrine of the mystical body of Christ, and in the process was developed and modified, as is characteristic of catholicism generally. Its deepest theological significance, however, lay in the fact that it inseparably linked ecclesiology and christology together and thus made the Church an integral factor in the salvation event.

Nowhere is this more apparent than in the letter to the Ephesians, which for that very reason has become the classical document for all doctrine concerning the Church. Here even the connection between ecclesiology and christology is given a sacramental basis, so that becoming a disciple of Jesus is no longer the basis but the consequence of being a Christian. The Church grows as it were out of baptism, and in the celebration of the Lord's Supper it is constantly reunited out of all the dispersion to which its members are subject in everyday life. The decisive factor here is that men do not act on their own but are passively joined to the salvation event. As the sole actor, Christ mediates himself to those for whom he died and over whom he chooses now to reign. The drama of salvation is not concluded with Easter. Rather, precisely for the sake of the Easter event, it has an earthly continuation, because the exalted one desires to manifest himself as Lord of the world. The sacramental presence of Christ in the Church for the world – that is the central motif of the early catholic doctrine of redemption. For this the 'saving facts', the Incarnation, the Cross and the Resurrection, form the presupposition.

Even this view can claim a precedent in Paul. He did in fact make the sacramental incorporation into the worldwide body of Christ the criterion of being a Christian, and thus rejected a mere historical or ethical connection with Jesus of Nazareth as this criterion. For him also the lordship of Christ on earth rests on the fact that the exalted Lord, present in the Church, binds his own to himself and to one another. By endowing them with the Spirit, he makes them capable of permeating the old world as the inbreaking of the new, following his own precedent, and thus of demonstrating his omnipotence in every place and time.

To be sure it does not suffice to show at what points early catholicism could take up Pauline motifs and develop them further. One has to keep in mind that this procedure involved substantially only that side of Pauline theology which the Apostle shared with the preceding and contemporary Hellenistic church,[4] since for this church the view of the sacramental presence of Christ in his Church is characteristic. It is not the view as such, but its modification which determines the distinctiveness of Paul. However, his successors no longer recognized the importance of the Pauline modification, to say nothing of retaining it. Again I can only briefly exemplify a matter which deserves to be developed comprehensively.

Surprisingly enough, the great and weighty statements about the Church as the body of Christ in the genuine letters of Paul are presented in an exclusively parenetic context, and as entirely obvious and almost incidental. As a matter of fact, it is astounding how scanty the explicit ecclesiology is in these letters, compared, for example, with the anthropological discussions. This fact should not be taken as innocuous. Whatever explanation is offered for it, it is by no means to be concluded from the texts that the doctrine of the Church constantly occupied the apostle and forms the secret centre of his theology. Ephesians is another story, and it is not accidental that there, as in all deutero-Pauline letters, anthropology correspondingly recedes. It is begging the question to ask whether one is permitted to harmonize here instead of recognizing a shift in the centre of interest. Historical criticism will insist that it is the texts themselves that are decisive, not an image of Paul which we find desirable.

Of no less consequence is the modification which the Apostle made in the Hellenistic doctrine of the sacrament. For he no longer combines in a naive, i.e. undifferentiated way, participation in the Cross and in the Resurection of Christ. To be sure, he viewed the new obedience, to be verified in the everyday situations of life, as the proof of transformed existence and the beginning of the eschatological world. However, since he regarded it as only a sign of future resurrection, he distinguished himself from enthusiasm, which sees the sacrament as guaranteeing freedom from jeopardy. For Paul the

[4] The significance of the Hellenistic church has recently been contested on the basis of a curious foreshortening of the perspective provided, of all things, by the book of Acts (cf., e.g., Schoeps, *Paul*, pp. 16ff.; B. Gerhardsson, *Memory and Manuscript*, Uppsala, 1961, p. 297). It seems to me to be one of the enduring contributions of R. Bultmann that he has given us a clear and, in my opinion, secured view of this church.

jeopardy of temptation is the place of true worship and genuine discipleship of Jesus. For him, the sacrament grants no guarantee of salvation, but it makes possible the overcoming of the world effected by the Spirit through a faith under threat by the world. It therefore opens up the dialectic of Christian existence, which is both under temptation and determined by the Lord at the same time. The reality of the new life stands and falls with the promise that God remains faithful and does not abandon his handiwork. Therefore statements about the sacrament are paralleled, and in a certain way even paralysed, by others about the gospel or faith. The Church is the world under the promise and commandment of the heavenly Lord, the host of those placed under the word and thus summoned ever anew to the exodus of the people of God. This means that Christian existence is no manageable phenomenon within the bounds of a clearly defined cultic society, and the effect of the sacraments cannot be described by the formulas *φάρμαχον ἀθανασίγς* or *ex opere operato*. For the Giver cannot be separated from his gift and, on the other hand, he is not identical with his means of salvation, but he remains Lord and Judge over and in his gifts.

There is for Paul no extension of the earthly Jesus in the Church as the earthly deputy of the exalted one.[5] It is just where he speaks of the body of Christ that christology and ecclesiology are not interchangeable. The Lord's domain manifests the Lord, but it does not stand in his stead and take possession of him. The body is the field and instrument of the Spirit, not its substitute or its fetters. Paul is utterly misunderstood if one regards the primacy of Christ over his Church as meaning anything other than the exclusive lordship of Christ. If the Pauline motif is used in another sense, the apostle necessarily, though against his will, becomes the pioneer of early catholic Christianity.

The contrast is especially clear when it comes to the concept of ecclesiastical office. Characteristically, the genuine letters of Paul mention neither ordination nor the presbytery, but leave the functions of the Church to charismatics and address every Christian as a charismatic. That is not to say that certain duties were not more or less firmly bound to persons suited for them. Nonetheless, in their

[5] This follows most pointedly from the Pauline doctrine of the Spirit, which, precisely when it enters man and pervades the Church, preserves the externality of the Lord and of salvation (cf. Gal. 2.20). Far from being voided, the *extra nos* receives its keenest expression in the *in nobis*.

positions these people counted as special representatives of the universal priesthood, to which baptism with the gift of the Spirit calls the Christian and for which the Spirit qualifies him ever anew. To put it pointedly, but without exaggeration, the Pauline church is composed of nothing but laymen, who nevertheless are all, within their possibilities, at the same time priests and officeholders, that is, instruments of the Spirit for the enactment of the Gospel in the everyday world.

Correspondingly, Paul knows no Christian cult in the strict sense, although he presupposes the Old Testament cultic law, the concept of an almost cultic intercession of the heavenly Christ for his own, and above all, of course, the cultic societies of his environment. He alludes to these from time to time in terminology and motivation. The earliest Christian services of worship, and the celebrations of the Lord's Supper which, as a rule, may be assumed to have been connected with them, cannot be used as opposing evidence. To be sure, the letters of Paul themselves show that the Hellenistic churches made cult celebrations of these worship services in the sense of the mystery religions; they viewed the sacraments as mediating a share in the destiny of the dying and rising divinity and understood themselves as a cultic society. Paul, however, had to battle against this distortion constantly. He did it not least by designating the Christian's everyday life as the sphere of true worship (Rom. 12.1f.). The boundaries between profane and sacred, which elsewhere are marked by holy times, places, celebrations, persons and functions, do not exist for him. As far as he is concerned, the gatherings of the Church are the occasions for preaching the word, teaching (rehearsing doctrine), and praising God. They are the place where the Christian reflects upon his everyday service, so far as enthusiasm can be restrained, and receives his readiness and strength for it. They call him into community and mission, for which every Christian must be prepared in his situation. In this we perceive a comprehensive conception of personal responsibility and congregational discipline, whose clarity and grandeur are fascinating.

It must be pointed out with even greater emphasis in this case, that such a conception, apparently even during the lifetime of the apostle, was never more than imperfectly realized. Already in the next generation, even in the area of Paul's own mission, it was replaced by another. This is shown by the Lucan writings and the Pastorals, which give instructions for church order in letter form, so as to be able to claim for them the authority of the apostle. Here we find, it seems to me, the monarchical bishop, surrounded by presbyters, deacons and other co-workers bound by vow. The office is conferred by ordination and, because it is regulated by disciples of the apostles, placed in apostolic succession. The Lucan work as a whole is totally incomprehensible if it is not seen that only in the stream of apostolic tradition does one also belong to the one holy Church as the earthly realm of salvation. I Clement and the letters of Ignatius display the same tendency. They already differentiate between office-holders and laymen and are important milestones on the way to a fully developed cultic praxis.

In this hasty sketch my only interest has been in characterizing the revolution which occurred within half a century after Paul. The historical necessity of this transformation should not be overlooked. The Pauline understanding of office, worship, Christian freedom and responsibility was apparently unable to curb the ferment of enthusiasm in the churches. It seems rather to have incited it so that it became a danger for the entire Gentile Church. Out of a pressing need, therefore, for which it knew no other remedy, this church grasped at those forms of church government which had stood the test in Jewish Christianity.

It is precisely in this respect, in my opinion, that the revolution can be called legitimate. For I think that the Holy Spirit manifests itself in the Church most clearly when, in the midst of the pressing need and perplexity of men, it awakens the courage and spiritual gifts for new ways which are appropriate to the situation. Apostles do not justify retaining old orders, when they can no longer serve contemporary life. That Church which does not stand ready at all times to break out of its traditional walls and is not willing to bear the risks inevitably associated therewith, cannot seriously appeal to her Master for her stance. To be sure, it should be asked what price has to be paid for such departures from tradition and in what way the necessary revolution can be justified. Herein lies the actual problem of early catholicism. I will go into this briefly again in my conclusion, after I have attempted to expose the problem of Paulinism as far as I can.

The necessity of new orders is conclusively demonstrated by the struggle against enthusiasm. Historically speaking, it was only in this way that the Christian churches were able to repel the assault and survive as churches of Christ. Nonetheless, they were not satisfied simply with taking the necessary measures. They thought that they also had to derive the legitimacy of these measures from tradition. For this they used the fiction of the authority transmitted from the apostles. This was not done by appealing to the Pauline preaching about the freedom of the Christian and the Church. Rather the new orders were presented as established by the apostle himself. They were based, then, on his office with its function of providing church order, and to that extent on a principle of tradition and legitimacy. In this process there was now involved the power of a constructive fiction, the reception of which was made dependent on the illusion of a demonstrable continuity immanent in the Christian realm.

It can be shown, of course, that in actual experience such revolutions never occur and succeed without fictions and illusions. Nevertheless, the theologian can hardly be content with that, if he does not wish to declare faith to be simply a religious form of behaviour and to subordinate it to the canons applicable thereto. His concern should be directed precisely toward preventing faith from becoming this. For illusion imperils him more than vice. That is well demonstrated by the price which early catholicism had to pay for the preservation of the Christian Church in the defence against enthusiasm.

In borrowing from Jewish Christianity, the Church was compelled to bind the Spirit to the office. The Church had to be placed under an authority which would no longer allow its right and power to be constantly questioned and which would no longer require that both of these be derived from its proclamation. At this juncture the institution as such received authority, right, power and Spirit. Henceforth, it is responsible for preaching, determines doctrine, and tolerates the priesthood of all believers only within the boundaries which it sets.

Into the new cult, which was in the process of establishing itself, the legacy of the Jews as well as that of the ancient mystery religions was taken up. The latter, since it was still flourishing everywhere, proved superior to the Jewish Old Testament legacy, which was allowed little more than the task of assuring the continuity of a sacred past for contemporary practice. The spheres of sacred and profane are now marked by times, places, persons and functions rather than by obedience and disobedience. The gospel and the freedom of the Christian are concealed under a religious metaphysics of heavenly-earthly orders. Christianity arises as a new religion with a divine founder, a cult which anticipates the heavenly celebration, faith in basic saving facts, and an ethic which strangely enough is nourished by Jewish Old Testament traditions and those of popular philosophy. From the writings of the Apostolic Fathers one can conclude that this ethic was no less effective in appealing to the environment than the Christian proclamation of salvation. They also show, however, that from this time on the goal of Church education was the pious man, and the Pauline doctrine of the justification of the ungodly was stripped of its paradoxical character.

There remains the task of drawing a conclusion from our discussion. Does it not consist of a dilemma in the final analysis? The historical-critical approach leads to disillusionment. That at least, in my opinion, it has in common with the gospel. We have seen that the subject 'Paul and early catholicism' does not indicate the historical centre of earliest Christian history, but at best only an exemplary fragment from its bewildering variety. It is extremely complex even in itself. For not even the question who Paul really was has yet been adequately explained. One can hardly deny that, among other things, he helped prepare the way for early catholicism. Willingly or unwillingly, we all serve the current that carries us along. Both as missionary and as theologian Paul had little direct and lasting influence on the subsequent development, though this stands in flagrant contradiction to his own claims. Indeed he was and remained an individualist, doubtless one of the most significant in church history and surely the most controversial even in earliest Christianity. The later period was able to assimilate him only by setting the image of a saint in the place of his actual life. In this way some substantial features of his existence and history could be retained and put to good use. Nonetheless, the connection between Paul and the later period rested largely on misunderstanding. The apostle to the Gentiles was seen as the actual founder of the worldwide Church and its first order. And even in this he was regarded only as the extended arm of the original apostles. Thus he appeared to be an indispensable connecting link within the *Una Sancta* on its supposed continuous and controllable way from Jerusalem to Rome and into the world.

Alongside this image of Paul, to which the ecclesiastical future belonged, there is, however, the real Paul as well. This Paul remains confined in seven letters and for the most part unintelligible to posterity, not only to the ancient Church and the Middle Ages. However, whenever he is rediscovered – which happens amost exclusively in times of crisis – there issues from him explosive power which destroys as much as it opens up something new. His historical existence and activity is then repeated. The gospel of the unknown God who justifies the ungodly and none but them, and who deals with us only in this way, then comes into conflict with the Christian religion which is concerned about the piety of the pious. Then the one Lord, with the demand of this exclusive lordship, shatters those authorities which claim to be his earthly deputies. The Church becomes the creation of the word, instead of being the mother of the faithful and possessor of the truth. Worship in the secularity of the world replaces the Christian cult. Faith in him who is always and exclusively the one who awakens the dead replaces the superstitious belief in history and salvation history as sources of revelation. The universal priesthood of all believers rises up against the sacramentally guaranteed office, which claims authority on the strength of tradition. The freedom of the Christian man and of the Church of Jesus breaks through the ecclesiastical ethic and uniformity. Mission pushes aside pious self-admiration and self-assertion.

It is never long, to be sure, until orthodoxy and enthusiasm again master this Paul and banish him once more to his letters. However, the Church continues to preserve his letters in her canon and thereby latently preserves her own permanent crisis. She cannot get away from the one who for the most part only disturbs her. For he remains even for her the apostle of the heathen; the pious still hardly know what to make of him. For that very reason his central message is the voice of a preacher in the wilderness, even in Protestant Christianity, which today stands much nearer early catholicism than it supposes or is willing to believe.[6]

[6] The satisfaction of Catholic theologians over the rediscovery of catholicism in the New Testament has been most notably expressed by H. Küng, '"Early Catholicism" in the New Testament as a Problem in Controversial Theology', in *The Council in Action*, 1963, ch. 12, pp. 159–95. I gladly join in his appeal to the common ecumenical task, though with less enthusiasm. To the catholicity of the early catholic church one may attribute the fact that she did not exclude Paul from the canon (187), provided the double motive of God's providence and human error, and perhaps the pressure felt from the heretic Marcion, are not forgotten. I wish that Küng would retain his trust in the early Church's discernment of the spirits, which he believes cannot be improved upon. The historian has learned, not without cause, to approach all tradition at first with some mistrust. The spirits have too often been confused in tradition for us not to have to face the risk ourselves, without proxy, in questions of life and death. That the total context of the Scriptures aims at speaking 'in one form or another of Jesus Christ and his Gospel' (185) cannot very well be disputed. It is pointed out to us often enough in our own camp. But who does not also intend that elsewhere 'in one form or another'? The 'evangelical' form is much preferable to me here. I hear the motto: 'To be Catholic is to be evangelical' (183). Would to God it were so, but surely it cannot be so or

become so, if the statement may not be reversed. My protest is in fact directed against the Catholic Church (183) in and outside of the Roman Church, inasmuch as here the one thing necessary is not the whole to which Küng summons. The whole Church and the whole Scripture – but that can surely be said in the strict sense only eschatologically, especially if one observes that Jacob and Esau still today contend with one another everywhere. In view of the conclusion of this essay, we must perhaps first of all come to an even clearer and more pedantic understanding of how much the 'whole Paul' causes us distress and joy. That would at least be an unusually provocative touchstone for genuine Catholicity and original Protestantism.

XIII

UNITY AND MULTIPLICITY IN THE NEW TESTAMENT DOCTRINE OF THE CHURCH*

All New Testament statements about the Church have their particular historical location. They are therefore subject to continual change, they are compressed into various key images and mark stages and new departures within primitive Christianity. The New Testament does not present us with an *ecclesiologia perennis* but offers us instead certain ecclesiological archetypes. My first task is to provide the outline of a justification for this historical judgment.

We are faced at the very beginning with the most difficult problem of all. We know that Jesus made fellowship possible to and among those who followed him. On the other hand, he did not found any organizationally apprehensible and clearly defined communities, and withdrew from the people of God as much as he involved himself with it. He certainly did not create a Church in our sense of the word, embracing both Jews and Gentiles; according to the conviction of many New Testament scholars, he did not even express any desire that such a Church should exist. The rule of God which he proclaimed is not adorned in any later ecclesiastical dress. This applies not only to him but to the community of the days immediately after Easter, which is still totally determined by its connection with Old Testament salvation history and awaits, in apocalyptic expectation, the re-establishment of the messianically renewed people of the Twelve Tribes; this people, however, is composed only of Jews – with the inclusion, of course, of proselytes. Later Christianity did not adhere to this conception in its original and central sense, not even – indeed, least of all – when it picked up and used the motif of the

* A lecture given at the Fourth World Conference for Faith and Order, Montreal, 16 July, 1963, and first published in *Ökumenische Rundschau*, 1964, pp. 58–63.

people of God in a transferred sense, now including Gentile Christians in its framework of reference.

Thus a great gulf had to be bridged if the step was to be taken away from this beginning and out beyond the limits of the Jewish people. This step is associated with the name of the 'Hellenists', the leadership of the Seven, and the emergence of Antioch as a new headquarters of the Christian religion. Where Gentiles become disciples without previously becoming (Jewish) proselytes, it is not possible to talk seriously of the renewed people of God, but only of the new in antithesis to the old. The prophetic promise that, after the redemption of Israel, the Gentiles, too, would come in, is now no longer the mighty act reserved for God alone. It now becomes a task to be realized by Christians. Such a transformation is possible because the time of the End, with its signs and wonders, is seen as already dawning. A corresponding change takes place in christology: Jesus is no longer the Son of Man hidden in the heavenly places until his return but the exalted Lord, already reigning in triumph. Over against his glory, as the trial of Stephen surely demonstrates, Temple and Law lose, at least for the Hellenists, their absolute validity. It is no longer Israel alone, but the world, which belongs of right to the risen Lord. Faith as personal decision is now the real criterion of the Christian; and the Church, as the company and sphere of the faithful, is now the kingdom of Christ on earth, which cannot be understood except as the work of the Spirit.

This Christianity which is in process of disengaging itself from the ties of the Jewish religion is, on the evidence of the letters to the Corinthians, determined – and threatened – by enthusiasm. Because it, too, cannot survive without some organizational structure, it evolves a self-understanding based on the analogy of the mystery religions by which it is surrounded. Christ becomes its cultic God, bestowing upon it freedom not only from demonic forces but also from the limitations of current earthly ordinances. In baptism it experiences the power of the Resurrection working psychosomatically. The eucharist is celebrated as the banquet of those who have been removed from the assault of the world. Religious ecstasy limits and devalues Christian service. The battle to overcome the very present threat of this enthusiasm was a long one. It has always remained latent in Christianity; wherever the sacraments press into the foreground of the saving happening, the cultic law of the Old Testament regains exemplary significance and produces a privileged priestly ministerial caste, and the Church is unable quite to throw off the character of a Christian mystery religion and will therefore be marked by withdrawal from the world.

Paul is in the position of having to guard equally against Judaism and enthusiasm. He therefore only continues to describe the Church as the people of God when he is setting it in antithesis to unbelieving Israel. Continuity with the Old Testament history exists for him only as a gift of faith. It is a continuity of promise and miracle only, a continuity which seems to be criss-crossed again and again by the history of unfaith. It cannot be controlled by any power immanent in the community, as the example of Israel itself shows. The rule of Christ is the realm in which God shatters all carefully cultivated piety and acts as the one who raises the dead and as Creator *ex nihilo*. It is by these very means that he makes us the instruments of grace in Christian brotherhood, common humanity and world-wide mission. The Church as the Body of Christ is the sphere of operation of this grace, extending as it does throughout all space and time and thus, out of its rich store of *charismata*, leaving no time and no place without its promise and without its challenge. The post-Pauline epoch makes it clear that no successful resistance to enthusiasm can be maintained while the reception of the Spirit is bound exclusively to baptism, and Christian service in the community and in the world is interpreted exclusively in terms of the universal priesthood of all believers. The development of a ministerial office transmitted by ordination becomes the criterion of this new direction in the Church. Jewish Christianity has a ready-made form of presbyteral government out of which the monarchical episcopate very quickly grows. The Spirit given in and with ministerial office authorizes the recipients to administer the apostolic inheritance and calls the bearers and interpreters of the sacred tradition into an unbroken succession. When the Pastorals compare the communities ordered in this way with domestic life, the conception of the Church as the household of God which is once again a throw-back to the primitive Jewish Christian outlook, can be discerned. It is designed, of course, for a Christianity which is taking up its entrenched positions against enemies within and without. The idea of mission becomes, in this situation, of secondary importance. As in Colossians and Ephesians the very existence of the Church is the real divine witness to the world. That is true even of Acts, which tells a story of the coming into existence of the worldwide Church and equates it with the history of mission.

Here, too, primitive Christian eschatology pales into insignificance in the light of ecclesiology. As the area in which miracles and the gifts of the Spirit operate, the Church is the institution of salvation. It is also becoming so independent of christology that it is itself the continuation of the history of Jesus. That is historically valid. For the Church is the possessor and the transmitter of Gospel-truth, because the twelve apostles, in their role of eyewitnesses of the life and Resurrection of Jesus, are the guarantors of its message. The one holy and apostolic Church embodies, equally as an historical entity and as distinguished by the rule of the Spirit within it, the continuity of salvation history. We have arrived on the threshold of early catholicism.

The Fourth Gospel (again!) mounts a remarkable counter-offensive against this development; it contains no explicit idea of the Church, no doctrine of ministerial office, no developed sacramental theology. Correspondingly, there is a strange compression of preaching, the effect of which is to bring 'Christ alone' into strong relief as the one thing necessary and to play this idea off even against the fathers who represent holy tradition. Admittedly, the theme of the Church is actually touched on in the farewell discourses. But this occurs in a characteristic context as answer to the question how the earthly community of the time after the Passion and Easter, in its separation from its Lord, can yet abide with Jesus. The 'presence of Christ' as the unqualified master theme of the Gospel is thus bound to the Word of Jesus as the true bearer of the Spirit with a tightness not paralleled anywhere else in the New Testament. 'Church' denotes here the company of those living under this Word and determined by it alone.

The picture I have drawn has been of necessity sketchy, and some details in it may well appear questionable. But the fact that there is an incessant process of change going on within New Testament ecclesiology can hardly be disputed; and this process naturally brings with it corresponding changes in eschatology, soteriology, anthropology and the doctrine of ministerial office. Theology never grows in the vacuum of abstraction, untouched by contemporary history. While this fact is generally admitted, it is nevertheless frequently deprived of its offending sting. Changes and tensions are explained as necessary phases of an organic development in terms of the different personalities, groups and epochs involved. Things which, considered in isolation, are disparate, regain connection, teleology and unity when considered from a common central point of vision. The justification for this approach is obvious. Every historian is well acquainted with the law of life: what is obsolescent dies to make room for what is new, but the new always connects with something that has gone before. The process which is broken off here will have a chance to continue in another form there. Spirit and tradition must not be identified, but neither are they mutually exclusive. At various points in time and space, the same thing creates for itself differing, and, in extreme situations, even opposing, forms of expression. Because unity presupposes differentiation, it is never uniformity, which would produce sterility and the death of all common life. Even life and fellowship in the Holy Spirit expresses itself as unity held together by tensions.

But to say all this is not enough. Christ and the Christian Church are not cyphers which can be combined with any and every form of religious organization, every possible theological conception and the luxuriant growths of devotional practice: still less can they be used as trimmings. Joy in the manifold manifestations of the historical and the will to solidarity with all God's creatures may not legitimately lead to the postulate that the Holy Spirit is indiscriminately present nor to the surrender of criteria for the testing and the distinguishing of spirits. Christian unity and Christian incompatibility are complementary, or else belief and unbelief are merely psychological phenomena. The question of Christian unity is identical with the question of Christian truth. Only docetism can afford to ignore the fact that Jacob and Esau live in constant proximity without ever becoming one, and the scandal of the Cross awakes the old Adam simultaneously with the new. Even theological outlines provide documentation for this, and such documentation is already present in primitive Christianity. For the Church has never been the pure community of authenticated saints but always the field in which tares have been sown.

No romantic postulate, however enveloped it may be in the cloak of salvation history, can be permitted to weaken the sober observation that the historian is unable to speak of an unbroken unity of New Testament ecclesiology. In that field he becomes aware of our own situation in microcosm – differences, difficulties, contradictions, at best an ancient ecumenical confederation without an Ecumenical Council. The tensions between Jewish Christian and Gentile Christian churches, between Paul and the Corinthian enthusiasts, between John and early catholicism are as great as those of our own day. Onesided emphases, fossilized attitudes, fabrications and contradictory opposites in doctrine, organization and devotional practice are to be found in the ecclesiology of the New Testament no less than among ourselves. To recognize this is even a great comfort and, so far as ecumenical work today is concerned, a theological gain. For, in so doing, we come to see that our own history is one with that of primitive Christianity. Today, too, God's Spirit hovers over the waters of a chaos out of which divine creation is to take shape. So it is right to emphasize yet again at this point that Jesus' proclamation of the dawning of God's kingly rule may have conjured up many ecclesiologies, but it remains strangely transcendent over them all and is by them all at best brokenly reflected and not seldom totally distorted.

Now in conclusion: in spite of all its vicissitudes, its tensions and its contradictions, primitive Christianity proclaimed the one Church, not in the sense of a theory of organic development but in the name of the reality and the truth of the Holy Spirit. How was this possible? How can we take up this task in our own day? How can our insight into this diversity of ecclesiologies deepen and clarify our confession of the unity of Christ's Church rather than destroy it? That is the central problem which we now have to put to ourselves. I am convinced that the solution of this problem lies neither on the historical plane nor at the level of organizational strategy. The unity of the Church was, is and remains primarily an eschatological property, to be enjoyed only as a gift, never as an assured possession. The unity of the Church cannot be apprehended except by faith which hears the voice of the one Shepherd and obeys his call to form one flock, his flock. The one Church lies behind us only as we participate in the exodus of the pilgrim people of God out of its old encampments on its way to the kingdom of Christ. For the Church is the kingdom of Christ on earth, and this kingdom is always ahead of our earthly organizations, theologies and devotional practices. We can never catch it up. It captures us and then sends us out to seek it, to live it out, to bear witness to it in fresh ways. It is itself the way on which we cannot stand still or even turn back. But we must so tread this way as not to rest in theological ease at the point where we simply ask what the sufficient marks of the kingdom of Christ are. Let me therefore end with certain questions I find the New Testament putting to me when I try to discern the unity and truth of the kingdom of Christ through all its ecclesiologies.

Is not the supremely important thing that the Lord should remain sovereign over his servants, the head over the members, and that our picture of him and his lordship should not displace, overshadow, seem to correct his own? If this were realized in practice, then the relationship of Christ and his Church would never be reversible and the unity of the Church would then require of us that we should not place ourselves on the same footing with him nor think to complete his work nor make ourselves in any way independent of him. We should have to decrease, in order that he might increase. Christology is the permanent measure of all ecclesiology. Does not the kingdom of Christ mean, secondly, that Christ alone becomes the Lord of us all? But surely, this in turn must mean that he must have permanent and unrestricted access to each of his members and they must have similar access to him, and not be shut off from him by any power, even the maternal power of the Church. To give his Word free course and to facilitate for every obedient hearer immediate passage into his presence – this must therefore be the paramount concern and the inviolable limit of all ecclesiastical authority, and the fruit of Christian common life. Does it not follow, thirdly, that all tradition and all ministerial office within the Church can possess authority only as long and as far as they help us to hear Christ addressing us; as far, that is, as they continue to be servants of the promise of the Gospel and of the means of grace designated in the New Testament? Naturally, the question immediately arises, fourthly, as to the source to which we are to look for the interpretation of the Gospel and the validation of what is preached. Is there any answer possible other than the christological one – namely, that, with the Baptist, we must look to the one on the way to the Cross? For he alone is the end of our wilfulness and the source of all grace, the Judge of the devout and the salvation of the godless. And here, fifthly, we have the most radical determination of the true being of the community of Jesus. Can it really be a religious association among others, measurable in terms of piety and morality, of cult and organization, of profound speculations and wide influence? Doubtless, this is what it looks like from outside, and this is how its members, corporately and individually, very frequently understand it. But what has all this to do with the Jesus who associated with tax-collectors and sinners and died for the godless. Is not the only relevant criterion here whether or not this community follows him? That would liberate it from staying put in earthly camps and despatch it at once to the far corners of the earth, there to show forth God's solidarity with his creatures. In following the crucified one, it would have its part in the glory of the Christ. To sum up: the worth of every ecclesiology, even in the New Testament, can be estimated precisely. The criterion is the extent to which it succeeds in declaring the royal freedom and the lordship of Jesus Christ who, according to Eph. 2, is himself alone the unity of his Church.

XIV

THOUGHTS ON THE PRESENT CONTROVERSY ABOUT SCRIPTURAL INTERPRETATION*

(For Ernst Wolf on his sixtieth birthday – a token of gratitude and friendship)

THE RELATIONSHIP of Church, Scripture and scriptural interpretation has suddenly become a burning question in many circles. In my view, we ought to be glad that an important theological theme of this kind is no longer the preserve of academic interests but has been taken up by local congregations. It is true that, like every science and every skill, theology has its own problems, methods of working and presuppositions, the logic of which it is not easy to make comprehensible to outsiders. But, on the other hand, theology is not a form of esoteric doctrine. The Christian community has put this work out to contract, as it has other work; it is therefore both allowed and indeed obliged to call theology to account, and ought to be in a position to inform itself about theology's central questions, the upheavals which take place within it and, from time to time, about its characteristic trends. Now this cannot happen if this community, for its part, is not prepared to take seriously its duty to listen and to do its own share of thinking. Theology has, after all, to do with thinking, and there is no skill and no science which can be grasped painlessly without effort. The most serious difficulty in the confrontation which is brewing today is that community and theology have grown apart; and for this both parties are certainly to blame. The contemporary battle will prove to be meaningless, if it does not reunite us, or at least bring us closer together; that is, if theology does

* 'Zum gegenwärtigen Streit um die Schriftauslegung', a lecture given to the Westphalian Federation of the Evangelical Alliance, 12 March 1962, and first published in *Das Wort Gottes und die Kirchen* (Schriften des Evangelischen Bundes in Westfalen 4), 1962, pp. 7–32.

not acknowledge its responsibility to the community nor the community its responsibility to think more deeply and more far-sightedly in company with theology. An irresponsible theology and a community void of ideas must of necessity continue to be strangers, even when they fight with and against each other. I want now, in my own way – very frankly, very aggressively and, as I hope, in the apostolic sense of the word, very edifyingly – to show that a theology determined by historical criticism, which is the kind of theology I represent, is not necessarily bound to lack responsibility over against the community. I shall lapse only infrequently into the role of exegete. The problems with which we are concerned here can in general be discussed without donning the heavy armour of the specialist. But I am not going to renounce my claim to speak to you as a teacher, even if many do see me rather in the role of defendant. There are far too many people today pontificating about scriptural interpretation who have no real knowledge either of Scripture or of interpretation and who therefore are the first who need to learn.

The accusation levelled against historical critical theology runs as follows: it destroys the community and its faith, instead of building them up. The rights and wrongs of such an accusation cannot be decided without first clarifying the issue as to what the community in the evangelical sense really is and, consequentially, what are the fundamental characteristics of evangelical faith. The answer seems to me a simple one: in the evangelical conception, the community is the flock under the Word as it listens to the Word. All its other identifying marks must be subordinate to this ultimate and decisive criterion. A community which is not created by the Word is for us no longer the community of Jesus. That is a polemical statement. Of course, it is self-evident that Christian fellowships and churches look to Scripture. But this can be done in very different ways. The distinguishing mark of the Reformation and its disciples is the exclusive particle, the word 'alone'. In this discussion, too, this exclusive particle is not expendable. Concretely expressed, the relationship of the community and the Word of God is not reversible; there is no dialectical process by which the community created by the Word becomes at the same time for all practical purposes an authority set over the Word to interpret it, to administer it, to possess it. Naturally, the community has always the task of interpreting the Word afresh, so that it can become audible at all times and in all places. In a certain sense it has also the task of administering it, inasmuch as it creates ways and means for the Word to make itself heard. But possess it – never. For the community remains the handmaid of the Word. If it makes the Word into a means to itself as an end, if it becomes the suzerain of the Word instead of its handmaid, the community loses its own life. The community is the kingdom of Christ because it is built up by the Word. But it remains so only while it is content not to assume control over the Word – a temptation which has been a constant threat to the Church. The freedom of a Christian man remains in existence only when, and as long as, he belongs not to himself but to his Lord. In precisely the same way, the community retains the character of the kingdom of Christ only when, and as long as, it subordinates itself to the Word, leaving in the Word's hands all the power and absolute freedom of action. Even a congregation which calls itself Christian is devoid of any authority at all – indeed, must be called to order and repentance – when it makes itself the measure of the evangelical Word it is charged to utter and makes its own believing state the basis of proclamation and, derivatively, of theology. We do not have to take seriously in Christian territory any and every complaint that proclamation and theology are destroying the foundation of the community and of faith. For that was often enough the very task of prophets and apostles, as we can learn equally from the beginning of Jeremiah and from the letters to the churches in Revelation, even if we are no longer prepared to learn it from the history of the Reformation. I should actually prefer to express the same thing from the other angle, the positive: if the essence of the community is and remains its posture as a hearing community, then the community exists in no other mode than that of pilgrimage. In evangelical thought we know no sacred times, places, persons, institutions to which the Word could be inseparably bound and on the basis of which it could be handed on and authenticated. On the contrary, with Abraham, with the people of the wilderness, with the prophets and apocalyptists of the old Covenant, with Jesus and his disciples we live in a continual condition of exodus, for ever being called from traditional ties and established camps out onto the road of promise. It is no good relying on the fact that we did once hear the Word: we have to abide in this hearing. A Church, whose exodus has come at some point to a definite end, is no longer a congregation under the Word, whatever traffic it may have with this Word. But if this is really true and grounded directly in Scripture, there ought hardly to be so many unthinking and light-hearted attempts as there are today to call scientific theology to repentance without considering the damage which is being done to the community.

But as my immediate purpose is simply to set up a few guiding lights, I am going now to turn first to the second half of the question I have posed. You will undoubtedly have noticed that so far I have spoken frequently of the Word, sometimes of Scripture, but not at all of the canon. This, of course, was not accidental. Certainly, for all Christian churches, the Word of God and the canon belong together. But they are in no way identical, as orthodoxy in its various forms would have it. They cannot be so, as even a quite superficial consideration will show. First: which of all the possible canons is to be our authority? The Hebrew, Greek, Latin and German Bibles cannot simply be equated. On the contrary, each new language and each new translation alters the Bible, as anyone can test for themselves. Secondly: it is also altered, however, on the basis of new discoveries and improved insight into the original Greek texts, which lies behind all the translations. Such alterations take place mostly unnoticed, but they are permanent and by no means unimportant. Thirdly: even if one day we were to find ourselves in the position – which can, in fact, never occur – of having in our hands an assured original text, this text would still contain an abundance of passages which were incapable of unambiguous explanation and would very frequently allow of the most diverse interpretations. Even the most learned specialist scholars find themselves unable to agree about the sense of certain words, statements and viewpoints. There is no canon established, or capable of being established, once and for all. To pretend that we have it, is to lull ourselves to sleep in the arms of a treacherous illusion. We never have anything but a provisional form of the canon and even this is qualified by being subject to conflicting interpretations. The truth of this statement can be demonstrated alike in every evangelical fellowship and in the theological faculties, among the exegetes in their own circle and among exegetes and systematic theologians engaged in dialogue. That the Church lives in a constantly renewed state of exodus can also be seen from its commerce with Scripture. We possess Scripture only as those who are always receiving it afresh. If we want to possess it on any other basis, we shall make it a closed book to ourselves. We all know by experience that it changes its countenance according as to whether the child, the adolescent, the adult or the elderly, the pedantic, the despairing, the self-confident is looking within it. The unused, unexpounded book as such can only become an object of superstition. But even the book in use and exposed to interpretation still does not remain exactly the same for any one of us throughout the whole of his life, let alone for all of us taken together. The canon (so long as we do not mean by this a thing between two covers) exists, but not separably from its hearers and readers, and each Bible reader can at any time, by himself or with others, become aware of the same truth as the researcher recognizes in his specialist activity. When we are dealing with Scripture, we are not dealing with a firm and settled possession but with a never-ending task. Of course there are the congregations and the Bible-owners for whom there is no problem, because they know it all in advance. These may well contend for the canon as if for a reliquary. But there can be no genuine controversy with them because they are standing not under, but upon Scripture – which was certainly *not* given to us as a platform.

This brings the third section of my theme into focus – the matter of interpretation. I must now be somewhat more circumstantial, because here we reach the central issue of the contemporary confrontation. I begin with a postulate and a thesis. It is undeniable that today, both in the world around us and also in the Church, the passion for 'restoration' and indifference on the part of the positivist elements are both prominent. But this situation serves to obscure the characteristic Reformation approach to the understanding of Scripture; and it was not fortuitous that this approach expressed itself originally in criticism of a reigning ecclesiastical tradition. Anyone who is still prepared to learn from the Reformation must recognize that knowledge of the Gospel can never be gained and maintained otherwise than critically. If we possess the canon only by continually rediscovering it, we experience the Gospel in the same way. The Yes and the No here are fundamentally incapable of being separated. Thus Paul summons his hearers in I Cor. 14.29 to exercise a critical judgment on prophecy or, as we should say, preaching. In I Cor. 12.11 he calls the power of discrimination between spirits a gift of grace, and he himself exercised this gift by waging a life-long battle against legalism and enthusiasm as the two great adversaries of the Gospel. To sum up: the Gospel begets the critical faculty and creates the critical community, whereas the absence of criticism is the sign of spiritual impoverishment and deprivation. In this connection we have to remember that the letters to the Seven Churches in Revelation satirized such spiritual poverty precisely from the religious angle and cast it up as a reproach in the face of congregations correctly ordered in the ecclesiastical sense. To be critical means: to have criteria. When we enquire about the correct criteria for Scriptural interpretation, we face what in technical language is called the problem of hermeneutics. When today ecclesiastical circles become disturbed because they believe the authority of Scripture to be threatened, this is only taking up over a wider field and at a different level the controversy about the hermeneutical problem which has already been going on for a long time in academic theology. Pietism appears here in the role of spokesman and its right to intervene cannot properly be contested. In point of fact, while this whole matter is the concern of us all, it is specifically the concern of Pietism. For the congregations of West Germany, as they actually exist, have for the most part been moulded by pietism in so far as they have any life in them at all. It is not pietism's right to take part in the debate which presents problems; but, in my view, it is the way in which it does it and the position it is defending.

To produce evidence for this, I have to go back to origins. Right at the outset, we have to remember that a profound crisis has gripped our whole spiritual life and our sociological structures. Next, we have to see that Pietism, too, has been affected by this crisis, and indeed particularly so. It developed along with middle-class society and has always been very closely interwoven with it. But this society is disintegrating at an increasing pace, as the revolution of the technological age asserts itself more strongly. We are all conscious of this and have only to think how the form of family life which has hitherto obtained in our own close circle, in our households themselves, is now collapsing. Islands are more and more taking the place of the firm mainland and how extensive these islands are has not yet been put to the question. But it is hardly an exaggeration to state quite soberly that our whole Church life today is almost everywhere confined solely to these islands. That could not be said – at least for the villages – even sociologically fifty years ago. Quite plainly, like the Church in general, Pietism in particular cannot cope with this new situation. Its power has by no means been broken: but it is exercised more and more from a position on the defensive rather than on the attack and without any doubt at all its field of manoeuvre is becoming increasingly restricted. In consequence, what in its dawning and in its hey-day was specifically modern has now become conservative, even reactionary; and, in turn, the nervous reaction to this is to look for a scapegoat. This process is seen most clearly in the relationship with theology. The tension between pietism and scientific theology has always existed since orthodoxy lost its hold, and the incontestable appeal of pietism over against enthusiasm, vary as it may have done according to time and place, has not only continually fed this tension but has occasionally raised it to fever pitch. On the other hand, I readily concede that in the field of professional theology, as in every science, all kinds of experimentation go on, not always happily conceived. He who constructs, thinks and lives cannot succeed without making experiments and taking risks. Science is no more fool-proof than any other form of existence, and theology is no exception to this rule. Combustible material for a conflict is therefore always present on both sides; and sometimes it is only a question of whether the slow match will be put to it or not. In my opinion, this is possibly being done at the present moment in thoughtlessness and panic – in so far, indeed, as fire-raisers are not involved. Yet, speaking generally, for the last hundred years there has never been a generation of theologians so strongly orientated towards the empirical life of the Church as ours. Not everyone is able to take a synoptic view of the actual circumstances. But everybody who is even vaguely familiar with them knows that the Liberalism which prevailed for fifty years has been routed in the theological faculties and will never rise again, at least in the old form. A much greater threat is the possible revival of a compromise theology of the old brand under the banner of speculation in terms of salvation history and, above all in systematic theology, of a confessional orthodoxy. The most radical criticism is undoubtedly to be found assembled on New Testament territory and is represented there by the circle of Bultmann's pupils. But can we overlook the fact that we too, and precisely at this point, have almost all passed through the Church Struggle; we have spent half our adult days in the practical life of the Church and could not free ourselves, even if we wanted to, from the mark they have left upon us? We have as yet no need of witnesses to testify to this. Once this is made clear, it cannot be seriously maintained that the face of theology in the universities has so altered in the last few decades as to bring harm upon the Church and ever increasing anxiety to Pietism. The situation is exactly the reverse. But why then, the sudden passionate flaring-up of conflict instead of the armed neutrality or the mutual indifference which about fifty years ago to a large extent characterized both sides? It seems odd that one can be branded as a fanatical churchman *and* as the destroyer of faith and the local congregation, both within the space of a bare twenty years – and the latter not always by those who were formerly on the same side. I have even heard that a new Church Struggle was being proclaimed, directed against us who are in a more exhausted state from the first one than we should like or than is good for our work.

Such an outbreak of feelings and demonstrations only becomes comprehensible when we analyse our situation today with our eyes on its challenge and its historical necessity. We can scarcely deceive ourselves any longer into believing that our generation is exempt from the call to a new exodus out of familar surroundings into the land of an unknown future. In ages past, churches were extinguished over wide areas, although we are reluctant to remember this, rather as if God had not been acting according to the book. However this may be, uproar is a necessary concomitant of any exodus. There are always those who do not want to 'let go' and are unable to die; there are always those who die stubbornly in the last ditch before the collapsing temple of their fathers and call that obedience; above all, there are always the professional mourners whose hour this is. If there is anything which may be said to the credit of contemporary theology, it is this: where it has not wholly decayed into an occupation for the specialists, it is trying to create a way and a land for the Church of tomorrow and thus, with greater or less decisiveness, returning to those basic principles which once came in with the Reformation. Both are equally difficult and nobody can reasonably be required to jump over his shadow. Yet anyone who finds himself on the other side of this yawning abyss ought at least to consider whether he is not obliged to participate in this enterprise. What does this mean when we apply it to the question of scriptural interpretation?

Let me formulate it in such a way as to start out from the decisive point: the Reformation did in fact recognize the Gospel as an energy of criticism over against the world of the religious man – that is, the piety of the devout – and drew conclusions from this in regard to the canon also. We need not be primarily concerned here with things like Luther's aversion to the Epistle of James or Calvin's non-comprehension of Revelation. Far more important were the critical attitude towards extensive tracts of the Old Testament, which laid down Israel's way of life and the fundamental distinction between Law and Gospel. But there we have a pointer to one contrast with the practice of today's Church which is by no means perceived at a deep enough level. The biblicism which for the most part determines the life of our congregations is not in the true Reformation succession, is scarcely acquainted with it and is still less able to acknowledge it. In practice, and frequently enough in principle, the whole Bible is held to be the Word of God and the Gospel to be only its innermost core. Even if everything in the canon is not put on the same level, it is pictured as at least constructed in a series of steps leading up to the Holy of Holies. This state of affairs is illustrated very clearly in the Herrenhut Readings: God's Word meets us whenever the Bible is opened and it meets us in statements which can be removed from their context. It is no part of my purpose to discredit the Readings. I honour their history, so rich in blessing. I would only point out that here Scripture is being regarded and handled in a manner different from that of the Reformers. This fact has, however, unusually far-reaching consequences. That distinction between Law and Gospel, which was for the Reformers the key to the understanding of Scripture, can now be no longer seriously observed. Everything is Gospel, even if not always in its ultimate depth and glory. It is no accident therefore that both pietistic history and the kind of preaching which prevails today show clearly how emphatically life and proclamation have fallen into legalism. 'By grace alone', against its Pauline sense, is made into the foundation of the piety of the devout and hence of necessity it becomes at the same time the wall of separation erected against the lostness of the godless, instead of forming God's bridge for both him and us to tread. Does this not make the community of Christians into the bearer of one kind of religiosity among others? Is its relation to the world not being turned upside down here? For the religious community, which distinguishes itself from the world by its piety, is the watchword which goes forth from Qumran, but not from Jesus.

Finally, let us ask what such an understanding of the Bible means for hermeneutical practice as such. It will not be unfair if we sum up the ideal of piety among Protestant congregations in the formula: every man sitting down with his Bible in front of him! Undoubtedly this conception does point towards the nature of the Church as the hearing and obeying community. And it is also a fact that every Christian must find his own way into the Bible because the categories of personal appropriation and responsibility cannot be eliminated from evangelical Christianity. But in laying down these postulates it must never be overlooked what pressures and difficulties arise when this demand is expressed in such a generalized and isolated fashion. The Bible is a document which embraces a thousand-year-long history and was concluded eighteen hundred years ago. How can the individual Christian overcome the historical distance which separates him from such a document? How can he comprehend the historical contexts of every page and every passage in his Bible, how can he master its contradictions? In this situation is the Scripture not bound to be regarded as one single enormous book of random texts and the Holy Spirit as the means to historical knowledge and the power which enables historical gaps to be bridged? But is this a true description of the function of Bible and Holy Spirit according to the confessional documents of the Reformation? Very many will return a straightforward, untroubled and bold affirmative to this question and appeal to their own experience and the illumination they have received for verification. Now we may freely grant that no man plunges into Scripture without drawing out blessing therefrom and yet at the same time, looking at the sects which arose on this very basis, still find that for us the hermeneutical problem remains completely unsolved. It would certainly be a rewarding exercise to devote one visitation entirely to eliciting the theological content of the Sunday sermons and the weekday Bible studies and fellowship meetings. We should establish the existence of a more than Babylonian confusion of voices but at the same time we should arrive at a common point of departure and a common denominator for these voices: wherever the canon in its totality is accepted as the Word of God and biblicism reigns, the personal piety of the individual will turn the scale. But is the devout man the key to the interpretation of Scripture? If this were really the position, at least there would be no need to mount a campaign against historical criticism. The truth is, that we should then be faced not by what is felt to be an arbitrary and unbelieving assault on God's gift of salvation, but by an arbitrariness confined to the pious. I cannot see that the difference is very considerable and, in my view, the contestants are very close together, not in their theology and doctrine but in their ordinary practice and in their sins. All the outcry which is being raised today cannot do away with this involuntary solidarity in their traffic with Scripture. For the most part, the only possible alternative to the scientific method is violence done by the devout.

This brings me to the end of the first part of my review, in which I have sought to clarify the positions from which the battle is being fought out. I shall now go over the same ground again; though very much from the opposite direction, with the object of delineating the task and the solution which seems to me the best. In dealing with the problem of interpretation, I am bound to argue as an exegete who is keeping his eye on the primary fundamental consideration of hermeneutics in the New Testament itself: the Pauline distinction of *pneuma* and *gramma*. This antithesis can be translated into German only with difficulty. For it does not denote, as both classical and modern idealism would understand it, the opposition of letter and spirit, where 'letter' refers to that which is experienced as external, contingent and rigid and, as such, cannot be straightforwardly assimilated by the spiritual mode of existence. In this connection, 'spirit' was similarly interpreted as the human capacity for self-awareness and for making sense of the world and of history. As a Jew, Paul saw in the written crystallization of the divine will no hindrance to personal appropriation but rather an advantage over against the diverse, changing and ambiguous 'unwritten laws' whether of nature or of human reason. Thus, in his usage, *gramma* does not refer to something which is essentially form, such as we immediately think of when we hear the word 'letter', but to the divine law as the sum of its individual injunctions – the conception which went down to defeat in the Old Testament. *Gramma* is thus closely connected with *graphe*; more exactly stated, it is a quite specific form of *graphe*. On the basis of the antithesis we may make this formulation: *gramma* is 'Scripture' isolated from the Spirit, and not understood or interpreted according to the intention of the Spirit. The Jews value just that blind obedience which does not ask questions but follows the ordinance for God's sake, even when the human being in question no longer has any understanding of the will which is manifesting itself in the ordinance. Against this, the New Testament conceives of open-eyed obedience as the attitude of the child who knows the father's heart and will and can therefore act out of love. Thus *pneuma* is for Paul something different from what it was for the Greeks. It is not divine or human self-consciousness but the energy of the eschatological new covenant (II Cor. 3); it alone can produce the circumcision of the heart (Rom. 2.29) and it alone lies at the root of Christian obedience. Summing up, we can say that *pneuma* is for Paul the divine power which conveys the righteousness of faith and therefore stands in opposition to the law of the old Mosaic covenant. These brief statements, which really demand a lecture to themselves, will have to suffice. The point here is that Paul does not leave the reader of the Bible to his own devices, but says to him that Scripture demands to be interpreted in the light of a specific presupposition and of a specific goal. *Pneuma* and *gramma* are the two mutually exclusive possible ways both of Christian life in general and of the understanding of Scripture in particular. The Scripture becomes *gramma* when it fails to be illuminated by the power which creates the righteousness of faith and is understood instead, as the Law was understood by the Jews, to be a call to a piety of merit and achievement. The Bible is therefore for Paul in no way, in itself and apart from its use, Gospel. But it can become Gospel, when, and in so far as, it is rightly interpreted. This happens when we listen to it obediently in its capacity as the proclamation of the righteousness which is by faith and which is the criterion for discriminating among the spirits. And this criterion operates not only over against the prophets in the early Christian assemblies but also over against Scripture itself. Paul's immediate concern was with the Old Testament. But there can be no question that, as he is using his terms, they apply equally to primitive Christian prophecy and to the New Testament. Thus the door is barred to every form of arbitrary interpretation which enthusiasm can beget. It is not permissible to read into Scripture what we should like to be there.

It is not even permissible, if we are really looking for the Gospel, to accept uncritically from Scripture everything which is written in its pages. As Jesus adopted a critical stance towards the Mosaic Law and its requirements for purity instead of appealing to the letter of the Old Testament, so Paul's aim is the critical Bible reader and the critical congregation, both able to distinguish between the will of God and the letter. The following formulation of the position is extremely dangerous, but we need this kind of exaggeration today: it is the Spirit alone who makes possible a critical and proper hearing of Scripture. We have very frequently misused this insight, because we have not always understood by 'Spirit' precisely what Paul understood. But both Christian and congregation are inevitably exposed to this danger, because they stand between Christ and Antichrist. God's real action and will is not identical with our wishes and illusions – not even our pious wishes and illusions. Nothing is 'Spirit' which does not set us within the righteousness of faith, i.e. the justification of the ungodly. God's dealings are with the ungodly; always with the ungodly, and most of all when he is dealing with the pious. It is this, more than anything else, that we have to learn from the narratives of the Passion and of Easter, if we desire to hear and understand their message aright. The Gospel does not establish a new religion for those who want to be pious, but salvation for the ungodly; and Christians are not pious people resting safely on grace but ungodly people standing under grace. No one who has not learnt this lesson has any claim to make judgments in the name of faith and the Christian community about Scripture and the right interpretation of it. Here, and here alone, is the point where the Church stands or falls, and everything else with it. What is decisive is not whether we acknowledge the whole Bible but whether we remain clear and unshakable on this point.

It is from this standpoint that the current debate about the Bible requires to be seen and carried on. Hitherto, however, it has not generally been conducted on this assumption and for this very reason has produced the particular kind of confusion in which we now find ourselves. There is a readiness in certain camps to unleash a 'Church Struggle' about the Bible without even having grasped the difference between Gospel and Bible. They are fighting about the Bible as if it were a reliquary, or a book of oracles speaking directly across two thousand years into our own present. It is vital that I should be quite explicit here, otherwise we shall be failing to communicate with each other. It is not compatible with the Pauline view of Scripture and Spirit to stick a pin into the Bible and then to regard the passage thus marked out as a piece of guidance for oneself. To do this would be to make the Bible into an object of superstition and to compel God to speak whether he pleases or not. Only the heathen can compel their gods to appear, to speak, to come to their help. The Father of Jesus Christ is not bound in such a way as to be at our disposal whenever it suits us.

They must be very strange Bible-readers who have not yet observed that it is possible for God to keep silence in the Bible concerning our confusions and our questions; and that at least he is frequently silent in certain writings, pages or phrases so far as certain generations are concerned. Many sermons bear witness to the fact that God has not spoken out of his Word but has kept silence there; and I must make it clear that this applies frequently to so-called edifying and orthodox sermons! The sects provide evidence that God is also capable of blinding us and hardening us by means of the Bible, although, and precisely because, we boast of observing the letter of the Bible. Indeed – and whatever contradiction and annoyance I may cause by saying this – not everything that is in the Bible is God's Word. In the last resort the contemporary controversy is about the truth or falsehood of this proposition. If, in the view of my adversaries, by using it I am threatening or destroying the very foundation of faith, then I see in this my categorical duty – the categorical duty of the Protestant theologian. For a faith orientated in this way is, in my opinion, and, as I believe, in the view of the Reformers, superstition. But to separate faith out from superstition is the primary business of the theologian. It is not the covers of a book which authenticate revelation. God *may* take up his dwelling between the covers of a book, just as he did within the crib and the swaddling clothes. The experience of the Church bears witness to this. But he does not remain so imprisoned therein that it is possible for us to possess him and manipulate him like an object. He himself bears witness to us of this when he does not on every occasion speak to us out of this book, nor out of all its pages, nor always out of the same pages. In other words, the Bible does not render him superfluous and thus we do not, like the Moslem, believe in a book even if that book is the Bible. It is possible to detach the Bible from God's will and presence, and make it into a holy thing, a disposable content, an inanimate object. Then a divine 'it' is speaking out of its pages. The Bible, however, is only holy when, and to the extent that, the Lord speaks out of it, the Lord who does not allow himself to be taken possession of like a piece of loot. No gift is fruitful in which he does not give himself, and in all his gifts it is primarily himself he is giving and not 'something' – a something which is sacrosanct in its own right. He will therefore be heard as being himself the measure of the Bible; which is to say that the Bible has, and preserves, its authority from the Gospel and is, for the rest, only one religious document among others. Indeed, no other kind of outlook in dogmatics can be integrated into the historical findings which are accepted today by theology in all its ramifications, even on the Catholic side, as being fundamental. Of those I am going to select at this point only some of the most important. Within the local congregation it is not usually made clear that the Bible does not speak directly to our present situation as if the two thousand years in between did not exist. It speaks directly only to the men of its own time. When I say this, I am referring to it in the round and in its various contexts; for naturally, as with other ancient books, it is possible for anyone who has a knowledge of Hebrew and Greek to understand immediately individual words, narratives and sections. But even the mere fact of translation into German is an attempt to bring home to me that to which I have no direct access – in other words, it is preaching. The reader of Luther's Bible actually hears the Biblical message only in the adaptation and translation made by Luther in his capacity as preacher, and thus this message does not by any means coincide at all points with the original. Anyone who has struggled honestly with Romans, for instance, knows what a labour it is even to understand Luther's translation and what a significant help translations in the language of our own day can be. This kind of example shows that the Bible is essentially an historical document in which we listen to a conversation conducted over some two thousand years, and mainly to a sermon on Christian faith and obedience. Thus Luther called the oral Gospel the real Word of God and declared that the Bible was only necessary because otherwise this oral Gospel would miscarry and be falsified. The Bible is for him essentially an emergency aid, precisely because, in his view, God's Word is not susceptible of being confined in a book.

Secondly, we must remember that only a very small selection of the primitive Christian discussion has been handed down to us in the Bible. Because we can so frequently reconstruct only badly or not at all the historical context, the specific allies and adversaries, the time and the place, we only relive a minimum of what actually happened and that mainly in the form of a very often delayed echo. There has also been a process of selection in operation, both accidental and intentional. Thirdly, this process continued into the fourth century, even though it may be true that the canon of the New Testament had already been in existence, so far as its essentials were concerned, for one hundred and fifty years. But this in turn means that a conditioning factor in the construction of the canon was the judgment of the second and third centuries about what seemed to them correct and incorrect, important and of doubtful validity, and that the canon taken as a whole is thus a product of the early stages of the 'catholicization' of the Church. It was filtered through the historical and theological perception of the Church of those days. From this angle it is comprehensible that II Peter found a place in the canon, athough even Schlatter acknowledges it to be pseudonymous, its date of composition is about A.D. 150, and it represents an early catholic dogmatic tradition; while the Apostolic Fathers, which are in part considerably older, remained excluded. Fourthly, as early a writing as I Corinthians shows that there were already violently disputing parties and confessions within primitive Christianity; it shows also how the road trodden by this Christianity leads from Jesus to early catholicism and how this road becomes visible in the New Testament. Though it might be an exaggeration, it would not be a baseless one if we were to postulate that the canon as such is the foundation not of the unity but of the diversity of the Christian churches. Every man can find something in it to square with his own dogmatic theology.

All these absolutely assured findings are normally not taken seriously by the devotion of the local congregation or, worse still, not even known to it. This devotion finds no difficulty in exposing itself to the technological age so far as its piety is concerned, but its historical and theological approach has remained stationary in the eighteenth century. For, broadly speaking, it has taken no part in the development of theology since the First World War, a development which has brought us back to the questions posed by the Reformation. I would even go so far as to say that to a great extent it participated in the Church Struggle simply on the basis of a conservative and partly reactionary attitude. A similar explanation can be advanced for the fact that today tendencies towards a return to the past are to be observed everywhere. It is hardly possible to acquit pastors and teachers of having insufficiently grasped and exploited a task which properly devolves on them. They may throw the blame on to the training they received at the university; and, as it seems to me, with some justification. I must, of course, immediately say that such justication is only valid on the basis of two observations: that there has been an extensive failure of theological education in the past and present can hardly be disputed, even if it can be explained and even shown to be in large measure inevitable. Above all we must at last frankly admit that the university course overstretches the capabilities of a very considerable percentage of our theological students and has long ceased to be viable as the exclusive channel of entry into the ministry of the Church. Obviously, one cannot, in the practice of the ministry, pass on and embody in one's own person what one has not really been able to take in and work over for oneself. If we are to speak the truth, we have to say that these are the pressure points at which the problems of university theology became visible. We may place the responsibility and the blame where we like; the fact is that the piety of the local congregations today, generally speaking, is located about half-way between the Reformation and contemporary theology, equally remote from both, not only historically but doctrinally.

To ascribe the present-day controversy to the opposition between the piety of the local congregations and a theology which has become unbelieving, is completely to miss the point. In reality two theologies, which have gone their separate ways for about two hundred years, are now at war with each other – pietistic dogmatics, and those of the Reformation (or, more accurately, the dogmatics which, starting from that point, are pushing forward into the present). This formulation can hardly be interpreted in any other sense than a provocative one. But I cannot suppress the passionate question: 'When will a Church community which calls itself evangelical and protestant at last be ready and willing once again to do some real theological and dogmatic study along this line and to think, re-think and think again, instead of adopting the defensive role of possessor and guardian of the truth over against this challenge and making itself into the protector of reaction?' In all conscience, it is true that it is not only the one side which is in need of repentance and conversion here. A theology which lacks the courage to call the community in the very spirit of the Bible to conversion and to an exodus into the school of the Reformers is not worthy of the name. For we are not pursuing our own private interests and studies; we are using our studies on behalf of today's, and still more tomorrow's, Church. Herein lies the continuity with what we were doing from 1933 to 1945. If you will allow me a personal word: for fifteen years I was simply the pastor of my congregation, nor did I want to be anything else. When I look back on that time, I cannot escape the conclusion that the Church Struggle scarcely led us a single step forward out of our defensive posture into the freedom of an attacking position. I cannot acknowledge as an authentic partner in dialogue anyone who does not feel deep sorrow and concern when he thinks about this. It was this anxiety which led me to take up theological work again, this time in the form of historical criticism. If we are going to compound today with a situation in which basically everything remains as it has always been, then we are throwing away what is perhaps the last chance which will be given to us to break out of the state-protected monopoly of a religious merger into the wide open spaces whither the mission of Jesus is calling us. Spiritual and ministerial self-satisfaction is the most intolerable of all evils within the Church and the busy activity of officials does nothing to improve this state of affairs. What has happened to a Church and a Christendom which are no longer ablaze with the promise of the first and fourth beatitudes?

In the matter of the controversy about the Bible, let the community be clearly aware of the context in which it has been set. That there are pseudonymous writings in the Bible, more non-apostolic than apostolic, even early catholic dogma, and that therefore there is and must be historical criticism of the Bible: all these things prove only that God's Word, when it issues forth, does not translate us into heaven, it sets us firmly on earth. A canon in which there were not some unevangelical doctrine could only be a book fallen directly from heaven. For where on earth should we find a congregation composed only of believers, of those who were obedient, of those instructed purely by God, of the saints? If primitive Christianity had been like that, if it did not belong to our sort of history, we at least could not identify ourselves with *its* history. But it is Scripture itself which tells us that Jacob and Esau, on earth and within God's earthly people, belong indissolubly together. Even if I did not see this to be true historically, I should still have to say it was true doctrinally. Those who hold the canon to be without error of any kind, perfectly evangelical, inspired in whole and parts alike, have a docetic understanding of it; this will necessarily lead them to a docetic understanding of Jesus; and then, like all Docetics, they will no longer comprehend the Cross, they will make faith into intellectual assent and the Church, which is admittedly now becoming restricted to the pious, into the flock of the blessed. All is interconnected here, as church history shows, even if dogmatic theology has not made it clear to us long ago. On no account are the lowliness and the hiddenness of Jesus on his way to the Cross to be retrospectively removed by a fundamentalist understanding of the canon, nor faith to be transformed (at this one point at least) into freedom from temptation. The Bible, too, preserves after its own fashion the lowliness and the hiddenness of the crucified Jesus. God speaks through it, as through the earthly Jesus, out of the darkness and hides himself in it as in the earthly Jesus, and his Cross. Only by building on this foundation shall we be able to hear God proclaiming the Gospel from within the canon. Otherwise we are bound to lose the Gospel for the sake of the canon, as undoubtedly happens in practice. For the Law is not the Gospel, Moses is not Jesus, James is not Paul, II Peter is not the first beatitude, and the Bible is no substitute for God.

I might well conclude at this point; for it is now quite clear how I understand Scripture, on what basis I interpret it, and why, as a theologian, I employ the procedures of historical criticism. It will also be quite clear that I am not prepared to make even the slightest compromise here, because if I were to do so, I should of necessity cease to be a theologian. But to conclude at this point would in fact be to remain in the realm of theory. The question of the interpretation of Scripture, however, must be authenticated by standing up to the test of practice. It is from this source that the congregations must be faced with what they have to be and to do. Thus I return to my original starting point. In the understanding of Scripture which I hold, what is the place and the task of the local congregation? John 17 seems to me to express this most clearly. We read there of the flock which follows the voice of the good shepherd, that it is in the world but not of the world. Not of the world – the context shows that this is said only in connection with the Word which is being addressed to us. It is not we who are, or are to become, heavenly. Nevertheless, under the Word we do cease to be 'world' in quite the same sense as all men are 'world'. We become again God's world, the creation in which God's Word is heard afresh and the way which is Christ himself has its beginning. If we ask whither this way and this discipleship lead, we receive a very remarkable answer. John 17.15 says: 'I do not pray that thou shouldst take them out of the world'; while 17.18 continues: 'As thou didst send me into the world, so I have sent them into the world.' The place and task of the Church, therefore, is – the world. In no other way than by working out this mission can it be what it is called to be.

It is the glory of Pietism that it has been the pioneer of overseas mission in the Evangelical Church. But obviously the time during which this work can be carried out as it has been hitherto is at, or near, its end. But this cannot possibly mean that the mission of Christ will come to a stop, because the Church would then no longer be the Church and Christians would no longer be Christians. To be the Church, to be a Christian – these stand or fall by this mission which would not *be* the mission of Christ if it were anything less than mission to the world. This is not necessarily to exclude denominational life and personal devotion. But in any case the current is running obviously and, in this sense, for the first time against us, where for one thousand nine hundred years it seemed to be running for us and did at least offer us room for manoeuvre, together with world-wide opportunities. It is disturbing to see how little our congregations have any concern for international politics. I am not saying that in every situation they ought to rush into some action or other. But at least they ought not to neglect altogether reflection, recollection and the kind of repentance which leads not to a crushed withdrawal into a closet but to a listening for a new commission, of a kind possible and, indeed, mandatory into today's conditions. The rapid increase of population in Asia and Africa by itself would already be a factor sufficiently hostile not only to the white man as such but to Christendom, let alone the certainty that the first atom bombs would be likely to fall on the countries round about us. The space we have for manoeuvre becomes daily more restricted. Blindness to this state of affairs cannot be excused on a plea of faith in God. It is not on to be blind, mentally lazy and apathetic when it is a question of the task laid upon us. Mission which goes no further than our kith and kin, than the community in which we live, is no longer the authentic, total mission of the Church. Correspondingly, a Christianity which allows itself to be driven ever more strongly on to the defensive and there to bolt itself in, is no longer offering the total and authentic Christian promise. It is a fearful degradation when the area allotted to the Church under the shield of the State's protection becomes the limit of our field of operation. It is a caricature of the Church when the life of the Christian congregation is seen only inside the walls of our churches into which, I may add, fewer and fewer non-members are finding their way; when this congregation is concerned only about its own inherited religious possessions. Its only true and lasting inheritance is in fact the pledge of its Lord that he will lead it into freedom. Indeed, unless everything else is subordinated to this pledge, party strife is bound to set in about the administration of this inheritance and about the correct uniform. Then the most important characteristic of preaching will be, as it was with Schleiermacher, that it is 'adjusted to the congregation', quite regardless of whether the world understands the shibboleth of the devout or not.

The problem of our mission does not only come alive when we look at what is world-wide or far off. It arises also out of our own everyday life. It is quite impossible to deny that both in our church buildings and in the various church groups we are for ever meeting the same people; many may even think it is nice that we are left to ourselves in this way and that Church and world now meet only at festivals, at the graveside or at weddings. If we ask why this is, the answer is not difficult to come by: the world around us sees in us the representatives of a religion which possesses and offers, if nothing else, at least a few pious convictions. But for the majority of the human beings amongst whom we live it has suddenly become in an odd way a great nuisance to be called to have convictions of any sort. We have adopted this approach too often, and been too often disappointed. No faith as such is now able to move the masses, whether it be political, trade unionist, philosophical or even the faith of the Church. Men see any faith as in greater or less degree a means of catching them in a trap, even if they concede it some idealistic element or find it useful in some way. Over against the conformism of the political parties, of the classes and, unfortunately, of the Christians, too, there is growing up a conformism of those who are not going to be caught and involved and who are erecting around themselves a wall of defensiveness and indifference.

You must surely sense for yourselves how even our own families are being sucked into this whirlpool and especially how the adolescents, mistrustful of adult leadership, are creating their own groups in which they are at home among themselves. Every organization is seen as having a particular axe to grind and is tolerated as such. Naturally, a church which is understood along these lines as existing for the purpose of pushing religious propaganda can no longer penetrate at any deep level into the world in which it is set. The fact is that, over wide areas, the Church and its faith simply arouses no interest; further, it arouses least interest of all in the circles where the technological reality of tomorrow is taking shape. This state of affairs concerns us all even if many do not feel themselves directly affected. If it is not yet true of many of our congregations and fellowships, it is nevertheless a fundamental trait of our environment. It is more than time for us gradually to learn this plain truth, the more thoroughly and expertly the better. But it cannot be learnt in a spirit of resignation. Rather, it means that we must be concerned about the opportunities of the mission that is laid upon us *today* and no longer simply allow the law of our action to be prescribed from outside the situation. Perhaps there is little hope of theological and dogmatic unity. But surely there must at least be unity of the kind which moves us to ask together: 'What shall we do today, in so far as each and all of us bear the same commission which we cannot pass on to anyone else? What *is* mission here and now?' I believe that the first answer comes to us direct from Pietism. For the history of Pietism has been almost always conditioned by the fact that the institutional ministry had failed it. As a Lutheran, I reckon to know something of the purpose and the necessity of this ministry. But, also as a Lutheran, I ought to know at least as much of the priesthood of all believers. This latter rallying cry has always been muted by concern with the ministerial office. It seems to me that today necessity, if nothing else, is compelling us to reverse the emphasis laid on these two ministries even to the extent of giving it considerable visible form. Immediately, we can say that for a long time there has been good evidence that no pastor is now in a position to carry out the ever-increasing functions of his office. It will in all probability even become necessary gradually to write off the expensive and, for the most part, half or wholly ineffective common training for all pastors, and to take the corresponding risks. The Church, which never tires of commending to its members the risk of faith, can surely not wish to live and act as an organization without itself taking some risk – although this is just what it is always doing. Commonsense itself tells us that obligations laid on everyone alike do not call forth either the greatest devotion or the highest honour. Today as never before we have to take trouble about the gifts and potentialities of the individual Christian in order that as a body we may once again become mobile in the field. Theology is as little everybody's vocation and *charisma*, as is preaching or doctrine or visiting the sick or administration. The Christian community only begins to carry responsibility for all these ministries in an authentic way when it ceases to expect everybody to do everything or even to expect one man to do nearly everything and so to give nobody room to exercise the real freedom and authority of which he is capable. The concept of the ministerial office has been so overdone in theory and become so illusionary in practice that we are quite unable to carry out the universal mission in a sufficiently pluriform fashion. The risk, and the inevitable stabs in the back, will be no more serious than they are now. We must certainly be more inventive than we have been, and as only love is the mother both of necessity and invention and possesses the required powers of endurance, we must make more room for love both in our meditation and in our patient contemplation. To exaggerate: however serious and, at first sight, discouraging a situation it may be, if ever a community of genuine lay people were in demand, it is in our world as it continues to become, in a remarkably prosaic way, religionless. In no other way can we break out of our island existence, our ever-narrowing ghetto, into the places where, by virtue of our mission, we belong. The Church simply cannot surrender the world, retreat into its fastness and wait for visitors from the outside. That only means that at the present time it is not possible for it to become secular *enough*.

The Church could – and should – have become properly secular long ago. For, in contrast to Moses, it was Jesus himself who first put an end in principle to the sacral and Paul proclaimed in Rom. 12–14 the worship of God in the everyday life of the world – that is, in the secular. That the Church failed to hear this message, misunderstood what was being said to it and made for itself new sacral arrangements – these things sprang from the fact that its mission drove it into the world of the Hellenistic mystery-religions. It became, more unconsciously than consciously, more through the outlook of its local congregations than of its leading theologians, itself a mystery religion, and was then able to validate this process by appealing to the cultic law of the Old Testament. Once this law of tradition had gained assent, a mystery religion the Church had to remain so long as its environment was religious or at least unwilling at bottom to dispense with religion. But whatever we may say, our situation has altered, after a preparation lasting a century. A Church which addresses itself nowadays to the religious sentiment of the world around is increasingly making passes at the empty air, and ought not at any price to seek comfort by reminding itself that it has always been the 'little flock'. It may become or remain the little flock, but only as salt and yeast and, so far as I personally am concerned, as pepper too. Going on living for itself, left to itself, it ceases to be the Church. For, according to the Gospel, being the Church means being mixed with the dough. It is ineluctable death, certainly for the Church, probably for both Church and world when these two amicably and peaceably part company, as is so obviously what is happening today.

This, then, is the point on which all the things I have been talking about converge: the problem of the relationship of Gospel, canon and interpretation, of theology and congregational piety. If the Bible has anything to say to the realities of our own time, if the interpretation of Scripture must by critical necessity be orientated around one central point and if the Christian congregation is willing and able to do some real theological thinking about this, then what is at issue – not just theoretically but practically – is this: Jesus did not come primarily and solely to the religious. The central message of the Bible is that God deals always, indeed exclusively, with the godless, because before him no man is pious and just. When this is once more preached clearly, aggressively and passionately as the Gospel from our pulpits and believed and practised in the Christian community, then perhaps some may feel that they have a legitimate vocation to call the exponents of historical criticism to account. But as long as this is not the case, no one has the right to do this in the name of Jesus and the Gospel – and I acknowledge no other authority. The piety of a congregation which may be prepared to convert the godless but is neither willing nor able to live with them is perhaps showing a greater contempt for its Lord than a theology which pursues its academic discipline according to its own logic and in so doing maintains contact with its environment in space and time. On the other hand, a theology whose vocation and operation is confined to the ghetto is only of interest to a fat, complacent community, incapable of penitence. If anyone doesn't like this, he will have to lump it. This is a simple problem of drawing the correct conclusion.

As I end, I should like to pick up the word 'conclusion' and under this heading to sketch out yet again from another perspective what I felt it necessary to say today. If we read the signs of our times aright, we see clearly that neither among the local congregations nor in the realm of theology have we any reason or justification for the kind of religion which is a contemplation of our own navels. Faith, at least in the Christian sense, means not primarily belief, but obedience which is prepared to be sent out. We can see the meaning of this spelt out in Jesus. To begin with, his preaching was not like that of the scribes or of founders of religions. He gave his disciples the 'Our Father' but no creed. He did not make them recite his words by heart as the pupils of the rabbis had to do; he founded no religious party like the Zealots or the men of Qumran. It was sufficient for him that he gave help, spiritual and physical, even if the crowd scattered again afterwards. He walked thus in an amazingly matter-of-fact way with God and was anything but doctrinaire. Now we cannot and should not simply seek to imitate him. The duty of bearing witness to him led even his first disciples to sketch out credal formulae, dogmas, doctrines and theologies. Otherwise their witness would have been borne away on the wind. So, too, today – today especially – it is essential to know once again what we do believe and are not prepared to believe; and indeed to have a form of Christian doctrine which they can handle is more necessary for our congregations than their daily bread. Only, that is not the be-all and end-all of everything. Mission precedes faith, mission alone provides its basis and its motivation. Today it seems as if mission exhausts itself before it has got beyond faith. So at least most people see it, the godly and the ungodly, the congregations and, unfortunately, the theologians too. But this is the source of the decay in Christianity, for in Christianity mission must always precede faith, because otherwise our act of belief would replace the divine will and the godliness of the godly would replace our sonship to God.

Only where mission determines our faith and thus does not end with it do we regain the realm of freedom which in spite of all our favourable circumstances we are increasingly losing even in the West. The word 'freedom' has become a political word. But where in the Church today can we see and know the freedom of the Christian man as the one criterion for being a disciple of Jesus? Where freedom is not growing, Jesus has not yet arrived on the scene – this sentence has to be uttered in this exaggerated way in order for it to be heard at all in our day. Where freedom is not growing the Church is not really present even if the Bible is being defended with horns and teeth. To be pious is not the same as to be able to enjoy and to bestow freedom. Piety which neither possesses nor conveys freedom is certainly not sonship. The whole Gospel can be summed up like this: Jesus brought freedom wherever he came. For he dealt with men from his base as a child of God and set them where only children of God could stand, even when they did not will it. He lived and realized in his own person the first commandment which is in fact not a commandment at all, but a promise. If he had brought men piety he would not have died the death he did. It was because he called men to freedom and bestowed it upon them that he came to the Cross, and it was none other than the pious who helped to erect it. They were unable to tolerate the free man. But it is as *the* free man that he is the promise of the earth. Nobody has said this better than Paul who sees the world waiting for the revelation of the glorious freedom of the children of God and goes on soon afterwards to interpret the sighing of the Spirit in our worship as the cry of the children of God for their perfected freedom. Christian life as the exercise of the freedom which is the sign manual of sonship, the gift of the Spirit and the bridge to a world in which men may close the door to our faith but wait for the authentication of our freedom with all the passion of a restless longing ignorant of its own goal; Christian sanctification totally comprehended in the preservation and realization of the freedom of the children of God; this is what we owe to God and the world in equal measure. Where this actually takes place, the Church does not remain in a little corner; there comes into being that solidarity with the godless which is so full of tension, but from which Jesus lived, the Christian fellowship grew and the first beatitude was vindicated. Life lived in the freedom of the children of God is a miracle which does not pass unnoticed. It was at this point that the mission of Jesus emerged into the light, without benefit of sacred times, places, institutions or persons. When are we finally going to get this message from Scripture, allow ourselves to be led by Scripture to put it into practice and to take all the risks entailed? Only the way of discipleship, the sign manual of which is the freedom of Jesus, is indispensable even today. But that is the way of those who have the capacity to put freedom into effect, instead of limiting it and taking it away. A controversy about the correct interpretation of Scripture, which is not from the beginning a controversy about the nature of this way, is not being fought on the basis of Scripture and under the banner of the Gospel, but on the basis of religious self-preservation and is thus, Christianly speaking, nothing but a religious noise by which we are not going to allow ourselves to be disturbed.

XV

THEOLOGIANS AND LAITY*

THE THEME WHICH I have had prescribed for me is in every way relevant to our own time. There is an ecumenical lay movement in existence and, as the Vatican Council shows, it has its Roman Catholic counterpart. Further, there is on both wings vehement lay criticism of the theologians, their activity and their training, of the kind which is especially familiar to us in Württemberg. Appearances suggest that a great majority of the Churches in the world might be brought together with unusual speed and unusual depth of encounter if a single article of faith were to be spoken forth into the midst of all their conversations: I believe in one apostolically founded episcopal office. Only a few know and sense all that is at stake here, and a single evening is far too short a time in which even to hint at the questions which press in upon us once the subject is raised. A few marginal critical observations must suffice. The proper celebration of a centenary entails not only retrospective thanksgiving but the kind of forward-looking dissatisfaction which asks 'What can we and must we be doing today?' If we want to honour the past, we have to give the present the same thing which drove our fathers out of the old paths into a new land. It is only because they broke out of their accustomed pastures that we can celebrate this centenary today. But it is too easy just to celebrate without once again being ready for new departures. To behave like this would be to misunderstand the very thing our fathers were saying and to disqualify us from being their true successors.

Let me immediately lay down in advance my most important thesis and, in doing so, make it quite clear that, so far as the theme which has been set me is concerned, I am no neutral referee but a participant committed up to the hilt. As I see the contemporary

* Hitherto only in duplicated form. A lecture given at the centenary of the Christlicher Verein junger Männer (The YMCA) at Tübingen, 6 May 1963.

situation and desire to help to shape it, I acknowledge only one true Christian community – a community of lay people who have pledged themselves to service and in which the theologians have a special task. For every Christian has been called by virtue of his baptism to the holy priesthood, every Christian stands over the whole range of his life and in full personal responsibility in the estate of discipleship, of witness and of sacrifice, or else he is not really a Christian at all. There is between theologians and so-called lay people absolutely no fundamental difference such as could encourage any limitation on, much less any exemption from, the task which is common to all; such as could justify all the activity's being on one side, all the passivity on the other. The New Testament teaches us that there are only active Christians, or to express it better, Christians in mission, sent out as the messengers of their Lord. Every passive Christian dishonours his Lord and his Lord's community. That must be said as sharply as possible today, because the Church in our time is in large part composed of passive members, whether we are thinking of worship or of witness in daily life. Their distinguishing mark is that they pay the Church taxes, go with greater or less frequency to hear sermons, are baptized and confirmed, married and buried; in short, that they belong to a religious fellowship as to a club, a trades union, a party, something in which paid officials do all the real work. But such a Church is a disgrace to Christ in our world, however smoothly it may function: and the ordained ministry, of which the theologians are the paid officials, is then in practice the guardian of a prevailing religious usage. The situation is not changed merely by securing the occasional, or even the regular, collaboration of lay people. This simply shows that the organization is going well. But we are concerned not primarily with the organization but with the mission of each and all. Anything less means that the whole object of the exercise has failed.

Immediately excuses will begin to be made. We live in a complicated world. Behind us is a history in which established orders, customs and divisions of labour have come into being. We live an everyday life in which we are all more often directed than free to take firm steps of our own volition. Life is rationalized like a factory. How can the Church escape the effects of all this? Many will at once protest that if they are to take part in any more Church activity they will be compelled to neglect their work, their family and other obligations. And besides, ought things not to be left to those who have been trained for them? Otherwise, will not lay people be exposing themselves to the suspicion of wanting to put themselves forward? Or from the ministerial point of view, is it worth the effort that has to be expected when we think of the errors which will inevitably be made by beginners and lay people? Doubtless these and similar questions are in large part justifiable and must be heeded. In the Church, as everywhere else today, it is mainly the specialist who is in demand and from whose narrow angle of vision everything is measured; and naturally lay people operate only with great difficulty in this situation.

Certainly we cannot remain content with it. Even if the Bible permitted it, the nature of our times would forbid it. For something is happening now which in my judgment has never happened before. When we speak in our day of ecumenism and mission, we have always in front of our eyes the picture of a Church extending throughout the world which is going on growing even in spite of bad setbacks. This picture, at least taken in isolation, is false or even merely the deceptive superficial appearance of a highly alarming reality. It seems to me that we ought rather to be seeing Christendom under the sign of a world-wide dying and of closing doors. In Asia, Africa and South America the number of non-Christians produced simply by the population explosion is increasing so rapidly that we cannot keep pace; and the young nationalist movements, as well as the renascent indigenous religions, are still further restricting our sphere of influence. Sixty years ago men could promulgate the slogan 'the world for Christ in our generation'; but in the end that has turned out to be an illusion. Humanly speaking, such a watchword will never be possible again. On the contrary, should we be overtaken by an atomic war which would presumably hit Europe and America harder than anyone else, all Church organization would break down even in the so-called Christian countries.

I do not want to paint the picture too black. But we must see the signs which observant eyes can no longer overlook. For the first time in remembered history the tide is running against us, and for the first time since the early days of Christianity it is possible seriously to imagine that the vision of the Book of Revelation is literally being fulfilled: that the Antichrist is enthroned visibly and universally on the graves of the saints and only in the desert is there any room for the people of God! But if this is what the present and the future hold for us, it must be the concern of every individual Christian. The preservation of the Church is God's affair, not ours. We must of necessity enter with Christ into the dying of the Church in the particular form in which it is unavoidable for ourselves. We are not proposing to surrender a single inch prematurely, before necessity demands it. For instance, in a highly technical world we cannot simply dismantle organizations just because they could not be maintained in an emergency. The development of new forms of fellowship need not be our most pressing concern while those we have inherited still remain in existence and function more or less effectively. What is really at stake is this: we ourselves must become alert and, indeed, so must all who want to remain Christians. Let me make this point by means of a very shocking image: it is time we prepared ourselves for partisan warfare in the service of Christ. The more complicated the structures of modern life become and the more they necessitate the services of specialists, the more dangerous they are. Only the true human person can survive when the technicians fail. Only a minority remains flexible. In time of need Christ is always at hand where the individual Christian is holding out. Our task is so to live that all can and may collapse around us except one thing – the word of Jesus: 'What is that to you? Follow me.'

But if this really is the state of affairs, the question arises once again; what have we actually to do, each one of us as an individual, in our own station and on our own personal responsibility? It would be easy at this point to indicate the yawning gaps of various kinds which we feel to exist over the whole range of Church activity and especially in every aspect of Christian service. Yet that would necessarily be once again understood as above all a cry for specialists. The kind of discipleship which I am trying to outline is not, however, limited to specialists, great as its need of them may be. We are doing no more than patching up if we merely look at the points of acute shortage and forget that it is the shortage of Christians which leaves these and many other posts unmanned. The Church has no need to be ashamed of patching up; only, she must not be content with this expedient. We are asking the wrong question when we begin with the visible gaps in the Church's work and then look for perfection or, less often, for a suitable outlet for our own strength or weakness. Exactly the reverse process has to take place, or, before we can turn round, we shall be back again in the old dichotomy between specialists and laymen, of which that between theologians and laymen is a logical consequence.

Over against this we have to remember that it is discipleship which is laid upon us all and nothing else. But in the same measure as discipleship takes hold, everything else follows of its own accord; the gaps where there is a particularly urgent need fill themselves and, not least important, specialists appear for every kind of employment. Again, in the same measure, the questioning about what we ought to do and what we can do stops. When we are following Jesus we no longer need to ask this question. Too much falls upon the disciple to allow him to stand idle in the marketplace. Even at the eleventh hour his Lord calls him. At this stage there is no need to look round for work to do. Men come to one of their own accord with their need and their difficulties.

I think of the example of the Master. How often the Gospels use the expression 'Jesus passed by'! He goes about seemingly without objective but, as if drawn by a magnet, meets with those who have need of his help. He moves them in a remarkable way to follow after him again, instead of setting up established local groups, as did the religious people of his own time and the Christian community after Easter. He is completely given up to the present moment, as if that alone mattered. It seems to me that this state of affairs will be reproduced everywhere where there is someone following Jesus. He does not need to engage in much activity to call attention to himself. He has only to be there. He may carry on his daily work like everybody else. But upon him will be fulfilled the promise of the city on the hill which cannot remain hidden and the other, of those who bear light in a perverse generation. He will always like the Samaritan, be stumbling over those who have fallen among murderers, and always have around him joyful folk with whom he will laugh and sad folk with whom he will mourn. He will appear to others as a rock in the stormy waves, as a reserve of freedom in a world locked up in itself, as a stronghold of peace (which is a higher value than reason) even if he himself does not notice any of this. The real service of Christ begins and ends with the discipleship which has no need of publicity and does not push itself forward into the limelight. It shines of itself and is offence enough in itself. Jesus still moves the world, from within its hidden places, today. Our church towers are far too tall, even if high-level building is slowly overhauling them: our worship is much too religious not to resemble every other sort of gathering and to be supplanted by them; our organizations are far too powerful not to hide him rather than to manifest him; our propaganda is much too loud to allow his voice to get through. The more ceremoniously we treat him, the less recognizable the Man of Nazareth becomes. At the point at which he receives the maximum publicity, he is hanging on the Cross. Now of course we have no need to ignore the fact that Pentecost did happen and the world mission did come into being. Only, we should not forget that since Pentecost there has been another Christianity in which Jesus has become invisible: a name for religious activity of which the world was full before and remains full, without any reference to him. We ought to be even more strongly on our guard than before against a piety which advertises itself. The duty of witness need not go unacknowledged, but it is the mark of a witness that he should suffer. In our world there is such an inflationary volume of pious chatter and such a suspicion of mere words that silence is very nearly a virtue and at the very least an act of prudence. Our primary witness is our life. Words and persuasive arguments without this life simply irritate people. The Church would have a better image if it talked less and did more, if we were seen to be seeking for room among the ranks of the disciples rather than at the public address system.

Does this not mean then that I am prepared to dispense altogether with what we usually call ministry and ministries and, as a necessary consequence, to play down the task of theology over against general discipleship? Now, I am a theologian myself and intend to remain one, so this danger cannot possible be as great as may appear at first sight. But everything depends on giving ministry and ministries their proper place. They can never be something external to, and imposed upon, the general body of disciples but always a specific concrete realization of its life. But if we are to understand this process aright we must first of all be clear that, while discipleship is commanded for all, yet the content of its doing and becoming is never the same for all. In our discipleship we do not cease to be men who have their own particular excellences and weaknesses. Christians so often lack a sense of reality. They are for ever imagining that they have to be idealists and therefore addressing impossible demands not only to themselves but to others as well. Out of this situation arise conflicts which obscure the serious business of discipleship on both sides, tearing apart the fellowship and destroying the credibility of the Christ. But it is a property of the gifts of grace to open our eyes to reality in so far as we have not already distorted it by our presuppositions. For us Christians guilt is an unavoidable companion of reality and we only learn that Christ reigns in heaven by learning first that he is the fellow-traveller of the guilty. At the precise point at which he brings himself down to the level of our humanity, he reveals himself as the Son of God. To set him in the ranks of the saints is to take away his glory and no one whose prime concern is to move among saints or among those who most nearly approach sainthood can really be a disciple. If we were actually to discover such people in our own street, we should certainly not come across Jesus of Nazareth there – he would have gone elsewhere. For he remains for all time the companion of sinners; and this shows each of us where we belong. We have to learn to bear each other's burdens and to endure each other. When and how does this happen? When we strip off our uniforms (we Germans have always been particularly fond of uniforms) and stop trying to impose uniforms on others – even, if possible, our own which has been shabby for a long time. Christ differs from men and from death in not being concerned with uniformity. Otherwise the Bible would have to be other than it is, for no one person in it is like another. Just for this reason it is not the dull book we so frequently make it. Solidarity exists only among those who are unlike. Those who are alike cannot help each other, nor do they have anything to communicate to each other. There is so much boredom in our church because we expect and demand far too much conformity. We are well aquainted with Sunday faces and Christians are generally thought of as people who put on a decent Sunday face and understand the technique of showing it to others. The Psalms cry out against this kind of behaviour, weep over it, mock at it, even curse it. Either it must grieve the good God, or he must laugh at our folly when he sees how we are continually trying to create a mask which can fit us all and be interchangeable, behind which we can hide our everyday humanity. Naturally it is his will that we change our lives under the impact of his Word. But what does this really mean?

In discipleship a man remains a human being among other human beings and yet himself becomes other than he was before when he allows himself to be called by Jesus into his ministry of brotherly representation. A Christian is a man who 'stands in' within his own sphere for the Lord Christ and at the same time for all his brothers. For the Lord Christ! Yes; this is how Christ rules the world: he lets no earthly realm be without some of his people and is always filling new places with them. For his brothers, too! No one can do everything and no one needs to will many things at once. Discipleship means: to will completely the one thing which is in our power to do and at the same time to give our neighbours time, energy and room to do in their station what they are called to do. The flock huddled tightly together is not an appropriate image of the Christian community, because there each one is fighting the other for space. Certainly, in taking upon ourselves the law of brotherly representation, there are two dangers to be guarded against: we must not be continually yearning for wider scope than has been given us, neither must we be continually looking out of the corner of our eye to see whether our neighbour is also fulfilling his quota. In the former case there is an unchristian Christian rat race in which what could be done is neglected because we are too busy dreaming of what might be done. In the latter, we meddle in someone else's job and spoil his zest for his ministry. It belongs to our humanity that even Christians do not like being perpetually told what to do by busy-bodies. Enough, indeed a frightening amount, of our efforts and of those of others will go wrong. But this happens quite inevitably. It is our God's good pleasure not to work with perfectionists. The society which, according to the biblical witness, he has sought out for himself is in general not as impressive as in our opinion it ought to have been. We should hardly be impressed by it ourselves. But Christendom has so far been invariably unsuccessful when it has tried to correct him. To it belong alike the strong and the weak, the wise and the foolish, the old and the young, all possible classes, talents, temperaments, each with their own errors and sins. Its appearance cannot be chequered enough if it is to do justice in any degree to the model of the biblical figures.

How does this affect our subject? In this way; that there may, and indeed must, be differences. Indeed, there must be what from an earthly point of view are complete opposites, such as tax-collectors and Zealots. Our common discipleship gives free course to each one of us and does not exempt anyone from the challenge to go himself. It takes seriously each individual and what he can do. This is the origin of that community in which there is abundance of opportunities for service and each man guarantees his neighbour freedom to praise the Christ with his body and his own particular endowment. In concrete terms, this means that not everyone is bound to preach. There are enough theologians who never learn to do it. Not everyone is able to get alongside children, young people, adults, the sick and dying, those who have made a mess of their lives, workers, countrymen, academics. What is important here is using one's eyes and one's common sense, and exercising humility and determination to see what one is good for; and to leave the way open to others. Why else has God given us eyes and common sense, and called us to humility and determination? It is equally important to accept counsel, help and correction from others who have been given better eyes, sharper minds and the gift of leadership. Why else have they, too, been set in the community? Again, all this will not happen without tension. Tensions are part of life even in Christianity, and only dead Christians stop annoying each other. Above all, we must grasp the fact that each Christian in his own field has from time to time something to say to all the others and mostly gives them something to think about. We do not only exist to rub each other's corners off or to set each other to rights. We do not stand in a row of interchangeable individuals. There are some who move and have their being in a quiet corner, some who operate in the public street; some who are allowed to walk the well-trodden paths, others who have to experiment; there are the preservers and there are the innovators who plough new furrows. Each has a particular destiny, each is open to a particular danger. Christians are always men at risk, irrespective of the place in which their lot has fallen. This is why we should be free over against each other, certainly, but not leave each other unsupported; and the community is as such responsible for each of its members. The solidarity of the community with all its members corresponds with the representative activity of the Christians among themselves. But solidarity here can only mean recognizing and calling out the gifts others have received, awaking the sleepers, strengthening the tired and so helping each to bear the responsibility of his gift that he comes to see it as his part in the task of representation. With this, we have at last arrived at the question of the ministry and the ministries within the Christian community. They are nothing if not discipleship in action, representative service on behalf of the community and within it, its limits set by a specific place in the body, by particular men and women and their particular gifts, bestowed or promised.

I propose now to clarify this last sentence in terms of the office of the theologian. If my thesis so far has been correct, his position, in the community and at the same time over against it, is exactly the same as that of any other Christian in *his* particular calling. But the particular task of the theologian is directed towards seeing that God's Word is rightly heard and expounded today. In this Word God so addresses us all that each one of us is enabled to see the opportunities and dangers of our own station. The theologians must therefore combine, as well as distinguish, the whole and the parts; he must concern himself about the heartland and the frontier of Christian existence; and all this with his eye continually on what is requisite and possible at this precise moment in history. Because his only source for this is Scripture, he will never cease from trying to open a way for Scripture into the present. This is nothing over and above what is laid upon the whole Christian community and upon each one of its members at his own station. The theologian, too, exercises a representative ministry. It is not therefore possible to draw nice neat dividing lines between theologians and so-called lay people. Many a layman supplements his pastor's weakness, and many are passionately moved by specific theological problems. These are not unmixed blessings. Conversely, there are quite enough pastors and alleged theologians who do not know their job, are making a nonsense of it and are in urgent need of help. We have reason to be suspicious of the proverb 'To whom God gives office in the Church, to him also he gives understanding.' We ought rather to orientate the bestowal of office according to the understanding which we can recognize in the individual beforehand, even though understanding alone may not be sufficient for any office. We have in the last resort to take into account the fact that, as in all other analogous activities, many threads run together, many presuppositions exist, many different capacities are required both for the office of pastor and for the work of theology; men vary in their bent, their vision, their temperament and thus cannot all be measured by the same standard. The one ministry exists here also only within the diversity of ministries and gifts. The pastor, the theologian *tout court*, is an abstraction. When we speak as if this were not so, we are only indicating that there is, and must be, a centre of gravity for these ministries. Where then is the centre of gravity for what we call theology?

As there are many contradictory views on this question, I shall simply state my own opinion: a man becomes a theologian in the true sense by dint of that capacity which is called in Paul 'the distinguishing of true spirits from false'. We have behind us a Church history of some two thousand years. Within this history Jacob and Esau have always been inseparably bound together. Jesus has been witnessed to as well as betrayed, we have separated ourselves wilfully from the world or else lost ourselves in it for lack of real roots. The theologian ought always to keep this history in mind and to understand that, from the perspective which it gives him, he can counsel, comfort, encourage and warn the present. The generations stand together under the word of the Bible. But the Bible is an endless building with many corners and little rooms of which only comparatively few are inhabited. The theologians should be more or less thoroughly acquainted with its time and its plan; he should open up those doors which are bolted and take care that we do not go astray in the mazes or settle down happily in the outer courts. Finally, we live in a world which is re-erecting the tower of Babylon and in which tongues have once again become confused, even ecclesiastically. For we see around us a multiplicity of separated churches, confessions, sects, contradictory traditions, convictions, attitudes. The theologian should be concerned about the one thing needful, yet at the same time he should keep lines of communication open so that this one thing can be heard by each one in his own language. Then it will indeed reach each one at his station, give each one strength to serve and leave none without a line of vision into the open heaven.

But how could the theologian engage in this activity unless he had previously experienced the painful ebb and flow of history as something to be borne within himself? – unless he set his own sights in the silence on the thousand problems of Scripture? – unless he had swept with his own eyes the boundless horizon of today's world from end to end and discerned its characteristic signs – according to the measure of his knowledge? Slogans are useless here. This task requires a study in depth, however it may actually be structured. It is also necessary to institute experiments which are not immediately comprehensible to others. Neither experience nor a break-through into the future are to be had without false trails and blind alleys. We know that every life, even the Christian life, is for ever going astray in both these ways and we shall therefore not hold against the theologian his participation in the universal lot of mankind. We cannot distinguish between spirits which have never before been conjured up and therefore to the menace of which we were never before exposed. History, the Bible, the present movement – these are the battlefield of the spirits. It is not necessary for every Christian to expose himself voluntarily to their assaults, their seductions and their terrors. But it *is* necessary that some should do this in special measure on behalf of the rest of the community, and live and die on the job. For the Christian society is always called, like the people of God in the wilderness, to press forward out of the old camps into the world which lies ahead. It becomes unfruitful and ceases to follow its Lord if it entrenches itself in the familiar haunts of its fathers and grandfathers. Christ is the promise for the world of today and not merely for the world of yesterday or of a hundred or two thousand years ago. But today's world, exactly like that of yesterday and of a hundred or two thousand years ago, is a heathen world, even if it seems to be Christian over whole areas of the earth.

We should not be asking ourselves primarily this evening how we can create more opportunities for the laity to realize their vocation, how we can bring pastors into closer contact with everyday life and make what they say and do more comprehensible, how we can give the theologians greater sensitivity to the feelings of the local congregations and the congregations greater trust in the theologians; how we can make the Church's administrative machine more genuinely flexible, deploy the specialists to better advantage or guard against their being too powerful. Such considerations are certainly useful and, in their place, necessary. But if we begin there, we are thinking as the technological world thinks, that is, bureaucratically and organizationally. Furthermore, such questions are only meaningful in limited circles which look beyond difficulties and expectations and are able to carry through what obviously needs to be done. What we have to think about this evening is the kind of discipleship which allows itself to be led by Christ out of the old into the new, out of the past into the present: that means, out of the groups in which we have come to know and understand each other, speak the same language and share in the same outlook into situations where life is lived without Christ. For he himself goes to the tax-collectors and the Zealots, to Herod and Pilate. To him no less than Abraham comes the command 'Go out from your father's house and from your friends into a land which I will show you,' that is into a heathen land. What is now necessary is that we should understand and lay hold of this passage with all the passion of brave and steadfast hearts, as being particularly ours in our discipleship.

But we have scarcely begun to do this. If we do not start to learn it of our own accord, we shall be taught it by force. Christianity is dying already the whole world over and that is the sign that even at a jubilee celebration we have to think seriously about our position. Christianity is dying of its own failures in everyday life. For thither is it called to be given its mission in the world: there is the place it incurs guilt if it takes flight. The promise is only ours for as long as we campaign in the world.

Because this is so, theology must today be the unease and the scandal of the local church which persists in the old ways. Many misapprehensions, follies and blameworthy actions on both sides make understanding difficult. But we should be seeking too cheap an accommodation if we were to concentrate mainly on this gap and think only of how it could be eliminated or narrowed. For we should then be remaining within the limits of the self-contained community always looking inwards, always measuring everything by its own standards. The tensions between theology and the community today, however, have their deepest roots in the fact that theology, by the very nature of its task, has to be concerned with the call to follow Christ out into our alien world, into that contemporary world over the whole face of which Christianity is dying and heathen religion is everywhere celebrating its own resurrection. We cannot set out on the way from the old camps into an unknown future where we shall encounter Christ anew, unless we begin to think. The representative service of theology for the community consists in doing some new thinking when such a situation arises and thus engaging in something of that daily repentance and conversion which is laid upon all Christians. It is from this standpoint that the guilt of the community over against theology as one of its ancillaries becomes visible: this community, over wide areas, cannot and will not think because it is under the illusion that it knows it all. It cannot liberate itself from the conceptions of its fathers and therefore itself becomes ever more alien to the viewpoints of its children. It listens to words which call it to faithfulness and to the defence of its inheritance and forgets in so doing that today, too, Christ strides out into the wilderness, as, according to the Epistle to the Hebrews, he has always done. If the price of understanding between the two partners, at present at such violent loggerheads, were to be that the local church should be spared rethinking and new thinking, then theology would be doing the precise duty laid upon it by leaving such a church behind it. The rearguard does not decide the direction the march shall take.

The moral rights of theology over against a community which is making no effort to free itself from the past and is still looking for Jesus in Palestine instead of in the Swabia of today, cannot be asserted strongly enough, even when enmity and mistrust and calumny result. The Bible is full of emnity and mistrust and calumny of religious parties. No one who strives for the truth is spared something of this kind, and our own time can hardly remain exempt. Yet we must remember in the face of all this the promise with which the Old Testament ends: 'the hearts of the fathers shall be turned to the children.' What a stumbling-block at the heart of this promise! It is the fathers who have to begin with conversion and that in the direction favoured by the children! What a programme of education lies locked up in this sentence! What radical rethinking we shall have to do, what experiments we shall have to allow, we who are so desirous of peace and safety! Then, and only then, will the hearts of the children turn to the fathers. This promise stands at the turn of the Old and New Testaments, and its realization comes when we allow ourselves to be led from the Old Testament into the New. There is no other discipleship: out from the well-sung land of the fathers under the sign of the Cross into no-man's-land, and on into the world of the heathen. This is true for us also. This is the conversion to which we today are once again called. In it we go forward into the future, not back into the past, and out of it the new people of God comes into being. If Christianity comes to the point of perceiving and treading such a way of discipleship again, then the theologians are likely to make a terrible number of silly mistakes. They, too, will then have to return home to the community or else cease to be theologians. But just so long as the community remains stuck on the threshold between the Old and the New Testaments and thinks itself obliged to make an Old Testament out of the New, just so long the theologians will continue to disturb the community. They will do it in virtue of their commission, in the representative role they are commanded to exercise and as a part of their own discipleship. It is a matter of following Christ out of yesterday into today and tomorrow and of keeping each other alert so that we do not become tired and slothful. The questions of organization and research are questions of method which have considerable significance but may never be allowed to settle or to obscure the real question, i.e. what discipleship means and does not mean today. No one can discover this single-handed and without much trial and error in many places and in many different ways. This does not happen without tensions between theologians and laymen. But when discipleship does not exclude thinking and thinking remains mindful of discipleship, then such tension is profitable for us and fruitful for our common universe of discourse. For then no one is exercising priesthood and right faith and true religion for himself alone. Then we are a community of genuine lay people in which each has his own particular non-transferable function and all praise the Christ together, each in his place.

ment today. [illegible] of the future, shall be [illegible] to the children? What [illegible] the basics of [illegible]? [illegible] and that in the [illegible] movement [illegible]? What is a [illegible] of education [illegible] this [illegible]? What radical rethinking we shall have to do, what [illegible] we who are [illegible] only then will the [illegible] to the [illegible] of the 'Old' and 'New' Testaments and [illegible] when we allow ourselves to be [illegible] from the Old Testament into the New. There are no more di[illegible] from the well-sung land of the fathers [illegible] and enter into the world of the heathen. This is true for us also. This is the conversion to which we [illegible] are called [illegible] in always [illegible] into the future, not [illegible] the past, and out of it the new people of God comes into being. If Christianity returns to the point of [illegible] and of [illegible] of discipleship again, then the theologians are likely to have a terrible [illegible]. They, too, will then have to [illegible] to the community of the [illegible], for just as [illegible] community cannot [illegible] on the threshold between the Old and the New Testament and thus itself be used to make an Old Testament out of the New, just so long the theologians will [illegible] the community. They will do it [illegible] of their [illegible] representative role [illegible]. It was a matter of [illegible] yesterday into today and tomorrow and of keeping [illegible]. The questions of [illegible] and questions of method which [illegible] be allowed to [illegible] really [illegible] what discipleship means and does not mean. [illegible] this [illegible]-handed and [illegible] many places and in many different ways. That does not [illegible] between theologians and [illegible] discipleship does not exclude thinking, and thinking [illegible] discipleship, then each [illegible] is profitable for us and [illegible] of theology. For then no one is [illegible] and right faith and [illegible] for [illegible]. We are a community of [illegible] people, in which each has his own [illegible] and all [illegible].

INDEX OF NAMES

INDEX OF BIBLICAL REFERENCES